SAILOR-DIPLOMAT

Medal presented to Captain James Biddle for capture of the
Penguin, 1815. Courtesy of The New-York Historical
Society, New York City.

SAILOR-DIPLOMAT

A BIOGRAPHY OF COMMODORE JAMES BIDDLE, 1783-1848

DAVID F. *oster* LONG

NORTHEASTERN UNIVERSITY PRESS
BOSTON   1983

Editors, Robilee Smith & Anne Lunt
Designer, Janice Wheeler
Maps, Bill Frigosi

Northeastern University Press
Copyright © 1983 David F. Long

Library of Congress Cataloging in Publication Data

Long, David Foster, 1917–
  Sailor-diplomat: a biography of Commodore
James Biddle, 1783–1848.
  Bibliography: p.
  Includes index.
    1. Biddle, James, 1783–1848.   2. United States—History, Naval—To
1900.   3. United States—History—War of 1812—Naval operations.   4. Admirals—
United States—Biography.   5. United States Navy—Biography.   6. Diplomats—
United States—Biography.   I. Title
E353.1.B5L66   1983   973.5′092′4   [B]   82-22236
ISBN 0-930350-39-1

Printed in the United States of America
87 86 85 84 83   5 4 3 2 1

TO MY SON CRAIG

CONTENTS

LIST OF MAPS

LIST OF ILLUSTRATIONS

PREFACE

Many authors would agree with the old saw that "one book leads to another." That is certainly true in this life of Commodore James Biddle. While conducting research for and writing my previous naval biographies of David Porter and William Bainbridge, Biddle's name constantly appeared, commencing with the shared experience of all three as nineteen-month captives of the bashaw of Tripoli after the USS *Philadelphia* had run aground there late in 1803. Further investigation revealed that no full-length biography of Biddle had ever been written. This seemed to me a gap worth filling; many of his colleagues in the early Navy had been so honored, among others, James Barron, Stephen Decatur, Isaac Hull, James Lawrence, Thomas Macdonough, Oliver H. and Matthew C. Perry, Edward Preble, John Rodgers, John D. Sloat, Robert F. Stockton, and Thomas Truxtun.

I was already familiar with the forty-seven-page article by Nicholas Biddle Wainwright, former editor of the *Pennsylvania Magazine of History and Biography,* entitled "Commodore James Biddle and His Sketch Book," published in the January 1966 issue of that journal. After rereading it, I immediately sent him a letter, asking if he planned to write a full-length life of his ancestor. When he replied that he did not, the way opened for me. There would be no lack of documentation for such a study. A huge number of Biddle family papers has survived, and it was primarily upon them that Wainwright had based his long article.

As the episodes of Biddle's life unfolded, a pattern emerged. This small, slender perpetual bachelor, reserved and aloof, immersed in the affairs of his large and affectionate family circle, periodically found himself involved in arresting and sometimes even melodramatic circumstances. The courage that he demonstrated in the USS *Wasp* against HMS *Frolic* in 1812 was pronounced, as was his adroit gunnery while commanding the USS *Hornet* against HMS *Penguin* in 1815, followed immediately by the consummate nautical skill he evinced in escaping from the potent enemy ship of the line *Cornwallis*. He weathered three almost simultaneous crises in 1822—a horror-filled onslaught of yellow fever that eventually killed about one-third of the men under his command in the frigate *Macedonian;* his forced apology to avoid a duel with Captain Arthur Sinclair; and a helpless night passed on a beach at La Guaira, Venezuela, fearing that the single cable securing his frigate *Congress* would snap during a hurricane that shattered all twenty-three of the other vessels in that harbor. His vividly described escape from going down with the frigate *John Adams* at Pensacola in 1825; his tribulations with unruly and drunken midshipmen while commodore of the Mediterranean Squadron in 1829 and 1830, and while governor from 1838 to 1842 of the Naval Asylum at Philadelphia, which he ran as a forerunner of the U.S. Naval Academy; and toward the end of his career, his physical assault by a Japanese soldier at Yedo (Tokyo) Harbor in 1845 while his two ships were surrounded by hundreds of armed Japanese barges round out the picture of a courageous man of action. Along the way he sustained perplexing relationships with the two women who evidently were in love with him.

Between these periods of excitement and stress he lived placidly in Philadelphia or abroad while quietly attending to his many diplomatic duties for the Department of State. The most meaningful of these was: tightrope walking between Spanish royalists and Chilean and Peruvian rebels from 1817 to 1819 in order to save from confiscation large numbers of American ships and cargoes, while freeing many of his fellow countrymen from prison. During 1818 he temporarily left his work there to make a quick voyage to Oregon where he laid claim to that country for the United States. During 1822 and 1823 he fruitlessly negotiated with Spanish officials in the Caribbean while endeavoring to eradicate piracy in those waters. He maintained American neutral rights during the Brazilian-Argentinian War of 1826 to 1828. He joined others in writing the first Turkish-American Treaty at Constantinople in 1829 and 1830. On his last cruise, from 1845 to 1848, he completed the ratification of the first Sino-American Treaty, while establishing the U.S. legation at Canton and the Shanghai consulate. He went on to Japan, where he prepared the way for Matthew C. Perry's resounding success seven years later; he then sailed to California, where he oversaw American naval operations against Mexico in the Pacific. In 1823 he suffered embarrassment and frustration while carrying abroad Caesar Augustus Rodney, his sizable family, and their ludicrously abundant luggage. The situation was highly comical, but most assuredly Biddle failed to see any humor in it.

Intellectual, self-contained, class conscious—even snobbish, but with a saving grace of understated humor—patriotic, paternalistic toward his sailors but touchy and oversensitive with his equals or superiors in the naval and diplomatic hierarchies, Biddle is a personality worth studying. His contributions to his nation are, I hope, ample justification for this work.

While specific identification of sources is of course in the chapter notes, the bases of my research should be mentioned here. The most essential manuscripts were those to and from Biddle at Andalusia, the family estate near Philadelphia. Mr. Wainwright very kindly arranged for them to be moved for my convenience to the Historical Society of Pennsylvania, and later I was able to make a quick trip to Andalusia for a final check on the papers and to see the estate for myself. Other sources at the society were additional papers of James Biddle, those of Nicholas and James S. Biddle, many of great interest in the Cadwalader Collection, and scattered items from the Connaroe, Dreer, and Gratz collections.

Biddle's seagoing career could be followed in the hundreds of letters passing between him and the secretary of the navy in the microfilmed Navy Department's Record Group 45, as well as other departmental files still in manuscript form at the National Archives. There I studied Department of State materials, especially the microfilmed Consular Despatches, for information about Biddle's diplomatic career. Important information was unearthed in many collections at the Manuscript Room at the Library of Congress. I also personally inspected manuscripts and newspapers at the U.S. Naval Academy; the American Antiquarian Society; the New-York Historical Society and the New York Public Library; the Massachusetts Historical Society; the New Hampshire State Library; the libraries of Dartmouth College and Harvard, Yale, Princeton, Hong Kong, and New Hampshire universities; the Peabody Museum and the Essex Institute at Salem, Massachusetts; and the town libraries at Portsmouth, New Hampshire, and Newburyport, Massachusetts.

Letters to, from, or about Biddle were sent to me from the American Philosophical Society; the Franklin D. Roosevelt Library; the historical societies of Delaware, Maine, New Jersey, and Oregon; Haverford College; and the universities of Indiana and Michigan. The Samuel F. Du Pont letters at the Eleutherian Mills Historical Library at Wilmington, Delaware, were of particular value.

In addition to those individuals identified in the notes as helping me, I am especially indebted to the research librarians at the University of New Hampshire, seldom stumped by even the most esoteric

questions; the Central University Research Fund of the University of
New Hampshire, which provided me with a grant for my basic research in Philadelphia and Washington; and my wife, Susan Robinson
Long, who proofread my manuscript while at the same time sacrificing her own interests to provide me with essential time for writing
and research.

David F. Long
Durham, New Hampshire

SAILOR-DIPLOMAT

PROLOGUE

The wind was picking up sharply and the rain was beating down harder on the ship of the line *Columbus* as she cut through the rollers about halfway home from Rio de Janeiro on the last leg of an eventual 69,000-mile cruise that had commenced almost three years before. In his cabin Commodore James Biddle, recently in command of first the U.S. Navy's East India Squadron and then the Pacific Squadron, sat at his desk studying a letter from his nephew, Lieutenant James S. Biddle, stationed at the Philadelphia Navy Yard. The wizened little commodore felt old and tired and ill, but as the needs of his relatives always revitalized him, he summoned up enough energy to answer his nephew's request for a biographical sketch of his naval career. But how could he summarize forty-eight years in the service without staying up most of the night? Chronologically? No, that would take too long. Instead he would let his memory, still keen, take him where it would.[1]

He dipped his pen into an inkwell and started in his execrable penmanship: "*Columbus* at Sea. Feby 12, 1848—My dear James . . ." The names of places he had been, many more than once, popped into his mind: Europe and the Mediterranean—Britain, France, Spain, Portugal, Italy, Turkey, Sicily, Malta, Gibraltar, the Balaeric Islands, Tunis, Tripoli, and Algiers. Latin America—Colombia, Brazil, Uruguay, Chile, and Peru (he forgot Venezuela). The West Coast of his own country—California and Oregon (he neglected to say that it was he who had laid his nation's claim to that vast area in 1818). Asia and the Pacific—Hawaii, China, Macao, Hong Kong, Japan, and the sprawling Dutch East Indies. The West Indies—almost all of the European islands there, as well as the two black countries of Hispaniola. What did this impressive globe-trotting add up to?—"once around the world, five times round the Cape of Good Hope, three times round Cape Horn, and crossed the Equator twenty times."

He thought for a moment: was there any major sea command which he had never held? Yes, although he had flown his commo-

3

dore's broad pennant over the Mediterranean, Brazil, Pacific, East India, and West India squadrons, luckily he had never had to endure the rigors of the African Squadron nor the ennui of the Home Squadron. As an American diplomatic representative he had signed the first U.S. treaty with Turkey, exchanged ratifications of the first U.S. treaty with China, and if he had failed in similar efforts in Japan, he was satisfied that no one could have done better with that xenophobic people.

How much did his nephew need to be told about his combat experience? Not much, for any American naval officer would recall the details of his two bloody engagements during the War of 1812. Second in command of the USS *Wasp* when she annihilated HMS *Frolic,* he had been the first to reach the mast of the shattered enemy, personally hauling down her flag. Two and a half years later he had commanded the sloop *Hornet* when she shot to pieces HMS *Penguin,* after which he had masterfully engineered his escape from the 74-gun HMS *Cornwallis.* So he wrote only the laconic comment: "During the war with Great Britain, I was in two actions, both of them successful." The searing impact of the bullet in his neck which he had received after the *Penguin* had surrendered he dismissed as simply, "once seriously wounded." Ranging back to Tripoli from 1803 to 1805, he wrote no more than that he had been "upwards of 19 months a prisoner," after William Bainbridge, his friend and mentor, had surrendered the USS *Philadelphia.*

Biddle went on to itemize some of his personal distinctions. He was the only officer still in service during 1848 who had commanded a combat vessel in the War of 1812. His promotions had come so rapidly as to make him, within fifteen years of his entry into the navy as a midshipman, a "post captain," the highest official rank for an American officer ("commodore" was a courtesy title given to a squadron commander). Certainly few, if any, of his colleagues could boast that he had "never fought a duel, never was tried by a court martial, never drank a glass of grog." Wine, of course, was quite another matter.

Next he jotted down a few of his honors: one silver and one gold medal from his government, a sword from his home state of Pennsylvania, a silver service from Philadelphians, a "public dinner" by New Yorkers. Dishonor? Yes, and most undeserved. He had been "slandered by the Legislature of Delaware, and burnt in effigy by the people of Wilmington." The episode still rankled after a quarter-century. He thought back to 1823 and the lies that Caesar Augustus Rodney had spread about him after he had transported that ailing and aged diplomat on a mission to Argentina, via Europe, accompanied by Rodney's wife, her maid, their son, and nine unmarried daughters, for all of whom he had to find accommodation. Worse, Rodney's party had brought along such a huge amount of excessive supplies and dilapidated furniture that some of it had to be stored on deck, turning the immaculate frigate *Congress* into a floating junkyard, the laughingstock at every port she visited.

Should he mention others whom he ranked in Rodney's category? The inefficient and perhaps corrupt Captain Isaac Hull, whose Charlestown Navy Yard he knew had been responsible for the lethal outbreak of yellow fever in the frigate *Macedonian* in 1822? The pompous, devious, and cowardly John Rodgers who had covered up for Hull? The touchy and pettifogging Arthur Sinclair who, about the same time, had tried to get him court-martialed? The crude, hotheaded, and insubordinate David Porter, on whose court-martial in 1825 he had sat and whose conviction he had approved? Above all, the rabble-rousing Jacksonians who he still believed, despite all the evidence to the contrary, had driven his brilliant and beloved younger brother Nicholas out of his presidency of the Second Bank of the United States and into eventual bankruptcy and premature death?

No, let them be.

He scrawled a few afterthoughts: his mercantile voyages to China in 1807 and to Portugal four years later while furloughed from the service; his diplomatic mission to France, also in 1811; his trip abroad as a tourist in 1824 to accompany an ailing brother-in-law.

Drained, he sat back in acknowledgment of his failing health and the late hour. He must end it and get to bed. What, beyond his devotion to his relatives, had been the chief motivation of his life? Why, of course . . . He picked up his pen and closed with a patriotic flourish: "There is but one country in the world that I wish to see again, and that country is my own. I am now on my way to it. Shall I ever leave it again? I think not, certainly not willingly."[2]

CHAPTER 1
ANCESTRY, BOYHOOD,
AND EARLY NAVAL CAREER,
1783–1805

Although the name Biddle may be thoroughly associated with Philadelphia today, that family did not arrive there until roughly a half-century after its founding. The English Biddles, originally "Biddulph," began their upward mobility with Commodore James's great-grandfather, the first William Biddle. A Quaker, he had been subjected to the increasing intolerance toward his sect typical of the Stuart Restoration, and migrated to America during 1680 and 1681. As one of the proprietors of West New Jersey, he was affluent enough to take over a large farm called "New Hope," on the Delaware River near Bordentown. He prospered, partly through his political connections as a member of the Council of Proprietors, the Governor's Council, and the Assembly. His son, the second William, inherited the estate in 1711, and contented himself with acquiring more land and attending to his brood of seven surviving children, dying in 1743.[1]

During its next American generation, the family divided between the offspring of the third William, the eldest son, and John, the youngest, starting what one breezy Philadelphia social historian calls the "Romantic" as against the "Solid" Biddles. Clement (1740–1814), the first cousin of Commodore James's father, was the most prominent of the early "Solid" Biddles, serving with distinction in the American Revolution, primarily as the aide-de-camp of General Nathaniel Greene, and a longtime fellow soldier and friend of Washington. He then engaged in Pennsylvania politics and established a prosperous dry-goods business. Family genealogies shrug off Clement's younger sister Ann with the single comment, "married General Wilkinson." Surely he was worth additional information, for he was none other than James Wilkinson, the murkiest American of his time, congenitally corrupt and untruthful. He had been "clothier-general" during the Revolution, holder of top U.S. Army commands for decades, paid agent of the Spanish government in the Floridas, fellow conspirator with and turncoat against Aaron Burr, and inept tactician in the War of 1812. Yet he was repeatedly whitewashed by courts-martial before he died in Mexico in 1825. Commodore David Porter, who had unpleasant associations with Wilkinson at New Orleans from 1808 to 1810, accurately summarized him as "Genl Puff . . . a man of duplicity meanness and cowardice." Ann, who died in New Orleans in 1817, somehow "never lost faith" in her shady husband, and never "failed to share his wanderings." Wilkinson's besmirched reputation may explain why Commodore James never mentions his second cousin by marriage in all his voluminous correspondence.[2]

Of John's "Romantic" Biddles, five of the third William's generation need mention: James (1731–93) was colonial admiralty official and later a Philadelphia judge, for whom Commodore James was named; John (1736–94), who fought in the French and Indian War and was a colonial financial bureaucrat at the time of the Revolution, was the only Tory Biddle; his property was confiscated and he fled to Nova Scotia, where he died. Edward (1738–79), another French and Indian War soldier, Speaker of the Pennsylvania Assembly, and a member of both Continental Congresses, suffered a disabling injury in a personal fracas in 1774 from which he never recovered, and which kept him out of the army and hastened his early death. The lives and characters of Charles (1745–1821) and Nicholas (1740–78) are examined below.[3]

As for the third William himself, his life was tragic. He was comfortably well off at first, and his future might have seemed secured in 1730 when he married the socially prominent Mary Scull, daughter of Pennsylvania's surveyer-general and one of "the prize beauties of the city." He moved to Philadelphia and underwent some business reverses, but apparently was saved from disaster by the large share he inherited in his father's estate in 1743. Yet he continued to be helpless in his dealings with predatory competitors. After posting bond for a bail jumper he went into bankruptcy, and died embittered in 1756. He left his widow practically penniless with nine children, of whom four had to be supported at home. Somehow she struggled through, taking in boarders, working at a tavern, catering, and selling maps from her father's collection.[4]

Commodore James's father might have been called "Charles the Pugnacious" before settling into a more humdrum way of life. He was a merchant marine captain during his early years. In his *Autobiography* he narrates a continuing saga of adventures, replete with shipwrecks, drownings, rescues, mutinies, plagues, surreptitious landings and precipitate departures, battles public and battles private. He admitted to a murderous temper, especially toward his men. On one occasion he struck a laggard seaman over the head with a belaying pin so ferociously that the blood began flowing from the prostrate sailor's mouth. Luckily the wound was not mortal, but Charles resolved that henceforward he would assault no member of his crew with anything "but a piece of rope." During the Revolution he was briefly a prisoner of war, and upon release still retained enough bellicosity to challenge a Georgia militia officer for an alleged insult to his brother Nicholas, recently dead; only the officer's abject apology avoided a duel. Charles then seems to have quieted down in order to pursue a thriving mercantile career and to participate in politics, becoming vice-president of the Pennsylvania Supreme Executive Council in 1785, eventually serving under Benjamin Franklin as president.[5]

In 1778 Charles married Hannah Shepard of New Bern, North Carolina, and eventually settled with her just north of Philadelphia's city limits. He described his union as "the most happy circumstance of my life." Perhaps, but the biographer of Nicholas Biddle, the Revolutionary naval captain, calls her "timid and shy with strangers," implying that she may not have been the ideal mate for a rising entrepreneur and politician. At least she triumphantly fulfilled another marital duty by providing him with ten children:

1. William (1781–1835), a lawyer in Philadelphia, boyhood companion of Nicholas the future banker, but almost never mentioned in Commodore James's family letters;
2. James (1783–1848), commodore, USN, and the subject of this biography;
3. Edward (1784–1800), midshipman, USN, who died at sea during his first cruise;
4. Nicholas (1786–1844), the nation's premier banker and target of the Jacksonians during the 1830s, the most famous Biddle and James's favorite brother;
5. Charles (1787–1836), a lawyer who settled in Tennessee, and something of a rarity—a supporter of President Andrew Jackson throughout, and selected by him to survey routes across Central America during the 1830s;
6. Thomas (1790–1831), USA officer, able fighter during the War of 1812, and army paymaster in St. Louis after 1820. There he was involved in a spectacularly absurd duel with U.S. Congressman Spencer Pettis, in which both were mortally wounded;
7. John (1792–1859), a War of 1812 veteran who later moved to Michigan, where he became the territorial delegate to Congress and chairman of the state's constitutional convention;

8. Richard (1796–1847), a Pittsburgh attorney, two-term U.S. Congressman, and considered the family intellectual after publishing his biography of Sebastian Cabot;
9. Mary (1798–1854), married to her cousin, Clement's son John;
10. Ann (1800–63), married to Francis Hopkinson.[6]

James Biddle was born on 18 February 1783, while the family still resided north of the city proper. When he was three his father moved into downtown Philadelphia, taking over a two-story house on Market Street between Sixth and Seventh; there he grew up. Immediately anyone writing his life meets with disappointment. Unlike the subjects of so many late eighteenth- and early nineteenth-century biographies and autobiographies, no concrete information remains about his boyhood. One looks in vain for the usual narratives of stern but loving parents; of childish pranks, followed by the inevitable trip to the woodshed for paternal correction; of successes and failures at school; or of harrowing accidents and prostrating illnesses.[7]

Nevertheless, we can conjure up some probabilities about young James's formative years. Reared as he was in the stability afforded by a large, affectionate, and affluent family, love for his relatives quickly became one of his most enduring characteristics. He was fortunate enough to reside in the nation's political, social, economic, and intellectual center. Philadelphia, with almost fifty thousand inhabitants, was by far the country's largest city, as well as its capital until 1801, when it was superseded by the new Federal City at Washington, D.C. It was the banking and commercial metropolis of the United States, with worldwide oceanic trade routes—to Europe and the West Indies in particular, but also to China, thereby facilitating James's own two visits to that remote empire, separated by almost forty years. The Biddle house was close to the waterfront, and the brothers doubtless spent endless hours reveling in the sights, sounds, and smells of a busy seaport.

James would have been drawn toward the armed forces by his family's recent history. He might well have chosen the U.S. Army; two of his younger brothers entered that service, and his elders must have told many a yarn about his two uncles who had fought in the French and Indian War. Yet the lure of the navy had even a greater attraction. His father could not have been reticent about recalling seafaring adventures, and above all, the great magnet drawing him toward the navy must have been the career and dramatic death of his Uncle Nicholas.

Nicholas Biddle, the third William's fifth son, earmarked himself for the sea while barely in his teens. After sailing with his brother

Charles on voyages to Canada and the Caribbean, he decided to avail himself of the finest naval education extant. He traveled to England, where, through family connections he managed to enter the Royal Navy as a midshipman in 1771. After a couple of cruises he was recommended by his commander for a much coveted assignment. He sailed in the sloop *Carcass* (British naval nomenclature of the time is often inexplicable) on a two-ship polar expedition from June through September 1773. A vast icesheet off Greenland blocked progress farther north, but Nicholas reveled in the voyage, on which sixteen-year-old Horatio Nelson, the future victor at Trafalgar, was a shipmate. Back in England, he learned of the Boston Tea Party, resigned his commission, and hastened home. Young as he was, his Royal Navy training unquestionably made him one of the most professionally adept officers in the new American revolutionary navy.[8]

His rise in the service, first in the Pennsylvania and then in the Continental Navy, was rapid. Following irksome "row-galley" duty, he was given command of the 14-gun brig *Andrew Doria*. After he seized two Scottish transports carrying much needed munitions and then picked up six prizes in the West Indies, he was ready for a better assignment. As the fifth-ranking captain in the Continental Navy (at that time John Paul Jones was only the top-rated lieutenant), he was awarded the 32-gun frigate *Randolph*. On the prowl during late 1777 and early 1778, he nabbed five enemy vessels.[9]

On his last cruise he was the commodore of a five-ship squadron, and departed from Charleston accompanied by the ship *General Moultrie*, 20 guns, and the brigs *Notre Dame*, 16; *Fair American*, 16; and *Polly*, 14. Off Barbados on 7 March 1778 a large man-of-war was spotted bearing down rapidly on the squadron. Conflicting evidence fails to reveal whether Nicholas realized that she was a much more potent ship of the line rather than a frigate roughly equal to his own strength. When they closed just after dark she was unmistakably revealed as a battleship, the 64-gun *Yarmouth*. The *Randolph* poured in the first broadside, and during the first few minutes seemed to have the better of it; one eyewitness later testified that the American was firing "four or five broadsides to the *Yarmouth*'s one." This was no wind- and wave-directed naval ballet of exquisite seamanship, but a simple slugging match at point-blank range. Marines on each side could "throw their hand grenades from the tops into one another's decks."[10]

Total American guns under Biddle's direction added up to 98 as opposed to the British 64, but the four smaller U.S. warships proved useless. Indeed, the *General Moultrie*, firing aimlessly in the general direction of the battle, sent some projectiles into the *Randolph*. After about a quarter-hour, Nicholas was hit by either a bullet or a splinter in the thigh. Refusing to go below, he was sitting in a chair while a surgeon dressed his wound when the *Randolph*'s magazine exploded with an ear-shattering roar, raining masts, timbers, and shrouds on her stunned adversary. Nicholas and three hundred other Americans died at once; a few days later four lucky survivors were picked up by the *Yarmouth*.[11]

The twenty-seven-year-old commodore quickly became a national hero. Toward the end of the Revolution two ballads honoring him were published, and a half-century later James Fenimore Cooper hailed him: "There is little question that Nicholas Biddle would have risen to high rank and great consideration had his life been spared. Ardent, ambitious, fearless, intelligent, and persevering, he had all the qualities of a great naval captain, and although possessing some local family influence, perhaps, he rose to the station he filled at so early an age by personal merit."[12]

His death was naturally a grievous blow to the Biddle clan, but gradually their shock and sorrow were replaced by pride. Certainly his memory must have had a lasting imprint upon his nephew James. Authentication is missing, but it is most unlikely that he would have been unaware of his uncle's credo as a naval officer, expressed in a letter written during 1776:

> I fear Nothing but what I ought to fear. I am much more afraid of doing a foolish Action than of loosing [*sic*] My Life. I am for a Character of Conduct as well as courage. And I hope never to throw away the Vessel and Crew merely to Convince the world that I have Courage. No one has dared impeach it yet. If any should I will not leave them a moment of doubt.[13]

There is some scanty information about James's education. He may have been tutored at home intermittently, but according to the archivist of the University of Pennsylvania, he attended "the preparatory division of the University in 1792–1793." Then follows a gap in those records until 1798 to 1800 when "Biddle doubtless *did* attend collegiate classes for at least a year or two . . . but our records are, unfortunately, deficient for the very years we need and are only complete for *degree recipients*." Confirmation that he attended but did not graduate from the university was provided by two service journals in almost identical biographical sketches of him, as well as a nineteenth-century work on well-known Philadelphians. In classes there he concentrated on the classics, and soon developed a love for literature which he maintained for the rest of his life, both aboard ship and through several long intervals awaiting a seagoing assignment.

He bought books continually; by 1845 his personal library contained 2,329 volumes. But he was hardly out of his mid-teens when scholarly activities began to pall, and he concluded that his country might be able to use his services.[14]

By 1799 belligerent action in the so-called Quasi-War between the United States and France was drawing to an end. The alliance that had been made by the two countries in 1778 had begun to disintegrate a decade and a half later. American resentment over the meddling and mendacity of "Citizen" Edmond Charles Genet, revolutionary France's first minister to the United States, had been matched by French indignation about the Anglo-American Jay Treaty, signed in 1794, which Paris considered so signally unfriendly an action as to break off relations. French privateers (semipublic, semiprivate vessels licensed by their government to prey upon enemy commerce) began seizing American merchantmen. Following the failure of President John Adams's "XYZ" mission to Paris in 1798, hostilities mounted, but neither side found it advantageous to declare war. Therefore, on an informal basis, Franco-American fighting was restricted to clashes between armed vessels of both sides, in American waters no further north than the Carolinas.

The new Constitutional Navy, under the energetic direction of Benjamin Stoddert, the nation's first secretary of the navy, was sent into action to protect American shipping against French predators. Captain Thomas Truxtun, commanding the frigate *Constellation,* 38 guns, became the Quasi-War's hero after forcing the surrender of the French 36-gun equivalent, *L'Insurgente,* during February of 1799. Almost a year later he trounced the much stronger *La Vengeance,* 52, although his crippled adversary managed to limp away.

Whatever lure the sea already had for James would surely have been enhanced by his father's close association with the bluff, aggressive, short-tempered, and (as his letters suggest) somewhat paranoid Truxtun, who was a frequent visitor at the Biddle home. Charles Biddle was the captain's agent, handling for him all financial matters pertaining to the prizes he captured. Both James and his next oldest brother, Edward, must have found the seafarer's flamboyant stories engrossing. They badgered their father for permission to enter the navy to serve under Truxtun, and reluctantly he agreed.[15]

Late in 1799 Truxtun urged his agent to contact Secretary Stoddert at once in order to procure their "warrants" if the two boys wished to join him in the frigate *President,* sister ship to the 44-gun *Constitution* and *United States,* being fitted out in New York City. On 14 February 1800 James and Edward were commissioned U.S. Navy midshipmen. Not until summer, however, was the *President* ready for sea, and Truxtun advised Biddle to bring his sons to that city "shortly after the 4th of July." On 9 July, according to their father, he left them at the house of Aaron Burr, soon to become vice-president, although Burr's papers make no mention of it. Early in August Biddle and his wife came to Truxtun's home at Perth Amboy, New Jersey, where the frigate was loading water. Mrs. Biddle was almost inconsolable about the imminent departure of her sons, but became more reconciled to it after Tom, their "faithful black who had been born and brought up with the family," agreed to go along with them. "The parting scene between Mrs. Biddle and the boys was an affecting one; to me a very painful one," their father reminisced later.[16]

Sometime early in September they went on board the *President* to begin a rugged, and effective, naval education. Not only was Truxtun personally awesome, but his lofty status as the ruler of a man-of-war had no nonmilitary parallel in their contemporary world. David Porter, whose career would often crisscross James Biddle's, had served under Truxtun as a midshipman in the *Constellation,* and many years later referred to him as a "little tyrant," who dared not unbend "lest he should lose that appearance of respect from his inferiors that their fears inspire. . . . A man-of-war is a petty kingdom, and is governed by a petty despot."[17]

As might be expected, Truxtun was a stickler for discipline and would apply any means that he thought necessary to achieve it. Yet for all his bully and bluster he used his power fairly and for his underlings' welfare. When Porter protested about his shipboard treatment, threatening to resign from the service, Truxtun bellowed at him:

> Why you young dog! If I can help it you shall never leave the navy! Swear at you? Damn it, sir—every time I do that you go a round on the ladder of promotion! As for the first lieutenant's blowing you up every day, why, sir, t'is [sic] because he loves you and would not have you grow up a conceited young coxcomb. Go forward and let us have no more of your whining.

It seems likely that Truxtun would have dealt out an even greater amount of profane criticism to James and Edward in order to demonstrate his impartiality. According to his biographer, the captain decided to make his ship a de facto naval academy, accepting almost twice as many midshipmen for training as a 44-gun frigate usually carried. "Here indeed was a school of the sea, provided for young gentlemen who aspired to the command of a ship the best that the Navy could offer in the way of precept and example." The chaplain was assigned to teach classes in the mathematics essential to navigation, and even though he proved to be so unpopular with the senior officers that he was dismissed within six weeks, no doubt Truxtun made sure to find another instructor.[18]

The *President*'s cruise into early 1801 was uneventful as far as hostile actions were concerned. The Quasi-War was in the process of being concluded by the Treaty of Mortefontaine (Convention of 1800). But on the personal level, tragedy struck. In December Charles received a letter from one of the frigate's midshipmen telling him that the sixteen-year-old Edward had died at sea the previous month. Many years later he wrote about "the inexpressible anguish this fatal letter gave me. I cannot at this time think of it without being greatly, very greatly affected." Its impact upon his wife was even more pronounced: "It was a long time before we could get her in any way composed; her screams even now seem to strike my ear, and I shall never forget this melancholy scene."[19]

Although Charles gives no cause for his son's death, and implies that it happened during a single night, another account states that he had succumbed to a "fever" after a few days of illness; in the West Indies it would probably have been yellow fever. Edward was described in the Philadelphia press as "elegant" and "finely proportioned," standing "near six feet." His mathematical ability had been his most pronounced feature: "So great were his acquirements" in this "abstruse and difficult" field "that at the age of fifteen, when he quitted school, there was not a teacher in the city who could yield the least assistance." He had even "made himself a complete master of Sir Isaac Newton's *Principia* without the help of a tutor." Truxtun mourned to a naval colleague that Edward was "without a vice of any kind, or even a foible that I ever heard of, his disposition was of the most friendly, & benevolent kind, his education, Mental qualifications, studious habits, becoming Pride, discernment, and good sense, bid fair to make him a Naval Ornament." It could only have been a staggering blow to James, for he must have been in constant attendance, only to watch his brother die in painful delirium. He later told his father that he had been unable to write to him about the matter for he felt "too much distressed."[20]

He appears to have mastered his grief by incessant hard work during the remainder of the *President*'s cruise. "James has been very hearty," Truxtun assured Charles. The Navy Department judged his record commendable enough to retain him in the service as one of the 150 midshipmen worth keeping in its postwar cutback—204 others had been dismissed.[21]

Once the ship had docked, however, he was placed on inactive status until early 1802. A silhouette dating from that year portrays him at the age of nineteen. Dressed in his high-necked midshipman's jacket, he is saved from a "too handsome" designation by a bulging back of the head and a slightly bent nose. A single errant strand of hair falling over his upper forehead offers a contrast to the firmness of his mouth and chin. His earliest surviving letters date from this period, both pertaining to the romances of Nicholas. In a bantering elder-brother style he reported that a "Miss Lewis [?]" had "talked a great deal about her dear sweet charming darling Nicky Biddle and how much she loves him." A month later he was back on the same subject, but concerning another girl. He warned Nicholas (aged fifteen) to expect the amorous advances of Miss Johannah Turner, and went on to "advise you, on receipt hereof, to read some piece against Early Marriages, in order to strengthen yourself against the *All Powerful* charms of the *All Accomplished* Miss Johannah—Amen." James would heed his own admonitions in this sphere; early or late, he never married.[22]

In his first letter to his brother, James had mentioned in a postscript that "Tripoli seems to have declared war against the United States," echoing many months of American uncertainty as to whether such hostilities had really commenced. Yusuf Karamanli, bashaw of Tripoli, had learned to his infinite displeasure that the dey of Algiers and the bey of Tunis received greater amounts of tribute than he to save American shipping from the corsairs of these Barbary dependencies of the Ottoman (Turkish) Empire. His efforts to get a larger payoff having failed, on 14 May 1801 he declared war and sent out his raiders to seize American merchantmen and enslave their crews.[23]

The new Jefferson administration equivocated as to how to meet this ambiguous threat, for no official word had been received that Tripoli had gone to war. During 1801 a squadron was dispatched to the Mediterranean under Commodore Richard Dale, but his orders placed him in such a quandary as to guarantee failure. He could defend himself against attack, but could initiate no hostile actions himself unless he was sure that the bashaw had begun to fight. By a stroke of luck when his squadron came into Gibraltar he found two of Tripoli's best warships at anchor there and blockaded them so successfully that at length they had to be abandoned. But his efforts to bring Yusuf to his knees by either diplomacy or naval pressure were unavailing, and he was summoned home to be replaced as commodore by Richard Morris.

Early in 1802 James Biddle was ordered to join the *Constellation*, under Captain Alexander Murray, and proceed to the Mediterranean as part of Morris's fleet. He was so well educated a midshipman that he was charged with keeping the *Constellation*'s journal on a day-by-day basis during her entire eleven-month cruise. From early June to early September the ship lay off Tripoli, trying to blockade its harbor. This exercise proved to be an ordeal of boredom, broken occasionally by pursuit of a sail that turned out to be a neutral, and a single inconclusive engagement with Tripolitan ground forces on 29 July. This duty ending, the frigate plowed back and forth between Malta, Tunis, Syracuse, Palermo, Naples, Leghorn, Toulon, and Malaga on diverse supply, communicative, and visiting errands. In Malaga on 11 December, the "agreeable news," as Biddle put it, was received that the *Constellation* was called home. She left Gibraltar late in January of 1803 and dropped anchor in Chesapeake Bay on 15 March.[24]

Although Biddle had nothing to say about it, the cruise had been a disappointment, and Murray was a major reason. He had been a Revolutionary War privateersman, partially deaf from the accidental detonation of a gun, and very likely suffered from failing eyesight. He was inept enough to merit the caustic remark of William Eaton, at the time U.S. consul in Tunis and later the invader of Tripoli from Egypt, that the government "might as well send out Quaker meeting houses to float about the sea as frigates with Murrays in command."[25]

As personal matters are by nature rigidly excluded from warships' journals and logs, Biddle's experiences during his first Mediterranean cruise must be surmised or taken from secondary sources. In the sonorous prose of the *Port Folio*, a leading American naval magazine:

> The islands and shores of the Mediterranean present such interesting remains of antiquity, and so many places consecrated by great events, and the eloquence of classical writers, that a young man whose studies rendered their names familiar to him, finds among them a rich fund of instructions and gratification. Mr. Biddle availed himself of all his opportunities, and was frequently enabled to indulge the enthusiasm of a scholar when he treads upon classical ground.

Certainly the opportunities had been there for him, and it is reasonable to assume that he took full advantage of them. His journal reveals that he had time enough to visit the neolithic remains on Malta, the Carthaginian ruins near Tunis, the recently begun excavations at Pompeii, and the magnificent Byzantine mozaics at Palermo. His sojourn at Malaga, however, was too short to permit him to travel to Granada's Alhambra.[26]

Biddle remained home in Philadelphia only a few months before being assigned to the *Philadelphia*, Captain William Bainbridge's crack 38-gun frigate. Departing on 28 July, she pulled into Gibraltar on 24 August. During the voyage a picture of Biddle as an officer was provided, and it could hardly have been less flattering. In 1808, a shipmate, marine private William Ray, published a book entitled *Horrors of Slavery, or, American Tars in Tripoli.* In it he describes an episode involving Biddle and two marines. Evidently it was etiquette in Bainbridge's frigate to answer naval officers with "here, sir," while marine officers received no better than "here." According to Ray, "Mr. B. of Philadelphia was to muster the marines and inspect their hammocks," when the two privates answered their names with only "here." "O, fatal hallucination! O, impudent fellows! . . . The little captious, amphibious animal flew into the most outrageous passion, and seizing the end of the mizzen hallyards, gave each of those audacious wights twenty or thirty blows with all the strength of his little arms. . . . Luckily for them he was no Mendoza or he might have pounded them to jelly." In Ray's list of excellent officers who had been kind to the crew, Biddle's name is conspicuously absent.[27]

This castigation of Biddle cannot be shrugged off, for Ray was serving in a capacity far below his talents. A printer and editor facing debtor's prison, he had escaped by enlisting in the U.S. Marines at the age of thirty-two. A sharp-eyed and disillusioned observer, he looked down on his naval superiors from his lowly station. He was appalled at the power that officers, even midshipmen in their early teens, had "to command, to insult, to strike in the face men old enough to be their grandfathers." He ripped into Porter, who had joined the *Philadelphia* as first lieutenant in the Mediterranean, as mercilessly sadistic, driving the crew almost to the point of mutiny. He found Bainbridge remarkably indifferent to the sufferings of his bluejackets during their Tripolitan captivity. On the other hand, he lauded Stephen Decatur, who often bypassed the lash in favor of grog curtailment, as one so loved by his men that they "would almost sacrifice" their lives for him.[28]

But if the Biddle limned by Ray may be largely accurate, it is partially explicable and certainly temporary. After all, the nineteen-year-old youth had been thrust from a wealthy, intimate, and supportive family into a harsh world ruled by terror. Most officers and even some of the sailors themselves were convinced that a warship, often facing blood-freezing peril during weather- or combat-caused emergencies, could function with any efficiency at all only through an immediate and almost instinctive obedience to orders. The one way to ensure this essential response, they felt, was by the maintenance of a system of punishment so inevitable and so painful as to guarantee compliance. Men so brutalized often became brutal themselves. Officers referred to their sailors as "rabble" or "the dregs"; and some of these characterizations were accurate. If many of the "tars" of that period had been attracted to the service by the simple patriotism so noticeable at that time, the hope of prize money, or a sense of adventure, a sizable percentage were castoffs from the merchant marine, fugitives from justice, or, increasingly, deserters from the Royal Navy.

No advanced degree in psychology is required to infer that with his aristocratic background, the slightly built five-feet, four-and-a-half-inch Biddle would have been baited and otherwise well tested by his sailors. He seems to have overcompensated for his physical unimpressiveness by extreme assertiveness, shows of bravado, and a spurious ferocity. As he gained maturity and confidence he outgrew such proclivities. The logs and journals of the ships he later commanded, as well as hundreds of his captain's and squadron commander's letters to the secretary of the navy, testify that he resorted to flogging less than many of his fellow officers, Porter and Bainbridge included.

The *Philadelphia* arrived overseas supposedly in time to participate in what would be the single energetic U.S. naval campaign against Tripoli, but disaster struck instead. Morris had proven even more slothful than Dale, lallygagging around the Mediterranean from port to port with his wife and little boy. When he roused himself to some spasms of activity, they were largely useless. He was recalled in favor of Captain Edward Preble, a dour, irascible, but electrifying commander, despite the ulcers and tuberculosis that would kill him within five years. While Preble was en route to attack the bashaw, he was briefly sidetracked by the grim possibility of war with Morocco. Late in August the *Philadelphia* had intercepted the disguised Moroccan cruiser *Mirboka* with a captured American merchantman in tow. Bainbridge had discovered papers proving that the Moroccan government was issuing licenses permitting its raiders to operate against American commerce. Informed of these hostile intentions, Preble gathered his squadron off Tangier and overawed the sultan of that country into making a lasting peace with the United States. Congress eventually appropriated five thousand dollars to reward the *Philadelphia*'s people for the capture of the *Mirboka,* but Biddle's share as a midshipman could only have amounted to a few dollars.[29]

Preble then dispatched Bainbridge to patrol off Tripoli Harbor, in consort with the 12-gun sloop *Vixen.* For a couple weeks in October the two ships tried to seal off that city. On the 19th Bainbridge made an inexcusable error. Acting on a vague rumor that Tripolitan men-of-war were at work off Tunisian Cape Bon, well to the northwest, he sent the *Vixen* to hunt for them, leaving himself alone on an enemy coast. A savage storm drove the frigate far to the east, and it took a week before she could regain her position off the bashaw's capital.[30]

On the morning of the 31st a Tripolitan raider was spied trying to sneak into the harbor, and the *Philadelphia* pressed after her, but by eleven o'clock it became clear that the quarry had escaped. Bainbridge then came about to head for open sea some four miles east of the city proper when the ship ran atop Kaliusa Reef, mostly of sand, which was unmarked on American charts. Attempts to drive her forward only embedded her more solidly. Trying to back her off failed, as did efforts to lighten her by jettisoning most of the guns. The stricken frigate listed more and more to port, rendering her few remaining cannon inoperable. Tripolitan vessels began sniffing around, but remained at a distance, for they wished to possess an intact prize. Bainbridge ignored the boatswain's mate's suggestion that they consider kedging—carrying a heavy hawser tied to an anchor well away in a boat, dropping the anchor, and inching the ship along by turning her capstan. Granting the probability of failure with Tripolitan men-of-war in the vicinity, kedging might at least have been attempted. And the question has to be asked: Could not 307 well-armed and desperate Americans have resisted a little longer? It so happened that a day and a half more was all that was needed; a mere forty hours later shifting winds and tide refloated her. Furthermore, had the shallow-drafted *Vixen* been retained, she probably would have chased the enemy that morning; even if not, she might have held off the enemy for that short time or at least saved some, if not all, of the *Philadelphia*'s men from their forthcoming ordeal.[31]

At 4:00 P.M. Bainbridge called all the officers into council. They were "unanimous of opinion" that to prevent unnecessary bloodshed, the ship must be surrendered. Ray claims that some of the crew wanted to continue to fight, but that they were overridden by the officers. Frantic efforts were made to render the prize worthless to the foe. Portables were tossed over the side, but scuttling failed, for being aground she could sink no farther. The American flag was hauled down, although the hovering Tripolitans seem not to have recognized the significance of the act. Porter and Biddle were given the harrowing task of rowing out in a boat to announce that their resistance had ceased. As they approached the nearest enemy gunboat, their forthcoming misery was previewed:

> Nearly twenty men of ferocious appearance, armed with sabres, pistols, and muskets, jumped into the boat and at once commenced their work of insult and plunder. Two of them snatched Mr. Biddle's sword, pulled off his coat, and began to fight for it, until at length, probably to decide their dispute, they returned it to him. His cravats were violently torn from his neck, his waistcoat and shirt opened, and his breast exposed, for the purpose, as he very naturally inferred, of perpetrating their horrid vengeance, though their intention, it appeared, was only to search for

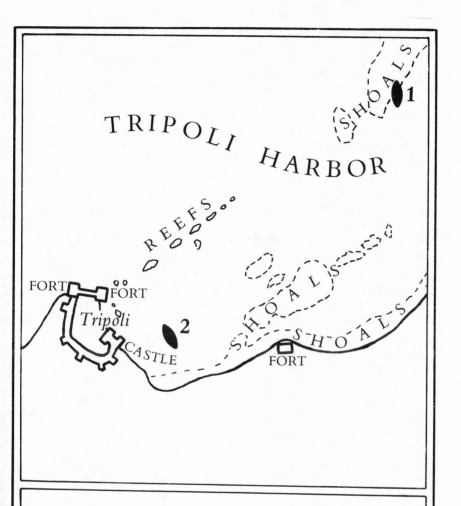

TRIPOLI HARBOR
1803–1805
1. *Philadelphia* Surrendered
31 October 1803
2. *Philadelphia* Destroyed by Decatur
16 February 1804

valuables that he might have concealed about his person. They searched all his pockets and took all his papers and money, except twenty dollars in gold which he had slipped into his boots and thereby secured. The officers and crew were then carried on shore, conducted amid the shouts and acclamations of a barbarous rabble to the palace gates.[32]

Biddle and Porter were hurried into the presence of the bashaw, Yusuf Karamanli; they remained there alone with him, his ministers, and well-armed guards, to be interrogated about their frigate and the other ships of Preble's squadron. While this was going on, Bainbridge and the others had been receiving the same rough treatment aboard the *Philadelphia,* the captain risking his life by forcibly resisting the attempt of one Tripolitan to strip away a locket containing "a miniature of his young and beautiful wife." The officers were reunited in front of the bashaw, who was reported to be, temporarily at least, in an excellent mood. He had just apprehended about one-third of the total American naval strength in the Mediterranean at that time, and come into possession of more than three hundred hostages, who should realize a handsome ransom. Later that night, Nicholas C. Nissen, the resident Danish minister and a tower of support for the Americans throughout their incarceration, managed to round up some bedding for the officers, as well as permission for them to live in the abandoned U.S. consular building.[33]

Thus commenced a year and a half for Biddle and his fellows as Yusuf's unwilling guests. The officers fared much better than the men, who were subjected to harsh discipline, cramped quarters, little food, and onerous physical labor. For the first two weeks even Bainbridge had to admit that the accommodations at the consulate were "tolerably comfortable." They were allowed servants; adequate, if coarse, food; and even occasional horseback rides. But following a report that Preble had mistreated some Tripolitan captives, the enraged bashaw subjected the officers to a day of terror in mid-November. They were sent forcibly to the nearby large stone warehouse, already jampacked with the men. "When fatigued from standing up, we were obliged to lay down on the filthy ground," Bainbridge complained, but late that evening the bashaw relented and permitted them to return to the consulate.[34]

Three months later, when Stephen Decatur wormed his way into the harbor in the USS *Intrepid,* a converted Tripolitan cruiser, in order to incinerate the *Philadelphia* at anchor, their housing changed permanently for the worse. Until liberation sixteen months later they were incarcerated in the bashaw's castle in "dark and smoky" quarters with little air and less light. As one of Biddle's fellow midshipmen wrote, their situation was "beyond description, nearly Six Months Solitary imprisonment have elapsed since the doors of our prison have been opened for any other purpose than supplying us with our daily sustenance." In a letter to the U.S. consul at Leghorn, Italy, Biddle referred to the unpleasantness he was experiencing and the further "rigor" that he anticipated. Near the end of his ordeal, he called his conditions still "hateful."[35]

Filling idle hours became their greatest necessity. Biddle's crony, Midshipman Richard Jones, complained of "the dull uniformity of a prison" and its "total lack of interesting intelligence." The mail situation was unusually aggravating. Evidently none arrived from America until the summer of 1804, and then it stopped. As late as two months before their release Bainbridge lamented that he had not "received a line" from home since that time. Biddle's first surviving letter from Tripoli was sent only seven weeks prior to his regaining freedom. Yeoman efforts were made to relieve their tedium. Lieutenants Porter and Jacob Jones set up a "College" for the midshipmen, stressing some cultural subjects, especially foreign languages, but primarily to instruct them in mathematics and naval tactics. For the latter they duplicated ship movements with blocks of wood pushed around the floor to study battle strategy. The ever-helpful Nissen brought them books, among them a volume of famous dramas. With this they began a series of theatrical presentations, building sets and making costumes. Because of his good looks and small size, Biddle probably had to suffer through leading female roles, perhaps having to undergo near strangulation if compelled to play Desdemona in *Othello*. After each performance they criticized one another's acting, which "kept them alive, and sometimes cheerful for a fortnight, and now again they began to prepare for another play."[36]

All their schemes to escape primarily by tunneling through the walls to swim out into the harbor, failed. Once they hoped to seize a passing Tripolitan boat, and on another occasion to meet a British frigate erroneously reported to be passing outside the port on a particular day, but neither opportunity could be realized.[37]

During their shared misery, Biddle made the captain his most cherished elder friend. Bainbridge needed all the support he could get, for he had plunged to the nadir of despair during his first few days of captivity. Prior to 1803, in the short history of the Constitutional Navy, only two U.S. warships had lowered their colors, and Bainbridge had commanded both. In 1799, believing that no sizable French men-of-war were in the Caribbean, he had brought the USS *Retaliation,* his first command, under the guns of two French frigates and been forced to surrender. When he was captain of the USS *George Washington* on a humiliating tribute-bearing cruise to Algiers during 1801 and 1802, the dey, Bobba Mustapha, had made him replace the American standard with the Algerian, and sent him off to Constantinople transporting the dey's mission to the sultan of Turkey. Now he had surrendered his third ship. From Tripoli he had to write Preble: "I have zealously served my Country and strenuously endeavored to guard against accidents, but in spite of every effort, misfortune has attended me throughout my Naval Life—Guadaloupe [*sic*] and Algiers have witnessed part of them, but Tripoli Strikes the death blow of my future Prospects."[38]

But he was only partly correct. He may have been the early service's unluckiest officer, but he was also its most adroit. In each case he had turned apparently irredeemable disaster to his own advantage. This came about in part by the realization of his superiors that his abasements could have happened to anyone, and partly through his own masterful ability to serve his nation well during the immediate aftermath of each misadventure. For instance, in Guadeloupe he had lied to the French commodore about total American firepower and thereby saved two U.S. warships from capture, as well as exposing the hypocrisy of French colonial officials in the West Indies, hitherto only suspected by the John Adams administration. In regard to Algiers, it was recognized in Washington that had he refused the dey's orders he would have started an unauthorized war. Moreover, he had cleverly bluffed his way past the Turkish forts at the Dardanelles and gone on to Constantinople. There he had made a close friend of the Turkish fleet admiral and brother-in-law of the sultan. On his return to Algiers he had used his new authority to overawe and abase Bobba Mustapha. He would repeat this process of turning defeat into triumph in Tripoli.[39]

There was no way that Biddle could avoid falling under Bainbridge's sway after his captain had written him at some point during their captivity: "I request that you will not only consider me as a commander who respects you as an officer . . . but as a friend who sincerely esteems you. Therefore request of me as you would your father. My friendship you have, my purse and services are at your command. I will keep you with me until I consign you to the arms of your family." Bainbridge, while acerbic enough with his naval equals and superiors, was a model teacher and mentor for most of his younger colleagues, emphasizing the importance of educating them socially and morally beyond the more obvious necessity of promoting their training in the strategy and tactics of seamanship. The junior would emulate this interest of his senior; for the remainder of his career Biddle deeply involved himself in attempting to mold his midshipmen into ideal officers. To a large degree Bainbridge has a claim to have been a father of the service's educational advancement, while Biddle from 1838 to 1842 would change his somewhat informal school established at the Naval Asylum in Philadelphia into a direct forerunner of the U.S. Naval Academy at Annapolis (see chapter 9).[40]

The news of what had happened to the *Philadelphia* and her people did not reach the United States until early in March of 1804. Naturally to Charles Biddle and his family, the realization that James was in the hands of the bashaw was a "severe blow," especially following so closely the death of Edward. It is doubtful whether their anxiety was very much eased by Truxtun's breezy assurance that "James is young and will only consider it a frolic." Charles briefly considered dashing to Tripoli himself to obtain his son's release, but instead turned for help to the resident British consul. Phineas Bond was a former Tory who in 1778 had fled to England, where he stayed for many years establishing commercial ties between the two countries before coming back to Philadelphia in his new capacity. Bond promptly wrote to the secretary of the navy asking him to "pay particular attention" to the plight of his "young friend Mr. James Biddle, if it be practical and proper," adding that he had set up a credit of five hundred pounds for him in London.[41]

When James had departed in the *Philadelphia* he had taken with him Bond's letters of introduction to British naval officers and diplomats in the Mediterranean. Of these Sir Alexander Ball was the most helpful. A close personal friend of Lord Nelson, he had besieged and taken French-held Malta, then rescued its inhabitants from starvation, for which he was rewarded with the governorship of that island. He assured Charles Biddle that he would utilize all his powers to assist James. Even though Ball's diplomatic endeavors in that direction came to nought, he was able to provide young Biddle and his colleagues some much appreciated luxuries. James wrote his brother Nicholas, who was residing in Paris, that Ball had sent him "no small quantity of Porter, Cheese & Wine—Tea, Coffee & Sugar." The ale and the wine were the most welcome, and promptly put to good use. Biddle, Midshipman Richard Jones, and Lieutenant Theodore Hunt hosted a party at which James was reported to have been "under the influence of the Libations." Here is the one recorded instance of Biddle's life at which he even approached temporary sottishness; for the rest of his life wine at dinner seems to have been the limit of his indulgence.[42]

Freedom for the *Philadelphia*'s complement neared during the spring of 1805. Although U.S. diplomatic activity aiming at their release had started almost as soon as their predicament became known, for about a year and a half a monetary accord with Tripoli to ransom the captives could not be reached. This impasse was broken by General William Eaton. He invaded Tripoli from Egypt, accompanied by Yusuf's brother Hamet (the rightful ruler), an American naval officer, nine U.S. Marines (hence "to the shores of Tripoli" in the Marine hymn), and some five hundred men made up of nearly all the nationalities of the eastern Mediterranean. On 29 April, amid international astonishment, Eaton's improbable little army captured Derna, the bashaw's easternmost city.

For a time American decision makers debated among themselves whether to support Eaton in a drive straight for Tripoli proper, or to sign a less-than-satisfactory treaty with Yusuf. A pivotal factor in opting for peace rather than war was the bashaw's almost paranoid fear of the threat posed to his rule by his brother, Hamet. Moreover, he still had three-hundred-odd Americans upon whom to vent his rage and fear. Historians still argue about the reality of the danger faced by Bainbridge, Biddle, and the others, but the evidence appears to show that their lives were indeed at stake. Certainly Bainbridge thought so. Dr. Jonathan Cowdery, whose journal is one of the main sources about the *Philadelphia*'s loss and its aftermath, noted that after the fall of Derna, the bashaw had declared that if his capital were threatened, he would "put every American prisoner to death." A little later he repeated his initial observation: Yusuf had cried "with great passion" that if Hamet tried to replace him, all of his captives would be "burned alive." Final confirmation of the real peril faced by the hostages was provided by Robert Smith, secretary of the navy, after they had come home. He told President Jefferson that "many of the officers, late prisoners in Tripoli," had informed him "that the Bashaw made up his mind to massacre them while our forces were laying waste the town. He again and again was heard to say that having killed his father and a brother, he could not have any scruples about killing a few infidels."[43]

So the appeasers were able to prevail: Bainbridge; Tobias Lear, U.S. consul-general in Algiers; and Commodore Samuel Barron, who had replaced Preble before being in turn succeeded by John Rodgers during mid-May. Eaton was never permitted to assault the city of Tripoli, and the war was ended by a treaty signed on 3 June and made effective the next day. Yusuf came off very well, for he was allowed to keep his throne (thereby dooming Hamet). Furthermore, all American forces would be withdrawn from Tripoli and the bashaw received a carefully stipulated "payment," not a ransom, of sixty thousand dollars for the prisoners. All that the United States gained by the agreement was the liberation of Bainbridge and his people, the freedom of American merchantmen from Tripolitan harassment, and the status of a most favored nation (all privileges won by one most-favored nation would be automatically extended to all others in the same category).[44]

The jubilant captives were released on the 3rd, but the men held so drunken a debauch that their departure had to be delayed a day. Bainbridge, Biddle, and most of the officers debarked on the USS *Constitution*, Rodgers's flagship, which headed for Sicilian Syracuse, arriving there on the 7th. A court of inquiry, demanded by Bainbridge, was convened on the 29th to pass judgment on his surrender of the *Philadelphia*. It was held on the USS *President*, with its members, Captains Stephen Decatur, Hugh G. Campbell, and James Barron (Samuel's brother), the latter presiding. Porter as first lieutenant was the main witness, and his testimony was all in Bainbridge's favor; the others merely parroted his version of the disaster. Late in the day Biddle was called, and stated that he could add nothing to what had already been said. The sending away of the *Vixen* was passed over and nobody mentioned the failure to try kedging. After the captain was permitted to make a lengthy self-defense, the outcome was easily predictable. The court found that he had acted throughout "with fortitude and conduct in the loss of his ship . . . and that no degree of censure should attach itself to him from that event." This decision was enthusiastically endorsed by the American people. For the third time in six years Bainbridge had managed to transform initial humiliation into eventual acclamation.[45]

Biddle and his captain sailed home in the *President*, entering Chesapeake Bay on 10 September. They were greeted as if the guns of the *Philadelphia* had knocked down the walls of the bashaw's castle and her people had successfully stormed the city. Hampton Roads, Virginia, set the tone for all the welcome-back ceremonies, featuring testimonial banquets and extravagant compliments. In a private letter Bainbridge described how he, Biddle, and the others were treated with "feasting and indulging in all the Luxuries of Epicurus, and the flowing libations of Bacchus." Richmond, Fredericksburg, and Alexandria all followed suit, with the climax a gala affair in Washington on the 25th. Shortly thereafter Bainbridge was able to fulfill the promise that he had made to Biddle in Tripoli—to "keep you with me until I consign you to the arms of your family." Late that month Biddle arrived in Philadelphia "in perfect health," to the "infinite joy of the family."[46]

In the midst of his exuberant receptions, Bainbridge found time to evaluate his officers for the Navy Department. Biddle was one of the only four whom he mentioned by name as hoping to have under his command again. He summarized him briefly: "James Biddle from his high sense of honor and talents must one day be conspicuous in the service of his Country." It would prove to be an accurate forecast.[47]

CHAPTER 2
INTERBELLUM, 1805–1812

Even before Biddle returned from Tripoli, the Navy Department had planned immediate use of him. He was "but a short time home" before heading south to join the gunboat flotilla of Captain Alexander Murray, his former commander in the *Constellation*. These miniscule warships were the subject of controversy among American naval officers. The economy-minded Jefferson administration recognized that the army was indispensable for domestic security, particularly against the Indians, but they looked upon the navy as undemocratic, monarchical, and above all expensive. Nothing demonstrates this continuing suspicion of the maritime army better than the matter of the highest grades. It was 1862 before any of the navy's officers could assume the title of admiral, while the army had promoted scores to the rank of general.[1]

This negativism spilled over into shipbuilding. The Jeffersonians, dedicated to naval curtailment, refused appropriations for the construction of any ships of the line, additional frigates, or sloops of war. But gunboats, small floating batteries, could be justified as a sort of naval militia, readily available to protect the national coastline from invaders. And they were cheap. Congress, from 1803 to 1807, authorized the construction of 288 gunboats, although only 176 were actually launched, and some of those never saw active service. Their total cost was $1,584,000, an average of a mere $9,000 apiece. The four ships of the line and six frigates that Congress sanctioned in 1815 cost the government $250,000 per vessel—a powerful contrast.[2]

The typical Jeffersonian gunboat was between 50 and 70 feet long, 10 feet at the beam, powered by oars and a fore-and-aft or lateen-rigged sail, mounting a single 24- or 32-pound gun at the bow, and manned by between 25 and 45 men. Biddle thought that the gunboats that the navy had "borrowed" from the king of Naples had proven useful during the Tripolitan War. And some of the senior officers, Preble among them, agreed, emphasizing their potential value in sheltered American inland waterways. But others did not, partly because commands of such small vessels would go to junior officers, but primarily because they were so unseaworthy as to be useless in blue-water action. For instance, nine U.S. Navy gunboats had sailed across the Atlantic for service against the bashaw; one disappeared with all hands en route, and near panic afflicted the crews of the others. James Lawrence (later to die in action in the USS *Chesapeake* against HMS *Shannon* in June of 1813) "often told" Biddle that when he went to the Mediterranean in one of them, "he had not the slightest idea of arriving there." Stephen Decatur spoke for many of his colleagues when he wondered to Bainbridge whether it would be a "real national loss if all the gunboats were sunk in 100 fathoms of water."[3]

Still, they were all that were available for service during the post-Tripolitan War's cutback. The Navy Department, aware of an upsurge of French and other privateers off the shores of South Carolina and Georgia, ordered Murray (with a copy to Biddle) to "protect all vessels whatever, as well foreign as American, against the aggressions of the armed vessels publick or private of any nation." Biddle was given command of "Gunboat No. 1"—a most inauspicious designation, for she was the second to be so named. The first had been commissioned during the previous summer, and was at Savannah in early September when a massive hurricane swept out of the Atlantic, inflicting tremendous coastal damage all the way to Maine. When the wind and rain had finally subsided, a search began for the missing Gunboat No. 1. She was eventually discovered comfortably resting in a corn field eight miles inland. In Boston, delighted anti-Jeffersonian Federalists toasted the hapless vessel at a public dinner: "Gun-boat Number One: If our gun-boats be of no use upon the water, may they at least be the best upon earth."[4]

Biddle had no inclement weather with which to contend, only boredom, for Murray and his complement found little to do that autumn. The commodore reported to the secretary that he had "inquired into the proceedings of the French privateers," but none of them had "appeared off this Coast since my Arrival." He praised the diligence of one of his underlings: "Mr Biddle is very attentive with his gun boats, keeps out whenever the weather will permit, & when he goes in, he returns with a Suply [*sic*] of water & refreshments for us, by which means our present cruize is rendered . . . much more to our satisfaction."[5]

Matters continued quiet as the winter passed into the spring, and Murray's people began to be sent out on other errands. Biddle's primary chore was to examine the harbor at Beaufort, South Carolina, as a possible naval base. The nation had no such establishment south of Gosport (Norfolk), Virginia, except for the naval station at New Orleans, a site too far west for effective patrolling of Atlantic and Caribbean waters. Biddle's investigation at Beaufort was an analytic masterpiece. The task of composing his long report which filled almost four large pages (1800 words) was so fatiguing that three-quarters of the way through he jotted in the margin, "Here I break off to take Coffee and Beefstake [sic]." Beaufort's harbor was deep enough for any naval purposes, he found, and the sandbar near its entrance was passable even at low tide. The maze of rivers and inlets that surrounded the city offered both protection from attack and easy access to the interior should retreat be necessary. Drinking water and timber were excellent and abundant. Nor did he overlook negatives. He concluded that the terrain would not allow land fortifications strong enough for adequate defense. Nevertheless, the city should be able to ward off enemy incursions with the aid of gunboats. Summarizing, he recommended Beaufort as the best location for a naval base south of the Chesapeake. But the inflexibility of governmental economy pigeonholed his report. Beaufort never became a naval establishment, and New Orleans continued in that capacity until a base was founded at Pensacola in the mid-1820s.[6]

Biddle was well entertained during his frequent visits to Charleston, whose older inhabitants had not forgotten that it was from their city that his Uncle Nicholas had gone out to wage his gallant battle with HMS *Yarmouth* in 1778. Even so, his work in South Carolina had been tedious, and he welcomed a leave in May of 1806, remaining at home in Philadelphia for the next several months.[7]

But he soon chafed for a meaningful and more interesting assignment. The navy could offer him nothing, for almost all the frigates and sloops were harborbound or out of commission. With so many of its officers rusticating on half-pay and no foreseeable use for them, the department was granting furloughs practically upon receipt of their requests. Biddle decided to follow many of his colleagues into the merchant marine, which was ever on the lookout for skilled navigators and sea-trained administrators. He opted for China, where his second cousin George W. Biddle, Clement's son, had been living since 1804. James could renew his acquaintance with his relative while partaking in the risky but potentially lucrative trade with that exotic country which most Americans have found so absorbing from the beginning. During January of 1807 he asked for and was soon granted

a leave for that purpose. A month later he received his long-anticipated promotion to lieutenant.[8]

He finally sailed from Philadelphia on 30 April in the *Mercury,*
commanded by Captain Thomas Arnold, probably in the capacity of
supercargo (shipowner's representative). One authority speculates that
he may have gone out as an employee of Stephen Girard, an eminent
Philadelphia merchant, banker, philanthropist, and one of the country's first millionaires who was a giant in the early China trade. But
by 1807 he would probably have considered anyone named Biddle a
persona non grata. He had first dispatched George Biddle as his agent
in China during 1802, and was pleased enough with his performance
to promote him to his chief supercargo and send him back two years
later. By the time James was ready to head for Canton, however,
Girard had already become convinced that George was a larcenist. He
launched a lawsuit against his former employee accusing him of acting
in league with a Chinese merchant to mulct him out of precisely
$83,405.51. Furthermore, Girard owned neither the *Mercury* nor the
Pennsylvania Packet, upon which James returned. It is most unlikely
that he would hire as his agent a cousin of the man he was in the
process of ruining—let alone send him to and from China in some-
body else's ships. Probably James was acting for some other import-
export house in Philadelphia.[9]

James's voyage to China occupied approximately 145 days, undoubtedly by way of the Cape of Good Hope, India, and through the
Straits of Malacca to Batavia (Djakarta) in the Netherlands East Indies
(Indonesia), before proceeding to Portuguese Macao, some forty miles
west of Hong Kong and about ninety miles south of Canton. When
he arrived in China's southern metropolis, George was temporarily
absent but had left a letter for him, anticipating "the Pleasure I will
have by taking you by the Hand & hearing from our family. I am
much pleased by your coming this way altho the present prospect of
Gain is not very great. I think it will be much better than commanding
Gun Boats." He ended by telling his cousin to go to "Imperial Factory
No. 1" which would be "*your quarters*" during his stay and that his
"comprador [Chinese business agent] will take care of you until my
arrival."[10]

Ordinarily one would expect to read James's reactions to vistas
unlike anything that he had witnessed before. The waterfront, for
instance, as described by Sydney and Marjorie Greenbie in *Gold of
Ophir; or The Lure that Made America* (1925):

> The Pearl River was a never-ending scene of entertainment. Stately man-
> darin boats with lanterns swinging and flags flying, flower boats, with
> all their filigree carving, and a sound of music all day long floating back

amidst the uproar, like unfinished melody made with tinkling glass accompanied by the occasional banging of tin pans; luxurious canal boats, from far inland cities, with varnished sides and spacious cabins, bringing down the tea which was to load some American brig; or great sea-going junks moving out among the canal boats, setting forth for Luzon and Java and the Malay Peninsula, as they had been doing since the very dawn of history.

But sad to say, James's total commentary about his impressions of China add up to exactly three words. After his homecoming he told Bainbridge that he "did not like" Canton. He would enjoy that city much more when he returned thirty-eight years later (see chapter 10).[11]

At least the sort of business in which he had engaged may be surmised by what was listed when he cleared customs in Philadelphia on 12 April 1808. Some items seem slated for resale: "11 boxes of various teas, 6 bales of nankeen cloth," and "several boxes of Chinese porcelains." Others were clearly gifts to family and friends or for his own personal use: "feather fans, ivory chess sets, and a variety of lacquerware furnishings such as a desk and chessboard."[12]

James left China in late November on the *Pennsylvania Packet,* under Captain Edward Boden, which, after 140-day passage, docked at Philadelphia in April of 1808. He may have been accompanied by his cousin George, who "went home at the end of the tea season of 1807–1808, apparently in an attempt to extricate himself from his difficulties and obtain the release of his property that Girard had attached." In this effort George was unsuccessful, and in May of 1809, before he knew the result of his former employer's lawsuit against him, he had to go back to China. There he learned that arbitrators had awarded Girard $38,000. This blow, coupled with demands for repayment of debts which he had contracted in Canton, prostrated him with "anxiety and mortification"; he died in Macao on 16 August 1811. The Biddles tried to reassure one another that George's peculations were "very slight offenses," but the affair was unquestionably a stain on the family escutcheon.[13]

Hardly had the lieutenant distributed his presents and regaled his relatives with stories of adventures "east of Suez" than he began to crave some challenging professional activity. He learned from scuttlebutt that Bainbridge was about to ready the USS *President* for sea; he wrote the captain asking for a position with him, as he needed "a Cruize to rub off my merchant service ideas," adding that he preferred frigates to gunboats. But the rumor was premature, and after he had notified the secretary of his return from the Far East and his readiness for a new position, he was sent back to Murray's squadron, this time to command Gunboat No. 120 in Chesapeake Bay.[14]

If he had found unpalatable the operation of these small craft against nonexisting French privateers off South Carolina, his new duties were even less appetizing. The reason was the Embargo Act, which President Jefferson had pushed through Congress late in 1807. Britain and France, locked in the Napoleonic Wars, had been regularly seizing American ships and cargoes for alleged violations of their commercial measures against each other. British impressment of American sailors for compulsory service in the Royal Navy was an even greater irritant. Jefferson had repeatedly protested against these offenses against his nation's sovereignty, but to no avail. As his sea-going navy was moribund, the president had no forcible means to retaliate, except by resorting to his own variety of commercial warfare. He was convinced that the belligerents could not long withstand the loss of American goods and services: the Embargo Act forbade any American exports whatsoever, not only to Britain and France, but also to neutrals, for they might reship such produce to the warring nations.

The measure was almost hysterically unpopular in the maritime areas; merchants, sailors, shopkeepers, and anyone else engaged in foreign trade were promptly thrown into a crippling depression. Preventing violations of the embargo during its fifteen-month tenure provided massive headaches for naval officers. The experiences of Porter and Bainbridge may illustrate some of their difficulties. Like it or not, Biddle and his colleagues had no choice but to enforce it.

Porter's dilemma was caused by the act's complexity. One of his gunboats apprehended a Spanish schooner with the absurd name of *Precious Ridicule,* en route from Baton Rouge to Pensacola, both in nearby Spanish West Florida, laden with "wheat, cheese, oil, and clothing." Since the embargo barred only the exportation of American commodities, Porter had to decide what portion of her cargo was domestic and should be forfeited. In effect he threw up his hands, arbitrarily declaring that the wheat must be retained, while permitting the export of the rest as Spanish produce.[15]

Bainbridge, while in charge of the naval establishment at Portland, Maine (then still part of Massachusetts), encountered threats of violence, accompanied by smuggling on a sweeping scale. Portland's customs inspector notified Bainbridge that his subordinates were "nightly insulted and their lives have repeatedly been threatened if they persisted in that vigilance by which the laws of our Country they are commissioned to enforce." Moreover, "hundreds of disguised and armed men take possession of the wharves and thus with impunity load and convoy out of the harbor [for Canada] such vessels as are prepared and intended for smuggling." Bainbridge confirmed this when he told the department that the previous night he himself had observed two ships with American cargoes putting out to sea in "open violation of the Embargo laws." With only a single gunboat for patrolling, he added, there was no way in which he could stop such overt and widespread noncompliance. Luckily for the captain's self-respect, he was soon reassigned to Washington on other business.[16]

Biddle refers to his own experiences with the embargo in only one letter. During mid-September 1808 he had to ask a U.S. district attorney for advice in the case of the Swedish ship *Ann and Hannah*, about to embark on a voyage from New Castle, Delaware, to the West Indies. He had seen a newspaper item stating that all cargo-laden vessels, whatever their nationality, came under the act, but his original orders applied only to American-flag carriers. What should he do about the *Ann and Hannah*? No answer from the district attorney seems to have survived, but it is likely that Biddle emulated Porter, impounding American goods while letting the Swedish vessel clear port with identifiable commodities from abroad. To the great relief of naval officers and the maritime communities, on 1 March 1809 the Embargo Act was replaced by the somewhat less restrictive Non-Intercourse Act, outlawing both imports to and exports from the belligerents, but throwing open American commerce with the neutrals.[17]

By this time the U.S. Navy was slowly emerging from its post-1805 doldrums. The *Chesapeake-Leopard* affair had been the major catalyst for this renaissance. During June of 1807 Commodore James Barron had been peremptorily ordered to sail in the *Chesapeake* to assume command of the Mediterranean Squadron. His frigate was woefully unprepared for any hostile action. Because of the Washington Navy Yard's inefficiency and Master Commandant Charles Gordon's sloth while in charge of the ship prior to Barron's takeover, her decks were littered with a jumble of unsorted stores and munitions. Off the Virginia Capes lay Captain Salusbury P. Humphreys and his HMS *Leopard*. He knew that four Royal Navy deserters were in the *Chesapeake*; so intercepting her, he demanded the right to board and search for them. Barron tried to stall for time to ready his cluttered ship for action, but Humphreys poured in broadsides until the U.S. flag fluttered down. After removing the four he permitted the *Chesapeake* to put back into port with 3 killed and 18 wounded, Barron among them. American fury over this atrocity brought the two countries close to war, but soon abated with a realization of the national impotence. Barron, however, had to serve as the essential scapegoat for his country's humiliation. A court-martial early the next year found him guilty of having his ship unprepared for combat, and sentenced him to suspension from the navy for five years without pay.[18]

Aware from this incident that it was totally unable to meet any British maritime challenge, the Navy Department slowly began putting its larger warships back into commission. Bainbridge was given the task of outfitting the USS *President,* and early in 1809 Biddle received a most welcome letter appointing him second lieutenant of that frigate. The spring and summer were occupied with the myriad details of preparing a 44-gun man-of-war for blue-water duty, and by the autumn Bainbridge commenced a number of short shakedown cruises along the coast. Biddle says nothing about his experiences, but they could not have been enjoyable, for the *President* was continually battered by atrocious weather. Bainbridge summarized one voyage as no more than "Gales, Shoals, the Shores, rocks, Cape Hatteras . . . [and the] Gulph Stream." At one point—which must have been terrifying for Bainbridge and Biddle, with their memories of Tripoli—her pilot ran the frigate aground, but she was refloated without damage.[19]

Another cruise early the next year brought more of the same, with the captain carping to Porter that he was "heartily tired" of "Buffeting our boisterous Coast in the inclement Season." Biddle and his shipmates must have agreed. In March the ship went aground for the second time; this time her pilot accomplished the feat on a sunny, windless morning in Chesapeake Bay. She seemed so thoroughly embedded that preparations for kedging began, but a fortuitous shift in the wind refloated her, again without lasting harm to her hull. Bainbridge soon relinquished command of the *President* to engage in commercial voyages to Russia, and Biddle found himself once more seeking employment.[20]

While his movements from the spring of 1810 to the outbreak of war two years later may easily be outlined, details are scanty. Only three of his personal letters have survived, all pertaining to little more than trivial gossip about friends and relatives in Philadelphia. From other sources we discern that he briefly commanded the sloop of war *Siren,* went on one short cruise in the USS *Constitution* under Captain Isaac Hull, returned to the *President* with Captain John Rodgers, and during the spring of 1811 applied to the secretary for a furlough. He mentioned to Rodgers that he planned "to make a voyage to some port in the south of Europe." His destination turned out to be Portugal, but particulars—when he sailed, what he did there, when he returned—of his enterprise are lacking. Since he was back in the country by November of 1811, time would have allowed him to sail for Lisbon in any of the fifteen merchantmen leaving Philadelphia during that interim, and a roughly equal number were available for his passage back.[21]

Biddle emerges a little more clearly late the same autumn when Secretary of the Navy Paul Hamilton ordered him to report to New York City "with the despatches which you will receive from the Department of State." Master Commandant James Lawrence in the sloop *Hornet* would land him at Cherbourg, France, where he could expect further instructions from Secretary James Monroe. A second order, dated the same day, added a note of confusion. Biddle was, at the direction of President James Madison, to be accompanied in the *Hornet* by the noted munitions tycoon, "Mr. Du Pont de Nemours of Paris." Yet "Mr. Du Pont" is never mentioned in several newspaper accounts, all of which comment about Biddle's progress from Washington to New York, and his responsibility of taking official dispatches to Britain and France, as well as letters to London from Augustus Foster, British minister to the United States.[22]

The *Hornet*'s transatlantic passage was swift, for Biddle reached Paris on 4 January 1812. Apart from his official duties, how he occupied the rest of his time during a four-month stay in Europe is conjectural. A contemporary magazine tells of his "presentation to the Emperor Napoleon," and that he "attended all the parties given at the Tuileries." His observations about such momentous social occasions might have been expected to be retained, but evidently they were not. In yet another oddity, Lieutenant Charles Morris, Biddle's friend and fellow officer in the *President* less than two years before, was also in France during the same period. He described his sojourn there at some length, but Biddle's name is never mentioned.[23]

Biddle's business in Paris was with Joel Barlow, U.S. minister to France. This poet, publisher, land promoter, and leading radical had lived briefly in England, then in France from 1790 to 1805, becoming wealthy through speculation in French bonds. Madison had given him his appointment during 1811. Despite his long European experience, Barlow proved to be a most inept diplomat. Napoleon refused even to see him for two months after his arrival in Paris, and then hoodwinked the naïve American. Barlow had been instructed to get compensation for the many hundreds of American ships that the French had seized over the years. But the emperor lured him away from his mission by proposing instead a new commercial treaty between the two nations.[24]

A Boston newspaper announced that Lawrence (undoubtedly with Biddle, although his name is not mentioned) left Paris on 18 April, arriving at Cherbourg on the 27th, from which they sailed immediately. The *Hornet* docked in New York on 21 May after a twenty-two-day passage. Biddle raced on to Washington to deliver Barlow's report to the State Department. It made dismal reading, for it proved that Napoleon was obdurate about paying any claims, and "hope had to be abandoned for a settlement with France." But hostilities with England were on the immediate horizon, and as Biddle left for Philadelphia, he was probably as one with his naval colleagues in welcoming a clash with the arrogant Royal Navy, which professionally would prove the merit of the new American service, and personally would grant its officers opportunities for prize money and lasting fame.[25]

CHAPTER 3
WAR OF 1812 SERVICE,
1812–1815

Biddle's leave at home after his Paris assignment was of short duration, for the United States declared war on Great Britain on 18 June 1812. President James Madison had become thoroughly frustrated in his diplomatic endeavors to persuade London either to rescind its Orders in Council hampering American commerce or to stop impressing American sailors. He finally caved in to the demands of expansionistic and depression-ridden southern and western congressmen who felt that the only way to hurt the British was by conquering Canada, a feat deemed sure to succeed. The war measure was popular inland, but in the maritime areas only one congressman opted for hostilities. Furthermore, it was a masterpiece of bad timing, for the British repealed their Orders in Council only four days after the United States had declared war.

During the previous winter the administration had debated about how to use its miniscule fleet of some seventeen vessels that would have to face the eight-hundred-odd ships of the line, frigates, sloops, and lesser craft of the Royal Navy. Secretary of the Navy Paul Hamilton wanted to keep his men-of-war in port for coastal defense. Madison, however, reinforced by the appeals of captains William Bainbridge and Charles Stewart, overrode him, and declared that the U.S. Navy must be utilized offensively. This led to another controversy. Commodore John Rodgers argued that a single large squadron should be assembled to sail as a unit, for he was well aware that he would command it. Stephen Decatur and Bainbridge, on the other hand, urged that smaller units should do the fighting, either a frigate accompanied by a sloop or two, or each ship operating independently. The latter viewpoint eventually prevailed, especially when Rodgers's large squadron, made up of three frigates and two sloops put out on a cruise almost immediately after the war began and accomplished nothing of significance. The important psychological boost to the national morale brought about by three early American frigate victories aside, the navy should always have sailed as individual commerce raiders, avoiding battle whenever possible. Indeed, the smaller the American warship, the better. The greatest damage to Britain's essential and vulnerable merchant marine was done by privateers, next by U.S. Navy sloops, and last by frigates.

Biddle learned of the war while still in Philadelphia, and as he had no specific assignment, hastened to New York, where Rodgers was assembling his squadron, to offer his services as a volunteer. To his intense disappointment, he just missed his former chief; he even hired a boat, trying to intercept him off Sandy Hook, New Jersey, only to fail again. David Porter, commanding the little 32-gun frigate *Essex,* was to have accompanied Rodgers, but discovery of a rotting foremast and a fouled hull kept him in port for two weeks after the fleet had departed. As the *Essex* was the only warship remaining in New York, Biddle promptly asked to be taken on as a lieutenant. Porter agreed, but the frigate's other officers, knowing that Biddle had seniority over them, objected, and his request was refused. Contemporary publications imply that Biddle understood why he had been rejected and accepted it with equanimity, but that is not true. According to Porter, Biddle "expressed much chagrin," expostulated with him, and even threatened him. Prior to this confrontation there is no evidence that the Porter-Biddle relationship had been anything but amicable. After all, they had shared the experience of Tripolitan manhandling when they announced the *Philadelphia*'s surrender, and they had jointly withstood the rigors of the bashaw's imprisonment. But after this clash in New York, their association remained gelid for the rest of their lives.[1]

The disgruntled Biddle had no choice but to go home and wait. Late in July he received the welcome word that the secretary had assigned him as first lieutenant to Master Commandant (Commander) Jacob Jones in the *Wasp,* just into the mouth of the Delaware on the 17th, carrying dispatches from France. Both the man and the ship were first rate. Jones had an unusual background for his profession. Originally a practicing physician, then a clerk in the Delaware Supreme Court, he had entered the navy as a midshipman at the advanced age of twenty-eight. Biddle had been one of Jones's students at the "College" in Tripoli, and that had cemented their friendship. The sloops *Wasp* and *Hornet* (Biddle would command the latter from 1813 to 1815) were 18-gun sister ships, displacing approximately 450 tons, launched in 1806 and 1805 respectively. Alterations over the years would differentiate them slightly, but both would be undefeated in action against their British equivalents.[2]

August and September were occupied with overhauling and out-fitting the *Wasp* for a cruise, and it was not until 13 October that she was able to weigh anchor. By that time the exhilarating news had long since come in that off Halifax, Nova Scotia, Captain Isaac Hull's 44-gun *Constitution* had turned HMS *Guerrière*, 38, into a hulk; Jones, Biddle, and their fellows longed to emulate this stirring achievement. The *Wasp* headed southeast, and on the night of the 16th was tossed about by a strong gale that carried away her jib boom, killing two sailors.[3]

On the night of the 17th several distant sails could be discerned, and the Americans followed them. By daybreak seven ships could be counted, and Jones moved in to ascertain their nationality. They proved to be what remained of a fourteen-vessel convoy under the escort of HMS *Frolic*, 18, commanded by Captain Thomas Whinyates. He had spent the previous five years in various Central American and Carib-bean duties and had only recently heard of the war with the United States and the defeat of the *Guerrière*. The same storm that had hurt the *Wasp* had scattered Whinyates's convoy, and inflicted even greater damage to the *Frolic*, carrying away her mainyard top sails, and springing her main topmast.[4]

The *Wasp* bore down on a port tack to take advantage of the wind, blowing from the northwest, and both commanders hurriedly took down or reefed their upper sails to use "short fighting canvas." Whinyates ran up Spanish colors, but Jones could easily identify the stranger as an Englishman. At 11:32, when the two ships were only some fifty or sixty yards apart, action commenced. The seas were running very high and each commander took what advantage of them that he could. Whinyates, hoping to dismantle the American, fired rapidly from the crests of the waves, aiming high and ripping into the *Wasp*'s spars and rigging. Jones reported:

> Our main topmast was shot away between four and five minutes of the commencement of the firing and falling together with the main topsail-yard across the larboard [port] fore and foretopsail braces, rendered our headyards unmanageable for the remainder of the action. At eight min-utes the gaff and mizzen-top-gallant-masts came down, and at twenty minutes from the beginning of the action every brace and most of the rigging was shot away.

The *Wasp*, on the other hand, leveled primarily at the British hull and deck, letting go broadsides while coming down from the crests, on occasion so precipitously that the muzzles of her guns dipped under water. Nor did she fail to aim at the *Frolic*'s rigging. His "gaff being shot away, and there being no sail on the mainmast, the brig became unmanageable," Whinyates mourned.[5]

Although neither ship could maneuver effectively, the *Wasp* was still able to come down on her adversary, finally ramming into her with a "tremendous crash" which sent the British jib boom tearing in "between the main and mizzen rigging of the *Wasp*," directly over the heads of Jones and Biddle. The Americans were poised to board when Jones waved them back, for he had noticed that he was in a perfect position to rake the *Frolic*, that is, to fire down the length of her deck, a blow lethal to personnel. His ensuing barrage swept away almost every topside defender. Whinyates complained that at the same moment he was "unable to bring a gun to bear," while Jones asserted that as his men were "loading for the last broadside, our rammers were shoved against the sides of the enemy."[6]

At this juncture the Americans boarded. Jack Lang, an English-born sailor, was the first to leap across to the *Frolic*, with Biddle at his heels. When Biddle tried to clamber onto the jib boom, he tripped and started to fall, sure to be crushed between the two wallowing vessels. But an unnamed midshipman grabbed his coattails and yanked him back to safety. Recovering his balance, Biddle reached the British deck, followed by a mixed group of officers and men, raced past Lang, and reached the forecastle first. There he found Whinyates and two other officers, all wounded so gravely that they had to prop themselves against the rails in order to stand. The helmsman was the only man on the deck unhurt. No one resisted, and at 12:15 Biddle sprang to haul down the Union Jack by himself. The battle had lasted precisely forty-three minutes. Victorious commanders usually try to pass around the laurels as generously as possible, and Jones gave Biddle the highest grade: "Lieutenant Biddle's active conduct contributed much to our success, by the exact attention to every department during the engagement, and the animating example to the crew by his intrepidity."[7]

Although casualty figures of this fracas have never been agreed upon, it is certain that the carnage in the *Frolic* had been dreadful. She had something in the neighborhood of 110 on board when the firing commenced, and Whinyates estimated that only about 20 emerged unscathed. Biddle thought that the enemy had suffered some 30 killed and between 40 and 50 wounded. Historians have continued to differ slightly on the subject. James Fenimore Cooper surmises that the toll was between 90 and 100, Theodore Roosevelt's guess is 90; Captain Alfred T. Mahan's figure of 58, which was first given by a virulently

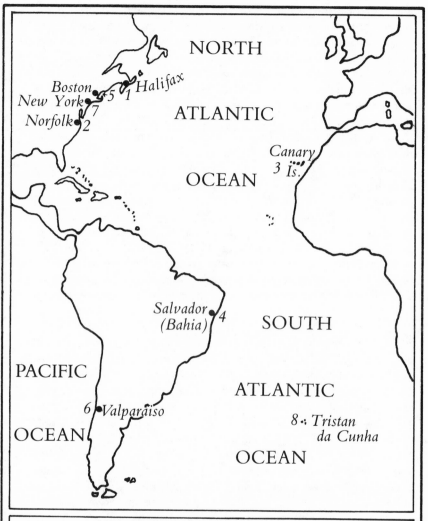

WAR OF 1812
Blue Water Naval Battles
(Mentioned in the Text)

1. *Constitution* vs. *Guerrière*
2. *Wasp* vs. *Frolic*
3. *United States* vs. *Macedonian*
4. *Constitution* vs. *Java*
5. *Chesapeake* vs. *Shannon*
6. *Essex* vs. *Phoebe* and *Cherub*
7. *President* vs. *Endymion* et al.
8. *Hornet* vs. *Penguin*

anti-American English source, is suspect. No one has quarreled with Jones's casualty report for the *Wasp*—5 dead and 5 wounded.[8]

There was also some later bickering about the relative strength of the two ships. Jones told the secretary that the *Frolic* was "stronger by 4 guns," and as this enhanced the victory, the American press trumpeted his exaggeration. Actually the British advantage was extremely slight. Evidently the *Frolic* carried a mere one gun more, and her advantage in tonnage and weight of broadside thrown was minimal. Furthermore, the *Wasp* had a larger crew and had suffered less damage from the prebattle storm. It seems fair to conclude that the contest had been between equals, and that the triumph of the Americans had been won by their more effective tactics and more accurate gunnery.[9]

Shortly after the British surrender, the two vessels drifted apart, with Biddle remaining behind to command his prize. Just then the *Frolic*'s mainmast and foremast crashed onto the deck. When Biddle had finished supervising a two-and-a-half-hour stint to clear the wreckage and extricate the dead and wounded from it, he spied an English ship speeding toward him. She was the ship of the line *Poictiers*, which even an intact sloop could be expected only to outrun, not to outfight. Since both the *Wasp* and the *Frolic* had been partially dismasted, they were easily taken. Admiral Sir John Beresford restored the wounded Whinyates to command of the *Frolic*—a later court-martial praised his courage and completely vindicated him for his loss. The *Poictiers* herded together the scattered convoy, escorting it and her two prizes into nearby Bermuda.

The outcome of the *Wasp-Frolic* duel reached the United States within three weeks. While there was some head-wagging about the ill luck attending the *Poictiers*'s inconvenient arrival, the country exulted in the victory, and the *Wasp*'s people joined those of the *Constitution* as the first Americans to be hailed as humblers of "the Ruler of the Waves." Jones's success was belatedly recognized as even more spectacular than Hull's, for he had beaten an equivalent, while the *Constitution* was demonstrably superior to the *Guerrière*.

Biddle and his fellows were "treated very politely" by the British in Bermuda. To contemplate a second imprisonment only seven years after the first must have been discouraging, but his enforced stay lasted little more than two weeks. Late in November an English cartel (a ship carrying exchanged prisoners of war under a flag of truce) brought the captives into New York.[10]

The celebrations started at once, generating the following doggerel, whose literary merit falls a remote second to its patriotic ardor:

The foe bravely fought, but his arms were all broken,
  And he fled from his death-wound aghast and affrighted;
But the *Wasp* darted forward her death-doing sting,
  And full on his bosom, like lightning alighted.
She pierced through his entrails, she maddened his brain,
  And he writhed and he groan'd as if torn with the colic;
And long shall John Bull rue the terrible day
  He met the American *Wasp* on a *Frolic*.

One may be permitted to elevate a skeptical eyebrow at the assertion that this "stirring song . . . was soon on the lips of singers at public gatherings, in barrooms, workshops, and even by ragged urchins in the street." One of the many toasts offered to the victors at a public dinner went: "Captain Jones, his Officers, and Crew: Their conduct proves that it requires British seventy-fours to conquer American sloops of war." Jones was the chief beneficiary of individual honors. He received "elegant swords" from his native state of Delaware and New York City, silver plate, a gold medal from the U.S. government, a quick promotion to captain, and a frigate command.[11]

Biddle was not far behind. He was given a sword by the Pennsylvania legislature, and Philadelphians presented him with a silver urn inscribed: "To Lieutenant James Biddle, United States Navy, from the early friends and companions of his youth, who, while their country rewards his public services, present this testimonial of their esteem for his private worth." He was elected a member of the United States Military Philosophical Society and an honorary member of the prestigious Society of the Cincinnati, the hereditary association founded by American Revolutionary officers. On 29 January 1813 the national government awarded silver medals to the *Wasp*'s officers. One hopes that Biddle did not daily await the receipt of his too anxiously—the secretary of the navy finally notified him that his medal was ready for presentation on 1 February 1837, a mere twenty-four years and three days after that honor had been bestowed. The payment of his prize money was not so long delayed. As the *Frolic* had been recaptured through no fault of the *Wasp*'s people, Congress appropriated $25,000 to compensate them. Biddle's share came to $416.67, and in a comparative marvel of bureaucratic speed he received it during 1818, only half a decade later.[12]

Some months of inactivity for Biddle ensued, broken by the welcome news that he had been promoted to master commandant. He could not have been elated toward the end of March to be informed by a private letter from the new secretary of the navy, William Jones, confirmed officially three weeks later, that he must report to the

Delaware River for gunboat duty protecting Philadelphia. But almost immediately he was spared this sterile responsibility, when Jones selected him to command the USS *Hornet* in New York and prepare her for a cruise. The sloop had been rebuilt during 1811, making her into a "very good sailer." Furthermore, she now carried two 12-pound long guns and eighteen 32-pound carronades, two more than her sister, the *Wasp*.[13]

By early 1813 the British were appalled at what had happened at sea in the American war. First the *Guerrière* had been lost, then the *Frolic*. Shortly after digesting this unappetizing news they learned that on 25 October 1812, a few hundred miles west of the Canary Islands, Decatur in the USS *United States,* 44, had not only hammered into submission HMS *Macedonian,* 38, but, eluding British patrolers along the Connecticut coast, had brought her into New London as a prize. Even worse, off Brazil on 29 December Bainbridge's *Constitution,* in the most bitterly fought engagement of the war between single frigates, had riddled HMS *Java,* 38, so thoroughly that she had to be scuttled the next day. The semiofficial London *Times* could hardly believe it: "The Public will learn, with sentiments we shall not presume to anticipate, that a third British frigate has struck her flag to an American. . . . Three frigates! Anyone who had predicted such a result of an American war this time last year would have been treated as a madman or a traitor."[14]

Strategically, of course, these defeats lessened not a whit Britain's overwhelming naval superiority, but their psychological effect was pronounced. They brought deliriums of happiness to Americans, compensating in part for the dismal record of the U.S. Army along the Canadian frontier during 1812, and consternation to the British. For two centuries and more the Royal Navy, even in the face of odds of two or three to one against it, had trounced Spaniards, Dutchmen, and Frenchmen with equal élan and efficiency. Its tally at sea against the French from 1793 through 1815 is astounding: the British lost 10 warships, the French 377. But because of the havoc inflicted by the American superfrigates, the Admiralty very sensibly ordered English 38s to avoid duels with the three 44s, unless compelled to fight for self-preservation or as parts of squadrons. Considerably more troublesome to Biddle and his colleagues, the enemy, under a conviction that the best way to deal with the emergency was to bottle up the American warships in port, strongly reinforced its blockading units all the way from Chesapeake Bay to the coast of Maine. They particularly congregated off New York as a convenient central location.[15]

Biddle reported to that city to assume command of the *Hornet,* where he was reunited with Jacob Jones in the former HMS (now

USS) *Macedonian* as the other members of a squadron led by Decatur in the *United States*. Aware that any exit southeast past Sandy Hook would be well corked, Decatur led his three ships into Long Island Sound, hoping to reach open sea between Block Island and Montauk Point on a commerce-raiding mission. Just when escape appeared at hand, a potent enemy squadron loomed up on the horizon, consisting of two ships of the line and escorting frigates, commanded by Admiral Sir Thomas Hardy, who had captained Nelson's flagship *Victory* at Trafalgar in 1805. The only option remaining to Americans on 1 June was run back into the sound and scurry into the well-defended harbor of New London, Connecticut.[16]

British reinforcements continued to arrive in the area until they totaled seven ships of the line and frigates, in addition to some smaller men-of-war. The three American vessels had to be taken eight miles up the Thames and protected by earthworks, dubbed "Fort Decatur," as well as by a huge chain obstructing access from downriver. As the months dragged through the summer and into the fall, constant drill with the guns and in the rigging kept the crews occupied, and a school was set up for the professional improvement of the younger officers. But this enforced leisure was agonizing for Decatur, Jones, and Biddle. New Londoners' initial adulation quickly soured, while the tightening British constriction dumped the area into economic stagnation by practically ending all maritime activities along the Connecticut shore. Many vented their anger on the officers, who found themselves the recipients of "scathing remarks implying cowardice, duplicity, and other invectives of the like."[17]

Stung by this attitude, Decatur resolved to take advantage of the shortened days and stormy weather of late autumn. As surreptitiously as possible he moved his squadron down to the mouth of the Thames, preparing to make a dash for it. All was ready on the night of 12 December when "blue lights" were observed shining from both sides of the river and at the harbor's entrance. The three officers immediately concluded that ultra-Federalist opponents of the war, so rife in the Northeast, were signaling the blockaders that an escape attempt was about to commence. Local inhabitants later scoffed at this theory, insisting that the "blue lights" were no more than those accidently "kindled by fishermen, or the gleams from country windows, or reflections from the heavens upon the water." The sources of these lights have never been determined, but whatever their origin, Decatur, "indignant at being betrayed by his countrymen," canceled his plans and made no further efforts to leave New London. The ensuing inactivity was peculiarly "irksome and vexatious" to Biddle, "who being now, for the first time, in command of a ship, was extremely

anxious to measure his strength with an enemy upon equal terms,"
but his repeated requests for permission to break through the blockade
were refused.[18]

By this time Biddle was viewing America's greatest naval hero
with a jaundiced eye. In a letter to his brothers he wrote: "Decatur
has lost very much of his reputation by his continuance in port. Indeed
he has certainly lost all his energy and enterprise." Perhaps Biddle's
social double-cross of his commander had already exacerbated their
relationship. Sometime during their compulsory sojourn at New London both men had gone to Philadelphia for the presentation of their
swords bestowed by the Pennsylvania Legislature. As Charles Biddle
told the story in his *Autobiography:*

> Decatur, not being a ready writer, was quite uneasy as to the set reply
> which he ought to make, and showed Biddle the result of his cogitations,
> asking his opinion of it. The speech was approved, perhaps with amend-
> ments. When the time came for the formal presentation, the junior officer
> of the two, according to rule, was to make the first reply. . . . To
> Decatur's dismay, Biddle responded by repeating, word for word, the
> speech which had been submitted for his criticism, and which a quick
> memory had enabled him to retain. The joke gave no offense, and all
> went off in great good humor.[19]

The last sentence is fatuous. If anything characterized Decatur it was
an acute awareness of his public reputation, and in the face of such
embarrassment, in all likelihood he took "the joke" with anything
but "great good humor."

During January of 1814, to relieve the boredom afflicting both
blockaders and blockaded, discussions were held on board the British
flagship as to the possibility of prearranged individual ship combat,
and Biddle was selected as the American negotiator. Learning that his
former ship, the *Wasp,* now renamed HMS *Loup Cervier* ("Lynx"),
was expected at any moment off New London, he became avid for a
mano a mano with her. Once she appeared, he and her captain, William
B. Mends, also eager for a bout, exchanged letters as to terms for
their duel. Sir Thomas Hardy, Mends's admiral, was agreeable, but
Decatur equivocated, insisting that the *Hornet's* crew be augmented
with picked officers and men from his frigates, assuming that the
enemy would do the same. This temporarily stalemated matters. But
when Biddle offered to remove his two-gun advantage and proposed
that each ship should fight with only her normal complement, the
last obstacle seemed to have been cleared away. Before the meeting
could take place, however, the *Loup Cervier* was ordered away on
another assignment, and sailed immediately. According to an English

naval historian, she "soon after foundered at sea, and every soul on board perished."[20]

Concluding that any effort of his entire squadron to evade the British armada massed off New London would be futile, Decatur ordered his two frigates back to "Fort Decatur." There the magnificent *United States,* sister ship of the ever-victorious *Constitution,* and the enemy prize *Macedonian* were ignobly "laid side by side." Their "topmasts were struck" and their "yards sent below." Useless, they remained in New London for the duration of the war. Only the *Hornet* was allowed to remain in commission, although another ten months of stultification still lay ahead. Biddle occasionally broke his do-nothing routine about which he continually chafed by visits to New York and Philadelphia. While writing to a member of the Society of the Cincinnati thanking him for his honorary membership in that organization, he seized the opportunity to add: "We look forward with impatience for the coming of long nights and blustering weather when we shall elude the blockading squadron, and get fairly out to sea." This he did on the night of 18 November, darting from New London to steer the *Hornet* safely through the British into New York.[21]

During Biddle's sixteen-month immobilization he and his fellow Americans had been alternately despondent and elated by the shifting fortunes of the war. The rest of 1813 had been highlighted by the loss of the USS *Chesapeake* to HMS *Shannon* (the first American frigate defeat), Oliver H. Perry's memorable triumph over a British fleet on Lake Erie, and mixed victories and defeats of the U.S. Army along the Canadian border. Once the trounced Napoleon had been sent into exile at Elba, however, the enemy could focus relatively unlimited attention on his transatlantic foe. The British planned to end the war on their own terms in 1814 by striking south from Montreal toward Albany, while simultaneously delivering a direct thrust into Chesapeake Bay. Thomas Macdonough's epic victory on Lake Champlain aborted the invasion from Canada. But in one of the most disgraceful episodes in American history, a small force of Britons brushed aside feeble resistance, captured Washington, and incinerated its public buildings. Baltimore's stout resistance, however, thwarted their strategic aspirations, and many of them sailed south. Andrew Jackson's unexpected annihilation of the English army at New Orleans was, of course, fought two weeks after the war was over.

The basic military and naval stalemate from 1812 to 1815 was reflected in the Treaty of Ghent, signed on 24 December 1814. Everything reverted to its prewar status, and the disputes that had touched off hostilities were either ignored or set aside for future discussion. The advent of peace, although starting some five weeks before Biddle had arrived in New York, was not known in the United States until February of 1815. Naval battles on distant seas would continue through the following spring.

Despite his inability, or unwillingness, to get his two frigates out of New London, Decatur remained the country's darling. He was given the *President*, 44, as his flagship, with the sloops *Hornet* and *Peacock* to round out his squadron, the latter commanded by Lewis Warrington, an able officer somewhat overlooked today. Biddle was furious to find himself once more under Decatur, for he had not forgotten his personal frustration for almost a year and a half, caused, he believed, by his superior's inexcusable lethargy. He groused to his brothers, "It is a most infamous arrangement that the *Hornet* and *Peacock* should be placed under the orders of Com^r Decatur."[22]

The squadron had been instructed to cruise against enemy merchantmen, first in the South Atlantic, with the isolated island of Tristan da Cunha as a rendezvous, and then into the Indian Ocean. Presumably to Biddle's delight, Decatur decided to split his command. Leaving behind his two sloops to escort the storeship *Tom Bowline* later, once repairs had been made, he slipped out of New York alone on 14 January. His pilot managed to ground the *President* the same night, injuring her hull so badly that she fell prey to blockaders on the morrow. After a somewhat less than spirited resistance, Decatur had to surrender his flagship to a four-vessel British squadron.[23]

The *Hornet, Peacock,* and *Tom Bowline* were luckier. According to their pilot, they were able to race by enemy patrolers in full sight and, aided by a strong and favorable wind, put out to open water on the 23rd. Even that late, Biddle and Warrington had not learned of the disaster that had befallen their commodore. Within a few days the ships separated until they would reunite in Tristan. Biddle's two-month solo crossing produced nothing more exciting than the interception of four sail, all neutrals. One of them, only a couple of days out of Tristan, told him that the war was over, but according to W.L. Brownlow, the *Hornet*'s marine lieutenant, his commander "did not believe it." Probably he did not want to believe it, for he admitted to his father that his purpose in cruising was to exact "some *retribution for the villainous blockade at New London.*"[24]

Biddle was readying to anchor at Tristan when he spied a stranger approaching from the northwest. She was HMS *Penguin* under Commander James Dickinson, mounting one 12-pound and eighteen 32-pound carronades, as well as two 6-pound long guns, a battery slightly inferior to the *Hornet*'s eighteen 32-pound carronades and two 12-pound long guns. A new brig-sloop, she had been commissioned in 1813, although the Napoleonic Wars' long drain on British manpower had kept her in port until the following June, when she was finally able to sail for the Cape of Good Hope. An English source claims that her crew was little better than third rate: "Her complement consisted . . . of the very young and old men; the former [im]pressed men; the latter discharged ineffectives." In South Africa illness had removed a few, so twelve Marines from a 74 were assigned to her, giving her a total of between 122 and 132, compared to the *Hornet's* approximately 140. The *Penguin's* duty was to track down and destroy the American privateer *Young Wasp,* which had recently picked off an East India merchantman in the vicinity of Tristan, although the official British report of the action says merely that she was on the lookout for "an American brig of war."[25]

On 23 March 1815, with a brisk wind blowing from the southwest and heavy swells, the two closed rapidly. In contrast to the situation between the *Wasp* and the *Frolic,* in this case the Englishman enjoyed the advantage of the weather gauge, but Biddle's seamanship was equal to the emergency, the details of which he reported to Decatur in his letter about the battle:

> I hove to for him to come down to us. When she had approached near, I filled the main-top-sail, and continued to yaw the ship, while she continued to come down, wearing occasionally to prevent her passing under our stern. At 40 minutes past 1 P.M. [the British put it at five minutes later] being within nearly musket shot distance, she hauled her wind on the starboard tack, hoisted English colours, and fired a gun. We immediately luffed to, hoisted our ensign, and gave the enemy a broadside.

As happened far too often for the British during the entire war, their shots went high, cutting into shrouds and sails, but in this instance without putting "a single round shot" into the *Hornet's* hull, while the returning American fire was "quick and well-directed." The *Penguin* drifted closer until the two ships slammed into one another, with the British bowsprit piercing into the American rigging on the starboard side between the mizzen and mainmasts—almost exactly at the same spot as when the *Wasp* crashed into the *Frolic.* The *Hornet's* "mizzen-shroud, stern davits, and spanker-boom" were carried away, but the *Penguin* paid a higher price. Her bowsprit snapped and her foremast came down on her port guns, rendering them useless.[26]

The leading contemporary English naval historian asserts that at this juncture the *Penguin's* ineffective "breech-bolts holding her carronades into place" began breaking and several guns tore loose. No other account confirms this, but if true, it is difficult to imagine a more unnerving development. The normal battle conditions on board a fighting sailer were hellish enough: the roar of broadsides, the sharp crack of the muskets fired by marines from the rigging, the whistle of ricocheting splinters as metal cut into wood, the heavy thwacks as hull collided with hull, and the incessant cacaphony as officers shouted orders and the wounded screamed for aid amid the moans of the dying. Heavy guns caroming across the deck, crushing the active and rolling over the fallen, would add a totally demoralizing element to the pandemonium. British officers later described the effect of one of the *Hornet*'s 32-pound carronade balls which smashed through the aft porthole on the port side, "carried away *six legs,* killed the powder boy of the division, capsized the opposite gun on the starboard side, and 'sunk in sullen silence to the bottom.' "[27]

As the two ships smashed together, Biddle perceived that the enemy was so badly hurt that he had but a single option for victory, and called his men to repel boarders. But nothing happened. One of the *Peacock*'s officers later learned that Commander Dickinson had snapped to James McDonald, his first lieutenant, "The fellows are giving it to us like hell! We must get on board!" Biddle asked McDonald after the battle why he had not boarded when he had the opportunity. He had tried to, the Briton replied, but when Dickinson yelled out the order, he "found the men rather backward—and so, you know, we concluded to give it up." Biddle's sailors now clamored for the chance to board themselves, but he coolly and wisely refused, for he realized that such derring-do could lose his victory, otherwise assured. He pulled his ship away instead. His face was already covered with blood from minor sliver wounds, and he later wrote his father that luckily he had decided not to wear his spectacles, for one splinter hit him in such a way that a lens would have been driven into his eye.[28]

Just as the two ships drew apart, Dickinson was killed, leaving McDonald in command of his stricken ship. Biddle understood that the lieutenant was calling across the short distance separating them that he wanted to surrender. After ordering a cease-fire, he sprang to the *Hornet*'s stern rail to confirm that fact, only to be shot through the neck and chin by a British marine, who was at once killed by his American counterparts. Instantly the *Hornet* swung away from the wind into broadside position, but McDonald reaffirmed his shouted surrender. The *Penguin* was "completely riddled with our shot, her foremast and bowsprit were both gone, and her mainmast so crippled as to be incapable of being secured." Biddle avowed that the British ensign came down at 2:02 after a mere twenty-two minutes of combat, but McDonald timed his surrender at 2:25. The American put his casualties at 2 killed and 11 wounded as against 14 and 28 respectively for the British; once again McDonald disagreed, listing his figures as 10 and 28.[29]

In a letter to Decatur, Biddle shrugged off his injury with the laconic statement, "I received a wound in the neck." A contemporary account assesses the damage to him more seriously: "The ball struck the chin directly in front with much force, and passing along the neck, tearing the flesh, went off through his cravat, waistcoat, and coat-collar." As he fell back, according to the embellishments of a naval journal, "two of the men took him in their arms, to carry him below, but finding that he would not permit it, one of those honest-hearted affectionate fellows, stripped off his shirt and tied it around his commander's neck to stop the bleeding. It is a circumstance honorable to the gallant young officer that his own wound was the last to be dressed on board the *Hornet*." Biddle's injury was less severe than it originally appeared, and his recovery was rapid. Within a few days he was able to tell his family that at first he had suffered "some pain and a little fever, but both are entirely gone." Another week and he could be even more assuring: "My own wound is doing remarkably well—It is nearly healed and indeed incommodes me very little." Doubtless recalling her extended hysterics in response to his brother Edward's death sixteen years before, he worried that his "dear Mother" must not make herself "unhappy" or "uneasy" about his injury, since it had never been close to a mortal blow.[30]

Of the *Hornet*'s ten other wounded, two marines and one officer had been the hardest hit, and Biddle most commendably extended himself for them. When he reached home he called to the secretary's attention that both marines "would be disabled for life and will be placed on the pension list. I would be most grateful if in consideration of their good conduct in action and their long & painful suffering" they could be promoted to corporal. He had no doubt that this would have "the happiest effect" upon them.[31]

First Lieutenant David Conner, already smashed in the hand, caught a grapeshot ball in the hip. Biddle told Decatur, "I lament to state that Lieut. Conner is wounded dangerously. I feel great solicitude on his account, as he is an officer of much promise, and his loss would be a serious loss to the service." Sixty years later, in a handwritten note beside Conner's last entry in the *Hornet*'s journal, his son added that he had been "desperately wounded in two places." Not for two weeks could Biddle report that his first lieutenant was "out of danger." Conner's convalescence was so slow that he needed special attention when he arrived in New York on 20 July. Biddle's "solicitude" remained so great that he obtained a nonservice doctor for him, billing the department for the cost. Secretary of the Navy Benjamin W. Crowninshield, who had succeeded William Jones in 1814, chided Biddle for not utilizing the navy's two authorized physicians in New

York, especially as one of them was "unemployed." But he grudg-ingly accepted the charge, while insisting that such deviations from the regulations of the service must not become established "prece-dent." Although he was compelled to remain on crutches for two years, Conner eventually recovered sufficiently to sail under Biddle once more, from 1817 to 1819, in the USS *Ontario*. At the end of his career he served with distinction as a commodore during the Mexican War.[32]

Historical commentary on the *Hornet-Penguin* imbroglio has been comparatively scanty, since it occurred after the war was over and was fought between sloops rather than frigates. Early nineteenth-century narrators tended to paraphrase or even copy directly the lives of Biddle printed in the *Port Folio* or *Analectic* magazine articles of 1815. Most modern historians have satisfied themselves with descrip-tions of what had occurred, without analysis, save for mentioning Biddle's accurate gunnery. Theodore Roosevelt and William James, however, have discussed the tactics of the encounter, the former briefly and the latter at some length.

In his long article about the War of 1812 in a British multivol-umed history of the Royal Navy, Roosevelt attributes the *Hornet*'s success to her commander's "utmost efficiency in every way." He amplifies his analysis in his *Naval War of 1812* (p. 431). It was Biddle's "cool skilful seamanship and excellent gunnery that enabled the Americans to destroy an antagonist of equal force in such an exceed-ingly short time." He is only partially correct, for in this case sea-manship was hardly an issue. It seldom was when sloop fought sloop. With no more than 2 long guns and 16 to 18 short-range carronades, it was imperative that combat be at close quarters. The frigates, on the contrary, mounting an abundance in both categories, could afford to choose between pirouetting maneuvers at a distance, taking ad-vantage of the wind to dismantle the enemy's rigging, or a sudden dash to loose carronade broadsides, with boarding as a final alterna-tive. But certainly Roosevelt is correct when he stresses the *Hornet*'s "excellent gunnery." Rapidity and accuracy of fire were unquestion-able American assets throughout the war. Not always, of course: in 1813 the superbly honed sailors of Captain Philip V. Broke's *Shannon*, trained together for seven years with almost daily drill at their cannon, pulverized Captain James Lawrence's *Chesapeake* with only a couple of broadsides before boarding. But usually when equal met equal American marksmanship resulted in victory; the American losses were likely to occur when sloops had to fight frigates or ships of the line, or when frigates fell in with enemy squadrons.[33]

The *Hornet-Penguin* mêlée permitted William James's anti-Americanism to flourish. His virulent animus evidently emanated from his experiences during 1812 and 1813. Trying to return to England from Jamaica, he was in the United States when war was declared, and was "detained for several months" before escaping to Canada. He repaid his captors for any unpleasantness that he suffered with two histories of hostilities at sea that maliciously denigrated every American victory and exaggerated every British triumph. Even an anonymous English commentator some years later could not tolerate James's overt bias: "The American character is the object of perpetual sarcasm; American officers of undoubted honor are charged . . . with falsehood and deceit; and the severest constructions are put upon almost every proceeding . . . of an American ship of war." Another source attributes James's hatred to his own ineptitude. He "for some time exercised the calling of 'veterinary surgeon' in the city of Philadelphia, but the mortality among his equine patients exposing him to imputations of malpractice, he returned to his native land, and devoted his skill to the studied depreciation of American commanders."[34]

James lashes into Biddle's report to Decatur, ridiculing his claim that he had suffered only two dead and eleven wounded. His evidence? British officers taken to the *Hornet* said that they had seen a body surreptitiously thrown overboard so that the victory would seem the more impressive. This accusation can be dispensed with quickly: no other authority has challenged Biddle's figures. James also declares that the American had lied when he reported that his ship was unhulled during the engagement. He varnishes his story by describing Biddle as "having drowned his native cunning in wine," admitting his fabrication to Britons after the battle, "in order to make the thing properly received in the United States." James is wrong on two counts. The *Hornet* was hit twice in the hull, but by HMS *Cornwallis*, 74, on 28 April, not by the *Penguin* on 23 March. He can provide no corroboration for Biddle's supposed lie and, moreover, not a shred of evidence exists that he was anything but abstemious. His single exception seems to have been his night of overindulgence in Sir Alexander Ball's ale while a teenager celebrating his liberation in Tripoli, a decade earlier.[35]

Hardly was the battle at Tristan over when the *Peacock* and *Tom Bowline* arrived. The ravaged *Penguin* was in no condition to be repaired and was scuttled the next day. The Americans remained at their South Atlantic rendezvous for another two weeks, anticipating the arrival of the *President* and the reuniting of the squadron. As mentioned above, although Decatur had lost his frigate off Long Island on 15 January, the two sloops and the storeship had sailed before that news reached New York on the 26th. During this interim at Tristan,

Biddle oversaw repairs to his masts and rigging, installed a new set of sails, and soon had the *Hornet* ready for further cruising. After enjoying Tristan's fresh vegetables and "fine fish," he and Warrington concluded that some disaster must have befallen Decatur, and they need tarry no longer. The *Penguin's* prisoners were placed in the *Tom Bowline,* and the storeship departed for Brazil. On 12 April the two sloops sailed together for South Africa and the Indian Ocean.[36]

They headed due east until the 27th, when they sighted a sail aiming toward them from the northeast. As she loomed larger the next day the American began exulting in the expectation of netting what looked like an East Indiaman crammed with her usual riches. The sailors were boasting that "they would have the birth [*sic*] deck carpeted with East India silk," while the officers were calculating their share in the apportionment of the "money, porter, cheese, &, &." that she should be carrying. Nevertheless, both sloops approached warily until the *Peacock* closed sufficiently to make out the stranger's alarming identity. Warrington frantically signaled Biddle that she was "a ship of the line and an enemy." An anonymous officer in the *Hornet,* whose "Private Journal" amplifies Biddle's official report to Decatur, claims to have been astonished at this startling revelation. But not his captain, who realized that British 74s and East Indiamen were approximately the same in size and appearance, although the gun ports of the ship of the line were real while those of the company vessel were painted on to discourage possible assailants.[37]

Rear Admiral Sir George Burlton was on board HMS *Cornwallis,* but operational responsibilities belonged to Thomas Bayley, her captain. He was the one who had to decide which of the two sloops to chase, for the *Hornet* dashed off to the southeast and the *Peacock* to the northeast. Correctly concluding that the *Peacock* was the swifter, he immediately set after the *Hornet,* some eight miles away. Sloops were expected to outsail ships of the line, of course, but occasionally, when the smaller vessel had been crippled in her rigging or when the right wind conditions prevailed, permitting the leviathans to utilize to the utmost their extra canvas, 74s could snap up sloops. This had occurred not only in the cases of the *Wasp* and the *Frolic* in 1812 but later in the war also to the USS *Syren* (or *Siren*) and the *Rattlesnake.*[38]

By 9:00 P.M. Biddle, "having taken in all steering sails, and hauled upon a wind," realized that the *Cornwallis* could keep him in view with night glasses until morning, and began to lighten his ship, burdened with extra supplies from the *Penguin.* Over the side went 24,000 pounds of kentledge (pig iron used as a permanent ballast)—"90 pieces, weighing about 50 tons"—a supply of heavy masts, and one of the two anchors and its cables. Biddle then tried a sudden tack to the

west, but his pursuer adroitly matched his every move. As the col-
orful naval historian and novelist C. S. Forester describes the chase:
"*Cornwallis,* as well as *Hornet,* was making every effort to discover
what particular trim gave her the last yard of speed at this time when
yards were of vital importance, the weather was squally, and with
the sudden variations, each ship gained on the other in turn."[39]

Bayley drew within range at 7:00 A.M. As he hoisted his colors
and Burlton's admiral's flag, he commenced firing with his bow guns,
but all were aimed too high, allowing Biddle to rejoice that he had
received "some thirty shot, not one of which took effect." Meanwhile
the *Hornet*'s sailors were frantically jettisoning the other anchor and
its ropes, the ship's launch, more shot, more kentledge, provisions,
spars, rigging, sails, and "every heavy article which was on board."
They had a brief respite while the enemy slowed to fire, but by 11:00
A.M. the Englishman was once again forging toward them, propelled
by a wind blowing from the southeast, the worst direction as far as
the *Hornet* was concerned. Biddle dispensed with his remaining spare
masts, the entire "forward forecastle," which had to be hacked away,
and all his cannon and shot, retaining only a single long gun and its
ammunition.[40]

By noon, however, every exertion seemed futile. The *Cornwallis*
drew within three-quarters of a mile, which should have allowed her
long guns to bore in accurately. For the next couple of hours "many"
broadsides thundered out, but only three times was the *Hornet* hit,
twice in the hull and once in the jib boom. The exhausted American
bluejackets were again called upon, this time to dump into the ocean
the armorer's forge, the ship's bell, and all the muskets and cutlasses.
According to the unnamed officer, they managed brief periods of rest,
lying on the deck during intermissions of running from one side of
the ship to the other as living ballast. Every foot proved essential, for
the *Hornet* pulled away a bit each time the *Cornwallis* swung into a
broadside position, and about 2:00 she ceased firing to resume the
chase. A half-hour later the breeze finally veered to the west and
steadily increased, now favoring the Americans. At sunset the 74 was
four miles away and at dawn of the 29th twelve miles behind. During
the midmorning Bayley gave up, "haling [*sic*] to the eastward, and
at 11:00 A.M. was entirely out of sight." Theodore Roosevelt sums
up Biddle's escape as meriting "the very highest praise for plucky,
skilful seamanship."[41]

So capably had the *Hornet* been handled that for once William
James was relatively tongue-tied, dredging up no more than a story
that the *Cornwallis* had stopped during the chase to pick up a marine
who had fallen overboard, grumbling that the British fire had been

"unskillful," and taking what pleasure he could in stressing that the American sloop had been so stripped of equipment that her career as a commerce raider had been terminated. But Biddle and his men were not to escape British ridicule altogether. The "Private Journal" of his officer, although captivating in the humanizing details so absent from his commander's matter-of-fact report, concludes with an amalgam of the miraculous and the lugubrious. He attributes the lucky shift in the wind that saved the *Hornet* to the "Divine Father—my heart with gratitude acknowledges his supreme power and goodness." Moreover, he has Biddle calling together his men while the *Cornwallis*'s cannon balls were splashing about them to praise their "conduct during the chase." The captain ended with the warning that "we might soon expect to be captured, &c. Not a dry eye was seen at the mention of capture; the rugged hearts of the sailors, like ice before the sun, warmed by the divine power of sympathy, wept in unison with their brave commander." *The Naval Chronicle,* London's service magazine, jumped upon this touching little account under the heading: "Amusing Narrative, or the Hopes and Fears of Jonathan." The reserved and class-conscious Biddle must have winced at the thought of British officers derisively picturing him blubbering amongst his lacrimose bluejackets.[42]

With his ship bereft of practically every seafaring necessity, Biddle proceeded at once to the neutral port of San Salvador, Brazil, arriving there on 9 June, where he was notified that the war had been over for almost four months. In a little more than a week he took on board enough gear and provisions for peacetime voyaging, and on 29 July was able to tell the department that the *Hornet* was just outside New York Harbor. He learned to his great satisfaction about the second of his wartime promotions; since 28 February he had been a "post captain," and no higher rank officially existed in the U.S. Navy.[43]

Biddle had to be cleared for the destruction of his movables in eluding the *Cornwallis,* and he asked for and received the secretary's appointment of a court of inquiry on the matter. The proceedings on the 23rd were entirely pro forma. Court president Captain Samuel Evans absolved him of "blame . . . [on account of] the loss of the *Hornet*'s armaments, stores, &c." Furthermore, he deserved "the greatest applause" for his "persevering gallantry and nautical skill, evinced in escaping, under the most disadvantageous circumstances, after a long and arduous chase by a British line-of-battle ship."[44]

Meanwhile honors had come Biddle's way, but understandably they were heaped upon him to a lesser extent than when he had helped Jacob Jones smash the *Frolic* with the *Wasp.* That victory had been only the second of the war at sea, and the first between equals, helping to bring the country out of the gloom attending the steady succession of U.S. Army disasters along the Canadian frontier. But another sloop triumph well after the fighting had officially ended generated a more muted national response. Nevertheless, New York City gave him a public dinner, and Philadelphia once more subscribed to a fund in his honor, this time for a silver plate service.[45]

The government was generous. Congress ordered a gold medal struck for him (it is depicted in Benson J. Lossing's *Pictorial Field-Book of the War of 1812,* p. 991). The obverse side has Biddle in profile with the inscription: THE CONGRESS OF THE U.S. TO CAPT. JAMES BIDDLE FOR HIS GALLANTRY, GOOD CONDUCT, AND SERVICES." The reverse side shows two ships wreathed in smoke firing at one another, and is inscribed: CAPTURE OF THE BRITISH SHIP PENGUIN BY THE U.S. SHIP HORNET OFF TRISTAN D'ACUNHA, MARCH XXIII. MDCCCXV." Compared with the quarter-century dawdling before he received his silver medal for the *Wasp*'s victory, the government's speed in this instance was commendable; his gold commemorative was ready for presentation within five years. Congress also appropriated in lieu of prize money almost $25,000 for the destruction of the *Penguin;* Biddle's share as captain came to a welcome $3,750.[46]

Biddle's wartime record had been superb. Valor in combat is the sine qua non for any officer in the armed forces, and in this sphere he had earned the highest grade. He had been the first to reach the *Frolic*'s deck and to lower her colors by himself. He had directed the *Hornet* against the *Penguin* with consummate professionalism. He had demonstrated the utmost seafaring artistry in outrunning the *Cornwallis*. Nor was it his fault that his battle experience had not been even more extensive. He had exerted himself to garner extra combat assignments: hiring a boat to chase Rodgers so that he might volunteer for the *President,* never forgiving Porter for denying him a like opportunity in the *Essex,* clamoring for action during his long confinement at New London, where he tried to duel the *Loup Cervier,* and repeatedly begging the department for permission to abandon the overly cautious Decatur and take out the *Hornet* alone. Yet he never permitted his craving for a fight to outweigh his prudence, as evidenced when he resisted the appeals of his crew to board the *Penguin.* His modesty and aloofness shine through his private correspondence and official reports—there is not a whimper about his painful wound. And during the last year of his life, when asked to review his wartime experiences, he considered it sufficient to say, "I was in two actions, both of them successful."[47]

CHAPTER 4
THE CRUISE OF THE *ONTARIO*,
1816–1821

Within two weeks of his homecoming Biddle began capitalizing upon his wartime record to seek a new command, preferably a frigate. The ever-victorious *Constitution* was his natural choice, and he put his father to work on it. Charles Biddle wrote to his fellow Pennsylvanian Alexander Dallas, secretary of the treasury, asking for help. Dallas replied the next day, expressing his hope that Secretary of the Navy Benjamin W. Crowninshield could "gratify him," as it would be a "popular appointment." These efforts failed, however, for the *Constitution* had sustained enough damage in her triumphs over HMS *Cyane* and *Levant* to be temporarily put in ordinary. Late that autumn the younger Biddle asked Crowninshield for the new U.S. frigate, *Guerrière,* but the secretary refused, as she was to be "kept vacant for some time for special service," by which he meant that she had already become Decatur's flagship for action against Algiers.[1]

Some months later, desperate enough to lower his sights, Biddle requested the sloop *Peacock,* only to learn that she was already slated for Master Commandant George Rodgers. That Biddle outranked his rival was inconsequential, since George was the younger brother of John Rodgers, president of the newly formed Board of Navy Commissioners, established in 1815 to aid the secretary of the navy. All these rebuffs, in part necessitated by the post-War of 1812 reduction in the service, made Biddle's pleas for another sea command premature, and he could do nothing but settle down in Philadelphia and wait.[2]

During this interim his portrait was painted by two eminent American artists. In 1815 Joseph Wood depicted him as a figure of almost consummate poise and self-confidence, coolly surveying the world from wide-spaced blue eyes, with dark hair carefully tousled in the manner popular during that period; a wide brow slightly frowning, a formidable nose, and well-shaped mouth and chin. In it Biddle is little short of handsome. Quite different is the impression given by the work of Charles Willson Peale. (He was the head of the country's most famous artistic family, for his brother James and his sons Raphael, Rembrandt, and Titian were all successful painters.) Biddle started sitting for him during May of 1816, and by the end of that year his picture was ready to join Peale's portrait gallery called the "Great School of Nature." Only with difficulty can the viewer conclude that the two artists had been looking at the same man. Peale provides a beady-eyed, tight-lipped, almost hooknosed Biddle, generating an aura of tension, far removed from Wood's serene commander. Possibly Peale's impression sprang from his tendency to paint his subjects' "eyes generally over-small and lips uniformly thin." But the small eyes, aquiline nose, and air of taut nervousness in a portrait painted of Biddle twenty-three years later by Thomas Sully seem to prove that Peale, not Wood, had been the more perceptive observer.[3]

During 1816, the famous "year without a summer"—so cold that a Boston paper forecast that it would be recalled for having not a single month "without frost"—Biddle warmed himself by playing chess (poorly, he admitted), taking short trips from Philadelphia, and following with rapt attention the sensational murder trial and execution of Lieutenant Richard Smith, U.S. Army. At the end of the war Smith had moved in with Ann Baker Carson, and then bigamously married her, for she was already the wife of John Carson, a captain in the merchant marine, who had been abroad for several years. When Carson returned and learned of the new housing arrangement he quarreled with Smith, trying to knife the lieutenant during their first meeting. A couple of days later Smith, accompanied by Ann, shot his unarmed enemy through the mouth, the victim lingering in agony for two weeks before dying. Although Ann was acquitted as an accomplice, Smith was convicted of murder and sentenced to be hanged. After unsuccessfully trying to bribe his keepers to allow him to escape, Ann cooked up an arcane plot. She hired two exconvicts and planned to kidnap and hold hostage in exchange for a pardon a child of Pennsylvania governor Simon Snyder's best friend. But forewarnings exposed her conspiracy. Once again that "most abandoned and wicked woman," as the press called her, avoided conviction, while Smith was "launched into eternity" at a public execution that attracted a huge crowd.[4]

Biddle, in a letter to a relative telling about Smith's hanging, thought that the victim had been anything but "resigned to his fate," because at the last moment he lost "all fortitude and manliness." It appeared that he had "too much cherished the expectation of a pardon and was therefore not well prepared for death." Biddle went on to complain about the "unequal distribution of punishments in this World," as "poor Smith suffered death for the killing of Carson," while Ann, the "guilty cause" of both men's demises, "should escape with her life." He closed on a metaphysical note: "She cannot be made to suffer in this life all that is due her offenses. Will not Vengeance therefore be pursued after death?"[5]

As the spring of 1817 arrived, Biddle was still avidly seeking active duty. When Bainbridge notified him that Oliver Hazard Perry was intending to relinquish the frigate *Java,* he at once applied for that command, but it turned out that no vacancy was forthcoming. On 12 May, however, Secretary Crowninshield finally ended Biddle's frustration by offering him the 22-gun sloop *Ontario*. She was relatively new, having been built and launched in 1813, displacing 559 tons, carrying two 18-pound long guns and twenty 32-pound carronades, with a complement of 150. Although one naval expert comments that she was "fast but did not steer well," Biddle seems to have found her seaworthy.[6]

The first of a number of conflicting orders came from the department at midsummer. Biddle was to meet in New York City President Monroe's recently appointed Latin American commissioners, Caesar Augustus Rodney and John Graham, with Henry M. Brackinridge as their secretary. He should transport them to South American ports, with Rio de Janeiro as their first stop and Buenos Aires as their "most remote" destination. The government's irresolution as to the precise nature of Biddle's duties was accentuated when the secretary sent him further instructions that same day. Now he should also carry to Argentina in an official capacity Judge John B. Prevost, a stepson of Aaron Burr and an intimate of the president, having served as his secretary during Monroe's ministry to France some years before.[7]

The *Ontario*'s departure was scheduled for 10 August, but was put off by the outbreak of typhoid fever among the sloop's people; Biddle estimated that about one-third had been stricken. Among them was Midshipman John Rodney, Caesar's son, and when he died his understandably distraught father was in no condition to fulfill his diplomatic responsibilities. Not until the following December were he and the rest of the commission able to leave for South America.[8]

Meanwhile the administration continued to alter Biddle's instructions. Information had been received that the war in lower South America between pro-Spanish "royalists" and rebel "patriots" was threatening American commerce in those waters. Biddle's cruise was extended so that he could take Prevost as a special agent of the government around Cape Horn to Chile and Peru, while he himself should protect the national shipping off Valparaiso and Lima. Finally, John Quincy Adams, the new secretary of state, had decided that something positive should be done about the festering quarrel between the United States and Great Britain as to the Oregon Country in the remote Pacific Northwest. His recommendation was accepted by the president that Biddle and Prevost should present London with a fait accompli by planting the American flag at the mouth of the Columbia River. Quite properly Biddle protested about these abrupt changes in and elongation of his itinerary, stressing to the department that "it is very manifest that a ship which may be in readiness for such a destination [Buenos Aires] may not be in readiness to sail to the Pacific Ocean and the Columbia River."[9]

His objections were shrugged off and on 3 October he was told to depart at once. He had no choice but to obey, and headed south the next day. At least he and Prevost did not want for delicacies during their lengthy voyage. Supplies originally earmarked for the Latin American commissioners had been transferred to the *Ontario,* including 15 gallons of cognac, 10 gallons of rum, 1,200 bottles of claret, 1,000 pickled oysters, 100 pounds of coffee, and 600 eggs, "packed in sand after having been dipped in hot oil."[10]

No international situation during the post–War of 1812 years provided a more puzzling dilemma for the United States than the Spanish-American colonial wars of independence. When Napoleon in 1808 had overthrown the Bourbon monarchy and installed his brother Joseph as king of Spain, that country's Latin American dependencies promptly refused to accept their new ruler, instead forming local juntas to carry on in the name of the deposed dynasty. But when Ferdinand VII was restored to power in 1810, habits of independence proved so irresistible that uprisings wildfired from the Rio Grande to the Straits of Magellan. In South America the greatest patriot triumphs were achieved by Simón Bolivar in the north and central areas and José de San Martín in the central and south. For a decade and more, however, Spanish royalists were able to put up a resistance so strenuous that the tides of battle fluctuated between themselves and the patriots until final rebel victory during the mid-1820s.

Almost everyone in the United States sympathized with the insurgents, for they were clearly modeling themselves upon American antecedents. But opinion divided as to time and circumstance of officially recognizing the new countries to the south as independent entities while Spain was battling so ferociously to retain possession of them. U.S. national opinion split on the issue. One potent wing insisted that recognition must be immediate—should not the one established republic in existence reach out its hand to aid the only others in the world? Its efficacy was soon sharply reduced, however, when it divided into two antagonistic factions. One was led by Henry Clay, the magnetic politician from Kentucky. He worked in league with Manuel Aguirre, special agent from Buenos Aires, and formulated the argument that the United States must recognize at once the government of Juan Martín Puerreydón, "Supreme Dictator" of Argentina, and a bit later that of Bernardo O'Higgins, who enjoyed the same title in Chile, both utilizing the martial abilities of San Martín.

The other bloc was headed by a triumvirate of Commodore David Porter, John Stuart Skinner, and Baptis Irvine, who dismayed the Clayites by blasting the de facto rulers of Argentina and Chile as pro-Spanish, pro-royalist, and pro-British. When Porter had been in Valparaiso in the *Essex* he had formed a warm friendship with José Miguel Carrera, the short-time ruler of patriot Chile during 1813 and 1814. But Carrera's dictatorship soon fell to that of O'Higgins, aided by Puerreydón and San Martín. To bring his friend back into power, Porter enlisted the aid of Skinner, postmaster of Baltimore, privateer owner, agricultural publicist, and deserver of a footnote in American history for advising Francis Scott Key, a fellow observer of the British bombardment of Baltimore, to publish his poem entitled "The Star-Spangled Banner." Irvine, the third member, was a former Baltimore newspaperman who was able to give Carrera, an exile in the United States during part of 1816, ready access to the press. Their spirited assault upon Clay's champions—Puerreydón, San Martín, and O'Higgins—first undermined and then derailed the Kentuckian's efforts to gain early U.S. recognition of Argentina and Chile, much to his displeasure.[11]

This division in the opposition gave President Monroe, Secretary of State Adams, and their supporters a welcome respite, for they felt that recognition must await, final and irrefutable proof that the patriots had won. Indeed, for a period after 1814 Spanish royalists reconquered Chile, leaving only Argentina beyond their control, and the rebels could not achieve total victory on the west coast of South America until a decade later. Premature U.S. recognition of republican insurgents might spark intervention from the pro-monarchical "Concert of Europe," formed by the powers that had whipped Napoleon, which had already used its potent armies to stamp out any opposition to "legitimate" dynasties in Europe, and might eventually do so throughout the world. Adams was particularly cognizant that recognition at any time from 1817 through 1821 might ruin his delicate negotiations with the Chevalier Luis de Onís, the Spanish minister in Washington, which eventually would gain American possession of all the Floridas and an acceptable Spanish-American transcontinental boundary. So procrastination became the Monroe administration's policy in regard to recognition, and what better way to come up with a persuasive apologia for it than to accentuate the need for accurate information about conditions in lower South America? Actually the necessity was real, as well, for news came only from unofficial sources. Prior to Biddle's cruise there were no fully accredited American representatives below Brazil.[12]

Monroe's fact-finding commission of Rodney, Graham, and Secretary Brackinridge, which had been told to concentrate upon Argentina, had originally been tilted toward Clay's viewpoint. Rodney, former U.S. attorney general, was recognized as his ally. Although Graham, chief clerk of the State Department, seems to have had no preconceived opinion, Brackinridge had already written a pamphlet supporting Puerreydón and San Martín. But the appointment of Judge Theodorick Bland, Skinner's father-in-law, gave the Porter-Skinner-Irvine bloc representation on the commission. Bland was on record as considering "Carrera and his followers as martyrs, the O'Higgins faction as despots, and the Buenos Aires government as robbers." He was also permitted to go on to Chile, where he spent most of his time recovering the four thousand dollars that his son-in-law had loaned to Carrera with the spectacularly ungenerous terms of 100 percent interest per annum. Certainly this quartet added little of value in the formulation of a consistent U.S. policy toward Latin American revolutionary regimes. Each member went his own way, and eventually all four published separate accounts and recommendations, confirming Adams's conclusion as to "the extreme difficulty of maintaining harmony in joint commissions." Yet the mixed nature of the reports muddled the question of recognition so thoroughly that the administration gained precious years for Adams to deal successfully with Onís.[13]

Biddle, Rodney, Graham, Brackinridge, Bland, and Prevost were not alone as American diplomatic representatives in lower South America. William G. D. Worthington and Jeremy Robinson were already there, the former a quasi-official "special agent" to Argentina, Chile, and Peru; the latter on an unofficial basis, although both would act as Prevost's subordinates. Worthington, a thirty-three-year-old enthusiast for democracy, served capably for a time. But Monroe was infuriated to learn that he had concluded an unauthorized commercial treaty with Argentina and written on his own a constitution for Chile, and had him summarily dismissed in 1819. Robinson had been appointed "agent for commerce" to Lima during July of 1817, but for some reason his commission was withdrawn. Undaunted, he sailed south anyway, hoping for later official restoration. He inundated the State Department with information about his work with Prevost, some of which was quite perceptive. His quest for a permanent position, however, was unsuccessful, and he returned home during the early 1820s.[14]

The *Ontario* had long since arrived at Rio de Janeiro in mid-November 1817 after an unexciting forty-five-day passage from New York. Biddle delivered dispatches to the U.S. consul there, and was presented to Dom João VI, king of Portugal and Brazil. The Russian North American Company frigate *Kutuzov,* under Captain Vasilii Golovnin, was also in port, and the officers of both vessels exchanged visits; they would meet again ten months later in California. The *Ontario* left on 1 December, rounded Cape Horn, and came into Valparaiso on 24 January, fifty-five days out of Rio. A painting in Biddle's Sketch Book shows his sloop listing dangerously to starboard in heavy seas, but the passage could not have been particularly difficult, for no untoward incident is mentioned, either in the ship's log or in the journals kept by Biddle and David Conner, who had sufficiently recovered from his wounds suffered while fighting the *Penguin* to serve once more as first lieutenant.[15]

From information that they already possessed, Biddle and Prevost could agree about their major responsibilities in Chile and Peru. They must try to liberate American ships locked into Valparaiso harbor by a royalist blockading squadron from Peru; enable some forty-odd U.S. whalers in the Pacific to get supplies along the west coast of South America, a quest that their masters dared not undertake because of Spanish men-of-war; free an unknown number of American citizens held in Peruvian jails; and as a favor to John Jacob Astor, foreign trader and fur tycoon, bring about the release of his merchantman, the *Beaver,* seized at the royalist-held Chilean port of Talcahuano. (The cases of the *Beaver* and the *Canton,* another American ship in the same circumstances, shall be discussed later in this chapter.)

As the *Ontario* sailed into Valparaiso harbor her lookouts were busy identifying the more than forty ships in port. Five were flying the American flag, and HMS *Amphion* was the single foreign warship. Cruising farther offshore was a Spanish squadron, under Capitan de Navio Tomas Blanco Cabrera, consisting of two frigates and two brigs, effectively closing off the city. Valparaiso was the exception, however, for Spanish sea power was too weak to seal off the entire rebel-held coast; Americans were correct in calling it a paper blockade, designed to throttle neutral commerce. Yet the royalists had every right to be concerned about foreign ships arriving full of munitions for the patriots.[16]

Shortly after she entered, Cabrera ordered the *Ontario* to halt and send a boat over to the *Venganza,* his flagship, for the port was under blockade. Biddle decided to bluff, telling the Spaniard that he commanded a U.S. man-of-war and that his orders compelled him to put into the city for supplies, instructions that he could not disregard. Cabrera replied that his interdict applied to public as well as private vessels. Biddle dispatched Conner to ask bluntly whether Cabrera "intended to use force to prevent my entrance," which was promptly denied. Although a Baltimore paper trumpeted that the *Venganza* was in "such wretched condition" that he could have easily taken her and her escorts, Biddle knew better. After entering the harbor the next morning, he willingly agreed to Cabrera's face-saving request: to put in writing that he had been officially notified that a blockade existed. Later Biddle admitted that had resistance been threatened he would have stayed out to sea. Furthermore, he concluded that Cabrera had been legally correct, for from the Spanish point of view, Chile was still the king's dependency, and the old "Law of the Indies," prohibiting foreign trade with his colonies without permission, remained intact.[17]

After dropping anchor Biddle informed Francisco de Calderón, patriot governor of Valparaiso, that he would salute the city, provided that the same number of guns be returned as a matching courtesy. The *Ontario*'s cannons thundered out, and although Calderón had promised that his men would return the salvo, they never did. Biddle resented the slight and vowed not to salute again in Valparaiso, a decision that would later embroil him in controversy. Shrugging off his annoyance, on 2 February he greeted General San Martín on board the *Ontario* with the punctilio that he was so adept in maintaining. A couple weeks later Luis de la Cruz, acting for "Supreme Dictator" O'Higgins, and a representative of Puerreydón were accorded the same honors. Agent Worthington, who had recently arrived in Chile, complimented the captain for his "manly and correct conduct" that had contributed so much to his "warm welcome."

Biddle's next problem concerned the American merchantmen trapped in port. While immobilized by Cabrera's blockaders, they had been preyed upon by the patriots. Until Chile could procure a navy, privateers had to take up the slack. American masters complained to Biddle that all of them had lost so many men, enticed by high wages and the prospect of prize money, that they were seriously shorthanded. Biddle interceded with San Martín and finally recovered some twenty of the absconders, while receiving a pledge that further

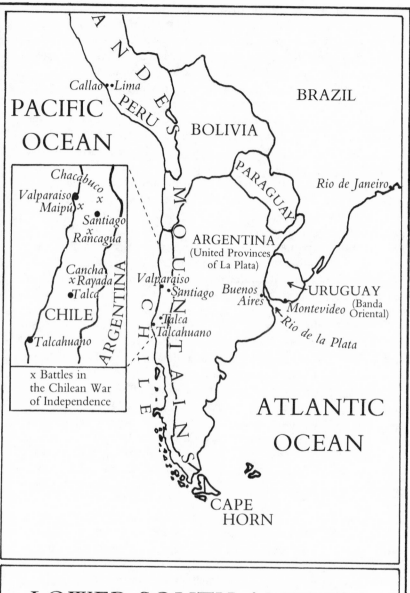

**LOWER SOUTH AMERICA
c. 1830**

recruiting would cease while the *Ontario* remained at Valparaiso. The captain was less accommodating to his fellow citizens when they begged him to convoy them past the Spanish squadron. He told them that he "did not deem it proper" to comply, although he went through the useless motions of asking Cabrera's permission to do so.[18]

Perhaps the most aggravating occurrence of Biddle's first sojourn in Chile happened on the night of 6 February. Six of his own men had the effrontery to steal a boat and row toward shore with the intention of signing on with Chilean privateers. The *Ontario*'s watch spotted them and opened fire, the noise alerting the harbor patrol, which took in the refugees. Biddle repeatedly demanded their return, but Calderón took so many months before complying that the captain was infuriated. This, coupled with the governor's broken promise about the salutes, made him doubt the reliability of Chileño patriots.[19]

Desertion continued to bring him headaches. During April, when the Argentinian representative de la Cruz asked that one of the absconders be permitted to join the rebels, Biddle was tempted to refuse, hoping no doubt to make an example of him through application of the cat before the crew. He saw, however, an opportunity to use the request to help Astor. That astute entrepreneur's ship *Enterprise* had been hired by the patriots to repatriate others who had been exiled by the royalists on remote San Fernandez Island for "five or six thousand dollars," of which only one thousand had been paid. Biddle gave up the deserter in return for a Chilean promise to settle Astor's claim, which was eventually kept. One night a couple months later, Biddle was willing to compromise his own high ideals of morality to help stem further desertions. Some of Valparaiso's ladies of easy virtue were stopped by local authorities from coming aboard the *Ontario*. Biddle protested to Calderón, and according to Jeremy Robinson, the governor ordered that "all the w———s in Valparaiso should repair on board the *Ontario* without delay." The captain does not mention desertion again as a problem.[20]

By this time Biddle was eager to leave for Peru, but when Prevost returned from a stay in Santiago near the end of February, they received appeals from both San Martín and the American mercantile community to remain until the royalist-patriot clash had been settled by combat. A week before the *Ontario*'s arrival, 3,500 troops from Peru under General Mariano Osorio had landed at Talcahuano and marched north, joined en route by some 1,500 Spanish soldiers in the vicinity. Osorio, who had ruled Chile from his victory at Rancagua in 1814 until San Martín had thrashed him at Chacabuco three years later, was an object of detestation and terror there. According to Biddle, his tenure had been featured by "the most odious tyranny and inhumanity." At Cancha Rayda, near Talca, on 19 March Osorio sprang a surprise attack upon the patriot army, which panicked and fled. His way to Valparaiso and Santiago appeared open, and foreigners were understandably apprehensive when he promised "an ignominious death" to every American and Englishman who fell into his hands, although Biddle suspected that his threat was designed to frighten them into flight.[21]

The captain knew that he had no authorization to start a Spanish-American war on his own initiative, but he was equally determined to protect the commerce of his countrymen. Just as he was concluding that his sloop would have little chance against Cabrera's *Venganza* and two brigs (the other frigate had departed), the 34-gun East Indiaman *Windham,* scheduled to be purchased by the patriots, came into port successfully. Biddle talked her captain into joining him, should it be necessary, to convoy the neutral ships by force through the royalist blockade before the city fell to Osorio. Biddle was confident that the combined firepower of the *Ontario* and the *Windham* could defeat Cabrera, but the reappearance of the second Spanish frigate ended those plans. He took advantage of the ensuing lull to persuade the patriots to buy the *Windham.* She was renamed the *Lautaro,* after a Chilean Indian who had rebelled against the Spaniards during the mid-1500s, and outfitted by men from the *Ontario* as a 44-gun frigate. Robinson says that San Martín thanked Biddle for his work in behalf of the *Lautaro,* "which could not have been done without him."[22]

The best of news came in during early April. San Martín had quickly reassembled his army scattered at Cancha Rayda, and on the 5th, in the decisive battle for Chilean independence, utterly routed Osorio at Maipú, killing, wounding, or capturing 3,500 of the royalists' 5,000 troops. Biddle expressed his exultation in a letter to his brother Nicholas, who thought it important enough to pass along to the president. After outlining his dilemma about maintaining neutrality versus his duty to guard American commercial interests, the captain went on: "The magnitude of responsibility which circumstances might have induced me to take made me wait with fear and anxiety the event of the battle, and the victory, relieving me from all my embarrassments, has given me a most lively joy. . . . The truth is, as you perceive, my interests as well as my feelings were enlisted on the side of the patriots." He suggested that "great commercial advantage" could be gained over the British if the United States "came out in favor of this people," and closed with a quick endorsement of his own role in the drama: "The strong sentiment of sympathy and kindness toward our government . . . has not been weakened by the presence of this ship." But this would prove to be the high-water mark of his amiable relations with the rebels.[23]

With the patriots thoroughly in control of Chile, there was no longer any reason to delay the *Ontario*'s voyage to the Oregon Country, with a stopover in Peru along the way. Biddle and Prevost left Valparaiso on 12 April and arrived on the 21st at Callao, Lima's port. By this time the two men were conversing only on essentials. Despite his reaction of "most lively joy" about Maipú, Biddle was increasingly wary of close involvement between his nation and the patriot Chileños, while Prevost remained steadfast in his devotion to the rebel cause. Personal chemistry was probably a more important factor in their growing estrangement. Both were sensitive and rank conscious; perhaps collision was inevitable, for their naval and diplomatic responsibilities were overlapping. When they first came to Chile, Prevost called attention to the captain's "honor, discretion, and service," but his attitude soon changed. Biddle later told Robinson that the judge had commenced interfering with his own decision-making rights, trying to dictate who should be invited to the *Ontario* and challenging his decision to anchor within range of Peruvian guns at Callao.[24]

The royalist government in Lima, headed by the suave and devious Joaquin de la Pezuela, viceroy of Peru ("Vice King" to Biddle), had not yet heard of Osorio's unexpected defeat at Maipú. That news, coupled with the realization that the acquisition of the *Lautaro* meant a threatening increase in Chilean sea power, led him to conclude that he must negotiate with the rebels, if only to gain time to strengthen his defenses. Felix d'Ochiavarriague y Blanco, a confidant of Pezuela, met Biddle at Callao and asked him and Prevost to come to Lima for a meeting with the viceroy about the possibility that the *Ontario* might carry a royalist diplomatic mission to Chile. Prevost warmly supported the proposition, telling Biddle that his cruise to Oregon was considered by Monroe and Adams secondary to calming roiled waters in lower South America. But the captain reminded Ochiavarriague that he was supposed to sail directly from Peru to Oregon, and he must have sufficient reason to justify any departure from his instructions. He would consider the lifting of the royalist blockade of Valparaiso and permission for American whalers to buy necessities along the west coast adequate compensation for the favor, he added.[25]

The viceroy was cordially personified to Biddle, at least when he met with him and Prevost on 27 April. The best he could do for the whalers was to have them officially notified that a blockade was in force, he claimed, but he would permit American ships to leave Valparaiso if they carried no rebel property. When the captain brought up the question of foreigners imprisoned in Peru, Pezuela promised to release the six American sailors and one Englishman currently held. In return, Biddle agreed to convey the altered blockade rules to Cabrera and carry the Peruvian mission to Valparaiso, as well as to send home four captured Chilean officers to start an exchange of prisoners. Throughout the conversation the viceroy focused his attention on Biddle, while treating the obviously pro-patriot Prevost "with great coldness." Pezuela admitted that he had formed "as good an opinion" of the captain as he had "unfavorable of his passenger." Undoubtedly Prevost's status as little more than a rebuffed bystander in further negotiations exacerbated the coolness of his relationship with his captain.[26]

Although he never admitted it, it is clear that Biddle had been duped by the viceroy, a circumstance that occurred rarely in his lengthy diplomatic career. Pezuela confessed his deceit: "I sent them [Ochiavarriague and Thomas Crompton, an English merchant in Lima] under the pretext of the exchange of prisoners." Their assigned responsibilities were to delay any Chilean naval offensive against Peru, spy on the patriots, and purchase arms for the royalists, known to be available from neutrals in Valparaiso. Furthermore, Ochiavarriague carried a letter addressed to a private citizen named "Don José de San Martín" rather than to "General José de San Martín, commander of the Chilean Armies," the final proof that Biddle was being used as a Spanish tool. Surely Pezuela had to be aware that any missive with such a salutation would never be accepted by the Chileños.[27]

When the *Ontario* entered Valparaiso harbor on 29 May, twenty-one days out of Callao, Biddle learned that only three days before the *Lautaro* had engaged the *Venganza* and a sloop, damaging Cabrera's flagship seriously enough to force him to lift his blockade. This allowed all the American merchantmen immobilized there to scurry away, save one, the *Two Catherines*. But much to the resentment of their masters, they had been compelled to sail shorthanded. Hardly had the *Ontario* left port for Callao than the Chileños recommenced raiding American crews, this time for the *Lautaro*. Although he launched no formal protest, down went the patriots another notch in Biddle's esteem.[28]

For the first week or so the Chileans hailed Biddle for his part in promoting the prisoner exchange. He, Ochiavarriague, and Crompton were escorted by an honor guard to Santiago and entertained "with every mark of respect and friendship" by O'Higgins himself. But Chilean applause turned to catcalls upon the presentation of Pezuela's letter to "Don José de San Martín," and royalist-patriot negotiations collapsed on the spot. The viceroy's agents were deservedly considered spies. Ochiavarriague in particular felt menaced, later reporting to his superior that only Biddle's protection had saved him from imprisonment. In gratitude the viceroy eventually issued a passport to the *Two Catherines* permitting her to leave for Peru with a cargo of wheat, ensuring a prosperous voyage. If outwardly Biddle continued to receive the ceremonial courtesies of O'Higgins and his cohorts, a modern commentator is right when he says: "This was the first step in his loss of prestige in Chile, and since he was the ranking United States Naval officer in the South Pacific, his loss of prestige was also that of the United States as a whole."[29]

At this point Judge Theodorick Bland appeared in Chile. The lack of unified opinion among the Americans there was demonstrated not only by the instant clash between the pro-Carrera Bland and the pro-O'Higgins Prevost, but also by the latter's dispute with Biddle, which had become public knowledge. First Lieutenant Connor noted that when they had returned to Valparaiso from Peru, Prevost "left the ship for Santiago, and I presume in consequence of a misunderstanding between him and Capt. B., he did not again join us."[30]

When the *Ontario* departed once more for Callao on 14 June, Jeremy Robinson had taken Prevost's place. This unaccredited diplomat, still yearning for a commission, had initially taken a most negative attitude toward the Biddle-Prevost collaboration. Somehow he had persuaded himself that their journeys to and from Peru were only camouflages for some nefarious commercial plot to their own advantage. Early in June he referred to their "mercantile scheme" which did "little to their honor as American officers." A couple of days later he carped that the captain was influenced "wholly by cupidity." On board the *Ontario*, however, Biddle turned on his considerable personal charm, and captivated his erstwhile critic. The day after sailing Robinson jotted down a comment that "Captain Biddle behaves with the most marked and gentlemanly politeness, bordering on friendship," and no more is heard about "mercantile schemes" before his departure at Callao on the 28th.[31]

Biddle's second sojourn in Peru was for two days only. He extended himself to aid the masters of two American trading vessels at anchor off Callao, one of which was Astor's *Beaver*. In Lima Ochiavarriague's account of Biddle's helpfulness in Chile affected Pezuela sufficiently to make him embarrass his American friend inadvertently. In a brief meeting at his palace the viceroy impulsively gave Biddle a handsome sword with a gold scabbard and a diamond-studded hilt. The captain, recognizing its value, very properly turned it over to the State Department when he came home, but that did not save him from castigation by the administration's enemies for accepting it. This concluded the first phase of his long cruise, and the government thoroughly approved of his actions to date. The eminent South Carolinian John C. Calhoun, briefly serving as acting secretary of the navy, complimented him: "The activity and zeal you have displayed in the execution of your orders merit the approbation of the Department, and you will be duly appreciated by your country."[32]

On 30 June Biddle commenced his long journey to Oregon. When calm seas and light breezes permitted leisure, he must have read several times his secret instructions from the Navy Department:

> You will . . . then proceed to the Columbia River, with a view to assert, on the part of the United States, the claim to the sovereignty, by some symbolical or appropriate mode adapted to the occasion. In the performance of this duty no force is to be employed, if in the attempt to accomplish the object any unexpected obstructions should occur. This last and important service being executed, you will proceed on your return to the United States.

He would also have mulled over what he already knew about that vast tract of some half-million square miles. The Oregon Country had long been the subject of a languid controversy among Spain (from California to the south), Russia (from what would become Alaska to the north), Britain and America (from Canada and the United States to the east), although by the mid-1820s Spain and Russia had dropped from contention.[33]

The remaining rivals had excellent claims by exploration: Captain George Vancouver and Alexander Mackenzie for London; Captain Robert Gray and the Meriwether Lewis–William Clark expedition for Washington. Biddle would have been thoroughly informed about the latter, for in 1810 his brother Nicholas had been selected by President Jefferson to edit the journals of Lewis and Clark. He would also have known that Britain could use the 1790 Nootka Convention with Spain to support its claim to Oregon.[34]

The two contenders also had claims, tenuous to be sure, to the Oregon Country by occupation, since for years their nationals had traded for furs along its coast. The Montreal-based North West Company, briskly competing in the fur business with the venerable Hudson's Bay Company, its British competitor in Canada until they merged in 1821, had already sent several expeditions into modern British Columbia and Washington State, hoping to bypass Hudson's Bay on the west coast. The "Nor'westers" also had to keep a nervous eye on John Jacob Astor, the farsighted entrepreneur who had decided to back an American challenge in Oregon. He organized the American Fur Company, and during 1810 and 1811 moved to occupy the valley of the lower Columbia, both overland and by sea. One party trekked cross-country to build and fortify a little settlement called Astoria near the river's mouth. But his seafarers met disaster. When their ship reached the northwestern shore, they were attacked by Indians they foolishly allowed on board. One doomed American blew up himself, his assailants, and his ship. Further affliction came to Astor's men when the Nor'westers informed them that the War of 1812 had broken out, and that Royal Navy men-of-war were en route to take possession of Oregon. In fear of losing everything without compensation, the Americans sold to the North West Company for $40,000 Fort Astoria, its accouterments, and a large cache of furs said to be worth $100,000 on the open market.[35]

By 1813 the Admiralty in London had learned to its consternation that Commodore David Porter in the little USS *Essex* had naval control of the Pacific, for no British warships were in that vast ocean; he was in the process of decimating London's whaling industry based at the Galápagos Islands off the coast of Ecuador. Captain James Hillyar was sent to the Pacific in the frigate *Phoebe,* accompanied by the sloops *Cherub* and *Raccoon.* His major responsibility was to destroy the *Essex,* but Oregon was also involved. Once around Cape Horn the *Raccoon* was to proceed alone to take possession of that country. There might have been an Anglo-American naval battle off the Columbia. Astor's agent, Wilson H. Price, in a futile effort to avoid selling out to the Nor'westers, sped to the Marquesas Islands, where Porter was briefly tarrying, and begged him to come to the aid of the threatened outpost. He refused, for that glory-hungry officer had already decided to return to Chile in quest of his pursuers. At Valparaiso on 28 March 1814 the *Essex,* outgunned and the victim of freakish weather, was hammered into surrender by the *Phoebe* and *Cherub.* It was an inexcusable miscalculation; Porter should have realized that his one small frigate harrying enemy commerce in the Pacific and perhaps the Indian oceans was worth any number of single-ship victories.[36]

A few weeks after Astoria had been sold, the *Raccoon* showed up at the Columbia. Commander William Black was as avid for laurels as Porter, and had been looking forward to some fun with his carronades. But once he saw that ramshackle settlement's feeble defenses, he complained, "Is this the fort about which I have heard so much talking? D——n me, but I'd batter it down in two hours with a four-pounder!" He proceeded to take official possession of the place, elevating the Union Jack and renaming it "Fort George," then sailed away. Unwittingly Black had confirmed the wisdom of Astor's employees when they made their sale to the North West Company. If they had not, their employer would have had to traverse a lengthy and tortuous course through a postwar claims court, with any restitution years away. Furthermore, when Black hoisted his nation's flag over Astoria he put it, at least potentially, on the list of British conquests, to be combined with tracts along the Canadian border in northeastern Maine, northern New York State, and the upper Middle West.[37]

The Anglo-American negotiators at Ghent late in 1814, grappling with the matter of wartime possessions, decided that everything taken should be given back, much to the advantage of the United States. But had Astoria been lost by the North West Company's legal purchase of it or by a Royal Navy officer's forcible conquest? Secretary of State James Monroe was convinced that the latter was the case, and in 1815 he told the British that his government planned to reoccupy Astoria in the near future. Nothing happened, however, until mid-1817, when Adams persuaded Monroe, then president, that Biddle should be further instructed to proceed to Oregon and reclaim the mouth of the Columbia.[38] Such was the state of affairs in Washington and London when Biddle sailed for Oregon on 30 June.

On 19 August, fifty days from Callao, the *Ontario* reached her destination. Biddle and his complement looked upon a sight to discourage the most dauntless navigator. A gigantic sandbar stretched across the Columbia's mouth and, as the captain put it: "The entrance of this River is rendered difficult to vessels as large as the *Ontario* by the shoalness [shallowness] of the water on its bar, by its sinuous channel, and by the strength and irregularity of its tide." He was right; attempting to proceed upriver was often a fatal mistake for sailing ships.[39]

As Biddle's orders forbade the use of force he had no need for his sloop's firepower. He went ashore with fifty officers and men in three boats, landing at the ominously named Cape Disappointment on the north bank. What ensued was fully documented by three eyewitness accounts: Biddle's Journal, amplified by those of lieutenants David Conner and James Aulick. According to the captain, he raised the American flag before a crowd of Indians. While the *Ontario* offshore rolled out a twenty-one-gun salute, "I turned up a sod of soil, and giving three cheers, I nailed up against a tree a leaden plate in which were cut the following words: TAKEN POSSESSION OF IN THE NAME AND ON THE BEHALF OF THE UNITED STATES BY CAPTAIN JAMES BIDDLE COMMANDING THE UNITED STATES SHIP ONTARIO, COLUMBIA RIVER, AUGUST 1818."[40]

The boats then fought the current upriver and, after looking in on an Indian village, crossed over to the south bank to visit Fort Astoria-Fort George. Biddle is silent about what occurred there, but Aulick registered his "mortification to see the British flag run up."

The settlement consisted of a handful of buildings behind a picket fence, protected by three guns, "although they have five or six more without carriages[!]." The grand total of its population was about fifty, equally divided between whites and Hawaiian Islanders—the Polynesians were often imported for physical labor by Americans and Englishmen alike. Apparently there was no confrontation whatever between Biddle and James Keith, the North West Company's manager, and the American stay was brief. Easing downstream along the southern shore, the little expedition stopped off at the Columbia's mouth for the captain to affix a wooden board with the U.S. coat of arms on one side and wording identical to that of his leaden plate at Cape Disappointment on the other. After a night in the anchored boats, Biddle and his men rowed out to the *Ontario*. Although neither the captain nor his two lieutenants mention any difficulty about reaching their ship, Jeremy Robinson noted in his diary that upon their return to Peru the officers told him that they had "a narrow escape from destruction in their boats near the breakers" over the Columbia's sandbar.[41]

Biddle saw no reason to tarry in Oregon. Asserting that he must have fresh water and provisions, neither of which were available there, he left that day for California, coming into Monterey on 25 August. In that port he was able to renew acquaintance with Captain Vasilii Golovnin, whose frigate *Kutuzov* he had visited in Rio. The Russian was passing off his cruise as a voyage of exploration, but Biddle suspected otherwise. He was aware that the Russian North American Company had, with Spanish permission, founded a settlement north of San Francisco called "Fort Ross"—a shortened form of "Rossiya," as that country was sometimes called in contemporary spelling. He had also "read in the English Newspapers" that the company had "taken possession of one of the Sandwich [Hawaiian] Islands and fortified it." He told his officers to make discreet inquiries of their Russian counterparts as to the truth of that rumor. They were assured that "there was no Russian establishment among the Sandwich Islands." Biddle doubted it, and passed his report along to Washington, "thinking it might be of interest to our Government."[42]

How much Golovnin and his men knew about their nation's ambitious if evanescent plans for imperialism in the Pacific, and the recent failure of those plans, is problematical. The company had tried to combine into a triangle Alaska's furs and shipbuilding with foodstuffs from California and tropical products from the Sandwich Islands, aware that furs and Hawaiian sandalwood should command high prices in the China market. A small fortified establishment on Hawaii's northwesternmost island of Kauai was started and abandoned during the single year of 1816. Fort Ross was maintained from 1812 to 1842 before being sold to American interests, and Alaska, of course, was finally sold to the United States in 1867. It requires little imagination to envisage how history would have been changed had Russia been able to plant itself permanently in Alaska, northern California, and Hawaii; Biddle was justified in concluding that knowledge of this far-reaching enterprise would be "of interest to our Government."[43]

Somewhere during her long passage toward Peru the *Ontario* passed HMS *Blossom,* sister sloop to the *Cherub* and the *Raccoon,* heading toward Oregon with none other than Judge John B. Prevost as her passenger. It should be recalled that Biddle had sailed from New York under secret orders to sail to the Columbia River. The administration hoped that the British would remain ignorant about the *Ontario*'s destination, but the king's chargé in Washington soon learned the truth and sent that information to London. More specific confirmation came from Simon McGillivrary, a North West Company partner who happened to be in New York. He wrote to the British minister in Washington: "My information is that the Captain of the *Ontario* has instructions to proceed ultimately to the Columbia River, and to seize or destroy the establishment and trade of the North West Company upon that Coast." Secretary of State Adams was evidently "embarrassed" at implications of deliberate concealment in regard to Biddle's mission, denying to the British minister that the United States had any such aggressive aims, and arguing that Astoria as a wartime loss should be returned.[44]

In London a report on the matter finally crossed the desk of Lord Castlereagh, British Foreign secretary. He decided, as one modern historian says, "to give the Americans what he referred to as 'an additional motive to cultivate the arts of peace,' and concluded that Astoria should be given back, 'provided it was made abundantly clear to them that this would neither recognize United States rights nor relinquish British claims to the territory.' " Orders were dispatched to Captain Frederick Hickey, operating off Chile in the *Blossom,* to sail to the Columbia and tell the Nor'westers that they must surrender their purchased outpost.[45]

At Valparaiso Hickey bumped into the stranded Prevost, and informed him that he was en route to Oregon for the restoration of Astoria to the United States. Delighted with this stroke of luck, Prevost hitched a ride, with the unlikely result that an American diplomatic representative came into disputed Oregon Country in a British man-of-war. On 6 October Hickey, Prevost, and the North West Company's Keith went through somewhat farcical ceremonies, during which the British ensign came down, the American went up, a salute was fired from the *Blossom,* and a transfer draft was signed, while uncomprehending Indians and Hawaiians looked on. Once Prevost and Hickey had departed, however, the Nor'westers continued to run that sleepy little backwater, for Astor had pulled out of the Pacific Northwest for good, concentrating instead on the U.S. Rocky Mountain fur business.[46]

The entire Oregon question was basically bypassed during the Anglo-American Convention of 1818. No final decision was reached on either who owned the area or what its boundaries might be. Instead it was determined that the country would remain open to both British and American settlers for ten years, a provision later extended annually through 1845. But Biddle's two-day sojourn and his claim to both banks of the Columbia, as well as Prevost's agreement with the North West Company, had at least some impact on Oregon's destiny. The leading specialist on the early history of that territory summarizes the meaning of what transpired during 1818:

> In British and also American diplomacy, Astoria was a symbol. It symbolized to the British government that side of the valley of the Columbia where the post lay—the river's southern watershed. Its restoration to the United States was a recognition, despite British intentions and protestations to the contrary, of American tenure in all that area. After the restoration the British government was never again able seriously to contend the American position south of the river.[47]

Sailing from Monterey on 30 August, Biddle arrived at Callao on 22 October to find that the cases of the American merchantmen *Beaver* and *Canton,* sources of concern for him since he had first entered the Pacific, were still in limbo. He at once set about trying to liberate them from royalist custody. Throughout, the issue of the *Canton* from Salem, Massachusetts, remained subservient to that of the *Beaver,* owned by the ever-influential Astor. The story of the *Beaver* commenced during the spring of 1817 when Richard J. Cleveland, a seasoned mariner who had already visited the Northwest coast, talked Astor into financing a commercial venture to take advantage of the revolutionary upheavals in Chile. Perhaps only Astor's well-filled purse could have provided the wherewithal for so costly an enterprise. The *Beaver,* "his favorite ship," was overhauled and refitted at an estimated cost of $50,000. She departed from New York with a variety of goods worth $140,000. Inconspicuously listed in her cargo manifest were 125 muskets and bayonets, plus 8,600 pounds of gunpowder, to be sold to the Chilean rebels. She put out from New York on 1 July 1817 with Cleveland as master and with the

Spanish-speaking Francisco Ribas as "Assistant Supercargo," earmarked for "Canton and the North West Coast"—South America was not mentioned—and insured for $80,000 against "participation in illegal trade."[48]

By the time the *Beaver* had rounded the Horn the entire Chilean coast was under patriot occupation, with the single exception of Talcahuano. With execrable luck that was the port into which Cleveland put for supplies during mid-October. Since firearms and gunpowder could hardly be more obvious as contraband of war, royalist authorities there impounded the ship and seized her cargo, the munitions going to the aid of their besieged army. The *Canton* had also blundered in and suffered the same fate. Although Ribas soon escaped to inform Astor what had happened, Cleveland had to remain at Talcahuano for several months before being able to make his way to Peru. Both men appealed to Pezuela for reconsideration, calling upon Biddle and Prevost for support. Prevost reported the incident to Adams, who told the U.S. minister in Madrid to protest to the Spanish government. In conversations with Biddle just before the captain had left for Oregon, Cleveland begged him to intercede with the viceroy. As that "opinion coincided with my own," Biddle was happy to concur, informing Pezuela that he and his country would be most interested to ascertain on his return from the Northwest whether the *Beaver* and *Canton* would be released. If not, he warned, it could have a most negative effect upon Spanish-American relations.[49]

Once back in Lima Biddle closeted himself several times with the viceroy. He wasted no time trying to argue that the seizures of the two ships had been illegal, but based his case on his knowledge that the royalists must depend entirely on American supplies if they hoped to ward off conquest by the rapidly augmenting Chilean navy. He commented that he had seen in the British press that retention of the merchantmen "had produced great sensation in the United States," and unless a quick and favorable decision about them was forthcoming, "the most unpleasant consequences could be apprehended." Meanwhile both Prevost and Robinson—each of whom later claimed credit for the successful conclusion of the affair—were busying themselves to the same end. Yet Biddle's intervention was paramount. The release of the *Beaver* and *Canton* on 30 November was the result of Peruvian supply needs, the threat of the *Ontario*'s battery (Biddle put it more diplomatically as "the presence of a public vessel of the United States"), and the amity that had developed between the captain and the viceroy. Pezuela also ordered that any portions of the cargoes from the two seized ships that could legally be returned should be, and that compensation for the unrecoverable shares should later be sought in prize courts. Cleveland wrote that he was "greatly indebted to Captain Biddle" for the *Beaver*'s liberation. Furthermore, he admitted, he would not have been able to sail on later profitable voyages for himself and Astor without the endeavors of men sent over from the *Ontario* to clean and repair his ship, which the royalists had left "very dirty in the extreme."[50]

Biddle lost no time in again trying to free his countrymen from foreign imprisonment. He was totally effective in having the door of Callao's jail thrown open for nine Americans apprehended while he was cruising to and from Oregon once he had promised to take them on board the *Ontario*. On the other hand, he was only partially successful in attaining the release of "upwards of thirty" Americans who had been found in the Chilean privateer *Maipú* when she had been picked up early in November by a Spanish man-of-war. Since there was no legal ground upon which he could stand, Biddle asked Pezuela to realize that they were naïve and uneducated sailors who had been "seduced and betrayed" into the rebel service, and certainly had "no intentional hostility toward Spain." He pledged that any men surrendered to him would be kept in the *Ontario* until she reached the United States. Pezuela replied that he had just received orders from Madrid that he must "keep in close custody" any foreigners apprehended in arms against Spain, and it was impossible for him to comply. However, he continued, as a personal favor to Biddle he would let him have "a few." The few turned out to be seven. Four had been among the deserters at Valparaiso the previous February (probably the last persons south of the equator who wanted to rejoin the *Ontario*), one a man whose father the captain knew in Philadelphia, another who has suffered with him in Tripoli, and a seventh who had once sailed under him on a cruise.[51]

Biddle was able to grant one last favor for American commerce in the Pacific before hoisting anchor for Chile. Just prior to his departure the master of the whaler *Eliza Barker* reported to him that his ship had been plundered in midocean of $1,200 worth of supplies by a Spanish sloop of war. Biddle shot off a protest to the viceroy who, accommodating as usual, promised to investigate the matter when the offending warship ended her cruise. If a wrong had been done to the people of the *Eliza Barker*, due compensation would be paid, a conclusion most satisfactory to both American captains.[52]

Throughout his tenure in Peru Biddle had been a shrewd and persistent diplomat. One must agree with the summary of his negotiations there provided by Edward B. Billingsley in his masterful *In Defense of Neutral Rights*, even though he overlooks Pezuela's sly use of him in the Ochiavarriague mission:

An understanding based upon mutual respect had been established with the viceroy. In his dealings with the latter, Biddle had not hesitated to clothe himself in the authority and power of the country he so proudly represented, nor had he shrunk from taking full advantage of Pezuela's precarious position in relation to the patriots. But he had carefully refrained from making unreasonable or exaggerated claims that would denigrate the authority of the viceroy or the dignity of his sovereign. On his part, Pezuela, recognizing in the naval officer a man of reason and integrity, was willing to concede any requests that could be justified under international usage and were not contrary to Spanish laws. Thus, Biddle gained significant concessions on behalf of his countrymen.[53]

The Chilean situation had changed drastically between the time that the *Ontario* had left for Oregon and the time she returned to Valparaiso on 27 December, twenty-one days from Callao. The patriots now boasted a stronger navy than the Peruvian royalists, and it was constantly being augmented by the arrival of purchased ships from Britain and America. Moreover, Lord Thomas Cochrane, later the earl of Dundonald, was the new commander of the Chilean fleet. He had written so scintillating a record during the recent Anglo-French wars that a plausible argument could be maintained that no other captain surpassed him in single-ship action. For instance, in the little HMS *Speedy* he picked off thirty-three enemy vessels in fourteen months, and then during 1801 with this 14-gun brig and a complement of only 54 he stormed and captured the Spanish frigate *El Gamo,* with 32 guns and a crew of 519. A leading British naval historian sums him up as "so wonderful—his judgment . . . so excellent—his resources so capable of surmounting any emergency."[54]

Yet Cochrane's personal failings came close to ruining him. He had an unerring ability to pick quarrels with those very superiors who could retaliate against him the most effectively. Henry Hill, U.S. consul at Valparaiso, described him as "almost always in hot water, being impulsive, headstrong . . . determined to have his own way. . . . His mind was not well-balanced." Cochrane's availability to command the Chilean fleet offers a case in point. While still a captain in the Royal Navy he was serving simultaneously as a leading radical in Parliament. He so assailed the mismanagement of those high in the Admiralty that they were bound to strike back. Their opportunity came in 1814, when he was accused of culpability in a stock market fraud engineered by his uncle, although many years later he was completely exonerated. He was tried, found guilty, and cashiered from the service. Adams called him "a swindling robber."[55]

Cochrane then signed on in Chile, serving from 1818 until late 1822. In this assignment he was emulating many other British and American officers, either disgraced, or more commonly, escaping half-pay status during peacetime doldrums by enlisting in foreign navies. Although he had been the patriot admiral for no more than a month before Biddle appeared, he was already stamping a Royal Navy hallmark on his new command, and he would be a source of contention for every American officer assigned to the southeast Pacific during his tenure.[56]

As soon as Biddle had made fast the *Ontario* he visited Cochrane in his flagship, the frigate *San Martín*. What exactly transpired between them is unknown, but Biddle, undoubtedly already aware of his unsavory reputation, came away with a lasting antipathy toward the domineering Briton. In a letter to his brother, Biddle asserted that anyone who could support Cochrane was "worse than a beast." A few hours later the admiral sent a letter to the *Ontario*, the first of five concerning salutes that would pass between them, starting a dreary and repetitive literary war, taking up two thousand words in Biddle's Journal and widely reprinted in the American press. Cochrane asked why the *Ontario* had not performed the courtesy of firing a salute upon entering port. He then alluded to a precedent at Gibraltar during 1802 when, he claimed, Admiral Lord George Keith, commanding British forces in the Mediterranean, had expelled Captain William Bainbridge in the USS *Essex* from that port for failing to do just that. Cochrane's implication was unmistakable: salute or get out of Valparaiso. Biddle, the proud and touchy representative of a proud and touchy nation, replied the next morning with a polite but definite refusal. He admitted that "it is customary to fire a public salute" when a warship comes into a foreign port. But when he had done so the previous January, Governor Calderón had not returned it. In view of such an insult he had resolved to dispense with that courtesy in any future entries into Valparaiso.[57]

Cochrane's second missive arrived within hours, reiterating his demand. Biddle's quick answer demonstrated his independence, for he defiantly told his adversary that now he would "excuse myself entirely from making the salute." Furthermore, he took sharp exception to the Briton's statement about Bainbridge and Keith in 1802, saying that his good friend would never have tolerated being ordered out of Gibraltar. Back came Cochrane, calling Biddle's attention to his inconsistency in first admitting that it was common usage for a foreign warship to salute and then announcing that he refused to perform that ceremony. Probably because the Briton had already said that any American salvo would not be returned with an equal number of guns, Biddle refused even to answer that letter, calling it "as ridiculous as it is vulgar." The matter of salutes had ended in an Anglo-American standoff.[58]

The last communication that passed between the admiral and the captain was a request that Biddle delay his departure from port, scheduled for 30 December, until the Chilean squadron could put out to sea on its way to attack Peru. Cochrane promised that this would involve no more than a day or two—but actually he did not leave for another fortnight.[59]

Biddle complied, setting the 31st as his sailing day. In this the American made a definite concession, for he had more on his mind than matters of naval punctilio. He had no desire to remain at Valparaiso a moment longer than necessary, for he knew that he was in the process of committing unneutral acts. Four of the five passengers he had brought from Callao were inoffensive civilians, but the fifth was a Colonel Olivarria of the Spanish Army, the viceroy's nephew, who needed transportation to Rio en route to Spain in search of reinforcements for the Peruvian royalists. Biddle recognized that he had no right to bring an enemy into a port at war under the protection of the American flag. He excused himself by admitting in his Journal that he "regretted very much" Pezuela's requested favor for Olivarria, and "felt reluctant to comply with it." But the cases of the *Beaver* and *Canton* were still under consideration at that moment, he argued, and they "would have been condemned" had he turned down the viceroy. He maintained that American national priorities called for him to achieve the liberation of the two vessels, even at the cost of breeching neutrality.[60]

A second situation that made Biddle wish to leave Chile at the first opportunity was the *Ontario*'s cargo of $201,000 in gold and silver. According to the captain's tabulation, forty-one thousand dollars was destined for America—$15,000 apiece for Astor and a Mr. Gracie in Manhattan, and $11,000 for an unnamed Boston shipowner—and $160,000 for Rio de Janeiro, dispatched by Peruvian merchants. Specie-carrying through waters often infested with privateers and pirates was a service frequently performed by both the American and British navies. The practice, tolerated by American law, was understandably popular with commanders, as they received a small percentage of the total delivered safely; in Biddle's case, $2\frac{1}{2}$ percent, or $5,025. He was therefore transporting royalist property into patriot Valparaiso under the aegis of his national ensign, a situation bound to be resented by the Chileños. To his further disquietude, he learned that rumors were sweeping the city that the *Ontario* was carrying not only an enemy agent but almost a million dollars in specie as well. There was always the danger that such an audacious and unscrupulous opponent as Cochrane might decide to board and seize such a treasure, taking his chances on later legal proceedings against him.[61]

Should battle be forced upon him, Biddle would face impossible odds, as Cochrane's fleet was composed of three frigates and a sloop. Chilean naval maneuvers on the night of the 30th seemed to be leading in that direction, and tension remained high among the Americans. While the flagship *San Martín* hovered offshore, the frigate *Chacabuco* dropped anchor so close to the *Ontario* that Biddle feared his rigging might be fouled. The following morning an American came on board to warn that Cochrane was planning to board the sloop should she attempt to depart so that her passenger list and cargo manifest might be examined.[62]

Biddle described both his perilous situation and his successful escape from it:

> Connecting the reports on shore and the maneuverings of the ships, with the character of Lord Cochrane, which is known to be destitute of principle and regardless of decency, it was quite obvious that there was either the intention to attack us, if we attempted to go to sea, or that the intention was to intimidate us from sailing. I did not choose to be deterred from sailing, whichever was the intention, and therefore at 10 o'clock in the morning, having cleared the ship for action, I weighed and stood out to sea, passing within half gun shot of the *San Martín* who made sail along with me, when I came abreast of her; and after I had got a few miles out, she & the *Chacabuco* tacked and returned to anchorage.[63]

Nothing out of the ordinary marked the *Ontario*'s voyage to Rio. There during late February 1819 Biddle loaded water and foodstuffs, using Astor's $15,000 in specie to pay for them, as well as providing his officers with their salaries. (The government eventually repaid the sum, with interest.) He then stood off Pernambuco (Recife) in northern Brazil where he tried without success to arrange the release from imprisonment of nine American sailors. Departing on 28 March, he came into Annapolis on 25 April.[64]

Following his much anticipated reunion with his "beloved family," Biddle might have been permitted to luxuriate in leisure after his exhausting cruise of 589 days, but that was not to be. Instead, he was forced again and again to pick up his pen in order to write yet another defense against accusations emanating from both South America and home. By mid-1820 he must have winced when he read yet another request from the secretary of the navy for additional "information."

His refusal to salute at Valparaiso caused his initial difficulty. Cochrane's interpretation of that confrontation had arrived in the United States almost simultaneously with Biddle's homecoming. The press divided on the issue as to whether he had insulted patriot Chile.

Administration organs shrugged off the allegation, but those favoring Clay's advocacy of a quick recognition of the South American rebel states criticized him for his stiff-necked and antirepublican behavior. Biddle, ever conscious of his public reputation, showed his discomfort when he replied to two brothers who had written to thank him for rescuing their ships from seizure: "I am very sensible of your kind and flattering expressions; particularly at this moment when my character is assailed in some of the newspapers, for a conduct which I trusted would not have incurred any public reproach." He iterated in his Journal that salutes were discretionary, not obligatory. He had so notified the Chilean authorities just prior to his departure from Valparaiso. Not only did they accept his explanation that his refusal had meant no disrespect for their flag, but they also considered the entire episode no more than a personal disagreement between Cochrane and himself.[65]

Much of the public discussion about the matter centered on Cochrane's reference to Bainbridge. Had he been ordered out of Gibraltar by Admiral Keith in 1802 for failing to honor the Union Jack? As Biddle moved to counterattack on this issue, Bainbridge sprang to his side, indignantly denying any such occurrence and pursuing the question further in the press. He stated that his dealings had been not with Keith, but with Admiral Sir James Saumarez. On his first stopover at Gibraltar in the *Essex* he did not salute because the USS *Boston*, preceding him into the harbor, had already extended that courtesy. On his second visit he had had a cordial meeting with Saumarez, during which salutes were neither requested nor given. Had he been ordered to do so, "Such a demand I would have considered absurd in the extreme."[66]

While basically correct, Bainbridge's memory erred here and there. Entries in the *Essex*'s journal during 1802 tell that he met Saumarez ashore on 27 February and 24 March; the admiral had come on board the American frigate on 18 April and was saluted with thirteen guns. As for Keith, on 16 April Bainbridge had saluted as he came into the Rock and the garrison "returned it." Nowhere in the documentation is there the slightest reference to any pressure on the *Essex* to perform such a courtesy, to say nothing about any ouster of that ship from Gibraltar. In short, the Biddle–Bainbridge collaboration proved that Cochrane's charges had been wrong. The leading American national weekly hailed Biddle as completely redeeming himself, as he had "put to rest all the stories circulated to his prejudice—and convinces us that he rightfully maintained the honor of the flag."[67]

There was no dispute on the subject of Biddle's accomplishments in behalf of American shippers and sailors in the Pacific, for everyone agreed that he had done splendidly by them. Eleven American "captains, supercargoes, and agents" in Valparaiso memorialized him: "We flatter ourselves that when it shall be known in the United States that nearly a million in American property has been saved from certain condemnation, and many American citizens from oppressive imprisonment, by your exertions, both our country and Government will duly appreciate and reward your meritorious services." Astor praised him in a letter published in the newspapers: "I congratulate you in your safe return from a long and perilous voyage . . . and in which you have rendered the most important services to your country, by having rescued and protected an immense property belonging to your fellow citizens, of whom I am one."[68]

There was, however, a negative barrage fired at Biddle by his erstwhile colleagues in Chile, who had been outraged by the *Ontario*'s precipitate departure from Valparaiso. Prevost outdid Worthington and Robinson in vehemence. He told Adams that Biddle's pro-royalist activities, especially in hauling specie, had damaged Chilean-American relations, much to the British advantage. He went so far as to persuade Joaquín de Echeverria, Chilean foreign minister, to protest officially about the captain's behavior. Specifically the Chileño accentuated Biddle's overt favoritism for the royalists and antagonism toward the patriots, to wit: smuggling Ochiavarriague and Crompton into Valparaiso as spies; accepting a costly sword from Viceroy Pezuela; bringing enemy persons and property into Chile under the neutral American flag (namely Colonel Olivarria and Peruvian specie, the latter setting a precedent that the British were quick to follow); and refusing to salute the Chilean ensign.[69]

In all Biddle had to write five explanations of his cruise, four to Secretary of the Navy Smith Thompson and one to President Monroe himself. When the House of Representatives on 31 March 1820 asked him for additional particulars concerning his specie-carrying, he availed himself of this opportunity to answer all the charges against him, with the exception of his overworked controversy with Cochrane about salutes. (Evidently he decided that he had already said all that was necessary concerning that topic in his widely circulated accounts in the press less than a year before.)[70]

His eleven-page explanation to Thompson on 2 April provided his best-reasoned defense. He stressed that he had transported Ochiavarriague and Crompton to Chile solely in connection with the prisoner exchange, and for no other reason. He had acted with perfect propriety in accepting Pezuela's sword, noting that he had not kept it for personal use but had turned it over to the State Department as soon as he had come home. With the viceroy still considering the cases of the *Beaver* and *Canton*, allowing Colonel Olivarria to board his ship was no more than an act of "kindness and courtesy" to Pezuela, with a clear implication that both ships would have been confiscated had he refused the Spaniard passage. In regard to specie-carrying, he argued that it was allowed by the U.S. law of 1800; the charge that he had broken the way for the British to perform the same service was asinine, for they had long done so.[71]

Biddle may have thought that this explanation would free him from further harassment, but only two days after writing it he was pilloried by the Speaker of the House of Representatives. Henry Clay, still doggedly pushing for immediate recognition of Argentina and Chile, had decided that behind Biddle's façade of a patriot supporter lurked a secret royalist sympathizer. Moreover, his discreditation might be used to impel the administration into precipitate recognition of Buenos Aires and Santiago. He drew a bead upon the captain's acceptance of Pezuela's sword, and—which must have been infuriating to the sensitive Biddle—turned the matter into a joke, barbed to be sure, but still a joke. In conjunction with a more serious House resolution to "outfit" ministers to South America, he introduced another calling upon the president to award Pezuela's sword to whichever patriot general in Argentina or Chile he deemed the "most worthy and distinguished."[72]

Clay showed what he really thought of his "sword resolution" by withdrawing it a month later. He did, however, emphasize that when he had heard that Biddle had accepted such an expensive present he was "greatly mortified" that the captain had not emulated the example set by the surgeon of the ship of the line *Franklin*. He had returned a $1,500 payment from a high-ranking Austrian whose broken leg he had set, while intoning that as "an American officer he had done nothing but his duty." Clay characterized Biddle's carrying royalist specie out of Peru as "highly improper." He concluded by calling Biddle "a gallant officer whose conduct has been inadvertent. . . . His errors, I am persuaded, will not be repeated by him or imitated by others."[73]

If Clay had expected to stampede Monroe and Adams into a premature recognition of Argentina and Chile by way of Biddle, he failed. Abetted by the opposition's continued division between the "Clayites" and the Porter-Skinner-Irvine faction, the latter still assailing the de facto governments of both countries as pro-monarchical and pro-British, the administration was given all the time and more that it needed to carry though its Latin American policy. The important Adams-Onís Transcontinental Treaty was signed on 22 February 1819, but exactly two years passed before it was ratified by

Madrid, and almost another two years elapsed before the United States finally recognized Argentina and Chile. Hence there was no need to sacrifice Biddle on the altar of diplomatic or political expediency (as befell Porter after his unauthorized landing in Spanish Puerto Rico in 1824, and Captain John Downes for exceeding his instructions by destroying the Sumatran village called Kuala Batu in 1832).

Indeed, the government ultimately gave Biddle its full support. In arriving at this decision the Navy and State departments were assisted by official word from both Spain and Chile that Biddle had given no offense; quite the contrary. During November of 1819 the captain notified Secretary Thompson that he had received a message from the Spanish legation in Washington that King Ferdinand VII was delighted with the prudent yet "exalted and gallant" manner with which he had conducted himself in Peru, and "His majesty . . . thanks you in his royal name." Even more to the point, in view of the opposition's charges that Biddle had been pro-royalist, during 1820 Worthington wrote the captain that about a week after he had left Valparaiso none other than Bernardo O'Higgins had remarked that "you were as good a republican as any one, and as for disputing about salutes, or search, his Government was too young to be so captious, and indeed treated it very lightly."[74]

Benjamin Homans, chief clerk of the State Department, summarized favorably Biddle's activities in South America in a note appended to the captain's letter to the president of 16 August 1819. Although Homans took issue with him on the matter of specie-carrying, stating that such a practice had not been completely sanctioned by the government until 1818, he concluded: "I cannot see cause of accusation against Capt. Biddle, his conduct . . . cannot be impeached. . . . Captain Biddle has violated no law or regulation of the Navy." Secretary Thompson carried the fight directly to Clay when he wrote the Kentuckian about "the benefit which has resulted in our trade, and the protection afforded . . . in the Pacific Ocean, and also the estimation in which Captain Biddle was held for services rendered." The State Department fell into line when Adams evaluated the efficacy of Biddle's work in Chile and Peru against Prevost's, concluding that the naval officer had outclassed the diplomat in diplomacy. Even though "Biddle's conduct was perhaps indiscreet, and not entirely disinterested," nonetheless, "he turned it to the account of his countrymen, for whom he saved and rescued property to a very large amount. He obtained the release of many citizens of the United States who were prisoners. Prevost had never saved a dollar nor obtained the release of a man."[75]

The cruise of the *Ontario* may be said to have ended with the efforts of Nicholas Biddle in mid-1821. He emphasized to the president that his brother had been utilized as a weapon against his administration by Clay and his minions; the best way to confound the opposition was to demonstrate confidence in the assailed captain by giving him an important new command. Early the next year his suggestion was adopted. Orders arrived that James should assume command of a frigate and move against the pirates who were harrying American trade in the Caribbean. The assignment, welcomed by Biddle, would prove to be a cruise through hell.[76]

CHAPTER 5
FRIGHT AND FRUSTRATION
IN THE WEST INDIES,
1822–1823

While Biddle was extricating himself from the charges emanating from the cruise of the *Ontario,* he was continually seeking a new seagoing assignment. For over a year and a half he toiled in vain, confessing to a midshipman also out of work: "I have applied for a command, but no command is at present vacant, nor is it certain when I shall obtain one." Meanwhile Nicholas Biddle wrote the president, accentuating that such was his brother's "zeal" for active duty, "that to whatever quarter he might be sent he would cheerfully accept the command." Monroe took six months to reply, blaming the illnesses of his children for his delay. While he had "confidence and respect" for the captain, he said, as well as "a perfect conviction" that he merited new opportunities, "it is not however in my power, to do every thing that my wishes dictate." Perhaps the president was able to exert some influence behind the scenes, for during March of 1822 Biddle was given the USS *Macedonian* and instructed to move against piracy in the West Indies.[1]

The 36-gun HMS *Macedonian* had been captured and brought into port by Decatur. She had been slightly remodeled to carry 38 guns, displaced 1,325 tons, and contained a complement of 362. She was one of the smaller and weaker of the Navy's frigates, for as the war had demonstrated, American fighting ships tended to be better built than their British equivalents. She had returned less than a year before from prolonged service off Chile and Peru. Captain John Downes, Porter's first lieutenant during the *Essex*'s wartime cruise and Biddle's successor to command the Pacific Squadron, had brought her into Boston during June of 1821 after a voyage of two years and nine months. Captain Isaac Hull, victor over the *Guerrière* and the Charlestown Navy Yard's commander, had the responsibility of cleaning her up and refitting her for another cruise. How effectively he did this work would be the subject of a furious controversy between him and Biddle.[2]

American commerce off lower South America, harassed during Biddle's tenure there, was more directly threatened by 1822 in the West Indies and the Caribbean. The tumult attending the Mexican, Colombian, and Venezuelan rebellions against their Spanish master was causing a continual flouting of law and order in those waters. Both sides had glaring naval weaknesses, and each turned to compensatory activities afloat judged illegal by Americans.

Spain, with its sea power exhausted by efforts to stamp out uprisings from Vera Cruz to Buenos Aires and Valparaiso, resorted to some of the most outrageous blockades in history. A classic example was the imposition of a 1,200-mile blockade of northern South America with precisely one frigate, one sloop, and one brig to enforce it. Such a miniscule force could not possibly police this extensive stretch adequately, so most of its ports remained wide open to foreign commerce. Any American vessel that strayed into a harbor where a Spanish man-of-war lurked, however, would be confiscated. Worse, Madrid augmented its weak navy by issuing commissions on a wholesale basis to so-called privateers, who were supposed to restrict their hostile endeavors to rebel Latin American shipping. Mexico and Venezuela followed suit by giving such licenses to operate against Spanish merchantmen to almost anyone who requested them. Spanish and rebel privateers alike seldom bothered to check the nationalities of intercepted ships, and in general they acted exactly like all the other pirates already infesting the area.

By the time of Biddle's appointment U.S. commerce in the West Indies was close to annihilation. A Philadelphian claimed that he had kept a careful account of the American vessels seized there from 1815 to 1822 and that they totaled exactly "3,002." This has the earmark of a considerable exaggeration, but certainly such occurrences numbered in at least the many hundreds. Biddle sent the department an account of eight American ships taken off Cuba during less than two months in 1822, some of them actually within sight of Havana's Morro Castle. In every instance the passengers and crew had at the least been robbed and beaten; some fared worse. When the merchantman *Leader* of New York was taken by "a piratical boat" about nine miles east of Havana, her master was "badly treated"; his wife was "taken by the pirates into a state room and there not only robbed of all her ornaments and clothing but otherwise shamefully and unfeelingly treated."[3]

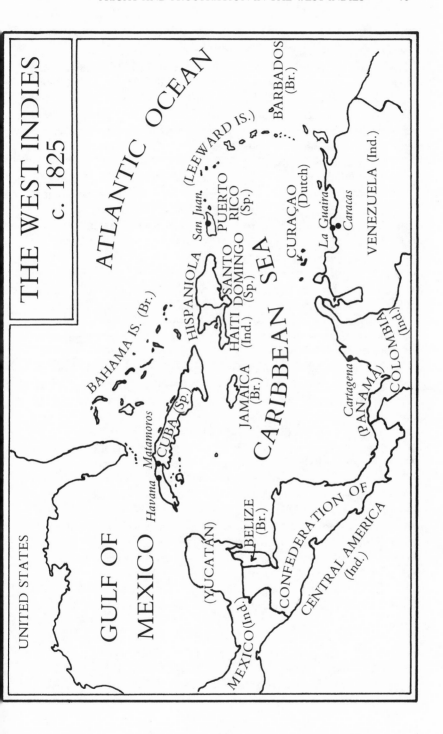

THE WEST INDIES
c. 1825

ATLANTIC OCEAN

UNITED STATES

GULF OF
MEXICO

BAHAMA IS. (Br.)

Havana   Matamoros
CUBA (Sp.)

(YUCATÁN)

BELIZE
(Br.)

MEXICO (Ind.)

CONFEDERATION OF

CENTRAL AMERICA
(Ind.)

JAMAICA
(Br.)

HISPANIOLA

SANTO
DOMINGO
(Sp.)

HAITI
(Ind.)

San Juan

PUERTO
RICO
(Sp.)

(LEEWARD IS.)

BARBADOS
(Br.)

CARIBBEAN SEA

CURAÇAO
(Dutch)

La Guaira   Caracas

VENEZUELA (Ind.)

Cartagena

(PANAMA)

COLOMBIA
(Ind.)

Accounts of such atrocities filled the columns of U.S. news-papers. *Niles' Weekly Register* of Baltimore carried dozens of stories similar to the following from Matanzas, Cuba, in 1821. An American brig, a sloop, and a schooner were all "CAPTURED *at the entrance of this harbor by a launch fitted out here!* . . . They killed the captain and two men of the schr . . . *they murdered all the crew of the brig, opened their entrails, hanged them by the ribs to the mast,* and afterwards set fire to the vessel and all were consumed! !" The people in the sloop were more fortunate, for they were only beaten and robbed.[4]

All the U.S. ports engaging in trade to the south were affected. A torrent of their protests and appeals for naval protection inundated the government, which as early as 1819 had responded, at least in part, by passing "an Act to protect the commerce of the United States, and to punish the crime of piracy." Under its terms the navy was sent to convoy merchantmen and to rescue U.S. citizens seized "upon the high seas." Warships were soon dispatched to the West Indies and for the next few years they operated individually and haphazardly. Centralized direction finally arrived during late March of 1822 when Biddle was given the courtesy title of commodore of the so-called West India Squadron. With the *Macedonian* as his flagship, all men-of-war assigned to that area were under his direction. Further re-inforcements were sent south over the summer and autumn until by November he commanded ten ships, mounting a total of 208 guns, among them two frigates. This impressive force, however, proved inadequate.[5]

Biddle's orders called for him to capture what piratical craft he could and to convoy American merchantmen throughout the West Indies and the Caribbean. Furthermore, he must request the Spanish captain general of Cuba (and later the Spanish governor of Puerto Rico), as well as the administration of independent Haiti, for per-mission to land along their coasts while in active pursuit of pirates. Operations ashore were essential if Biddle was to accomplish anything significant. The freebooters tended to congregate in shoal waters, darting out after their quarry. Unless they could be chased inland and cornered, apprehension would for all practical purposes be impossi-ble. But Secretary Thompson tied Biddle's hands when he warned him to avoid "all infringements upon the territorial jurisdiction of any foreign power."[6]

The *Macedonian* left New York on 4 April and came into Havana on the 28th. Two days later Biddle met with Captain General Nicolás Mahé and outlined his problem and his suggested solution of it: "The depredations have been committed chiefly in open boats, immediately upon the coasts, and off the harbors. . . . I have therefore the honour to propose that your Excellency should so far cooperate with me as to sanction the landings upon the coast of Cuba, of our boats and men, when in pursuit of pirates." The Spaniard's reply was predictable: "I cannot and must not consent" to such American violations of his territorial sovereignty. Furthermore, there was no need for any such incursions, since he had already taken "necessary measures . . . for the apprehension of outlaws." This was simply bombast; as his "necessary measures" consisted of no more than proclamations against piracy. Moreover, illegalities on such a massive scale could not have been carried out without at least the tacit acceptance, if not the active complicity, of the local bureaucracy. Mahé himself may have been innocent of such collusion with pirates but most assuredly many of his subordinates were not.[7]

Biddle nonetheless reported optimistically that he expected the captain general eventually to reverse himself, allowing Americans to land on unoccupied Cuban territory where "he is utterly incapable of exercising any authority." The commodore was too sanguine. Although he learned that corsairs had looted an American ship near Salt Key, an unpopulated sand flat off the Cuban shore, his request to Mahé for authorization to move against them unilaterally was denied.[8]

Biddle might have realized that the captain general was powerless to accommodate him in this matter without Madrid's permission. Except in cases of the most dire emergency, no government able to prevent it would grant to any other power a blanket allowance to violate its territory. Had Mahe acted on his own to grant Biddle's request, undoubtedly his superiors in Madrid would have first overruled and then punished him. The American stand was that a nation was compelled under international law to protect foreign persons and property within its domains. Should it be unwilling or unable to do so, some other power must act in its stead. This was the argument advanced by Secretary of State Adams when he defended General Andrew Jackson's ruthless invasion of West and East Florida during 1818. He asserted that the action had been necessitated by Spain's inability to police its boundaries sufficiently to halt the raids of Indians and escaped slaves into the southern states of the Union. But Washington gave Biddle no license to emulate Jackson's example. Instead, as he himself recognized, he would remain impotent to end the illicit assaults upon his nation's shipping off Cuba and elsewhere.[9]

Since he also failed to receive permission to go ashore after pirates in Haiti, he carried out what little remained for him to do. To be sure, his squadron scored some victories, picking up some thirty buccaneer vessels, but without any noticeable lessening of danger to his countrymen. He also set up a weekly convoy for American merchantmen running from Havana up the southern coast of Florida, down past the Bahamas as far as the Leeward Islands, back along Puerto Rico's northern shore, through the Mona Passage between that island and Hispaniola, down to La Guaira, west along the coasts of Venezuela, Colombia, and Panama, around the Yucatán Peninsula to Vera Cruz, up to New Orleans for new supplies, and back to Havana. He wrote to a friend in Philadelphia at the end of May: "I dislike Havana most cordially & shall leave it with no other regret than that I ever knew it, as a certain man said of his wife after they had been divorced."[10]

During this time Biddle was also involved in a somewhat bizarre plan to promote Cuban independence from Spain and annexation to the United States. Early in 1822 the American commercial agent in Havana told Senator Caesar A. Rodney of Delaware that "three-fourths or ⅔ of the white inhabitants of the Island, are decidedly in favor of being attached to the U.S.—as a *state* not as a *colony.*" He recommended that a naval force with a high-ranking negotiator should be sent to Cuba, the prevalence of pirates in its waters to furnish an adequate excuse for such a presence. Rodney passed on this letter to the president, who unofficially added that errand to Biddle's other responsibilities. Sometime during that summer he made contact with "several respectable and influential Cubans," notifying Monroe that one or more of them would soon be coming to Washington to discuss the matter with him. They also told him that but for the risk of civil war between the pro-independence forces and those remaining loyal to Spain, the island would long ago have rebelled. The wealthy Cuban planters feared that during this strife among the whites "the ascendancy of the blacks" might result in the ending of slavery there. As British public opinion was so abolitionistic that slavery could not be countenanced, and geographical considerations precluded the island from joining Colombia, Venezuela, or Mexico, annexation to the United States seemed to them the best option.[11]

During September a spokesman for these planters, known as "Mr. Sánchez," met the president in Washington. Monroe called a cabinet meeting on the subject. Secretary of War John C. Calhoun ardently favored the idea. Cuban annexation by the British or a slave rebellion there that might spread to the American South would be equally disastrous, he argued. He felt that there was no hurry, however, so Secretary of State Adams was able to persuade his colleagues that the proposal should be filed away for future consideration. He feared that an American Cuba would bring on a confrontation with the British, perhaps even a war for which the United States was totally unprepared. Therefore, he concluded, since Spain was retrogressing into a second-rate European power, the American policy in regard to that island must be to "adhere at present" to its "connection with Spain," while offering every resistance to any transfer of Cuba to Britain or France. His remarks carried the clear implication that someday the time might be ripe for its annexation. Indeed, Adams's recommendations in this matter were carried out from the early 1820s into the mid-1850s, when the Pierce and Buchanan administrations, confident of American power and hoping by foreign adventurism to divert the national attention from the impending sectional crisis, tried without success to "detach" Cuba from Spain.[12]

Biddle had more on his mind than Cuba's possible annexation or even the combined impact of privateers and pirates on American commerce. The officers and crew of the *Macedonian* were beginning to be infected by the onset of a most virulent form of yellow fever. In the annals of the U.S. Navy no more lethal service is recorded than that in the West Indies from 1822 to 1825. As one modern naval biographer puts it: the navy lost "more officers and men, in proportion, than any other service in which they were ever engaged," and the fact applies equally to all the nation's wars from the Revolution through Indochina.[13]

Porter, recuperating from the disease during 1823, complained that "it is occupation enough to keep one's self free from Musquitoes and Sand Flies." Of course nobody realized then that among the "Musquitoes" lurked the deadly *Aedes aegypti,* carrier of yellow fever, the great nineteenth-century tropical killer. David McCulloch, in his magisterial work *The Path Between the Seas: The Creation of the Panama Canal, 1870–1914,* gives a memorable portrayal of how the disease took hold:

> The patient was seized first by fits of shivering, high fever, and insatiable thirst. But there were savage headaches as well, and severe pains in the back and the legs. The patient would become desperately restless. Then, in another day or two, the trouble would appear to subside and the patient would begin to turn yellow, noticeably in the face and in the eyes.
>
> In the terminal stages the patient would spit up mouthfuls of dark blood—the infamous, terrifying *vómito negro,* black vomit. The end usually came swiftly after that. The body temperature would drop, the pulse fade. The flesh would become cold to the touch—"almost as cold as stone and [the afflicted] continues in that state with a composed sedate mind." Then, as a rule, in about eight or ten hours, the patient would die. And so great was the terror the disease generated that its victims were buried with all possible speed.[14]

Biddle first mentions the epidemic early in June, while his ship was still anchored off Havana, but by that time it was well advanced. A little eight-page private journal kept for a few weeks by Lieutenant Charles Gauntt tells a tragic story that emphasizes the rapidity with which "yellow jack" could strike. On 23 May "a party of American ladies" visited the *Macedonian*. The youngest, aged about sixteen, "a beautiful girl, full of health and spirits," was escorted by marine Lieutenant James Clements. Three days later he was dead, and she outlived him for only another forty-eight hours. When the frigate sailed for convoy duty on 4 June, fifty-one were on the sick list from the fever, "among them a large proportion of the officers." By the 18th Gauntt himself was stricken and transferred to another warship two days later, but he eventually recovered.[15]

As the *Macedonian* continued to follow her patrol route from Cuba to Haiti, to Cartagena in Colombia, and back to Havana, the death toll mounted steadily. Biddle assured the department that "all the means in our power" had been utilized to stem the horrid mortality, including "ventilation, white washing, fumigation, fire and letting water into the Ship," procedures that were completely useless. With his sick list skyrocketing day by day he belatedly decided to flee Cuba's murderous shores, heading for home on 24 July.[16]

During her passage the frigate was no more than a floating charnel house. Little imagination is needed to visualize what conditions must have been when some three hundred men, many of them delirious and vomiting, were trapped in the cramped living quarters of a warship. Biddle, naturally fastidious and with a lifelong devotion to his younger colleagues, was in agony as he recognized the first symptoms of yellow fever in one after another of his officers and men. He told Thompson, "I need not say, Sir, how deeply my feelings have been afflicted by this distressing mortality and sickness." The *Macedonian* crept into Chesapeake Bay on 8 August. When the final tally had been made, 101, almost one-third of her people, had died after spasms of *vómito negro*.[17]

Biddle was positive from the beginning where to place the blame for this tragedy: Captain Isaac Hull and his subordinates at the Charlestown Navy Yard. Despite the fact that she had been cruising for over two and a half years, much of the time in the tropics, the *Macedonian* had not been cleansed properly before being turned over to him, he was sure. He claimed that his own investigations during the voyage south from New York had shown that her ballast was covered with "darkness and dirt," salt provisions found in the hold were "in a rotten and putrid condition," and the stench from the bilges was totally "offensive." Nothing could be more obvious to him that Hull's sloth and inefficiency at Charlestown had caused the awful death rate among his complement during a cruise that had lasted only three months.[18]

These conclusions, which Biddle would never relinquish, seem ludicrous today. Unquestionably the fault was his, not Hull's, for he had erred seriously in keeping so close to the Cuban coast for so long a period. A Boston paper wondered "whether Capt. B. is not culpable after the early indications of disease which existed, for tarrying so long on a sickly station in the most sickly season of the year." But the commodore cannot be blamed for an inability to diagnose the basis of an illness that would not be properly identified for another three-quarters of a century. In his day yellow fever and other epidemics were commonly believed to be caused by "miasmic effluvias." Relief might come from ventilation and the other methods he had futilely used off Cuba, or even such esoterica as shooting off cannon "to clean the air." Had he suggested that mosquitoes were the carriers of "yellow jack" he would have been judged a lunatic.[19]

Biddle's account of the loathsome conditions in his flagship brought immediate official responses. Secretary Thompson wrote the day he first received the news that he felt "the strongest and most painful emotions" about "the silent and destructive operations of an irresistible disease." He ordered the *Macedonian* to proceed at once to the Norfolk Navy Yard, where its commandant and doctors would be available for "arresting the further progress of the disease." Speaking for himself and his colleagues on the Board of Navy Commissioners, Porter expressed their collective sympathy for the "wretched state of health" of Biddle's people, and assured him that "every measure in their power to afford you relief" would be taken. But the commodore's lips probably pursed when he read that although the commissioners had heard that the difficulty emanated from the ballast that had not been replenished at Charlestown, "This however cannot be the case." To be sure, Porter concluded, an official investigation would be held, but he and his colleagues "have every reason to believe that the ballast was taken out before the ship's hold was stored." To Biddle, a cover-up was getting under way.[20]

The Philadelphia Board of Health quarantined everyone in the *Macedonian* until the advent of cool weather. Biddle complied, ordering his subordinates to stay away from Philadelphia. He told the press:

> The mortality on board this ship has been very dreadful, and it has been deeply afflicting to me. Of the officers who have died, the only one of Philadelphia is my young and lamented friend, Midshipman [Alexander M.] Murray, a most deserving and promising officer, but the clothing and other baggage of Mr. Murray will not be sent from this ship until the summer months are past.[21]

Biddle was preparing to move against Hull for what he called "the villainous conduct of the officers of the Boston Navy Yard" when he tumbled into another kind of controversy with a fellow captain. This was the rule rather than the exception during the early 1820s. The upper echelons of the service may have been in the main sterling professionals, able navigators, ardent patriots, stout fighters, and at the same time deft negotiators in their frequently required diplomatic responsibilities. But they were also perpetually clawing after status and rank, ruthlessly selfish in elbowing aside rivals for choice assignments, ultrasensitive to any slight on their personal honor. They frequently engaged in duels, the curse of the service's first generation. Most officers would agree with Decatur who, after expressing the usual loathing for that anachronistic custom, nonetheless avowed that "the man who makes *arms his profession*" had no choice but to resort to private combat when no judicial decision could atone for a slur against his personal honor, real or imagined. The decade after the termination of the wars with Britain and Algiers in 1815 was the worst in this respect. Officers thwarted by slow promotions and the lack of command opportunities, with no potential hostilities in prospect for earning glory and prize money, vented their discontent on one another. Biddle swam in the mainstream, inside a few weeks managing to clash with three superiors—Hull, Sinclair, and Rodgers—almost dueling with two of them.[22]

Captain Arthur Sinclair was a veteran officer whose correspondence reveals a massively inflated idea of his own importance. He quarreled with Biddle over what the navy referred to as "the relations between" officers of the same rank with different titles and perhaps overlapping jurisdictions. Sinclair commanded something called the "Norfolk Station," entitling himself "Commander in Chief afloat," although he had no ships under his direction. Captain Lewis Warrington, however, was in charge of the Norfolk Navy Yard at Gosport. When the *Macedonian* had first come into Chesapeake Bay Biddle had communicated directly with Warrington and together they decided that the fever-stricken should be sequestered on nearby Craney Island. Sinclair took an instant exception to this arrangement, avowing that he had "ordered" just that, and complained to the secretary that Biddle had never officially reported to him about the change to Craney Island. Biddle, who understandably had more on his mind than the niceties of naval etiquette, learned through the press about Sinclair's protest. He overreacted in two angry letters to his superior, bluntly informing him that he "would not be instructed [as to] what I owe to my Ship's Company," and defiantly concluding that "I should not receive any instructions from you."[23]

Sinclair retorted that junior officers must obey the orders of a senior, and asked Biddle to "reconsider his letter and dispassionately determine whether or not it was written in terms and in a spirit of contumely and disrespect." Biddle unsuccessfully took his case to the secretary, asserting that he would have been remiss in his duty to his people had he awaited Sinclair's permission before putting them ashore on Craney Island. Sinclair lived some distance away, he pointed out, and his emergency required instant action. Sinclair asked Thompson, who remained noncommittal, to court-martial Biddle and even spelled out the precise charges that should be brought: (1) "Neglect of Duty" (in that he had not reported to his superior officer); (2) "contemptuous conduct to his superior officer" (by dealing only with Warrington); (3) "conduct tending to produce discord and insubordination in the Navy" (for writing letters refusing to obey further orders).[24]

During mid-September Sinclair sent Biddle a long and repetitive letter rehashing his previous communications and clearly intimating that unless Biddle apologized he would be challenged to a duel. Apparently Sinclair was not bluffing; at least, he had no objection to personal warfare. Some months later, while deciding not to challenge Lewis Warrington, he wrote that although he was *"morally"* and *"religiously"* averse to private encounters . . . yet there are cases where officers are compelled to it." Luckily Sinclair partially blunted his threat by suggesting that Bainbridge be asked to act as a go-between to encourage "proper explanations" from Biddle, thereby avoiding a duel.[25]

The prospect of combat between two high-ranking officers, especially so soon after Decatur's death in his encounter with James Barron little more than two years before, was wholly unpalatable to the president. Monroe successfully appealed to Nicholas Biddle for help in settling the matter. Both men realized that James must make some sort of an apology to satisfy his antagonist, and Nicholas acted upon Sinclair's suggestion that Bainbridge might serve as a peacemaker. With the aid of Caesar Augustus Rodney, Bainbridge prevailed upon his younger friend to express regrets, explaining to the secretary that they thought "the enclosed letter . . . ought to be deemed satisfactory, and that in consequence thereof the Charges exhibited by Captain Sinclair against Captain Biddle should be withdrawn."[26]

Biddle's note read: "I thought you interfered with duties, which had been assigned to me by the Navy Department, and in the invitation of this feeling, added to a state of mind already deeply excited, by the condition of my Ship, I replied to you in a style, which on reconsideration, I am willing to allow was not becoming either to you or to myself." Sinclair promptly dropped his court-martial de-

mand, chortling to a service friend that "*his high mightiness* was compelled to apologize, and no doubt thought he came well off to be
allowed to do so." To write such a letter must have been excruciating
for James. Nicholas devoted six full pages explaining to Monroe that
his brother had apologized only in deference to the president, but still
held strongly to the position that he had been right throughout the
controversy. "At every other post in the U.S. there is no officer in
command except the Commandant of the Navy Yard." As Sinclair
was calling himself " 'Commander in Chief afloat' where there is
nothing afloat," his situation was "a perfect anomaly in the service."
Hence his brother should have reported to Warrington alone. But the
Biddles were beating a dead horse in trying to reargue their case on
the basis of the issues involved. The fact remained that James had
crawled to avoid a duel, a decision more sensible than heroic.[27]

Having been so thoroughly bested by Sinclair, the commodore
fared no better in his efforts to have Hull found responsible for the
fever-wracked voyage of the *Macedonian*. His prospects looked favorable at first, for by early 1822 Hull was under heavy siege in
Boston. A cabal of his naval colleagues, headed by Commodore John
Shaw, was moving against him on several fronts. Bainbridge was
probably a member, for he had been ordered away from his command
at Boston's Charlestown Navy Yard for a most reluctantly under-
taken cruise to the Mediterranean in 1815. Since then he had tried on
four separate occasions to regain that post. But Hull, his replacement,
clung tenaciously to his command there, making frosty the relations
between the captains of the *Constitution*'s first and second great victories. Furthermore, Hull enjoyed the support of secretaries of the
navy Crowninshield and Thompson, as well as the enthusiastic endorsement of navy commissioners Rodgers, Porter, Decatur, and (after
Decatur's death) Isaac Chauncey. It is logical that the frustrated Bainbridge would try to take advantage of his opponent's plight, for if
Hull were removed from Charlestown, he would be the natural successor.[28]

Hull's troubles with the cabal had commenced when he recommended to the secretary that the courtesy title of "commodore" be
dropped from naval usage. Since he had never commanded a squadron
of as little as two ships, he much resented that he could only be
addressed as "Captain," not "Commodore," Hull. This suggestion
infuriated Shaw, Bainbridge, Biddle, and others who reveled in the
more prestigious title. They moved to take advantage of other allegations against Hull: he was accused of complicity with a clerk who
had stolen a large sum through kickbacks from Charlestown Navy
Yard employees (which could never be substantiated), and of charging

passengers "25 guineas"—possibly $1,200 in today's currency—for the short cross-English Channel trip while commanding the *Constitution* during 1811 and 1812. Shaw brought these and other accusations before the secretary, but Hull beat him to the punch by demanding and receiving his enemy's court-martial for "treating with contempt his superior officer" and for "Unofficerlike and ungentlemanlylike conduct."[29]

Shaw wrote several officers asking for supporting testimony. Biddle had nothing pertinent to offer on the peculation issue, but knew something about the excessive passenger fees supposedly assessed by Hull in the *Constitution*. When he had been in Paris during part of 1812, he said, the "exorbitancy of the price charged by Captain Hull for a passage across the British Channel" had been a common subject of conversation among Americans abroad at the time. "Mr. N. Hayward of South Carolina," since deceased, had told him that he personally paid the twenty-five guineas demanded. One European without sufficient cash had given Hull an expensive watch instead. Such was the nature of these reports, Biddle concluded, that they "seemed to preclude any doubt of their truth."[30]

Shaw's court-martial, presided over by elderly Commodore Thomas Tingey, met in Boston from 20 March through 12 April. (Biddle's first tour of duty in the West Indies made him unavailable for testimony.) The result was a debacle for the accused. All those who had provided Shaw with information that had encouraged him to harass Hull, Bainbridge among them, were struck either with second thoughts or sudden afflictions of cold feet. Everyone claimed on the stand that all they knew had been based on secondhand reports. Shaw was convicted and sentenced to a six-month suspension for "treating with contempt his superior officer" and for "Unofficerlike conduct," but with a truly remarkable linguistic precision, he was found innocent of "ungentlemanlylike conduct."[31]

No sooner had Hull surmounted this ordeal than the plotters against him tried again, this time inducing navy Lieutenant Joel Abbot to resurrect many of Shaw's accusations, while adding a few more of his own. By this time the department had made up its mind that Hull must be cleared, since no charges against him could seem to be substantiated. Secretary Thompson sent Commissioner Porter to interrogate Abbot. This he did in the manner of a prosecuting district attorney, and soon that unhappy lieutenant found himself before a court-martial in Boston on Hull's charges of "scandalous conduct, tending to the destruction of morals . . . of the Navy of the U. States." He too was found guilty and sentenced to a two-year suspension. How thoroughly the navy commissioners had thrown their collective weight behind Hull is verified in a letter Porter sent to Thompson just after Abbot's conviction: "The conduct of Cap Hull has been proven so pure and unexceptional[,] the charges against him so malignant and unjustifiable and the conspiracy to destroy his Character rendered both by the finding of the court in the case of Cap Shaw and the evidence and sentence . . . [in the Abbot trial] so manifest" that Porter demanded a new court-martial so that the lieutenant, rather than escaping with a two-year suspension, might be cashiered from the service. The department, however, allowed the sentence to stand.[32]

Despite the rout of his two most overt enemies, Hull remained in a glare of unfavorable publicity sparked by the old cliché about smoke and fire. The department acquiesced to his demand for a full court of inquiry about his entire administration of the Charlestown Yard. Thompson sent Rodgers to preside over the panel, the second commissioner to line up with Hull, and he and the other judges sat from 12 August through 15 October. Shortly before Biddle would have been called to the stand concerning the English Channel twenty-five-guinea fee, he abruptly about-faced, writing to Shaw: "My letter of March [February] last cannot I think in any way be material, and I should therefore prefer that it not be published. My testimony *in favor* of my brother officer will always be cheerfully volunteered, and it was with that view that my letter was written to you." His appearance would have been meaningless, since his knowledge about the matter was based solely on hearsay, but his switch was much resented by the anti-Hull intriguers as an act of cowardice and sycophancy. One of them, Captain Jesse D. Elliott, the early navy's most malignant officer, later wrote Shaw, sneeringly referring to how "that *high minded gallant little fellow Biddle treated* the Majesty of the board."[33]

Worse was to come. After Biddle had described to the court the nauseating conditions in his ship—caused, he insisted, by Hull's negligent preparations at Charlestown—Rodgers, speaking for the panel, brushed aside his entire testimony, declaring that Hull and his men had "manifested great zeal and attention" in fitting out the *Macedonian*. Moreover, he concluded, Hull's behavior throughout his tenure at the Yard had been entirely "correct and meritorious." Although entirely vindicated, Hull had had enough of Boston, resigning his command at Charlestown for active duty at sea. Not surprisingly, Bainbridge was his replacement.[34]

Biddle viewed with unrestrained fury what he deemed a ludicrous whitewash, made even more unbearable by the court's intimation that he himself must bear the onus for the horror on board the *Macedonian*. He at once elevated Rodgers to join Porter at the top of his list of most hated persons. Had not his controversy with Sinclair been reaching its climax at the same time he might well have challenged Rodgers to a duel. But he sensibly concluded that one prospective private war at a time was sufficient, and desisted. Still brooding over his humiliation some months later in the West Indies, he vented his rage in a letter to his brother Nicholas, referring to Rodgers's and Porter's "base gratification of personal malignancy, and by men who dare not in any manly way to gratify . . . [it]. I despise Com^r Rodgers as much as I detest his character."[35]

In a letter written the same day he asserted to a confidant in Philadelphia that Secretary Thompson had "determined to make the public believe that the *Macedonian*'s sickness was caused by the climate, or at least that it was not caused by any neglect at Boston." He said that the department had forbidden any ship of his squadron to go into Havana because of the "danger." Utilizing that word to attack Rodgers on the ground of cowardice, he went on:

Talking about danger always reminds me of a Navy Commissioner . . . who never liked to come within gun shot. I mean the man who mistook a sloop for a frigate and fired into her in time of peace [the USS *President,* 44, versus HMS *Little Belt,* 20, on 16 May 1811], & ever afterward *mistook* frigates for 74's and run away in time of war. I mean the man who resigned the command of the *President* when ready to sail & lying in New York, whence it is easy to get out, for the *Guerrière* then on the stocks and at Phila., whence it was impossible to get out. I mean the man who consented to accept the office of Secretary of the Navy during the war under condition that he was allowed to retain his commission as Captain, thus in effect stipulating only to be allowed to go to sea at the return of peace. [Rodgers's "condition" was not accepted.] I mean the man who chased the British frigate *Belvedere* in such a manner as to make it manifest that he did not wish to come along side. I mean the man who was insulted in his own ship by Decatur and had not the spirit to resent it. Do you know whom I mean?[36]

The rancor expressed by Biddle in the above was all too characteristic of the intraservice squabbling that so afflicted the navy's officer corps during this era. Editor Hezekiah Niles leaped upon a remark made by Sinclair that *"these feuds among ourselves tend very much to the injury of the service."* Niles agreed, stating that the real issue was the "renown, perhaps even the *efficiency* of the Navy . . . and if the officers by their 'feuds among themselves' destroy them, down they will go and them with it, great and meritorious as may have been their services." He ended with the warning that "the people will not be taxed because those paid and supported by them wrangle with one another." Niles's admonition was well taken, but the spate of courts-martial and courts of inquiry abated little if at all over the next few years.[37]

Fortunately for some peace of mind, Biddle had other problems to occupy himself. By late October he was preparing to return to the area that he had found so pestilential, displaying some black humor when he wrote Josiah Quincy, former Federalist congressman and later president of Harvard College: "The weather here begins to feel wintry, and I sigh for the climate of Havana."[38]

Dispatches from officers on duty in the West Indies during Biddle's absence gave evidence of increasing Spanish-American tensions there. A series of letters from Lieutenant Robert Spence, commanding the little USS *Cyane* at Puerto Rico from June into September, revealed the chasm between Spanish emphasis upon the maintenance of its own international rights and American stress upon Madrid's international responsibilities. A more direct confrontation occurred when Lieutenant Francis H. Gregory in the USS *Grampus* was told by the captain of the American merchantman *Coquette* that he had just been plundered by the crew of a Spanish privateer. On 15 August, a few days later, Gregory hailed the *Palmyra* (or *Palmira*), a ship similar in appearance to the one described as the assailant. There is conflicting testimony as to which combatant fired first, but there is no doubt as to the outcome. According to Gregory, his broadsides lasted only three minutes before the Spaniard surrendered, "a complete wreck, having one man killed and six wounded, and in sinking condition." Madrid protested vigorously about this incident, but after a series of trials and appeals up the American judicial ladder, Gregory's conduct was finally approved by the U.S. Supreme Court in 1827.[39]

When the tidings of these developments reached Washington from Spence and Gregory, they were deemed important enough to require a full cabinet meeting to mull over how they might affect Biddle's instructions for his second cruise. The major dilemma was whether to order the commodore to convoy American trading vessels through blockades imposed by local Spanish officials. Adams, who was very much in favor of granting such permission, noted in his diary that he had persuaded the more reluctant Monroe to go along with him. But Biddle's instructions when issued a few days later showed that the president had reconsidered. He was forbidden to escort U.S. ships through any sort of Spanish blockades. Furthermore, should he apprehend any suspected piratical craft he must "be careful that the case can be so clear and apparent as to meet any scrutiny which can be made, and to prevent the possibility of a well founded complaint from a friendly power." These restrictions went far to hamstring Biddle's efficacy during his second voyage to the West Indies.[40]

Well before the commodore had arrived at his station, one of his ships scored the last success his squadron would enjoy, but at the cost of an able officer. Lieutenant William H. Allen, commanding the schooner *Alligator,* learned that two American merchantmen had been taken well to the east of Matanzas on Cuba's north shore. Arriving there on 9 November, he found them being guarded by three buccaneer vessels. He and his men successfully stormed one and were going after the others when he fell, mortally wounded by two shots in the head. Four of his sailors also died. Although the remaining pirates escaped, Allen's sacrifice had resulted in one prize and the recovery of the two merchantmen.[41]

Biddle's flagship for his return cruise was the venerable USS *Congress,* 44, launched as early as 1799, displacing 1,265 tons and carrying a complement of 340. After a passage of twenty-two days she dropped anchor at Swedish St. Bartholomew's on 24 November. Biddle had been ordered to express to its governor in "strong but delicate terms" that he should do something to suppress not only pirates but slave traders using his island as a base. Of course the Swede affected total ignorance about any such activities. Biddle fared a little better in Puerto Rico, where the Spanish governor, avowedly helpless to end blockades there on his own initiative, assured him that Madrid would soon revoke any barriers to trade in his own jurisdiction, and that meanwhile he would make sure that American shipping would be spared further condemnations. Departing from San Juan on 11 December, Biddle proceeded to Haiti, where he could accomplish nothing, and came into La Guaira, Venezuela, on the 19th.[42]

The following night Biddle came within a single cable of losing his frigate and probably everyone on board. No mention of the near catastrophe has survived in his official or private letters. But eyewitness accounts were provided by Midshipman Samuel F. Du Pont, scion of the eminent Delaware munitions family and eventually a Civil War admiral; Midshipman Samuel Lockwood, who kept the frigate's Journal; and sailor David Winston.

While the *Congress* was moored in the harbor on the 20th, Biddle and Du Pont, leaving Lieutenant John D. Sloat in command, visited Caracas, the capital, some fifteen miles inland. Shortly after their arrival they received word that a gigantic hurricane was sweeping into La Guaira, annihilating shipping there. The two officers hastened back toward the port, having to hire three men to chop through the trees blocking the road. Du Pont described to his brother the terrifying sight he saw from the beach:

> We reached the Port about 6 O'Clock in the evening. The scene was really distressing, twentyone [*sic*] vessels had been driven on shore, some gone, others going to pieces, the sea breaking over the whole—our ship was that only one that had held on, but no one knew how long it would be so, as she was riding by the last cable[,] having parted two. The sea was rolling so high that there was no possibility of getting on board. I

set [*sic*] up the whole night watching the ship, expecting to see her coming on shore every moment, and had she started, she would have struck so far from the beach that very few indeed, if any, would have been saved. The next morning the sea had abated very much and by diving through the surf we got on board the ship. The wind favoring us, made sail, and stood to sea, glad enough to leave so detestable an harbor.

It is easy to imagine Biddle's agony as he stood bracing himself against the battering wind while staring helplessly at his frigate, expecting her single hawser to part at any moment, with the loss of his command and probably all her people.[43]

Midshipman Lockwood reported in the ship's Journal that the cables broke because they were "cut of[f] by a rock or an anchor at the Bottom," and claims that Biddle and Du Pont came on board at 7:20 A.M. in a boat sent in by Lieutenant Sloat at 6:30.[44]

Years later able seaman David Winston recalled the *Congress*'s narrow escape and credited Sloat with saving her:

> Commodore Biddle was ashore when an earthquake struck the southwest part of the city [no other account mentions an earthquake]. This was succeeded by a hurricane which drove from their moorings, and entirely destroyed twenty-two merchant vessels, and a Colombian man-of-war, with their crews, five only of the whole were saved, being picked up by a boat from the *Congress*. This boat and crew, consisting of a quartermaster and four men, were lost directly after, in endeavoring to bring further relief.
>
> At the beginning of the blow Lieutenant SLOAT ordered the boatswain to pipe all hands, when he urged us to obey the officers and stand by the ship—promising full pay and rations, till we should reach home, in case the ship was wrecked. We parted our chain and other cables, excepting the best bower [large anchor] which so dragged as to bring us near enough to pitch a biscuit on the rocks. I have never witnessed so hopeless a prospect as ours at that moment, and thank God we were able to ride it out. Soon as the blow abated, Commodore Biddle came aboard . . . and praised Lieutenant SLOAT in the highest terms, *for his skill in saving the Congress when every other vessel in the port was lost.*[45]

The frigate hastened into Dutch Curaçao the next day and spent some weeks in repairs. While there Du Pont made the first of several increasingly critical observations about his commander. He wrote his favorite cousin: "Capt. B. is a perfect gentleman, but there is not that fatherly affable way about him that characterize[d] Capt. [Jacob] Jones." During late January 1823 the *Congress* dutifully plodded on to Haiti and came to the waters off Cuba early the next month. This time the mosquitoes posed no threat, but supplies were beginning to run short. "For the past six weeks we have been wretchedly off for something fit to eat owing to our Bread becoming wormy," Du Pont mourned. Nevertheless, Biddle had no choice but to stay, for he had learned from the department that he must remain off Cuba until his replacement as West India Squadron commodore arrived. That this would be none other than the "detested" Porter must have sunk Biddle into deeper gloom.[46]

Save for the fact that he had not lost his ship in Venezuela, Biddle's second tour in the Caribbean had been sterile. Although he had cruised for "150 days[,] 112 of which we have been at sea" from November 1822 to April 1823, "we have taken no pirates," as Du Pont glumly put it. The commodore had to have been aware that privateering and piracy against American commerce in the West Indies had actually increased, especially off Cuba and Puerto Rico.[47]

Biddle's failure may be attributed to several factors. He had been given too many large ships and too few small ones, particularly light schooners and oared barges able to hunt down their quarry in the shallow waters which they infested. He was never able to get permission to follow the pirates ashore in any Spanish territory. Recognizing how this restriction had hampered him, he flashed his resentment with the laconic observation, "I despise the Spaniards." The department always seemed to couple its orders requiring his vigorous action with inhibiting qualifications, for Washington was fearful of embroilments with any European monarchy while the reactionary Quadruple Alliance abroad might be waiting for an excuse to intervene in the Latin American revolutions. Nor was he given the opportunity to cooperate with the Royal Navy, which by late 1822 had in effect been turned loose in the West Indies. The Admiralty in London had instructed its commanders to land in Cuba should the Spanish administration there be unable or unwilling to protect British shipping from pirates and privateers.[48]

Finally, Biddle himself appears to have behaved with a most uncharacteristic lack of flair and drive. Perhaps he was still dazed by his awful experiences in the *Macedonian,* embittered by his rebuffs at the hands of Secretary Thompson and navy commissioners Porter and Rodgers during his feuds with Hull and Sinclair, and unsure how he should interpret his often conflicting orders. His morale dipped to such a point that he wrote his brother and a friend venting his anger and frustration, using exactly the same wording in both letters: "Since there is so much cowardice & rascality at the head of the Navy, I have made up my mind, after this cruise, never again to ask for employment. It shall come unlooked for, if it comes at all." The years 1822 and 1823 were by no means Biddle's finest and even greater aggravations lay immediately ahead.[49]

CHAPTER 6
BIDDLE, RODNEY,
AND THE *CONGRESS*,
FLOATING JUNKYARD,
1823–1824

Researchers working in the hushed propriety of historical archives seldom find cause for hilarity. Biddle's plight, however, in transporting Caesar Augustus Rodney, Mrs. Rodney and her maid, nine daughters, a son, and a veritable Matterhorn of luggage to South America, via Europe, is hilarious, although most assuredly not to the captain himself. The episode made John Quincy Adams laugh "the tears out of his eye," and a similar reaction might be expected from those with a somewhat more developed sense of humor than the self-composed, self-righteous, and crusty secretary of state.[1]

The genesis of the *Congress*'s remarkable cruise was found in Secretary Smith Thompson's instructions to Biddle, still in the West Indies waiting for David Porter to succeed him in command of the West India Squadron. He was told to come home at once "for special Service," leaving behind an officer to communicate to Porter what he would need to know about conditions there. Shortly after his arrival at Norfolk early in April, Biddle received specific orders to proceed to Wilmington, Delaware, to pick up Judge Hugh Nelson, the new American minister to Spain, and Rodney, just appointed minister to Argentina. His itinerary called for him to sail first to Gibraltar (and perhaps Spain) to drop off Nelson, before proceeding to Rio de Janeiro and possibly Montevideo to put ashore Rodney and his brood.[2]

Prior to his embarkation, Biddle was given an opportunity to demonstrate the degree of still-burning animosity about his recent treatment by the Board of Navy Commissioners when they had supported Hull and Sinclair against him. While consoling his confidant Thomas Cadwalader, who had just been seriously wounded in a duel, he gleefully related how he had paid back its members, at least in part. He had asked Thompson to come on board the *Congress* at Norfolk, but when the secretary appeared he was accompanied by the uninvited commissioners Porter, Rodgers, and Captain Isaac Chauncey, Decatur's replacement. Biddle wrote: "You would have smiled . . . had you seen my reception of those fellows, for I treated them with the Respect due to their *characters* and not their vanity. Depend upon it, Chauncey is a small man, and as to Capt Rodgers I despise and detest him." His asperity was evidently so obvious that Thompson demanded an explanation for his "marked disrespect" to the commissioners, to which Biddle replied that he "entertained feelings unfriendly to those Gentlemen." The secretary still insisted that he offer a "disavowal" of his rudeness, and perhaps some kind of an apology was made, for the subject is dropped from further official communications.[3]

As Biddle contemplated his forthcoming cruise, he might have expected reasonably amicable relations with his two distinguished passengers. Hugh Nelson, born in Virginia in 1768, had enjoyed a notable career. A planter, lawyer, and state jurist (hence his title of "Judge Nelson"), he had served as a Democratic-Republican congressman from 1811 until his departure for Europe, and was an intimate of both Jefferson and Monroe. The record is not clear whether he and Biddle knew one another prior to their sailing together, but it is likely that they did, for Washington during the early republic was dominated by a small social, political, legal, and military coterie into which each would naturally gravitate.[4]

Caesar Augustus Rodney was unquestionably Delaware's favorite son. Born there in 1772, he had served, successively, as a Democratic-Republican congressman; U.S. attorney general from 1807 to 1811; an officer in the Delaware militia during the war; and a member of Monroe's fact-finding mission to South America in 1817 and 1818. Just before his new assignment to Argentina he had been briefly both a U.S. congressman and senator. He and Biddle had been on friendly terms. The captain would undoubtedly have sympathized with Rodney's unrestrained grief when his son, Midshipman John Rodney, had died while serving under Biddle in the *Ontario* in 1817. Their association in Chile the next year seemed harmonious. Finally, the captain must have recalled Rodney's cooperation with Bainbridge in helping him to avoid dueling Sinclair. Yet Biddle would have been bound to speculate nervously about the discomfort that lay ahead for him, if for no other reason than the size of Rodney's family. He tried to laugh off the matter in a letter to Cadwalader: "I have *official* information that *nine Miss* Rodneys are coming on board. This alone is sufficient to prejudice me against the Minister to Buenos Ayres, for it is not genteel nor respectable in any man to have nine unmarried daughters."[5]

The superfluity of Rodneys, however, temporarily took second place to a more immediate crisis. When the *Congress* came into Wilmington to receive the two diplomats, Biddle must have been stupified as he surveyed the baggage that must accompany the Rodneys. (A complete itemization of Rodney's accouterments appears in the Appendix.) In addition to "some articles" already put on board at Norfolk, there were no fewer than eighty separate entries listed at dockside that had to be crammed into the frigate. Some, because of their amount or peculiarity, stand out:

> 1 new Carriage with Harness; 1 old Phaeton with Harness; 1 old Cart with Harness; 1 Plough; 26 Trunks; 17 Tables; 11 Bureaus; 8 Pine Board Book cases (old); 107 Chairs[,] 47 old; 11 Bedsteads (old), 10 Beds (old), [but only] 4 Mattress' (old); 86 Boxes, 54 barrels, 16 Kegs, . . . "Contents of most of them unknown"; 3 Shovels (old); 1 Coffee mill[,] broken, . . . 4 dogs. 5 goats.

An unspecified amount of hay for the goats was the only article that understandably, Biddle refused to load, as "too hazardous."[6]

The *Congress* was soon packed to the bursting point. Biddle even had to have "no less than One Hundred Barrels" of ship's stores moved onto the berth deck, where the crew had to sleep, seriously interfering with their comfort and potentially their health. Even then it was necessary to secure in plain sight on the quarterdeck (a partial deck built from the mainmast aft above the main deck) what the captain referred to as "the refuse" of "Mr. Rodney's Garret and his Stable." The press delighted its readers with the result. A Massachusetts journal wrote about "the quarter deck covered with such necessities as an old cart and harness; carriages and carriage wheels; saddles; churns; chafing dishes; cradles; ploughs; drip-stones [part of a sill to carry off rainwater]; bedsteads; hearth-rugs; empty tea-chests; fish-kettles; andirons; shovels and tongs; and sundry other venerable accompaniments." A Philadelphia paper reported that the *Congress* "was visited by many of our citizens, who returned almost universally disgusted or confounded by the spectacle which they had witnessed. . . . The spectacle and inventory became common subjects of discourse at dinner and tea tables."[7]

These "venerable accompaniments" were by no means Biddle's only source of concern and vexation. Where could accommodations be found for Nelson, eight other passengers, and the Rodney entourage of thirteen in a vessel already carrying 340 officers and men?

Only the captain's quarters could be considered comfortable in American frigates of that era, when even the lieutenants lived in rooms little larger than prison cells. Nelson and Rodney had to move in with Biddle, while he put his carpenters to work altering "the after cabin and the Starboard State Room" for the Rodney women.[8]

On 8 June the *Congress*, by this time a travesty of what a fighting man-of-war should be, headed out to sea on her thirty-seven-day transatlantic crossing. For all concerned it was anything but a pleasant start. Midshipman Du Pont told his cousin about the commencement of the cruise:

> Sea sickness, that most tormenting of maladies, made its appearance with such fury that it threatened a long continuance. I wish I could describe the situation of our cabin and ship when we were bidding adieu to our Capes [Henry and Charles at the entrance to Chesapeake Bay]. Men groaning, women moaning, children bawling, cats squalling, and dogs howling.[9]

For the fastidious and privacy-loving Biddle the passage became almost intolerable. When he reached Gibraltar he mourned to his brother that "Mr. Rodney's Cot has not been taken down since we left the Delaware and it is quite horrid to see old boots and dirty clothes which are always kept hanging from it." After the Rodneys had gone ashore at the Rock, Biddle told his sister-in-law that his servants had kept busy with "soap and hot water" to "purify my Cabin. Ever since the 8th of June indeed my Cabin has smelt like a Portuguese Hospital" (surely a memorable simile).[10]

The Rodney children brought him no less exasperation. The younger ones specialized in caterwauling; Biddle wrote that his only consolation was that "we have never had more than two crying in the cabin at any one time." As a bachelor he "might not know what it is to hear one's own children cry, but I do know that it is not pleasant to hear the children of other people." Rodney's son gave him a different sort of headache. He found it necessary to point out to the eighteen-year-old George that it was not customary for midshipmen on active duty in an American warship to be served wine in the morning, a practice that the boy had commenced near the end of the voyage.[11]

Even worse was the continuous presence of several nubile Rodney daughters, who became instant sources of fascination for the six lieutenants and the twenty-one midshipmen attached to the *Congress*. He had, Biddle said, made every effort to see that "the Females on board have all the gratifications which the Ship affords—Every evening on the passage to Gibraltar the Young Ladies and the officers dance when the weather is good." It was predictable that romance would flourish under such conditions. Du Pont described himself as neither "remarkable, for my indifference, nor for any particular attention, to the ladies." As for his colleagues, "there were five regular courtships going on, and notwithstanding that there is considerable competition, but I believe that each of both parties, having chosen their favorites, and if we had a chaplain on board, I would not be surprised to see several matches." The very proper captain was sure that matters had quickly passed beyond dancing and even "courtships." He told his sister-in-law, "Some things have occurred on the part of the females so abandoned that I dare not name them," and then let loose his disgust: "I have never known any family so crass, vulgar, and indecent as this of Mr. Rodney." The result, as Biddle notified the secretary, was "proof how much the discipline of the Ship as respects the Officers was relaxed, which . . . I tolerated for the sake of the females of Mr. Rodney's family."[12]

When the *Congress* mercifully anchored at Gibraltar on 15 July, the captain was dismayed to see in the harbor a British frigate, a French brig of war, and an entire Dutch squadron. He lost no time in vacating his unhappy vessel, taking quarters on shore, following which, as reported by Du Pont, "he comes on board very seldom indeed." He did this not to escape the Rodneys, for they had also left the vessel, but rather that in this manner he could avoid having to invite foreign officers on board his junk-laden frigate. As he explained to the department, his quarterdeck, normally "the chosen part of a man of war," was now so unsightly with Rodney's miserable possessions that instead of "seeking opportunities of displaying to foreigners this Frigate which is one of the most beautiful in the Navy, I felt only chagrin and mortification & repugnance to seeing any stranger come on board. . . . I went to lodgings on shore as soon as the Ship was secure."[13]

Rodney's supporters later circulated a story that while Biddle was at Gibraltar he had tried to humiliate his unwanted passenger by "keeping Mr. Rodney's old Saddles constantly at the masthead." Not so, the captain avowed. The truth was that "one morning early at Sea when I was on Deck this old Saddle of Mr. Rodney's which was lying on the quarter deck was wet and offensive, and I made one of the men run it up to the Peak to dry—In about twenty minutes afterwards it occurred to me that this might be considered as done in derision and therefore I ordered it to be hauled down." It makes a charming mental picture to visualize the handsome USS *Congress*, slicing through the billows under a full spread of canvas, with a reeking saddle bouncing around at the top of the mainmast.[14]

Meanwhile the Rodney-caused irritations had to be put aside so that Biddle could act upon an immediate responsibility: to land Minister Nelson in Spain so that he might assume his diplomatic duties. The situation there made this task onerous. When the brutal, capricious, and underhanded King Ferdinand VII had been placed back on the Spanish throne by the British in 1814, he had launched a ferocious persecution of his more liberal subjects. Rebellious soldiers finally rose against him in 1820 and kept him virtually a prisoner for more than the next two years. The de facto overthrow of a "legitimate" monarch was anathema to the Concert of Europe (at that time composed of France, Russia, Prussia, and Austria, Britain having withdrawn from that alliance in 1822). Early the next year Paris sent an army to invade Spain that crushed the rebel defenders. By the summer only Cadiz remained outside French control, but that essential seaport was quickly hemmed in by the army ashore and under naval blockade. The city fell late in August, and Ferdinand was soon restored to full power.[15]

No sooner had they reached Gibraltar than Nelson pointed out to Biddle that conditions militated against his traveling overland to his destination. He asked to be taken to Cadiz in the *Congress*. Since this was contrary to his orders, Biddle thought that Nelson must assume the responsibility for such a departure, which he willingly did. Sailing on the 23rd the *Congress* approached a French squadron of two ships of the line and four frigates, only to be told by its admiral that she could not enter the harbor. First Lieutenant William L. Gordon was sent to the flagship to protest in vain that "public vessels" of a neutral country were not supposed to be affected by a blockade, and the frigate had to return to Gibraltar. Nelson eventually managed to make his way to Madrid, where he served as U.S. minister until 1825.[16]

A few days later Gordon mentioned to Biddle that he had overheard a rumor in a local tavern that Rodney, because "he had not been treated with the civility to which he was entitled," was trying to sail to Brazil on a chartered merchantman, rather than remain in the *Congress*. The astonished Biddle asked Nelson if he knew anything about Rodney's discontent, and was assured that "he had not before heard it and did not believe it." The captain notified the secretary that this "made on my mind a most unfavorable impression. Here was a person living in the same Cabin with Mr. Nelson and myself who without complaining a word to me, without any communication with Mr. Nelson, without the knowledge of any Officer of this Ship, allowed us to hear for the first time from the conversation at a tavern in Gibraltar, that he was so ill treated on board my Ship as to oblige him to take refuge on a merchantman." The fact that Rodney eventually decided to remain in the *Congress* for the voyage to Rio de Janeiro might lead to an assumption that the entire affair had been blown out of proportion, but that was not the case.[17]

Undoubtedly Biddle had tried very hard to be courteous to all the Rodneys and sincerely felt that he had succeeded. But there was no way that the resentments and disgust he so vividly portrayed in his private letters could not have been recognized by a man whose prolonged illness had given him "an uncommon degree of sensitiveness," as Nelson put it. Furthermore, Biddle was wrong when he said that none of his officers was aware of any strain between Rodney and himself. Du Pont wrote from Gibraltar that "the Captain has taken the most violent antipathy to the whole race, he does not treat Mr. Rodney with common courtesy." Hezekiah Niles, in a lengthy footnote to his four-column account of the Rodney-Biddle encounter, pinpointed with accuracy why a clash between the two was little short of inevitable:

> Captain Biddle was a very precise and particular man, attentive to the smallest matter of *etiquette* on board his ship; that Mr. Rodney knew nothing about etiquette, and could not understand it—and that his frank and friendly disposition, with the exceeding fondness that he had for his family, would continually interfere with captain Biddle's ideas of propriety in the regulation and government of his ship, on a long and interesting voyage. And indeed, to one who has been accustomed to have a *whole cabin to himself,* the ingress of a man and his wife and eleven [ten] children, all with equal right to possess it, could not be very pleasant. This may be said without disrespect to capt. Biddle, who is reported to be an excellent officer (and we know that he is a brave one)—fond of keeping things about him in a way [that] could not be expected to exist with such a family aboard.[18]

No sooner had Nelson left the *Congress* for Madrid on 3 August, honored by a fifteen-gun salute, than the frigate put to sea for Brazil. The Rodneys were all in place, and as Biddle confessed to the department, by this time he "no longer inquired nor cared" as to why they had changed their minds about chartering a merchant vessel for their passage. He continued: "For a few days after we sailed from Gibraltar Mr. Rodney and myself maintained a very formal and constrained intercourse from which I was soon relieved by a total and mutual silence between us." Although Nelson's absence made a bit more room in the captain's cabin, the strain must have been nerve-wracking for both men. Very likely Biddle could not hide his abhorrence of Rodney's odiferous cot, if not verbally than at least by facial expression. Finally, it is discreditable to him that in all his extensive commentary on their relationship, he never wrote a word of awareness of or sympathy about the fact that his unwelcome guest was seriously, indeed terminally, ill.[19]

At least the officers and the Rodney girls enjoyed themselves en route. Du Pont wrote from Rio that he had been grateful for their ability "to while away the dull hours at sea, but alas! we are going to lose them, they will not let us take them any farther." He said that "some of our gentlemen are certainly much smitten," repeated that he thought it lucky that no chaplain had been present or marriages would have resulted, expected that "salt water and a little absence" would make the officers forget their loss, and closed by hinting that Biddle may have been right in his acerbic statement about the girls' "abandoned" conduct when he reported that he must stop writing lest it lead him to describe "a little scandal."[20]

The *Congress* entered the harbor at Rio on 18 September, and Biddle later informed the secretary that he had "hastened to Lodgings on Shore as I had done at Gibraltar." He still felt that he could not entertain foreigners in his frigate "because of the condition of the ship." Yet the log of the *Congress* shows that on the day after arrival, she was boarded by a French admiral, the resident British consul, and Admiral Sir Thomas Hardy, commanding Royal Navy forces in those waters. He was the same officer with whom Biddle had negotiated unsuccessfully at New London during 1814 in his effort to arrange a single-ship combat between his *Hornet* and the *Loup Cervier*. Perhaps he avoided watching his guests' expressions of combined shock and amusement at his cluttered quarterdeck by assigning Gordon the chore of welcoming them aboard.[21]

The Rodneys remained in the ship for another entire month while arranging for a merchantman to carry their luggage south. Biddle's enemies in Delaware later asserted that he had deliberately abandoned the American minister and his family 1,200 miles from their destination, but this was unfair. Biddle correctly claimed that he and Rodney, while they were still speaking to each other en route to Gibraltar, had often conversed about the poor anchorage at Montevideo in what is now Uruguay and the dangerous passage from there to Buenos Aires when the *pampero* (a cold wind coming off the Andes) was blowing. And Biddle's rendition was confirmed in full by the Navy Department. The secretary, responding to Rodney's own request, had ordered the captain to drop off the family at Rio so that they could make their own arrangements for passage to Montevideo and Buenos Aires.[22]

Many days were required, of course, to transfer all of Rodney's luggage to the large ship hired to accommodate it. On 14 October Biddle was at last rid of his obnoxious passengers. He wrote to Washington that he had thought it likely that Rodney might wish to give some explanation for his hostility at the moment of departure. He assigned Purser Samuel Hambleton to stand by as a witness to anything that might transpire. As a fifteen-gun salute was rolling out, however, "I was present at the Gangway when Mr. Rodney left the Ship, but he passed me without looking or speaking to me." During the days before the *Congress* headed for home on 23 October Biddle presumably had his men fumigate his cabin to lessen its resemblance to a "Portuguese hospital." The voyage to Virginia was completed without incident on 17 December at Hampton Roads.[23]

Biddle had made another lasting enemy during the *Congress*'s unhappy tour of duty. Du Pont delivered his lifelong verdict about his commander and it was negative. He wrote his brother that "I am determined not to ask any favors of Capt. B. . . . His treatment of us all, has been so widely different from [my] last cruise, that I do not intend or do not wish to be under the least obligation to him." As soon as he could, Du Pont successfully applied to Biddle for permission to be switched to the ship of the line *North Carolina*. This initial antipathy strengthened; more than twenty years later he would refer to him as "that selfish little viper, Com. Biddle."[24]

Even before the *Congress* had arrived home the storm that had been brewing since the first reports about Rodney's misery filtered into Delaware began breaking over her captain. When Rodney had first boarded the frigate, Niles had informed his readers that "perhaps no man ever left a place with more sincere and honest wishes of the people for his health and happiness than Mr. R. left Wilmington. He was attended to the ship by a crowd of those who love him." The same source explained why he was so popular in his native state: "Mr. Rodney is beloved, as it were, by every man, woman, and child of that place, on account of his tolerant principles, kind manners, affectionate disposition, and strict integrity, as well as respected for his talents and public character."[25]

Most of Biddle's accusers concentrated upon his reputed discourtesy to Rodney and his ostensible abandoning of him and his family in Rio. Others circulated a spate of rumors: the captain had "once or twice . . . left him abruptly" while the two were conversing; Louis McLane, a congressman, and an enemy of Rodney in Delaware, had influenced Biddle against him; the captain had deliberately exposed Rodney's possessions to rain, ruining some of them; he had caused trouble for the family in getting their baggage through Brazilian customs; he had refused to allow the Rodney girls to go ashore in the ship's boats. Biddle either denied or explained away every one of these charges, but to little avail.[26]

Because of Biddle's "series of studied insults and contumely" toward its favorite son the Delaware House of Representatives demanded an official inquiry, declaring its "indignation at the unprecedented and disrespectful conduct of the commander of the *Congress*, toward a citizen, invested with the high character of a representative of this nation. . . . [This] is an insult offered to the national dignity and sovereignty, which requires a prompt and ample atonement." Although nothing came of this resolution, it sparked a brief journalistic war between Philadelphia and Wilmington. An editor in Biddle's home town sprang to his defense, focusing upon the inordinate amount of baggage involved, which, he said, "gave the decks the appearance of an auction ware house or *pawn broker's depository.*" Niles reprinted this comment along with Wilmington's castigation of Biddle, but sided with Rodney, declaring that the extraordinary number of his possessions had been mandatory "to provide every thing needful to the comfort of himself and his family." In addition, "all things should appear as fitted to the honorable rank and station that he held."[27]

Niles came up with a novel explanation for the variety and amount of the luggage that Rodney had insisted upon taking to South America with him. The British already enjoyed a lucrative trade there, in part because their ministers and consuls brought with them topflight examples of their nation's products, "to tempt the people to lay aside their old clothes, etc., and purchase new ones." Rodney had merely been trying to emulate this admirable diplomatic practice: "He wished to exhibit to the Buenos Ayreans some fine specimens of the talents of his countrymen, and in the most advantageous manner possible, that the stock of our commodities might be enlarged to carry on a profitable trade with them." The editor did not specify how the Argentinians were supposed to be stampeded into buying frenzies by Rodney's "2 large quilting frames, 6 sacking bottoms, and 1 fish kettle."[28]

Biddle tried to pretend that he was above such plebian squabbling in the press. He wrote Cadwalader: "*To lie like a newspaper* is as good a phrase now as it ever was. Having been slandered before by the papers, I have not as much sensitivity as before." Nor would he be provoked into any public retaliations against Rodney, since "my story of 'that *highly respectable citizen*' & of his family cannot be told without outraging public decency." He summarized Rodney as "that miserable old man."[29]

His outward aplomb was shaken, however, when he heard that he had been burned in effigy at Wilmington. He remained unmollified even though one letter-writer to a Delaware paper asserted that the deed had been done by "no respectable man" but by "a few mischievous boys." Shortly before his death, a quarter of a century later, Biddle recalled his symbolic burning at the stake with enough venom to list it as one of the more memorable episodes of his life.[30]

The Rodney affair naturally brought anxiety to the other Biddles. Probably that socially conscious family's greatest embarrassment came from the charge of "ungentlemanly behavior" against one of its most prominent members. Their closely knit group of friends in Philadelphia rallied around them. Charles J. Ingersoll, a politician, historian, and playwright, wrote to Nelson in Madrid for information about the matter: "The Friends of Captn Biddle have heard with regret that Mr. Rodney has complained of a want of proper treatment on board the *Congress*. Suffer me to inquire, if you had experienced anything of the kind." Nelson threw his full support to Biddle, avowing that he had never "perceived in his deportment anything but the most gentlemanly conduct." He went on to explain why he thought such unfair charges had been made: "Poor Rodney when he arrived at Gibraltar was in the most wretched health[;] indeed he was so low when we recommenced the voyage to the South that I really feared that he would never reach Buenos Ayres. I therefore made allowance for his feeble state of health." At first he had considered the rumors about the dispute at Gibraltar as no more than something to afford "a fruitful theme of table talk for the ladies, as likely to have but an ephemeral existence but certainly never to float across the ocean to disturb the existing harmony between Philadelphia and Wilmington." He concluded with a ringing endorsement: "For myself I must say that I saw nothing in the deportment of Capt. Biddle during the whole voyage which as his personal friend and friend of his public character and reputation I would have wished to change in the slightest degree."[31]

Lieutenant Gordon wrote his commander to reinforce the claim that all along Rodney had planned to sail no farther south in the *Congress* than Rio. Furthermore, he continued, "Mr. Rodney assured me both then (off Rio Janeiro) and at Gibraltar that should any opportunity present itself he would with pleasure do you any service in his power, notwithstanding the unfortunate misunderstanding that had taken place between you." The fact that Rodney, during the short time remaining to him (he died in Argentina on 10 June 1824), never seems to have registered any official complaint to Washington about the captain's treatment of him lends credence to Gordon's assertion.[32]

Meanwhile Biddle had been attempting to get from his government a verdict of innocent in his clash with Rodney, but without much success. In the aforementioned interview with the secretary of state he gained nothing more than the rare privilege of watching

Adams go into a paroxysm of laughter while listening to his angry recital of Rodney's horrendous luggage. He turned to Samuel South- ard, the new secretary of the navy, arguing his case in the 3,600-word letter of 13 February 1824 cited so often above, but he appears to have received no reply. It is possible that in private conversation Southard told Biddle to forget about the matter.[33]

A letter written to Thomas Cadwalader the following May by one high in the American governmental and economic establishment can be said to have ended the Biddle-Rodney fracas. Langdon Cheeves of South Carolina, a former congressman, recent president of the Second Bank of the United States, and "Chief Commissioner of Claims" arising from the Treaty of Ghent, praised the captain's public and private renown. He reported that "I mixed a good deal with the members of Congress & the Government [Monroe administration] during the last Winter, at Washington & I declare I never heard an injurious word uttered of him." He was sure that the affair would soon be forgotten with no lasting damage to Biddle. The public gen- erally, the "Government," and perhaps even Wilmington's "mischie- vous boys" who had burned him in effigy may have rapidly put into limbo the Rodney-laden cruise of the *Congress*. Not Biddle, however. He would remember it with resentment and distaste for the rest of his life.[34]

CHAPTER 7
COURTS-MARTIAL,
THE PHILADELPHIA
NAVY YARD, AND
COMMODORE OF THE
BRAZIL SQUADRON,
1824–1828

With the unlamented Caesar Augustus Rodney out of presence if not out of mind, Biddle remained in Philadelphia stoically awaiting what orders the Navy Department might be pleased to send. His first task was to appear as a witness in the court-martial of Commodore Charles Stewart, whom he had known since both served as midshipmen in the USS *President* in 1801. Stewart had returned from commanding the Pacific Squadron off western South America to face a number of charges, some of which Biddle had been forced to meet after his long cruise in the *Ontario*. Stewart was accused, among other supposed delinquencies, of illegally carrying passengers in his flagship, using public stores to aid privately owned American merchantmen, transporting specie in neglect of other responsibilities, and favoring the royalists against the patriots in Chile and Peru.[1]

During the trial, which sat in Washington from 18 August through 5 September, commodores John Downes and Charles Ridgley, other recent Pacific Squadron commanders, joined Biddle in supporting Stewart. Biddle's testimony was the most helpful for the accused. He swore that men-of-war were the only safe means for noncombatants to travel in those belligerent seas, that he himself had always aided his fellow Americans with supplies from the *Ontario,* and that carrying of specie in pirate-infested waters was mandatory duty for both the Royal and U.S. navies. As for favoring the royalists, Biddle was at his most perceptive when he pointed out that "I believe it is impossible for any commanding officer to be in the Pacific without giving offense to the one side or the other. The royal party, knowing the general feeling of our countrymen, are jealous of them; the patriots, on the other hand, expecting too much, are dissatisfied." Stewart was "most fully and honorably acquitted" of all charges.[2]

With nothing material being offered by the secretary, Biddle was free to involve himself in family matters. His cousin, John G. Biddle, son of Clement Biddle, who had married James's sister Mary, had for some time been in miserable health. His doctors recommended a European trip for him, but there were complications. Mary insisted upon accompanying her ailing husband but he, fearing that he might die abroad, would not let her come, lest she be left "without a protector" in a "foreign country." Between his sister and himself there had "always existed a close intimacy," so James asked for and received a leave of absence in order to accompany them. The trio sailed on a merchantman on 8 October for Leghorn (Livorno) and as James had hoped, John's physical condition improved enough to enable the commodore to remain in Italy for only a few months. He notified the secretary early in March 1825 that he had just returned from Europe and wanted employment "afloat." Unfortunately his expectations for his cousin's full recovery were dashed. James was commanding the Brazil Squadron two years later when he was informed that John had died in Paris on 30 August 1826. He mourned at how crushed with grief Mary must be: "I deeply lament my absence at this moment and the impossibility of my being able to return for some time yet to come."[3]

Later in March Secretary Southard tried to accommodate Biddle by offering him command of the Norfolk Navy Yard at Gosport. The commodore's reply from Philadelphia was a masterpiece of tact. He managed to get out of the assignment that he did not want and put in a claim for one that he did. He wrote: "It will give me pleasure to accept the command of any Navy Yard to which I may be ordered. As however you have the kindness to consult my wishes . . . I take the liberty to say that no situation on shore would be so acceptable to me as the Navy Yard here." He did not have long to wait. Early in May he was awarded, and immediately accepted, the Philadelphia Yard. He quickly settled into the duties of such a post: acknowledging receipt of departmental orders and printed material, passing along the secretary's communications to individuals, arranging for the delivery of supplies from the local navy agent, holding trials, recruiting sailors, and reporting four times a year on the efficiency and conduct of his officers.[4]

This routine was interrupted for several weeks during the summer of 1825 by the trial of Commodore David Porter for his recent invasion of Spanish Puerto Rico, and Biddle was appointed to judge his old enemy. As Biddle's successor in the West Indies during 1823 and 1824 Porter at first had scored some signal triumphs, for he had been provided with the means denied his predecessor, namely adequate light sloops and barges, which could control the shoal waters. By the latter summer he had pretty well cleaned out the pirates operating off Cuba, although he had less success in Puerto Rico. But in the process he had earned the unrelenting enmity of the thin-skinned secretary of the navy, Samuel Southard, for coming home without permission during a second attack of yellow fever, carping about his shipboard accommodations, and frequent bickerings with his subordinates that resulted in unnecessary courts-martial.[5]

When Porter, under protest, had returned to his command late in 1824, he overreacted in avenging an alleged insult to one of his officers by local Spanish authorities at Fajardo ("Foxardo" in contemporary spelling), a notorious piratical center at the eastern extremity of Puerto Rico. The hotheaded commodore promptly led ashore two hundred armed Americans, spiked defending guns, and extracted an apology from the town's officials at the cannon's mouth for the supposed offense, under the threat that Fajardo would be utterly destroyed should it refuse. A few hours later he sailed away, notified Washington what he had done, and settled back to await the public and private congratulations that he expected.

Instead the administration immediately recalled him and soon dismissed him as squadron commodore, while demanding a court of inquiry concerning his Puerto Rican invasion. The Monroe Doctrine had been announced little more than a year before, and while the danger of European intervention in the Latin American revolutions had abated, it was still there. Porter's occupation of Spanish Fajardo might offer a plausible excuse to a French fleet and transports to sail to America in order to help Spain recover its lost colonies. Monroe himself, who would be president until early March 1825, jotted some comments about such a potentiality a little later:

> This command was deemed a very important one . . . [and] I knew that it would attract the attention, not of Spain alone . . . but of the new governments, our neighbors, to the south & in certain respects of several of the powers of Europe. . . . [Porter's orders were] dictated by a desire rather to err . . . on the side of moderation, than to risk a varience [sic], with any of the nations concerned. . . . My intention was that the Commander of the Squadron, & all actions under him, should take nothing on themselves, but confine themselves to the duty especially injoined on them.

Secretary of State Adams was more vehement: "Porter's descent on Puerto Rico was a direct, hostile invasion of the island, utterly unjustifiable . . . it was one of the most high-handed acts I have ever heard of."[6]

Porter reacted with defiance to what he considered most unfair and outrageous treatment. He sent a series of letters to Southard and a couple to Adams, the new president, which were later labeled "insubordinate." During May a court of inquiry decided that there were adequate grounds for a court-martial. Porter then doubly infuriated the administration by publishing a long pamphlet entitled *An Exposition of the Facts and Circumstances Which Justified the Expedition to Foxardo*. He even had the effrontery to dedicate it to the president himself. The contentious commodore was then brought before a panel on two charges: "Disobedience to Orders" for landing in Puerto Rico and "Insubordinate conduct" for his caustic letters to Southard and Adams.

One way or another the court-martial was packed with Porter's enemies. His only sure defender among the fourteen judges was Commodore John Downes, for the two had been intimates since they had shared adventures during the *Essex*'s long wartime cruise to the Pacific. But Commodore James Barron, presiding officer; Captain Jesse D. Elliott; the government-appointed prosecutor, Judge Advocate Richard C. Coxe; and Biddle were all hostile to the accused. Porter had sat on Barron's court-martial in 1808 over the *Chesapeake* disaster and had questioned him more often and more intensely than any other judge, supporting the sentence of a five-year suspension that had almost ruined his life. Elliott, perhaps as abhorrent a character as ever wore the uniform of a U.S. naval officer, had fled the dueling ground at Bladensburg, Maryland, in March of 1820, leaving prostrate not only the dying Decatur but also the gravely wounded Barron, for whom he was the second. Twice Porter had physically dragged Elliott back to the field, once shouting at him, "You left your friend weltering in his blood on the bare earth; go back . . . and do your duty to your wounded friend!" From that moment Porter had made no effort to conceal his boundless contempt for Elliott's craven conduct, and the latter surely ached to retaliate. Coxe was a warm friend of Southard and had exhibited so much animus against Porter during the court of inquiry that he was the only one that the defendant challenged, but without success.[7]

Ever since Porter had refused him a lieutenancy in the *Essex* during June 1812 Biddle had "detested and despised" him. For the rest of his life Biddle's correspondence is studded with excoriating remarks about him, proving that Biddle could carry a grudge with the best of them. A few more examples from 1816 to 1825 come to mind. At the end of the war Porter published a book about the voyage of the *Essex*. In it he had some fairly steamy passages about the sexual experiences of himself and his men with the uninhibited Polynesian girls of Nuka Hiva Island in the Marquesas, for which he was taken to task by London journalists. In reply Porter wrote for publication in the press a long, paranoid letter accusing the British of attempting in this way to avenge his victories over their whalers in the Pacific. Biddle scornfully called to a friend's attention this "foolish letter." Porter also had some unkind things to say in the same work about the appearance and morals of Chilean women. While en route to Valparaiso in 1817 Biddle told the same correspondent of his fear that this might make the Chileños less "civil and obliging" to him and his people. He would try to rectify Porter's damage by "abusing his book" which he could do "with safe conscience."[8]

During 1824 Porter had involved himself in a controversy with Lieutenant Beverly Kennan, one of his officers in the West Indies, and had him court-martialed. The weakness of his accusations was spotlighted when the commodore chose to define the word "noted," which Kennan had used to describe him, as "notorious." The accused fought back furiously and effectively: "A Captain in the Navy . . . has put on the mask of the anonymous libeler, and wantonly, grossly, unjustly assailed the character of an inferior." The court agreed and Kennan was "fully acquitted" of all charges. Biddle was correct when he forecast that the case "will make great noise throughout the nation, and I think will disgust the nation with Capt Porter" In the same letter the class-conscious Philadelphian revealed the depth and breadth of his snobbishness. Porter had married the fifteen-year-old Evalina Anderson in 1808. Apparently there was some possibility that she and her widowed sister might visit the *Congress* at Norfolk early in 1824. Biddle jeered, "Cap. Porter's wife you know is the daughter of Anderson who kept a tavern in Chester [Pennsylvania]. I abhor the idea of having in my ship the two daughters of a tavern-keeper." (He might have condescended to mention that his mere "tavern-keeper" was William Anderson, who was well enough respected locally to have been a four-term Democratic-Republican congressman.[9])

Bainbridge, who was serving as president of the Board of Navy Commissioners, had been ordered to sit on the court-martial but managed to wriggle out of the assignment. He recognized which way Biddle was leaning on the matter of Porter's innocence or guilt when he wrote shortly before the proceedings began: "Have you seen Commodore P's book [pamphlet]? I should call it a *statement to the* public— as I understand no defense whatever was laid before the court [of inquiry]."[10]

Porter's well-publicized trial, one of the Navy's longest courts-martial, must have been an ordeal for all involved, since it dragged on for five weeks during the ferocious heat and humidity of the typical Washington summer. A plethora of witnesses was called by both sides, and as one of Porter's biographers put it: "Everyone concerned gave evidence at the greatest possible length. The prosecution dragged in everything it could think of, relevant or irrelevant, while Porter on the defense wandered far afield." The defendant indeed had room to roam "far afield." His defense, presented orally by his counsel, ran to approximately fifty thousand words. But he had wasted his time, for there was a definite pro forma air about the trial. The amorphous nature of the charges, forcing the accused in effect to prove his innocence, plus the composition of the court, rendered the verdict desired by Adams and Southard easily predictable. On 10 August Porter was found guilty of both "Disobedience to Orders" and "Insubordinate conduct."[11]

The sentence was astonishing, however, for he was given only a six-month suspension from the service at full pay and allowances. Conviction on two such serious charges could well have meant dismissal from the navy, or at least suspension of between two and five years without pay. Instead Porter was awarded a half-year's salaried vacation. Equally surprising, although his judges had deemed him a flouter of orders they said that his behavior at Fajardo had been motivated by "an anxious disposition, on his part, to maintain the honor and advance the interest of the nation and the service."[12]

The biographer of David Dixon Porter, the commodore's son, attributes this remarkably light sentence to the efforts of Downes and Biddle, who "so modified the verdict as to render it self-contradictory, if not flattering." Half of that statement is nonsense. In all likelihood Downes did exert himself in behalf of his much admired former commander, but surely Biddle did not. The transcript of the court's daily proceedings show that Biddle attended every session save that of 30 July, but asked no questions whatever of any witness, contenting himself with signing the guilty verdict along with all the other judges. Biddle may have been a man of sufficient character to rise above his hatred for the defendant and treat him fairly. But it defies credulity to envisage him actively working with Downes to arrive at a sentence that amounted to little more than the mildest of rebukes.[13]

Whatever their wording or the result, Porter never forgave his judges. Vowing that he would not again "associate with those who were led by men in power to inflict an unrighteous sentence," he broke irrevocably with such old friends and supporters as Bainbridge and Rodgers. In 1826 he resigned his U.S. Navy commission, which he had held for twenty-eight years, to accept Mexican employment as capitan de navio (commander of the ship of the line squadron, but in effect admiral of the Mexican Navy). He fought well against the

Spaniards for a time, but the internal schisms that shattered Mexican political stability soon drained away its financial resources to such an extent that Porter was plunged into a poverty abject enough to make him briefly contemplate suicide. He was not able to come home until 1829, but two years later President Andrew Jackson appointed him first chargé d'affaires and then minister to the Ottoman Empire. Save for a couple visits to the United States, he lived in Constantinople until his death in 1843.[14]

His business with Porter concluded, Biddle returned to Philadelphia to resume the humdrum responsibilities of his navy yard. But more excitement and danger than he wished to experience began in September, when the secretary ordered him, Bainbridge, and Lewis Warrington to sail in the USS *Hornet* to select a site for a "Naval Establishment" at Pensacola, Florida. They departed on 28 October, spent only a week in making the necessary choice, and put out of the harbor in the frigate *John Adams*. The usually reticent Biddle's emotional account of what happened underlines how narrowly he and the others escaped death:

> On the 7th instant coming out of Pensacola in this ship with light winds and considerable swell[,] she refused stays, struck upon the ground, knocked off the rudder, stumpt against the hard sand, & frightened all hands like [the] very Devil. She gave some tremendous crashes. Never before was [a] ship that escaped so near going to Davy Jones. We expected the masts to come down upon our heads, & the ship herself to break into many pieces, leaving those [on board] when the masts had sheared to save themselves by swimming, if they knew how [Bainbridge at least did not]. . . . We have now a bad ship, a bad rudder and a bad crew coming upon a bad coast in a bad season. Our country could illy afford to lose these three Post Captains that are on board.

Somehow the battered frigate managed to reach Savannah, where Bainbridge and Biddle (Warrington is not mentioned) thankfully left the ship and came home by other means.[15]

The winter of 1825 and 1826 passed quietly as Biddle attended to his chores at the Philadelphia Yard while, as always, awaiting a sea command. Late in March the secretary sent him a private letter appointing him commodore of the newly established Brazil Squadron, and Biddle at once expressed his delight in accepting the assignment. His only source of discontent was his flagship, the memory-haunted *Macedonian*, unquestionably the last frigate in the Navy that he wished to command. He told Bainbridge that he hoped instead to get the *Brandywine*, 44, just arrived at New York, but to no avail. By 21 April he had been replaced at the Navy Yard and during mid-May had completed preparations for his voyage, sailing for Rio late that month. His basic responsibility was to protect the national commerce from illegal interference from either side in the Argentinian-Brazilian War, fought between 1826 and 1828. It was a prize worth conserving, for U.S. trade with the two belligerents for 1825 amounted to imports of almost $3 million and exports of some $2.5 million.[16]

Political and military conditions along the eastern coast of lower South America had been more tranquil than those off the western shores of that continent during the post-Napoleonic years, and Argentina had won its de facto independence far easier than Chile and Peru. Brazil had been able to wrest itself away from Portugal without bloodshed until 1822, although that gargantuan colony had belonged to Lisbon since the mid-1500s. When the French swept into Portugal in 1807 its royal Braganza family fled to Brazil, where King Dom João VI remained until returning to his throne in 1822. He left behind as regent his son, who quickly rebelled against his father, and taking the title of Emperor Dom Pedro I, declared Brazilian independence later the same year. The Portuguese Navy was dispatched to restore Lisbon's rule. But Dom Pedro emulated the Chileans by hiring none other than Lord Thomas Cochrane (Biddle's former bête noire). That Scotsman's triumphs over the Portuguese in the Atlantic equalled in audacity and efficiency his efforts against the Spaniards in the Pacific a few years before. Although heavily outnumbered, he compelled a huge Portuguese fleet to evacuate the northern port of Bahia, and chasing it, cut out prizes so brilliantly that only thirteen ships out of sixty were able to reach home. By late 1823 he had cleared Brazilian coasts of the enemy. Perhaps it was fortunate for the normal flow of Biddle's adrenalin that the imperious Cochrane had quarreled with the Brazilians about the amount of prize money due him, and departed in a rage long before the American arrived.[17]

Ever since the earliest colonial times Spaniards and Portuguese had bickered over the ownership of the territory between modern Argentina and Brazil called "Banda Oriental" ("Eastern District"), or present-day Uruguay. By the early nineteenth century Spaniards from Argentina, aided by local Uruguayan sympathizers, settled much of that area, only to have the Brazilians annex it in 1821. Most of the backcountry remained in opposition, however, and the occupiers controlled only Montevideo and a couple of other Uruguayan ports. Late in 1825 Buenos Aires announced that it had incorporated the disputed territory, and Dom Pedro responded by declaring war.[18]

Once he had established shipboard routine, Biddle had time while en route south to peruse the secretary's instructions, which amounted to some 1,800 words. He was to watch out for slavers and particularly privateers, as Southard feared that the corsairs so recently routed by

Warrington and the British from the Caribbean might try to set up new bases off Brazil and Argentina. He must ward off any "illegal exercise of power" threatening American commerce, but he must also avoid "collisions" with either antagonist. He should protest against paper blockades while realizing that his nation was on good terms with both Brazil and Argentina and he must keep those friendly relations intact. As for specie, he could carry it but he must not advertise that service. The maintenance of his complement's health and discipline was mandatory. He should do what he could to keep his officers from assailing each other in the press, and discourage dueling. At the same time he must give "unceasing care" to the education, both professional and moral, of the midshipmen. If he had any time left over he should collect "specimens" of interest to American agriculture.[19]

On 11 August the *Macedonian* dropped anchor off the Brazilian capital to assume direction of his squadron. It consisted of the 34-gun frigate *Cyane* and the sloop of war *Boston* under Commander Beekman V. Hoffman, in addition to the flagship. The *Cyane* was commanded by Captain Jesse D. Elliott, who had been in that area for some time. Possibly it speaks well for Biddle's equanimity that evidently he did not clash with that mercurial and malevolent officer. The commodore's instructions to his subordinates amounted to little more than a rehash of the secretary's orders to him. This done, Biddle settled down to learning what he could about the Argentinian-Brazilian war.[20]

He found that the conflict was approaching a stalemate. Ashore, military movements were desultory and haphazard. At sea the Brazilians hurriedly slapped on a blockade of the Rio de la Plata's mouth, trying to cut off Buenos Aires from foreign commerce. This was challenged by the United States on the ground that no sufficient naval strength existed to seal off so vast a stretch of water, and that the blockade had been imposed without sufficient notification to neutral shippers. Condy Raguet of Philadelphia, the American chargé d'affaires at Rio, protested vigorously that the mere announcement that a blockade had been put in was not enough. Instead, ships should have been warned away from specific ports corked by the Brazilian navy. He added that the entire eastern coast of the continent from the Amazon to Cape Horn was under the interdict of one or the other of the belligerents and that the nearest neutral havens for foreign merchantmen were Valparaiso and Cape Town.[21]

A short time after the *Macedonian* had reached Rio Biddle learned of a particular sort of harassment that American carriers off lower South America might expect. The brig *Bull* of Philadelphia had been stopped on the high seas while en route from Gibraltar to Montevideo by a "Brazilian cruiser." Her captors decided that the *Bull* was actually destined for blockaded Buenos Aires, and put a prize crew aboard the merchantman. According to the Brazilians, five unarmed Americans attempted to retake their ship from twelve armed guards, which as Biddle said was "not probable." On the way to Rio the Americans suffered "brutal treatment" and upon arrival were sent to the prison ship in the harbor. But the efforts of Chargé Raguet managed to arrange their liberation and permission for them to board the *Macedonian*. Apparently the *Bull* was eventually released.[22]

Meanwhile Raguet kept inveighing against Brazilian seizures of American ships in terms so excessive—he called one apprehender a "barbarian and a monster" and described the Brazilians as not "a civilized people"—as to make himself so unpopular that he had to leave the country. Biddle permitted his friendship for a fellow Philadelphian to cloud his perception when he wrote the department, "Mr. Raguet has been a faithful, zealous & able servant of the government. No man at Rio within the diplomatic corps . . . is so much respected or deserves so much to be respected." President John Adams offered a more accurate portrayal of his man in Brazil. In refusing a later appeal that Raguet be given another chance, he replied that "to replace in the diplomatic service abroad a man of such a temper and want of judgment, who took blustering for bravery and insolence for energy, was too dangerous."[23]

Next the commodore had to handle a disciplinary problem. Elliott demanded that the *Cyane*'s Lieutenant Samuel B. Phelps be court-martialed, but Biddle was able to handle the matter without judicial proceedings. He told the secretary that Phelps was "addicted to habitual intoxication," and that he was accepting the lieutenant's resignation. He would be sent to Washington for final disposition by the department. Biddle's decision was approved early the next year when Phelps was permitted to leave the service without further punishment.[24]

A few days later a much more serious matter erupted, namely a brawl that might well have caused a rupture in Brazilian-American relations, the details of which were provided in a long report by Lieutenant Uriah P. Levy of the *Cyane*. An inspection had revealed that urgent repairs were needed on that frigate's mainmast and bowsprit. Elliott received permission from Brazilian Vice Admiral Francisco Antonio de Silva Pacheco, commanding the government arsenal at Rio, to land and have carpenters from the *Macedonian* make the essential renovations at the local dockyard. While directing the work, Midshipman John W. Moores told Levy that when a Brazilian press gang was passing by, he had been hailed by one of its members. Sailor William Hanson of the American ship *Rebecca* shouted that he had been shanghaied into the Brazilian navy. Levy passed on this information to Admiral Pacheco, who said that only Biddle, the commodore of the U.S. squadron, could approach him on such a subject. When Levy returned to the dock he found goings-on of "considerable excitement," as he put it with commendable restraint. Moores had tried to rescue Hanson single-handed, upon which the Brazilian escort commenced "beating him with their bayonets and swords, and dragging him toward the Launch," to be taken out to the prison ship. As the *Macedonian*'s carpenters were in the process of "coming down with broad-axes" to help the midshipman, Levy understandably found "great difficulty" in separating the warring factions.[25]

At this juncture hysteria was heightened by the appearance of Pacheco with "forty or fifty Soldiers, Citizens, and officers." When the admiral asked Moores for an explanation of his behavior he could not have been very much mollified by the reply, "You be damned!" Pacheco then seized the offender "by the back of the neck," upon which he was "struck" by the beleaguered American. "In an instant there was [*sic*] a hundred weapons, swords, bayonets, and sticks pointed against him." Although Levy kept calling at the top of his voice that the assailed was a U.S. naval officer and that it was "shameful for a hundred armed men to attack one defenseless boy," Moores was "beaten down." Only after Pacheco had "struck him several times with his cane" was he permitted to depart with Levy. The lieutenant offered an explanation for Moores's bellicose reactions: he was "a little excited by liquor."[26]

Biddle defused this potential international explosive with faultless reasoning. Normally he would have court-martialed Moores, he informed Southard, but in this case, should the verdict be an acquittal, the Brazilians would surely look upon it as a whitewash and the crisis would only be exascerbated. Moreover, Admiral Pacheco was "notorious for his violent deportment, especially toward foreigners." The best way to terminate the matter, Biddle wisely concluded, was to send Moores home for trial, adding, "I take leave to express the opinion that, considering Mr. Moores' youth, the sending him home under suspension from duty is perhaps punishment sufficient for his offense." His advice was not only heeded but Moores was promoted to lieutenant during the next spring, serving in that capacity until his resignation from the navy in 1841.[27]

More prosaic duties occupied much of 1827. Late the previous December Biddle had taken the *Macedonian* down to Montevideo, where the harbor lay so unprotected from storms that in almost two months he dared go ashore only twice for brief visits. He had not forgotten his unpleasant mnemonic association with Montevideo, writing his sister: "This you know is the wretched anchorage to which I was to have brought the still more wretched Caesar Augustus Rodney." He added a gracious little postscript to his sister-in-law Jane, chiding her for not writing: "When people are discontented, it is not unusual I believe to be most discontented with those they love most. Hence it is I suppose that man and wife so often fall out, and hence it is perhaps that I am now quarreling with you."[28]

Most of the year slipped by in routine patroling by the squadron along the 1,200 miles between Rio and Montevideo. Despite the Moores-Pacheco fracas and the continued apprehension of American merchant ships by Brazilian blockaders, relations between the two countries warmed sufficiently to bring about what Biddle called "the extravagant idea" of Brazil "applying to American vessels a doctrine in regard to blockades of a less injurious character than that which it would apply to British vessels." He was sure that such a concept had been "seriously entertained," but it quickly evaporated "in consequence of intimations from Great Britain that she would not submit to such a discrimination."[29]

The perusal of this and other letters from Biddle allowed President Adams to relieve some of his Anglophobic frustrations, for he was in the process of being thwarted by London in his efforts to open the British West Indies to American commerce:

> Cannon law is the law of Great Britain towards other nations. The principles which the courts of Brazil intended to pursue were just. They were to apply to each nation her own rules of blockade. Those of the United States, being favorable to neutral rights, were entitled to the benefits of them from the Brazilian tribunals. Those of Great Britain leaning only to the belligerent pretensions, she could fairly claim only the same measure which she meets [sic] out to others. But those are not their maxims. Belligerent, she tramples upon neutral rights; neutral, she maintains them at the cannon's mouth; and the Brazilian Courts have been awed into submission.

Despite Rio's inability to accommodate American aspirations more fully, a study of the cases concerning seven U.S merchantmen seized by the Brazilians from 26 April through 19 November 1827 seems to show that the admiralty courts in Brazilian-controlled Montevideo operated with less rigor than those of the Spaniards in the West Indies from 1818 through 1825. Four of the seven were released, one on the very day she was brought into port. Two were awaiting trial, and one that had grounded was caught in a naval skirmish between the

Brazilians and the Argentinians and burned after the discovery that she could not be refloated.[30]

Although Rio enjoyed naval supremacy early in the war, eventually Buenos Aires was able to lessen the impact of the blockade by the exploits of another seafaring expatriate, Admiral William Brown, a veteran Irish mariner who had emigrated to Argentina. By mid-1827 the outnumbered, sometimes defeated, and once badly wounded Brown achieved something close to naval equality, making it easier for American and other merchantmen to bring precious supplies into Buenos Aires. Biddle seems to have had no direct contact with Brown. His name does not appear in a day-by-day diary describing Argentinian exploits at sea from 1826 to 1828, and there are only a couple of noncommital references to the *Macedonian*. During November of 1827 Biddle did send Commander Hoffman of the *Boston* into Buenos Aires to confer with Brown in regard to the identification of American men-of-war should a battle be fought in their vicinity. He warned Hoffman to be most circumspect in showing favoritism to neither country, since "next to the Portuguese-Americans, the most suspicious people in the world are the Spanish-Americans." Hoffman completed his assignment without incident but complained that he had lost three bluejackets by desertion while at Buenos Aires.[31]

Toward the end of that year Biddle made a fast friend of the ailing John M. Forbes, U.S. minister to Argentina, letting him escape the heat of Buenos Aires by taking him in the *Macedonian* to cooler Montevideo. Forbes referred to this service in a letter to the State Department as the "distinguished honors and kind attentions" of the commodore and his officers. The two then cooperated in opposition to a new Brazilian proclamation. Rio threatened American commercial profits by requiring all foreign merchantmen to post expensive bonds promising "not to break the blockade of Buenos Ayres." Forbes was exasperated by what he referred to as "the lawless and unprincipled character" of the measure, and Biddle protested as well. On receipt of this information, Secretary Southard told Biddle to "be vigilant in doing everything in your power to prevent the execution of this injurious imposition, short of direct force." President Adams was willing to take an even stronger stand. He wrote: "The instructions now to be given to Commodore Biddle would be to disregard the decree in everything short of hostile conflict, and, if this should fail, the authority of Congress will be asked for the use of force." Luckily the need never arose for Biddle to put the president's bellicosity into effect, even though his letters to the department during early 1828 are filled with his complaints to the admiral of the Brazilian blockading squadron about the bonding requirement.[32]

By this time Biddle's tenure off lower South America was nearing its end, for the war itself was winding down. Neither side had the manpower, finances, or energy to win decisively. The original Uruguayan enthusiasm for their Argentinian supporters had waned in the face of Buenos Aires's refusal to accord them equal treatment. Urged on by strong British diplomatic pressure, the enemies agreed to compromise. By the Treaty of Rio de Janeiro, signed on 28 August 1828, Uruguay was granted its independence, each of its larger neighbors content to have it exist as a buffer state between them rather than belong to the other.[33]

During the early spring Biddle learned that he was to be relieved of squadron command, but it was some time before his replacement arrived. During the late summer he was able to sail in the *Macedonian* on her homeward voyage, writing the secretary late in October as he neared Chesapeake Bay that he was bringing the first news of the advent of peace between Argentina and Brazil. He was heading for Norfolk, but he had trouble aboard; Dr. Benjamin Tichnor, the frigate's surgeon, reported that of the twenty-three men in sick bay, ten were down with smallpox. Biddle, well aware of the apprehension of seacoast cities about contagion spreading from vessels newly arrived from infested ports, wrote in the same letter: "As the good people of Norfolk, like the people of some other *sickly* places, are timid upon the subject of imported-diseases, I shall be careful to let them know that we have the small-pox on board; and, unless they consent to it, I will not discharge any of our men there." At any rate, he himself was "impatient to leave the ship and impatient to reach Philadelphia."[34]

Biddle's accomplishment in protecting American citizens and property from illicit belligerent acts, while at the same time maintaining amicable relations with both antagonists, make up one of his most commendable tours of duty. Certainly his government thought so. Southard told him about "the satisfaction always felt by the department when the duties assigned to our Naval officers are performed with intelligence[,] fidelity and discretion. Accept my congratulations on your safe return to your country."[35]

Commodore James Biddle, painting by Joseph Wood. Courtesy of the Naval Photographic Center, Washington, D.C.

Commodore James Biddle, painting by Charles Willson Peale. Courtesy of the Independence National Historical Park Collection, Philadelphia, Pa.

Commodore James Biddle, painting by Thomas Sully. Courtesy of Nicholas B. Wainwright, Gwynedd, Pa.

Commodore William Bainbridge, painting by John Wesley Jarvis. Courtesy of the Arts Commission, New York City Hall.

Commodore John Rodgers, painting by Gilbert Stuart. Courtesy of the Naval Photographic Center, Washington, D. C.

Commodore David Porter. From David F. Long, Nothing Too Daring: A Biography of Commodore David Porter, 1780–1843. *Courtesy of the Naval Institute Press, Annapolis, Md.*

Capture of the British sloop of war Penguin *by the U.S. sloop of war* Hornet, *23 March 1815. Lithograph by Day and Haghe. Courtesy of Nicholas B. Wainwright, Gwynedd, Pa.*

H.M.S. Cornwallis, *74 guns, in chase of the U.S. sloop of war* Hornet, *27–30 April 1815. Lithograph by Day and Haghe. Courtesy of Nicholas B. Wainwright, Gwynedd, Pa.*

The U.S.S. Columbus *and* Vincennes *in Japan. Lithograph by Wagner and McGuigan. Courtesy of Nicholas B. Wainwright, Gwynedd, Pa.*

CHAPTER 8
MEDITERRANEAN
COMMODORE,
1829–1832

Biddle relished his eagerly awaited reunion with his kin for some six months, undoubtedly spending much of his time at Andalusia, the estate owned by his brother Nicholas and sister-in-law Jane on the banks of the Delaware River some sixteen miles above Philadelphia. His vacation ended in June of 1829 when Secretary of the Navy John Branch offered him command of the Mediterranean Squadron, to which he responded with an enthusiastic affirmative. He had reason to look forward to his new assignment, for the Mediterranean was the favorite posting of U.S. Navy officers and crews alike. To be sure, the West India, Brazil, Pacific, and East India squadrons had their particular attractions; but none could match the Mediterranean's generally agreeable weather; dazzling scenery; glamorous cities; fascinating ancient ruins, especially for those classically educated; variety of peoples; and readily available girls. Its very enticements, however, caused many disciplinary problems east of Gibraltar, and the new commodore would find himself well vexed by them.[1]

In early July Biddle notified the department that he was ready to sail as a passenger in the frigate *Constellation,* which lifted anchor at New York on 12 August. In the sharpest contrast to his crossing in the *Congress* six years before, he had amiable companionship throughout the voyage. Louis McLane, future secretary of state, was en route to London as the U.S. minister, and Biddle probably appreciated that he had been Caesar A. Rodney's chief political rival in Delaware. William C. Rives, appointed American minister to Paris, was equally affable. He was an influential Virginian, a long-time senator first as a Democrat and then as a Whig, finally serving in the Confederate Congress during the Civil War.[2]

After dropping off her illustrious diplomats at their respective destinations, the *Constellation* came into the Mediterranean. Off Minorca in the Spanish Balaeric Islands a man fell overboard, and according to a sailor eyewitness, one of the officers, identified merely as "Mr. B.," jumped in to save him. When both had been hauled aboard, Biddle "grabbed Mr. B. by the hand, gave it a hearty shake, and declared that he had not expected to have that pleasure again."[3]

On 18 October the frigate came into the U.S. naval depot at Mahon in the same group of islands, where Biddle relieved William C. Crane as commodore, elevating his broad pennant in the USS *Java*, 44. Impressive American naval power was congregated under his direction. In addition to his flagship it consisted of the *Constellation* and the sloops *Ontario, Lexington, Fairfield,* and *Warren.* Later the frigates *Brandywine* and *John Adams,* as well as the sloop *Concord,* would be sent to him as replacements for ships ordered home.[4]

In his first letter to the department after assuming command, Biddle enclosed his four pages of instructions to the captains and commanders of the ships in his squadron, in which, as usual, he basically repeated his own instructions from the secretary. They were to pass all official communications through him; transport specie provided that the service remained unpublicized; hold down the number of courts-martial in any manner possible; be most reluctant to make acting appointments unless absolutely mandatory; keep shore leaves at a minimum, since there had been recent clashes at Mahon between American and both Spanish and French sailors; maintain proper standards of health and discipline; and realize that U.S. relations with all the Mediterranean countries were excellent and must be kept so.[5]

Biddle's first major reponsibilities concerned two Barbary states. He was to look into Tripoli about a situation concerning a "Mr. Coxe," the American consul in that city. Some time previously an English officer, designated in the scanty documentation that exists about the case only as "Major Laing," had been murdered there. One of the bashaw's leading officials, Sidi Hassuna D'Ghies (very likely a close relative of the Sidi Mohammed D'Ghies, who had been Tripolitan foreign minister while Biddle was imprisoned there), was said to have been an "accessory" to the crime. Much to the bashaw's anger, Coxe first intervened in Hassuna's behalf, and then talked Commander Foxhall A. Parker of the USS *Fairfield* into taking both the Tripolitan and himself to Mahon. On 10 November Biddle went ashore in Tripoli and conversed about the case with the country's "chief minister," and on the next day met the bashaw, Yusuf Karamanli. The commodore admitted that Coxe had behaved improperly in spiriting Hassuna away from whatever punishment the bashaw

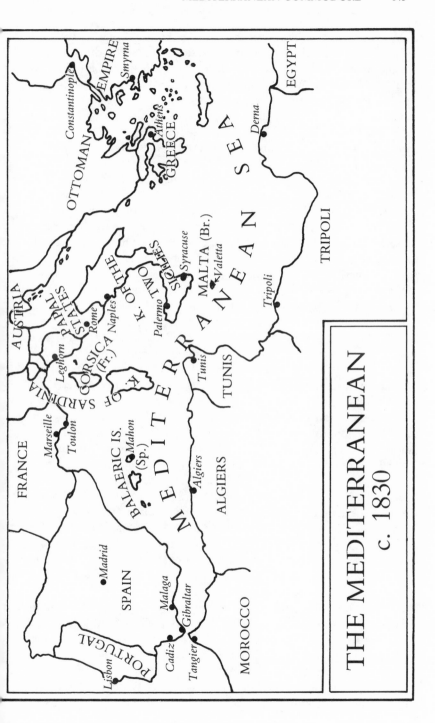

THE MEDITERRANEAN
c. 1830

wished to inflict on him, but the best that he could suggest was that Yusuf protest about it directly to President Jackson, which he did. Some months later Biddle groused to his brother that he had heard nothing from the White House about the bashaw's justifiable complaint. There the matter rested. The strangest aspect of the entire episode is that Biddle, neither in his seven-page letter about it to the department nor anywhere else, ever reminisced about his nineteen months as the bashaw's unwilling guest.[6]

Algiers was the other Barbary nation that preoccupied the commodore during his time in the Mediterranean. In 1827 the dey had lost his temper while talking with the French consul and slapped him across the face with a flyswatter, thereby giving the ensuing conflict the arresting name, "the Flyswatter War." After the dey's repeated refusals to make amends, a French expedition sailed to Algiers, landed, and deposed him. In order to protect the resident U.S. consul and other Americans who might be in danger, Biddle took the *Java* to that city. There he firmly endorsed the philosophy of the "white man's burden" by writing: "Algiers you know does not belong to the Algerians. The French have taken it and intend I believe to keep it. Without doubt the conquest of a civilized nation of these fine countries in which the imprint of ignorance and superstition will eventually be a blessing to the people." The commodore was correct in his forecast; after some initial hesitation France seized Algeria and kept it until 1962.[7]

Biddle could only have been under considerable nervous strain for many months during 1830 and early 1831. He received a letter from the secretary of the navy, written the previous February, in which Branch coldly asked him to respond to an accusation of political partisanship: "In a communication lately received from the Mediterranean by the Government, the following statement is made: 'I heard him, Mr Biddle say, in my presence, and in the presence of several Officers in his Cabin, that no language could express his detestation of the present administration.' " Such comments, Branch went on, were "subversive of the proper discipline of the Navy, and a violation of the laws enacted for its government." Biddle was invited to offer "such explanations as you may think proper."[8]

This menacing letter was not read by the commodore until 16 August and he replied to it the following day. He did not know who was the informant, he said, but "I declare unhesitatingly that his statement is utterly false, that self respect and the respect due from me to the Chief Magistrate of my Country equally forbid my using such language anywhere, but especially in the presence of Officers under my command." He should have been relieved when the secretary's reply arrived during the next February: "I have to state that confiding in your high character as an Officer and a Gentleman, I did not for a moment entertain the belief of your having used such expressions. I felt however from the source through which the information came, as well as justice to yourself and the Government to apprise you of it, and it gives me great pleasure to assure you that your letter is perfectly satisfactory."[9]

The secretary's statement that he had really absolved Biddle from the beginning was not true, and the commodore knew it. Actually Branch had asked the *Java*'s crew to evaluate their commander and even had their reply published in the press. Biddle was outraged, fuming to Nicholas:

> How miserable of the Secretary to publish the letter he received from the *Java*. Perhaps he wrote to my Crew to know what they thought of me, for I imagine at present the reputation of an Officer at head Quarters depends greatly on the opinion of the Sailors. For my own part I have always thought and said that it was extremely improper in Officers to address letters of approbation to their Commander, and God help the Service if Sailors are permitted or invited to do the same.[10]

Even though the commodore may not have expressed publicly and in those words his abhorrence of "the present administration," his above comments illustrate his aristocratic repugnance at the advent of Jacksonian democracy and the so-called "Age of the Common Man." His deep affection for his brother and his family would have impelled him along an anti-Jackson course in any event. Nicholas had been president of the prestigious Second Bank of the United States since 1823. Although he had voted for Jackson as a fellow nationalist in the presidential election of 1824, by 1830 he had become a strong antagonist of the new president. The skies were already lowering in anticipation of the struggle between the two over rechartering the bank for another twenty years, a fight that Nicholas was destined to lose. If anything, James outdid his brother in his dislike of the new political currents flowing through the nation. Anticipating that Clay would face Jackson in the election of 1832, he wrote: "The General I presume will go out of office as inauspiciously as he came in. It is quite impossible that the People can re-elect him." Fifteen years later he feared that the Mexican War might bring "the man who plants our flag upon the walls of the city of Mexico" to the White House, "tho' he be as unfit as was Jackson."[11]

Certainly James's friends knew his political bent. The ardent anti-Jacksonian John Robertson of Virginia wrote to him, aware that his opinions would find a sympathetic audience: "The immense patronage of the general government . . . and the unscrupulous manner in which it is used . . . [added to] the exertions and influence of dema-gogues—of selfish, professional, and designing politicians . . . [make America's national future] fatal to the continuance of our political institutions." Captain John D. Sloat, who had helped save Biddle's *Congress* during the terrible hurricane at La Guaira in 1823 and would be reassociated with him during the Mexican War, pointed out his former commander's partisanship by referring to the "Loco Focos." (They composed the Jacksonian left wing, called by that name ever since they had held a meeting in New York City by the light of early friction matches known as "locofocos.") "I have sent you . . . a small silver box with a steel attached to one side for striking fire to light cigars. I think you will find it more portable, convenient & agreeable than the Loco Focos you have been using especially as I know you dislike locofocoism in any shape." His record is crystal—Biddle would remain a staunch opponent of the Democratic Party and a dedicated Whig for the rest of his life.[12]

To return to the commodore in the Mediterranean—he was al-ways immersed in the minutia involved in commanding a large squadron on foreign assignment. He was constantly issuing orders to his commanders, reading their reports, checking with local navy agents as to the procurement of supplies, receiving and accounting for credits from London drawn on the U.S. government, ensuring that the ves-sels of his squadron remained shipshape, entertaining and being en-tertained by foreign dignitaries, broadcasting instructions about the health and morale of his officers and crews, and trying to keep a tight disciplinary rein on his unruly personnel.

One of his most widely self-proclaimed triumphs was his cam-paign against drunkenness. Near the end of his term as squadron commodore he notified the secretary that of the 1,107 men under his command, "exclusive of Commissioned and warrant officers," 819 were accepting cash in lieu of their grog allowance. "To encourage men to persevere, and to entice others to follow their example, the grog money is paid regularly and at short intervals. On board the *John Adams* . . . not a man draws his allowance for spirits." Biddle was so proud of what he considered a sterling accomplishment that he had the above statistics reprinted in a service journal when he returned home.[13]

Yet his temperance campaign may in no way be deemed an un-qualified success, among his officers at least. While at Smyrna (Edirne) in Asiatic Turkey, Biddle and his commanders were invited to dine on board a French frigate, along with two Royal Navy officers and a local British merchant. The same Commander Foxhall A. Parker of the *Fairfield* who had aided Coxe in Tripoli arrived "tipsy," and almost immediately upon sitting down to dinner "became intoxicated." While the others were still at the table Parker finally had to be carried to his boat "in a state of stupefaction." Biddle, although "very mortified," thought his drunken colleague to be "an amiable man" and claimed that he felt "kind feelings toward him, but believing as I do that he is addicted to this destructive habit, I am compelled, painful as it is, to make you this report." Possibly his talebearing operated to Parker's advantage, for the latter was retained in the service, remaining at least sober enough to achieve his captaincy in 1836.[14]

Alcoholic overindulgence was worst among the midshipmen, many of whom were barely past their middle teens. For instance, during September of 1831 two of them fueled up enough to turn the *Brandywine* into a bedlam. A court-martial convicted George N. Hawkins of getting "drunk on board" and making "great and scandalous noises thereby disturbing the Officers and Crew of the said ship." George Lansing was also found guilty, and only a barnyard analogy could describe his behavior; he did "scream out and make uncouth noises . . . such as the braying of asses, the caterwauling of cats, etc." Both were sentenced to be publicly reprimanded by the commodore in front of the people in every ship of the squadron. E. L. Greenwood, another midshipman, was also punished for lying when he asked for and received shore leave in order to "visit relations." Instead he caroused in a Smyrna tavern with friends, after which he became engaged in a drunken brawl with some Greeks for "treating one of their women with rudeness."[15]

Biddle had mixed results when he grappled with the sexual frustrations of his people. He occasionally permitted his sailors to go ashore so that they might enjoy "the pleasures" of Mahon. Such liberties were, however, curtailed when bluejackets from the *Ontario* and *Constellation* fell into a ruckus with Spanish sailors during the next September. The commodore was equal to the emergency, allowing whores to visit the men on board. Aloofly referring to them as "women of their own class in society," he apologetically called to the attention of the department that "this practice is not confined to our ships, it exists generally in the ships of war of all Nations. It is an evil which is tolerated as a preventive of greater evils."[16]

The officers were permitted no such release, which possibly explains some of the astonishing misdemeanors of the younger ones under Biddle's command. In his long article about the commodore, Nicholas B. Wainwright says that during his tenure the officers were "virtuous," but the records declare otherwise. Certainly he had made every effort to steer them in that direction, telling the secretary some months after his arrival:

> My duty to the Service exacts of me to enforce mildly yet strictly these views of the law and of the Department. To cherish honorable and gentlemanly feelings among the young Midshipmen, to stimulate their ambition, to aid their professional acquirements that they become qualified to fulfill the future hopes and just expectations of their country, I regard as the most important duties entrusted to me. On many occasions a Commander may employ his influence with more propriety and better effect than his authority.[17]

Sad to say, Biddle's praiseworthy aspirations seem to have been somewhat extraordinarily disregarded by what may have been an unusually raucous and rambunctious group of midshipmen, whose activities were programmed to gray the hair and line the face of any commander. There were at least twenty-six of that sort in the flagship *Java*, and enough others in the squadron's remaining vessels to force Biddle to flood Washington with descriptions and complaints about their disreputable and aggravating behavior. In a single letter from Smyrna during the spring of 1830 he gave particulars about what he daintily called their "ungentlemanly conduct":

> Mr. [Edmund] Burke and Mr. [Dominick] Lynch have been reported to me for being lousy. [!] Mr. [George M.] Hooe and Mr. [Franklin] Clinton for fighting with fists in one of the Ship's boats, Mr. [Joseph C.] Walsh for striking Mr. Burke, Mr. Burke for getting the wife of one of the Sailors into a state room on the berth deck, Mr. Burke and Mr. [Edward C. ? James E. ? William ?] Ward for punishing the men, when it is contrary to my orders for Midshipmen ever to punish any of the men, Mr. Walsh for calling Mr. Clinton a liar . . . and Mr. Clinton for striking . . . Mr. Walsh with his fists, Mr. Burke several times for being drunk and noisy. Six of the Midshipmen have fought duels. Reports innumerable have been made to me of neglect of duty of the Midshipmen while absent from the ship.

The same communication quoted the "School Master" as complaining that "but few of them had been disposed to attend instruction from him, and in particular that midshipmen Hooe and Greenwood had never attended at all.[18]

The commodore went on to itemize further delinquencies. During a single brief visit to Turkey, Hooe, Walsh, [Daniel B.] Ridgely, and "Tod" (either John G. or Oliver Todd) managed to quarrel so enthusiastically with "a Greek" that they tried to report him to the local Turkish pasha, but were not given an audience. Biddle was thankful: "No one is ignorant of the Turkish mode of finishing disputes between foreign Officers and a Greek; and it is dreadful to reflect that if the Pasha had received the Midshipmen's complaint it is quite probable without further inquiry he would have taken off the Greek's head."[19]

The evidence suggests that Midshipman Augustus B. Marrest was not enchanted with the personal and professional qualities of the *Constellation*'s Lieutenant Hiram Paulding. Other officers testified that in public Marrest had called his elder "a damned infamous scoundrel," "a damned puppy," and "a coward and a blackguard," epithets that Biddle justifiably called "scandalous to the highest degree." Certainly their commander had a right to take exception to the "great want of gentlemanly feeling" among his younger colleagues; indeed, it had been "greater than I have witnessed in any other ship."[20]

The disposition of the above cases would appear to show that naval justice did not operate with undue harshness on the accused. To be sure, Burke—vermin infested, quarrelsome, drunken, and either an attempted or actual seducer or rapist—was dismissed from the service, and Marrest was sent home to be cashiered for his somewhat negative commentary on Lieutenant Paulding. But even Walsh, whose constant fisticuffs with his fellows caused his commodore much "vexation and chagrin," managed to retain his commission after writing Biddle an abject apology and promising to reform. All the other midshipmen mentioned above were permitted to continue their naval careers, including Lansing, who on the very day that he was publicly reprimanded by the commodore had the effrontery to ask for permission to attend the opera in Syracuse that night, and was put out when his request was refused.[21]

To his further discomfort, Biddle soon discovered that the midshipmen were in the habit of running up sizable debts ashore, especially at Mahon. When he learned that the lice-ridden Lynch owed $150 and had precisely $18.29 coming to him in back pay, shore leaves for all the younger officers were suspended. Additional investigation proved that the "tailors, hatters, shoemakers, tavern-keepers and keepers of gambling houses have large sums due to them" from the midshipmen. Biddle listed eleven, whose debts ranged from a high of $133.77 down to two who owed merely $8.10 apiece. He accentuated to the secretary that such financial irresponsibility had not suddenly flourished since he had taken over command: "The practice of increasing debt on shore without the means or even the disposition to repay, is, I believe, of long standing in the Mediterranean Squadron. I shall endeavor to put an end to this disreputable practice." A few weeks later he pledged to employ "exemplary punishments . . . in aid of reproof and exhortation," but his labors here were futile. Even though he attempted to enforce a policy whereby no debt-ridden officer was allowed to go home until he had met his obligations, the matter crops up every now and then in his official correspondence over the next two years.[22]

With so much bickering, well inflamed by alcohol, it was predictable that the midshipmen would carry their hostilities from fists to pistols. Biddle mentioned that officers of the squadron had fought six duels before the end of March 1830, but provided no details. Such was not the case in the Bowie-McLaughlin encounter. Midshipmen J. K. Bowie and Cincinnatus Pryor had a minor spat. J. T. McLaughlin, a friend of Pryor, while trying to intercede for him, was slapped across the face by Bowie, following which a challenge was given and accepted. They went ashore at Smyrna sometime during the spring of 1831, and McLaughlin was "wounded severely," although in time he recovered. Biddle decided the case by suspending Bowie from duty and sending him home to allow the department to decide his fate. The elastic mores of the day concerning the acceptability of dueling, no matter what the laws in effect against it, permitted Bowie not only to remain in the service but to be promoted shortly thereafter.[23]

This bloodshed, and perhaps other such incidents, brought about a confrontation between Commander Philip F. Voorhees of the *John Adams* and some of his officers. While anchored at Mahon in December of 1831, Voorhees heard that a duel had been fought involving some of his underlings. He called all the officers together and informed them that if anyone died in "such disgraceful proceedings," he would put the survivors "in *double-irons*," ship them back to the United States, and "turn them over to the civil authorities as *murderers!*" He demanded that every officer under his command must give his "word of honor" not to participate, directly or indirectly, in dueling. When the assistant surgeon and three midshipmen refused to comply, he ordered them off his ship, forcing them to rent accommodations ashore. They appealed to Biddle on the ground that Voorhees had overstepped his authority. The commodore agreed and reinstated them in the *John Adams*. To be sure, Voorhees had every right to refuse shore leave for those he suspected might be planning an encounter, but he could not order them from his ship.[24]

Biddle's personal attitude toward dueling remains unclear. While he never wrote an approving word about that anachronistic custom, his correspondence carries no strictures against it. In this he was unlike many of his colleagues, even those who engaged in it. James Barron and Stephen Decatur expressed their antipathy toward private warfare even while planning the confrontation that would leave the former seriously wounded and the latter dead. The class-conscious Biddle may have been convinced that his status as "gentleman" set him and his social equals apart from "the rabble." Therefore he might have believed that court decisions, even in his favor, were insufficient to erase libelous or slanderous slurs against his personal honor, and that such stains could only be obliterated by a willingness to risk death. Although he apologized in order to avoid a duel with Sinclair, he seriously considered bringing Navy Commissioner Rodgers to the field in 1823; in 1836 he would second a relative in a bloodless encounter. Yet the utter senselessness of dueling should have deeply impressed him when he learned in the Mediterranean about the manner in which his younger brother, Major Thomas Biddle, had thrown his life away.

Thomas, born in 1790, had entered the U.S. Army as a captain of artillery and served throughout the struggles on the Canadian border during the War of 1812. According to a newspaper account, he fought well: "He entered very young into the army, was engaged in almost every battle on the northern frontier, and is mentioned in the official dispatches of the commander with distinguished honors. In the night assault of Fort Erie on the 13th of August 1814, General [Edmund P.] Gaines, in his official account, speaks of the activity and great efficiency of Captain Biddle's conduct, though he was then suffering from a severe contusion in the shoulder received from one of the enemy's shells." Shortly after the war he moved to St. Louis and by 1832 had served there for some time as the army paymaster.[25]

The strong political partisanship of the day impelled him into a quarrel with U.S. Representative Spencer D. Pettis, born in 1802, who served as Missouri's secretary of state from 1826 to 1828 and was elected a Democratic congressman a little later. While running for and winning reelection in 1830 he fell into a journalistic war with Biddle, an ardent anti-Jacksonian. The major castigated Pettis in a local paper and the latter retaliated with allegations that Biddle found intolerably offensive. Pettis asserted next that late one night his enemy sneaked into his room where, stricken with some unidentified disease, he lay trying to sleep. Biddle "there commenced beating me in a most violent manner. Is he not a *miserable poltroon* to come armed in the dark to attack a sick and unarmed man [actually Pettis admitted defending himself with a sword cane] in bed and asleep—not giving him a chance of defense?"[26]

Pettis then challenged Biddle, who, as the recipient, had the right to name the terms of their encounter. His extreme nearsightedness is offered to explain his incredible specification—pistols *at five feet*. Nowhere in the records is there any indication of what Biddle's wife thought about her husband's insistence upon committing suicide. They met on 27 August 1831 at four o'clock in the afternoon on an island near St. Louis. At this "murderous proximity" when their pistols dropped into place they overlapped. As they fired simultaneously, both fell mortally wounded: "Numbers of citizens of St. Louis lined the banks of the river opposite the scene of action, and I will leave you to imagine the feelings of the friends of the combatants, who were only partially concealed from their view, when they heard the report of their pistols and saw persons from each party run down to the river for water—thus showing that both were wounded." The effect of each fire was delineated: "Major Biddle is shot through the abdomen, the ball lodging within. Mr. Pettis is shot through the side just below the chest, the ball passing entirely through his body." The congressman's agony was "not so great" as his opponent's, but he expired the next day, "sensible, resigned, tranquil, and conversing with friends to the last." Biddle "lingered" for another twenty-four hours, dying on the 29th.[27]

Considering Biddle's assault in Pettis's room and the deliberate manner in which he arranged for his own demise by setting terms sure to be lethal for both antagonists, a newspaper letter-writer seems remarkably generous to him:

> In him the country lost not only a gallant, but a gifted and most estimable man. Something must be allowed to the habits of certain districts of country, particularly in times of high party strife and dissension. If, therefore, the matter of his death was rash, but a small portion of blame was his; in *chivalry,* none; for his conduct was honorable and manly throughout. And even there, the scenes of his lamented end, hundreds and hundreds who shared his friendship, or partook of his open hospitality like the thousands who knew and admired him elsewhere, will ever be ready to bear witness to the greatest sternness of integrity, courage and purpose, he united in private intercourse, the gentleness and amiability of a child[!].[28]

Always averse to airing his private emotions in public, James made only one reference to this ludicrous tragedy, and that most muted. He told the secretary near the end of a long letter written early in 1832: "While in quarantine at Malta I received information of the death of my brother at St Louis. On that account I declined the civilities offered me at Malta, and on the same account sailed from Malta sooner than otherwise I should."[29]

Biddle's depression over his brother's senseless death must have been deepened by his own failing health, for he had been suffering from severe, if spasmodic, illnesses since the summer of 1830. At that time he had been fulfilling in Constantinople his most urgent assignment while commanding the Mediterranean Squadron, the signing of the first Turkish-American treaty.

The eastern Mediterranean had not been overlooked in the frantic quest for new markets to replace those, especially in the British West Indies, lost when the United States tore itself away from King George's empire. As early as 1783 American merchantmen began showing up at Smyrna in Turkish Asia Minor, and by 1820 their cargoes had risen to a value of a million dollars annually. The Philadelphia entrepreneur David Offley had established his company at that city in 1811. Washington appointed him U.S. consul in Smyrna in 1823 in gratitude for his staunch efforts to reduce the exorbitant tariffs slapped upon American imports by the sultan's officials.[30]

Trade with the Ottoman Empire, however, remained without treaty protection and was barred from Turkish ports on the Black Sea, as well as from all of southern Russia. Tentative diplomatic overtures passed early between the two governments. Rufus King, U.S. minister to Britain from 1796 to 1803, worked with the Turkish resident ambassador in London about the possibility of opening treaty relationships. He persuaded President John Adams to grant William Smith, his minister in Portugal, the necessary authority to write such an agreement. Prospects for success appeared bright during 1800 and 1801, when Captain William Bainbridge brought his frigate *George Washington* into Constantinople on the distasteful errand of carrying the dey of Algiers's mission to the sultan. But while there he was befriended by the "Capudan Pasha," the Turkish admiral and brother-in-law of the sultan. This influential official became intrigued by the possibility of such a commercial pact and urged that Smith come on from Lisbon. But Washington reneged, perhaps fearful of embroilment in the heightened war in the Mediterranean caused by Napoleon's invasion of Egypt. In 1820 Bainbridge returned to Turkey on the same errand but erred in trying to use the tsar's ambassador to Constantinople to assist him in starting negotiations. Since the Turks were justifiably suspicious of anything the Russians suggested, Bainbridge had to come home with empty hands.[31]

Over the next few years progress toward a Turkish-American treaty was hampered by both political and economic considerations. The outbreak of the Greek uprising for independence from the Ottoman Empire in 1821 found the Turks resentful about outspoken American sympathy for the rebels. Another roadblock was composed of what can be stated bluntly as the question of bribery. Even to start treaty negotiations every outstretched Turkish palm from the sultan's down several ranks of his bureaucracy, had to be caressed with gifts, each carefully stipulated for each official. They were no baubles; the total sums required could range from $20,000 to $30,000. No pretense was made in Constantinople that presents exchanged should be of reciprocal value. Commodore Rodgers, for example, during the mid-1820s gave the sultan "a diamond ring and a diamond snuffbox," and received in return "a Turkish pipe, a shawl, two silk gown patterns, two handerchiefs and a small box of sweetmeats." Such difficulties help to explain the inability of naval officers, aided by Offley, special envoys sent from Washington, and local hirelings, to bring the project into fruition. Rodgers failed from 1825 through 1827, as did Commodore William C. Crane in 1828 and 1829.[32]

Slowly, however, the two countries sidled closer together, for each saw distinct advantages in opening formal relations. The Turks liked the possibility of using a third Western power as a countervailant to the omnipresent British and Russians. The benefits anticipated by the United States were particularized in the State Department's instructions to Rodgers: the rights to trade in all Turkish ports under the most-favored-nation status (with tariffs no higher than those paid by any European nation) and to appoint consuls in any Ottoman port desired, and access into and exit from the Black Sea.[33]

But a sudden and imperative need for Turkish naval replacements was fundamental in bringing them across a conference table with Americans. The sultan's attempts to crush the Greek rebellion had aroused international condemnation. Britain and France reflected the strongly anti-Turkish sentiments of their people, while Russia was activated by its long-standing desire to break though the Ottoman barrier at Constantinople to reach the Mediterranean. During 1827 a combined fleet of the three powers was sent to the Ionian Sea to help pressure the Turks into granting Greek independence. On 20 October, while negotiations were under way at Navarino in the southern Peloponnesus between the admirals of the allied armada and a hundred-ship combined Turkish and Egyptian fleet, someone commenced firing. The allies practically annihilated the sultan's navy. According to the secretary of the Turkish admiral, he lost on that single day "3 ships of the line, 76–84 guns; 4 'double-decked frigates,' 64; 15 frigates, 48; 26 sloops, 18–24; 12 brigs, 19; and 5 'fire vessels.' " After Navarino the highest priority of the sultan's government was the restoration of its shattered fleet.[34]

Such was the situation when Biddle, at Mahon, read the president's proclamation that appointed him, Offley, and Charles Rhind "each of them, jointly and severally, commissioners" to "confer, treat, and negotiate with the Sublime Porte [the Turkish government] . . . with full power to conclude and sign a treaty." This was accompanied by a second public announcement. Secretary of State Martin Van Buren itemized the commissioners' two major responsibilities: to sign a commercial pact and to gain the U.S. freedom of movement into and out of the Black Sea. The third communication was through the medium of a "secret and confidential" letter. Jackson told Biddle, by way of Secretary of the Navy Branch, that $20,000 had been set aside for him with the American naval agent at Gibraltar "to defray the necessary expenses," a polite way of saying "Bribe anyone you have to."[35]

This correspondence was delivered to Biddle in the Mediterranean by Charles Rhind, a Scottish immigrant who had established commercial connections in the Middle East early in his career. He had labored well as Van Buren's henchman in New York city and state politics, for which he was rewarded by his appointment to join Biddle and Offley. He also carried with him two unofficial letters, both in the name of Van Buren. Actually they had been written by the attorney and politician James A. Hamilton, son of the noted Alexander and acting secretary of state for a month at the start of the new Jackson administration before Van Buren was able to assume personal direction of that department. Although he was employed as the U.S. district attorney for southern New York state, Hamilton continued to act as if he were still directing the nation's foreign policy.[36]

One missive warmly commended Rhind as "a Gentleman of probity, intelligence, and industry," although Biddle would soon entertain grave doubts as to the accuracy of the word "probity." In the other, marked "strictly private," Hamilton asserted that the failures of Bainbridge, Rodgers, Crane, and their mercantile and local aides had been their inability to realize how sizable must be expenditures to entice the Turks into serious treaty-making. Brushing aside Jackson's $20,000 as little more than a bagatelle, he unofficially authorized the commissioners to spend considerably more to attain their objective: "a sum of 100,000 dollars[,] nay even 50 per cent more[,] for I am entirely satisfied that the nation would deem such a price a low one for the very great advantages that would result to us from the trade." Furthermore, Rhind should go on to Constantinople alone to meet Turkish officials. Hamilton did not trouble to spell out the obvious—Rhind could travel relatively incognito, while Biddle, as a high-ranking naval officer, and Offley, well known in the eastern Mediterranean, would be sure to excite British suspicions that active treaty negotiations were about to begin. London's ambassador to Constantinople was doing whatever he could to toss sand in American diplomatic gears, for his government had no desire for another commercial rival in the Ottoman and Black Sea trade. Russia, on the other hand, hoping to stem British influence in Turkey, instructed Count Orlov, its ambassador, to help the Americans.[37]

On 9 December 1829 Biddle and Rhind sailed in the *Java,* arriving at Smyrna on the 26th. Offley came on board to tell them to their "mortification and surprise" that "it was perfectly well known in Smyrna that we were commissioners." Nonetheless, there seemed to be no alternative but to send Rhind ahead on his own, as planned. Biddle ordered the flagship back to Mahon while he and Offley settled back in Smyrna to wait with as much patience as they could muster for Rhind to conclude his business. After taking the discouraging time of thirty-two days to reach Constantinople their colleague was not able to start negotiations until 8 February and could not achieve his objectives until 7 May. He narrated his experiences in a long letter to the president—more than eleven thousand words filling seventeen closely printed pages. Throughout, he told Jackson, he kept assuring the Turks that he represented a country whose national character was ever "candid," "frank," "open," and "sincere, in all our relations with foreign powers."[38]

For the first few days Rhind had been thwarted by Mehmet Sait Pertew, the "Reis Effendi" (foreign minister), who insisted that the United States must pay somewhat stiffer tariffs, at least for the present, than the European countries. But largely through the work of Count Orlov, Pertew was replaced by the eventually more compliant Mohammed Hamid but even so, weeks dragged by while the negotiators nitpicked. The Turk kept insisting that Americans pay slightly higher tariffs than their European competitors, and that their ships could not be admitted into the Black Sea until a treaty had been signed. The American went on asserting that his nation "would never submit to the indignity of being received on a footing less than the highest powers of Europe or paying more duties than the most favored nation." By April Rhind was beginning to erode Hamid's resistance, and on 7 May the treaty was finally completed, with one copy in Turkish and the other in French.[39]

Rhind shot off word of his success and a partial copy of his agreement to Biddle and Offley. They were a bit miffed that their colleague had gone ahead so completely on his own, and the erudite Biddle complained about the "bad French" in the translation. Nonetheless, they realized the necessity of a swift termination of such endless negotiations. More important, they had to admit that in the nine public articles that Rhind had sent them their national aspirations by and large had been met. The United States gained most-favored-nation status; full rights of navigation past Constantinople into the Black Sea on equal terms with the European powers; the privilege of appointing consuls in any Turkish port it wished; the principle of extraterritorial jurisdiction ("extrality"), whereby Americans accused of crimes committed in Turkey would be tried by their own consular courts under American law; and a shipwreck agreement.[40]

Biddle and Offley left for the Ottoman capital on 10 May, taking two weeks for the difficult and unhealthful passage. A couple of rude shocks awaited them. Rhind airily admitted that he had dispensed as "presents" jeweled snuffboxes costing $9,000 to essential Turkish officials. This bit deeply into Biddle's $20,000 appropriation, and since he was responsible for it, he resented not being consulted. Much worse, Rhind waited until four days after their arrival—the very day that they were to sign the treaty—to inform them that a secret provision had been inserted into it. The sultan had demanded American assistance in replacing the navy that he had lost at Navarino. Rhind had agreed, and, since "timber is abundant and strong and . . . the building expenses are there light and small," that "whenever the Sublime Government shall order the building and construction in the dominion of America of whatever quantity of war vessels, such as two-deckers, frigates, corvettes [sloops], and brigs," this should be done under contractual arrangements between the two governments as to designs and models, costs, times required for construction, materials used, and the means by which they should be sent to Turkey. Offley took immediate exception to this unwelcome information. Biddle reacted even more negatively, declaring that the secret article went against his country's long-standing policy to "establish no relations other than commercial with the natives of Europe." He was so incensed that he reverted to the subject of the snuffboxes, avowing that had he known about them he would have stayed in Smyrna. At this juncture Rhind blew up, as Offley observed, with a "violence" of such "long duration [as] appears to me to have greatly exceeded the cause," breaking off personal relations with Biddle before raging out of the room. Even though Rhind accused the two others of coming to Constantinople only "to mar the Negotiations," Offley continued to act as middle man between his touchier colleagues. After defending his naval provision as bringing great credit to the United States with the sultan, Rhind further antagonized the other commissioners by asserting that he had every right to sign his treaty unilaterally and "forbade their further interference in the matter."[41]

Infuriating as Rhind's overbearing manner was, Biddle and Offley concluded that their mission would be totally aborted should they refuse to endorse the treaty. Furthermore, the Turks might well retaliate with the imposition of even higher tariffs, thereby slashing American exports. So they scrawled their names upon it, in Biddle's case "with great repugnance." But he and Offley gained a measure of revenge on their highhanded colleague by refusing him the honor of carrying home the treaty himself. When informed that the document would travel to America at the first opportunity in a warship, Rhind responded with "an explosion of the greatest passion," and petulantly refused to sign his own treaty.[42]

Biddle and Offley explained the controversy to Jackson: "As there was a difference of opinion between us respecting the secret article," and Rhind "disagrees with us as to the propriety of forwarding these documents by a public vessel of the United States . . . we, therefore, forward this communication without his signature." The two thankfully left Constantinople on 9 June, arrived in Smyrna as early as the 13th, departed almost immediately in the USS *Lexington,* and on 12 July came into Mahon, where the commodore boarded the frigate *Brandywine,* his new flagship. Before he left the sultan's capital Biddle had summed up his feelings about his experiences there as "heartily glad" that he was through with "this Turkish business."[43]

He and Offley had correctly forecast that their government would side with them against Rhind concerning the naval provision. Ex-president Adams noted that "Commodore Biddle and Mr. Offley had both warmly protested against this article . . . declaring that they signed the treaty with great reluctance. . . . It is remarkable that my instructions to Offley and Crane had expressly forbidden their assent to any article incompatible with the neutrality of the United States." Even Rhind himself backed away from his original position. Some months after the completion of his work he shrugged off his secret provision, saying that he had "actually forgot[ten]" about it as "being considered as of no importance in itself." The treaty came up for senatorial approval early in 1831, amid much discussion about the covert naval proviso. The nine public articles were accepted by an overwhelming majority, 42 Senators in favor and only 1 against. The secret section was dropped, however, with 17 pro and 27 con.[44]

David H. Finnie, in his scholarly, well-written *Pioneers East: The Early American Experience in the Middle East,* evaluates the efficacy of the three American negotiators in bringing into being the first Turkish-American treaty. He sides with Rhind, emphasizing that had Biddle and Offley been attending the protracted negotiations they would not have accepted the naval article, and without it the Turks would never have come to terms. Finnie does recognize that Rhind's personality could hardly have been more prickly: "Unable in any way to cooperate with others, humorless, vain, sensitive on imaginary points of honor, quick to anger and slow to forget, it was his confidence in his own handiwork and his desire to monopolize all the credit for success which almost succeeded in marring the negotiations." Yet he concludes that Rhind's willingness to compromise on the naval question by giving the Turks what proved to be a meaningless victory was essential in establishing the first formal diplomatic relations between Washington and Constantinople. Perhaps this judgment, however, is colored by hindsight. At the time Biddle and Offley were confronted with the secret article it was anything but a "meaningless victory" for the Sultan. As Adams accentuated, its adoption would have meant a significant departure from the non-alliance tradition so strongly held in nineteenth-century U.S. foreign policy. Had the treaty depended on its inclusion, it never would have been ratified by the Senate. If Finnie deservedly praises Rhind for his part in writing the treaty, Biddle and Offley were equally important by ensuring, through their vociferous objections, the omission of the secret provision.[45]

Despite his desire to be done with "this Turkish business," Biddle still found himself concerned with at least some of its spinoffs. The secretary of state wrote him that William B. Hodgson, a youthful linguistic expert, was coming to the Mediterranean with dispatches for the U.S. chargé d'affaires to the Ottoman Empire. He must see that the two were transported to Turkey for the exchange of treaty ratifications in one of his warships. The chargé was David Porter, for whom Biddle had been expressing his distaste for some two decades. Porter's Mexican purgatory had been shared by his son, David Dixon, who had survived a desperate battle with a stronger Spanish man-of-war, following which he was imprisoned for several months. By 1829, however, father and son had managed to come home. The elder commenced besieging the newly elected President Jackson for a public appointment, finally achieving his ends as the U.S. chargé to the Barbary states, to be stationed in Algiers. With miserable timing he arrived in the Mediterranean just as the French were taking over Algiers, so he had no place to reside. After conversing with Biddle about the general international situation during the summer of 1830, he waited at Mahon until receiving word of his new position at Constantinople.[46]

There is evidence that Biddle felt a twinge of remorse for his role in convicting Porter in 1825. With one exception, none of his letters after that date repeats the continual slurs and snide remarks about him that dotted his earlier correspondence. Furthermore, when David Dixon Porter, an acting midshipman, showed up in the Mediterranean, Biddle went out of his way to help him. The younger Porter, for whom his father could do no wrong, had never forgiven those who had found him guilty. Biddle and Captain Alexander Wadsworth, commanding David Dixon in the *Constellation,* both fell into that category. He deliberately tried Wadsworth's patience with behavior that just skirted the edge of outright insubordination, to such an extent that his captain "refused to endorse young Porter's warrant as midshipman." Upon appeal Biddle reversed the decision, "perhaps as a friendly gesture to Commodore Porter." Biddle nevertheless remained implacably hostile to the elder Porter. When he was later approached for a contribution to build a "memorial" for him he refused, stressing to the requester the "blemishes in the character" of his old enemy.[47]

Eventually the elder Porter managed to receive his appointment as chargé to Turkey. In Constantinople during October of 1831 he exchanged ratifications of the first Turkish-American treaty. Although Rhind's secret article had been thrown out by the Senate, on an unofficial basis the United States contributed significantly to the resurgence of the sultan's navy. Porter brought over to Turkey the eminent American naval architect Henry Eckford, who had built a Mexican frigate for him, and the latter worked well for his hosts until his unexpected death in 1832. He was succeeded by Foster Rhodes, his foreman, who turned out a variety of warships over the next several years for the grateful sultan.[48]

For his successful efforts in helping to open formal diplomatic relations with the Ottoman Empire, Biddle paid a high personal price. Throughout most of his last two years as squadron commander he remained in fragile health. The cause, he was sure, emanated from his overland passages back and forth between the Turkish coast and capital in the summer of 1830:

> All my present sickness had its origin in my journies last year between Con¹ and Smyrna. These journies were performed on *horse-back,* during a spate of hot weather thru a very open country, with accommodations for travelers so wretched and filthy that from choice or necessity more properly speaking I often slept in the open air. A severe attack of chills and fever was the consequence, and they kept me so debilitated . . . that I suffered accordingly. In my present condition in respect to health I am convinced, and so are the medical doctors[,] that another Mahon winter would finish me forever.[49]

Through scuttlebutt Levi Woodbury, the new secretary of the navy, learned that Biddle was ailing, and notified him that he could relinquish command whenever he wished. The commodore was feeling somewhat better by the time he heard from Woodbury, and reported that he could remain, although he would appreciate the appointment of a captain to relieve him of some of his paperwork. He did manage to flee Mahon's cold and rainy winter, spending those months in the more congenial climate of Syracuse. Yet his improvement was short-lived and he continued to languish in poor health for the remainder of his time overseas.[50]

Before and even during his spells of illness, the comfortably well-off and artistically inclined Biddle was able to indulge his penchant for purchasing articles abroad, most of them gifts for his family. As he moved from port to port during his first four months in the Mediterranean he spent $1,465 on such presents, among them a shawl for his sister-in-law Jane, perfumery ("otto of roses"), "knives and forks," and "flower pots to send home." His most impressive acquisition was a bust of George Washington that he commissioned from Horatio Greenough, the premier American sculptor, who was living in Florence. His order was a godsend for Greenough, who wrote the artist and inventor Samuel F. B. Morse, "The 'violent pains in my pocket' have been relieved by the very liberal advancement (voluntary) of Com. Biddle of the full bust of W[ashingto]n which I am making for him." Four copies of this work are known to have been made, of which two have disappeared. One is at the Museum of Fine Arts in Boston, and although Nathalia Wright, Greenough's biographer, says that this is the only survivor, she is wrong. Biddle brought his copy home and it is still at Andalusia.[51]

By the summer of 1832 Biddle, feeling no better, informed the secretary that he was unable to go on to Constantinople as instructed, but must return home as soon as possible. He was turning over the squadron to Commander Matthew C. Perry, described by the commodore as an "efficient, capable officer." But the department had already dispatched his replacement. Commodore Daniel T. Patterson came into Mahon in the frigate *United States* on 25 August and relieved Biddle the following day. Perry took his commander in the *Concord* to Marseilles on the first leg of his return journey. Perhaps Biddle was unconsciously trying to rival Caesar Augustus Rodney in accompanying luggage; he took with him forty-two cases of personal possessions and five cases of wine. With but a single servant he traveled overland to Paris and Le Havre, where he booked passage in the packet *Francis I*. After enduring an unpleasant passage, he notified the secretary that he had come into Philadelphia late in November.[52]

Although still preyed upon by a number of ailments, Biddle had to expend what strength he still possessed in binding up some loose ends of his Mediterranean duty. For two months he bickered over his expenses with the Treasury Department's fourth auditor, who handled financial matters for the navy, before a satisfactory agreement was reached. Another matter needing adjudication concerned the *Brandywine*'s "slush fund"—money earned from the sale of excess ship's stores to buy small luxuries for the crew. A few of the flagship's men complained about the alleged mismanagement of it by Biddle and its administrator, Lieutenant J. D. Williamson. The secretary asked Perry to investigate the matter and the commodore received a ringing endorsement: "The crew was in a high state of discipline and appears to be particularly happy and contented. The regulations established by Com. Biddle enforced the greatest attention to the health and comfort of the men, and I am satisfied there is not the slightest foundation for the charges. . . . I believe also that but a small portion ever

signed or knew anything about the . . . charges." Following the receipt of several explanatory letters from Williamson, the acting secretary of the navy completely exonerated Biddle: complaints about
any maladministration of the slush fund were "without foundation
or any just cause of grievance."[53]

Praise for Biddle as a Mediterranean commander had already come
from the *Java*'s people, who coupled their admiration for him with
similar sentiments about Commodore John Downes, who had previously commanded that frigate. They commended "Captains Biddle
and Downes for the kind treatment they had received" and declared
that the navy "would never lack seamen while it had commanders
like Biddle and Downes." Yet Biddle insisted that a proper gulf must
always exist between officers and men. When he had transferred his
broad pennant from the *Java* to the *Brandywine* his former crew subscribed one hundred dollars to buy him a sword. Commander Philip
F. Voorhees of the *John Adams* wrote the commodore asking him if
he would accept the gift. He received a cold rebuff: "I disapprove of
officers receiving presents from the crew."[54]

Biddle's command of the Mediterranean Squadron from 1829 to
1832 could be assessed as reasonably productive, featured by both
victories and defeats. In diplomacy his major contribution had been
with Turkey, and he had performed well for his country there. For
three decades the United States had worried about the lack of treaty
protection for its burgeoning commerce in the eastern Mediterranean.
By 1831 its trade had been secured by the agreement between Washington and Constantinople, and he had played no small role in that
happy conclusion. As always, he had kept a sharp eye out for the
welfare of his men, working apparently with some success in abating
their chronic drunkenness. Despite his personal predilections he had
allowed them some sexual release, even if he had to call upon professionals for that service. His major failure seems to have been with his
younger colleagues, who obviously composed a standing affront to
what he depicted as the proper behavior for "officers and gentlemen."
Yet similar complaints seem to have been made by all other Mediterranean commodores. On a personal level he had emerged scot-free
from the charges of anti-Jacksonian comments, even though they
reflected his true sentiments politically. And it should be kept in mind
that for the last portion of his command he had usually been in execrable health. If the Biddle of 1829 to 1832 was not the superb captain
of the *Ontario,* neither was he the irresolute and distrait commander
of the *Macedonian* or the harassed and hard-hearted shipmate of Rodney in the *Constellation.*

CHAPTER 9
RECOVERY, INACTIVE STATUS, "GOVERNOR" OF THE NAVAL ASYLUM, AND FINANCIAL EMBARRASSMENT, 1832–1845

The commodore had returned from the Mediterranean close to death. Ten months after his arrival Nicholas informed Daniel T. Patterson, James's successor as commander of the squadron there, that his brother's "state of weakness" had made his "situation so very critical" that throughout the winter and spring of 1833 he doubted whether he could survive. James was still "extremely debilitated & unable to rise from his bed," even though he had been taken to the New Jersey shore to escape Philadelphia's oppressive heat, apparently spending part of the summer at Long Branch and part at Cape May. Too ill during July to write himself, James dictated a letter to President Jackson successfully recommending a midshipman's commission for his nephew, James S. Biddle. In it he commented on his physical condition, saying, "Since my return home I have been confined to my bed almost without intermission."[1]

Most assuredly the commodore had not lacked medical aid, for he was attended by a galaxy of Pennsylvania's most prominent physicians: Doctors Nathaniel Chapman, the aptly named Philip G. Physick, Thomas Dillard, and Thomas Harris, who had served with James as ship's doctor in both the *Wasp* and the *Hornet* during the War of 1812. With the imprecise medical diagnoses of that time it is hard to pinpoint exactly what ailed him, except that it did not appear to be a direct consequence of the fevers from which he had suffered during his journeys to and from Constantinople three years before. Dr. Dillard mentioned that his patient was afflicted with "inflamed glands" upon which Dr. Physick had applied "caustic" with some success. His sinuses, however, had "suppurated" and "discharged a good deal of pus." For a "swelling in the left thigh" he had already taken "nineteen" salt baths and would have to take seven more. Jane Biddle wrote her husband that James's ulcers were healing so slowly that it might be another two months before he could walk, and told him to notify their cook at Andalusia that he could now eat "fish, lamb, beef, or poultry & for dessert custard, rice pudding, stewed apples or anything else of that simple kind." He should be given a room on the ground floor close to the bathroom.[2]

In addition to a natural concern over his own painfully slow recovery, James worried about his old mentor William Bainbridge, writing a naval friend that the latter was reportedly "very low." The rumor was true. For a long time Bainbridge had been in such torture from a variety of ailments that for relief he had turned to narcotics, to which he had become addicted well before his death on 27 July 1833. The news affected James so adversely that Nicholas concluded that it had seriously impaired his brother's recuperation.[3]

Gradually, very gradually, the commodore recovered. During the late winter of 1834 he told a naval colleague that his health "continues to improve, but to reestablish it completely & renovate my constitution" he would summer in Virginia. During that August Dr. Dillard congratulated James for his decision to move about that state from White Sulphur Springs to Warm Springs, and wished him "a gay season" with "agreeable women in abundance at all the places you may visit."[4]

Dillard's remark about women gives evidence that this reserved, publicity-shy, family-oriented lifelong bachelor was anything but a misogynist. His letters show that from beginning to end his appreciative eye was always on the alert for an attractive female. And in at least one instance he may have been deeply loved. To be sure, nineteenth-century letter writers tended to express themselves in ways that would today be considered overly effusive and even maudlin. Nonetheless, the correspondence of Mary Randolph Chapman, James's second cousin by marriage, portrays a woman who, during the first of their few years at least, was much disenchanted with her husband. Simultaneously she was becoming enamored of the commodore. Unfortunately his replies have not survived, but her letters from mid-1833 to the summer of 1836, contained in the Biddle Papers at Andalusia, lead to that conclusion.

On 20 May 1833 Mary became the wife of John Biddle Chapman, a son of Dr. Nathaniel Chapman, one of the commodore's recent physicians. Perhaps the precipitate nature of their meeting and marriage presaged their future troubles. Biddle told a naval friend: "All the Chapmans have gone to Richmond to John's wedding. He is to be married tomorrow to Miss Randolph, a young lady of great vivacity and spirit to whom he became engaged after a nine day's [*sic*] acquaintance and in defiance of a rival who had long courted the lady with the approbation of her family." To worsen matters, John had been "inclined to worship Ellen Roberts" but dropped his quest because "George Roberts would not suit him for a father in law."[5]

The couple settled in Richmond and all the evidence suggests that John was anything but an ideal husband, standing convicted from his own and his wife's testimony as unintelligent, erratic, drunken, and quarrelsome. Her first letter to Biddle in the Andalusia files, written from Elizabethtown, New Jersey, only nine weeks after her marriage, shows that her marital difficulties must have started almost at once. She dramatically differentiated her present situation "from *our* pleasant *travelling*," and went on:

> But as we cannot have all our wishes granted, I yield to imperious necessity, with as good a grace as I can assume, and as my imagination is a fertile one, I have the vanity to think that by not looking at him, at least at nothing but his feet, I can metamorphose John into you, but all my attempts are in vain, for to begin with the most striking difference, he is as stupid as an owl and will not open his lips, so I have abandoned them in despair, and have resorted to memory, for a true and vivid picture of you, which is, I assure you, a much better likeness than John's feet.[6]

Sometime near the beginning of 1834 they met somewhere. On a Sunday night in January Mary admitted that she had already tried on three occasions to write him during that day, "for considerably more than a week has elapsed since we parted, and I have not yet told you in writing what a bitter parting it was to me." All that she had to look forward to was the coming spring when she would impatiently wait "for the arrival of that first little crocus which is to reunite us." She tossed another barb at her husband: "John is at his old tricks again; it is now nearly twelve o'clock, and he has not yet returned from a dinner to which he went at four. Ah! Commodore, what am I to do with him?" Knowing Biddle's affection for his sister-in-law, Mary asked for reassurance that Jane Craig Biddle was not "*very* interesting, nor *very* delightful & I shall be, *comparatively* speaking, happy, for I tremble for your allegiance. See how disinterested I am— Good night, dear, dear Commodore. God bless you." Some weeks later she mourned that she had not heard from him but would instead "reply to the *delightful letter* I received in my dreams last night. Do you know that I not only dreamt you wrote to me, but that we actually met in a ball room?"[7]

During May of 1835 the Chapmans had a daughter, whom they

named Gabriella, with the commodore as godfather. While insisting that his cousin must come to the christening, John demonstrated an unattractive callousness by the way he reported his family's present condition: "Mary and the baby continue to get well and squall, but I hope by the time you see her she will have squalled a quantum suff [*sic*—sufficient amount?]." Mary did have postpartum difficulties, perhaps psychological, certainly physical. Her husband wrote that she continued to suffer from "great disability . . . and a most troublesome pain in her back." On the same day Mary jotted a note to Biddle, commiserating with him about the death of his brother-in-law Francis Hopkinson, the husband of Ann Biddle. "Mere words of condolence are always commonplace, therefore I offer you none, but when one person is as much attached to another as I am to you, a much less misfortune would cause the string of feeling to vibrate, & make a kind heart sorrowful at the unhappiness of another."[8]

A few months later she was expansive with her compliments. Responding to his letter, she wrote: "I love of all things to hear from you; next to talking to you the greatest pleasure I know is reading your letters; for independently of the sort of intuitive conversation I carry on with you through that channel, your style, in my opinion, very much resembles that of my favorite author . . . I mean Horace Walpole." Her husband was his usual undependable self: "John went down . . . on a frolic today, & as I think it very doubtful whether he will return tonight, I send you ses amitiés."[9]

During the spring of 1836 Chapman managed to involve himself in one of the sillier duels on record. He and James Wickham, an old friend, were drinking together at the "Barbacue [*sic*] Club" in Richmond, and Chapman took exception to the other's diatribes about some mutual acquaintances. John told the commodore that Wickham "was drunk, but not sufficiently to prevent his knowing perfectly well what he was about. I was only moderately excited by the good juleps of the Club." With two such explosive tosspots concerned, the result was predictable:

> As my forebearance [*sic*] continued, his determination to browbeat me augmented & at least when he shook his fists near my face I ordered him to stand off, calling him a scoundrel—which he dared me in the most violent manner to repeat—on my doing so he seized me by the jacket & I beat him quite severely. After some persons had come up he called me a pitiful coward 4 or 5 times which I resented [?] by cracking him over the head with my cane.

Wickham of course challenged, and Chapman begged Biddle to act as his second.[10]

About the same time the commodore heard from John Brock-enbrough, either a close friend or perhaps a relative of Mary, who summed up the ridiculous affair admirably: "Two young & mettle-some young friends quarrel literally about nothing, while under the influence of wine." He too asked Biddle to stand up with John, as "my poor Mary's life depends upon the issue of this affair & I see no means by which it can be avoided consistently with the punctilious feeling of Mr. C. on the subject." Brockenbrough had also learned that Wickham's second would be John Dandridge, "a mischievous whelp who had been engaged in one way or another in some twenty duels." He himself was required to stay with "my poor child in her weakened condition," so Biddle must do what he could to bring about a bloodless resolution to the encounter.[11]

The duel took place on 15 September somewhere in Washington. Since Biddle as a second shared with Dandridge the right to set the terms under which they fought, apparently he was instrumental in reducing the odds that anyone would die. They were to stand back to back ten paces apart, and await the call: "Gentlemen, are you ready?—wheel—fire." The necessity of having to turn and aim before shooting enhanced the opportunity for error somewhere along the line, and lessened considerably the likelihood that either might be hit. Certainly these stipulations were far different from those of the Bar-ron-Decatur encounter in 1820. Bainbridge, Decatur's second, and Captain Jesse D. Elliott, acting for Barron, placed their principals only eight paces (twenty-four feet) apart, facing each other, and already aiming. At the word to fire they had only to press the trigger. As might be expected, both were seriously wounded, in Decatur's case fatally.[12]

The more lenient terms of 15 September became quickly obvious. As both turned at the word, Chapman shot but missed and Wick-ham's gun misfired, after which Biddle and Dandridge brought about an immediate reconciliation. The press treated the occasion as prac-tically opera bouffe. A New York paper provided a description similar to most others:

Another duel: An affair of wickedness and folly according to the true meaning of words, but of "honor" in the language of the world, took place at Washington on the 15th instant. The parties were young Mr. Wickham of Richmond, and young Mr. Chapman of Philadelphia, son of the eminent physician who bears that honored name. John Dandridge, Esq., of Washington officiated as the second of Mr. Wickham, and Com-modore Biddle rendered the same friendly office to Mr. Chapman. The affair ended without damage to anybody's bones or skin. Mr. Chapman fired without hitting, and Mr. Wickham pulled without firing, his weapon making no more than a snap. The friends then interposed, and Mr. Chapman did what he might as well have done at first—make a satisfactory explanation.

A Boston periodical carried much the same account, ending with an ironic "Sic transit gloria mundi."[13]

Mary, who had been kept in the dark about the matter until it was over, poured out her apprehension and appreciation to Biddle: "I have received a terrible shock. I try to struggle with it, & to suppress my emotion, but my whole nervous system is deranged, & my heart is sick[,] very sick." She thanked the commodore for "the noble part you have taken in my dear husband's late affair, & from the bottom of my heart do I thank my God that he had such a friend to look to. . . . My heart seems to expand, to double its usual size, in love for you." This is the last of Mary's letters to the commodore, for she died of unnamed causes during the next year. It is not easy to evaluate her relationship with Biddle. Obviously she had no possible future of any sort with Biddle, considering the mores of early nineteenth-century America. Nor do we know to what extent, if any, the commodore had reciprocated her outpourings of love for him. Quite possibly he looked upon her effusions as no more than a venting to an older relative about a marriage that at least initially was working out poorly. Nonetheless, the mere fact that he kept her letters for the rest of his life may imply a degree of affection for her well beyond the avuncular. At any rate his association with Mary Randolph Chapman humanizes the otherwise aloof and patrician portrait of himself that Biddle chose to present to the outside world, both publicly and in most instances privately.[14]

During this period of recuperation and concern with the Chapmans, Biddle had little contact with the Navy Department, for he remained on inactive status. There were, however, occasional exchanges between him and the secretary. A few of them were instigated by a war scare with France over that nation's refusal to pay claims owed to Americans, some of which dated back to the 1790s. In 1831 Paris had agreed to provide 25 million francs for that purpose, but in 1834 the French Chamber of Deputies declined to appropriate the necessary funds and soon defaulted entirely. In his annual message to Congress during December of that year an infuriated President Jackson threatened to impound all French property in the country, following which Paris recalled its minister to Washington. Biddle, along with other naval officers, had reacted enthusiastically to Jackson's bellicosity, and asked Mahlon Dickerson, the current secretary of the navy, for command of the frigate *Constellation*. Recalling War of 1812 experiences, he recommended that "our public ships cruise singly" rather than in squadrons. Even though there was a temporary spate of departmental activity, Dickerson appears to have ignored Biddle's request, perhaps unconvinced that the commodore had sufficiently recovered his health. The crisis simmered throughout much of 1835 until cooler heads prevailed on both sides of the Atlantic, and after the French met their financial obligations, the matter ended.[15]

During the next spring Biddle managed to wriggle out of a potentially unpleasant assignment. Captain George C. Read, his close friend, was coming up before a court-martial and Biddle had been named as one of his judges. Read must have possessed some attractive personal qualities to merit such intimate association, not only with Biddle but with Bainbridge and others as well. Evidence, however, is plentiful that he was merciless to his underlings. William C. Murrell, who served as a sailor throughout Read's long cruise in the frigate *Columbia* during the late 1830s, characterized him as a "sea monster," afflicted with "pride, hatred, and revenge." This might be written off as the carping of a malcontent had not Murrell justified his epithets with such entries as: "This morning there were two hundred and forty lashes served out in a short period of time. The boatswain's mate afterwards acknowledged to me that his arm was never so fatigued before." Months later the sailor avowed that "I myself counted eight hundred and thirty seven lashes before breakfast."[16]

Read even bullied his officers. While commanding in the Mediterranean in 1834, he had ordered one of his midshipmen to climb the mainmast, apparently an unreasonable demand, for the man refused. Read then had him forcibly hoisted up it. This and other such behavior led to his court-martial in Baltimore during June of 1835. Dickerson harkened to Biddle's appeal that he be relieved of this duty because of the recent death of his brother-in-law Hopkinson and his doctors' insistence that he be free to travel to cooler climates during the approaching summer, or "it would be injurious to me." As he took no part in finding Read guilty of the charges and sentencing him to a one-year suspension, Biddle was able to retain him as a friend.[17]

When Congress passed an act allowing disability pensions for officers wounded while on active duty, the commodore demonstrated his personal integrity. He applied for one in 1837, calling to the department's attention that he had suffered neck and facial wounds in the *Hornet* while shattering the *Penguin* twenty-two years before. But he ended his letter with the honest admission, "I deem it proper to add that I now experience no disability from my wound." As he must have expected, his claim was quickly rejected.[18]

He was also peripherally concerned in the planning for the combined naval and scientific exploratory expedition to the Pacific and even Antarctica late in the decade. The government had concluded that such would not only bring great advantages to American whalers, sealers, and the national commerce generally, but would also enhance the country's scientific reputation throughout the international community. Its purpose had been grandiloquently stated: "Towards the United States Surveying and Exploring Expedition are turned the eyes of all Europe; and your successful labors . . . will . . . enlarge the bounds of knowledge, and diffuse the blessings of civilization and Christianity among nations now unknown." England, France, and Russia now had expeditions afloat, "and that nation which wins the prize by pushing her discoveries farthest . . . besides reaping the rich harvests on present and contingent commercial advantages, will acquire the proud distinction of Benefactor of the Human Race."[19]

Yet from the start the project was plagued by a host of difficulties concerning both supplies and personnel, while rivalries and animosities were rife among naval officers and scientists alike. Captain Thomas ap Catsby Jones, its first commander, eventually resigned in disgust over the apparently insoluble troubles facing him. Biddle, Isaac Hull, and James Aulick were appointed by Secretary Dickerson to find his replacement, but every top-ranking officer approached for the Pacific assignment turned it down. Finally its command devolved upon Charles Wilkes, a mere lieutenant. He, nonetheless, was able to hector and chivvy his ships around the world during a cruise of almost four years, and decades later volumes based upon the expedition were still being published. It is impossible to say whether Biddle participated in selecting Wilkes, but if he did his role must have been small. William Stanton, whose well-researched *Great United States Exploring Expedition of 1838–1842* is the most authoritative work on the subject, does not even mention him.[20]

By this time Biddle's career had been long and noteworthy enough to grant him the privilege of choosing his assignments, and for him there was no middle ground. He would either be on active duty at sea or would rusticate in the environs of Philadelphia, close to Nicholas and Jane at Andalusia. Repeatedly he refused to accept appointments to head navy yards, opportunities enticing to most other commodores because of the small percentage they could retain from governmental appropriations for their command. Only the Philadelphia Yard, which he had directed during 1825 and 1826, allowed him to live at home, so in 1835 he lost little time in turning down Secretary James Paulding's offer of the Washington Navy Yard.[21]

Three years later, however, Paulding came up with a request that he did not refuse. In a letter marked "Private," the secretary told him that "various complaints" had been referred to him "against the administration of the Naval Asylum at Philadelphia." He thought that it should be directed by "some officer of high rank in the Navy." Would he accept this position with the title of "Governor"? The commodore not only agreed to serve in that capacity but within three weeks was in residence, for he considered his appointment ideal for eventually promoting a coordinated system of education for the midshipmen.[22]

The idea of a Naval Asylum dated back to 1799, when Congress passed an act setting up a "hospital fund" to which sailors had to contribute twenty cents a month out of their pay. The matter lay dormant until the mid-1820s, when an estate near Philadelphia was bought to set up a refuge for incapacitated or superannuated mariners. A cornerstone for the main building was laid in 1827, when Bainbridge proclaimed floridly: "A home will be established for the faithful who has been worn out or maimed in fighting the battles of his country. A comfortable harbor will be secured where he may safely moor, and ride out the ebb of life free from cares and storms, by which he has previously been surrounded." The cost for land and construction was given as $212,600, and the first pensioners moved in during 1831.[23]

The asylum remained until 1838 under the direction of the Philadelphia Navy Yard's commandant, and its early administration was chaotic, with responsibilities shared by Commodore James Barron, immersed in the minutia of running his yard; Lieutenant James B. Cooper, in residence at the asylum; and Dr. Thomas Harris, in charge of the inmates' health, who apparently seldom attended to that duty. Cooper had written the rules under which a sailor could be admitted: "The pensioner must be so injured or infirm as to be unable to contribute materially to his own support to be eligible." Those who had served for twenty years and were somewhat less incapacitated by "old age or infirmities" were also admissible, provided that their difficulties had not been in consequence of "vice, intemperance, or other misconduct." Those whose naval careers had lasted fewer than twenty years were eligible only if they had "distinguished themselves by gallantry in action or some other highly meritorious conduct." They were provided with clothing and naval rations as well as lodging, but had to work on the grounds to the extent that they were able. By the time that Biddle opened his "naval school" at the asylum in 1839, "about one hundred" pensioners occupied one wing of the main building, well away from the raucous younger officer-students who inhabited the other.[24]

The main building was in the Greek revival style, so popular with

Americans during that era, but as one commentator sourly pointed out: "This fashion has fastened upon the country a great number of solid and costly buildings, utterly unsuited to our climate, as well as being unsightly, from the very lack of fitness." He described this edifice as being "constructed in greyish white marble, with a granite basement. It is 380 feet in length, and consists of a centre, with a high broad flight of marble steps, and imposing abutments, and a marble colonnade and pediment, in the bastard classic style which was the fashion at the period of its erection." A more recent Philadelphia guidebook is kinder: "The main building is three stories high, built of Pennsylvania marble and embellished with a handsome portico of eight Ionic pillars. The wings contain verandas on each story." There were four main structures and "numerous outbuildings," with "fine walks, flowers, and trees adorning the grounds."[25]

During his tenure Biddle improved the facilities. According to the letters he sent the Board of Navy Commissioners during his term of almost four years, his major contribution was in arborization. While Barron had been in charge a severe local shortage of wood in 1836 and 1837 resulted in the shearing of the trees that had sprinkled the lawns. Biddle asked for permission to plant new ones, "so that the comfort and appearance" of the place "would be greatly improved," and set to work right away. During the next summer he was visited by the Philadelphia diarist Sydney G. Fisher, who applauded the results: "Biddle has planted the grounds with trees, 20 or 30 feet high . . . and has been very successful, losing only three out of fifty. They were set out last autumn and are very flourishing."[26]

The commodore introduced some other improvements, such as building a new wharf on the Schuylkill River, bringing drinking water directly to the main building, putting in new bathrooms, and constructing a more adequate icehouse. Two seven-foot "colossal granite balls," brought from the Dardanelles and donated to the asylum by Mediterranean Squadron Commodore Jesse D. Elliott, where they remain today, made conversation-sparking additions. About the only defeat that the "Governor" suffered in regard to his surroundings concerned their roads and sidewalks. "During my first winter here, I could not walk on our pavements," he complained to the commissioners. Furthermore, the sidewalks were made of brick and are "a great disfigurement to our noble portico." Toward the end of his assignment he was still dissatisfied with the "unsightly" bricks and wished them replaced with "flagging."[27]

Biddle had been in residence at the asylum less than a year when its chief purpose was shifted from being primarily a haven for retired sailors to being a progenitor of the U.S. Naval Academy at Annapolis. Like Bainbridge and many other senior officers, Biddle had long worried about the dismal state of naval education, in stark contrast to that of the army, which had been served by the U.S. Military Academy at West Point since 1802. For more than forty years the national opinion that somehow an army was more democratic as well as more essential than an expensive and aristocratic navy thwarted efforts of the seagoing service to match West Point. Some kind of catch-as-catch-can instruction had always been given at navy yards and in warships, usually with the chaplain doubling as the teacher of mathematics and navigation. Bainbridge's "school" in the ship of the line *Independence* at Boston from 1815 to 1820 had been widely noticed and sometimes copied by his colleagues.[28]

Furthermore, by the 1820s high-ranking officers ashore were often given the task of conducting examinations upon which promotions partially depended. Midshipman Samuel F. Du Pont described one series of tests that he took in 1823 as having "nothing at all on seamanship, but all mathematics," as well as on astronomy, necessitating a knowledge of "the processions of the equinoxes." Off and on during his career Biddle had been an examiner, and while on inactive status during the mid-1830s had been "President of the Board of Examiners," which met annually at Baltimore.[29]

Aware that he had ample room to set up a naval school of some sort at the asylum, Biddle notified the secretary on 28 June 1839 as to that possibility. Paulding asked for specific information about "the number of Midshipmen" who "could be accommodated." He could take some "forty or fifty," Biddle replied, stressing that having them congregated in one location would bring about a "more effective control" over the students than when they were scattered among several ships or navy yards. About the same time, David McClure, a prominent Philadelphia mathematician and scientist who had just been turned down for an administrative position at Girard College in that city, applied similar pressure on the department so that he might be employed. He had been lauded in a private letter as "a man of propriety and worth who has the confidence of those who know him best," and whose "experience and habits of clear and careful thought" would make him an ideal professor of mathematics.[30]

By November of 1839 McClure had been duly appointed, and the asylum's Naval School opened with Biddle as the sole administrator and the professor as a one-man faculty. This situation remained the same until the following September, when Biddle recommended to the department that a French instructor be assigned to him. Paulding not only approved but increased the offering by naming Julius Meiers as the teacher of French and Spanish, who commenced his teaching the following October. His courses were not compulsory, however, and it is doubtful if many of such an unruly group of students availed themselves of these opportunities.[31]

Notices were posted that those midshipmen not on active duty at sea and entitled to promotion might apply to the school for admittance to a term of eight months. They would remain on full salary and rations, but twenty dollars per month would be deducted for their room and board. Seventeen midshipmen formed the first class, among them three future Civil War admirals: John L. Worden, who would captain the USS *Monitor* during her epic battle with CSS *Merrimack*; Stephen Decatur Trenchard, honored for his part in the capture of North Carolina's Fort Fisher early in 1865; and Reed Werden, who commanded the Union's East Gulf Squadron late in the war.[32]

They met for instruction, six days a week at first and then five, from nine o'clock until two. Before it was transferred to more salubrious quarters on the ground floor, their classroom was in the dank cellar, described by student Daniel Ammen, another admiral-to-be, as "furnished with two blackboards and a large rough table in the centre of the room," chairs, and "an old sextant, to explain its adjustments, and no [other] apparatus whatever." Practical "seamanship" was stressed, but the students were also responsible for: "Bowditch's *Navigator*, Playfair's *Euclid* (Books 1, 2, 3, 4, and 6), McClure's *Spherics*, Spanish or French language texts, mental and moral philosophy, and Bourdon's *Algebra*." Each June Biddle would receive from the secretary word for word the same letter as to the correct procedures for the school's final examinations. He would preside over a board of examiners consisting of himself and four other senior officers. McClure would ask the questions, but could take no part in the final grading. The midshipmen were to be tested on "seamanship, navigation, and mathematics." The comments of the language instructor would be taken into consideration. A "general report" about each student's "moral and general character" must be appended to the academic results.[33]

The class of 1839–1940, the school's first, upon graduation thanked McClure for his efforts in their behalf, expressing their "strong attachment" for the "moral rectitude which you have so impartially shown during our professional career with you." Evidently this "strong attachment" went only so far. On one occasion they marched, two by two, into the classroom, all smoking "Turkish cherry stem pipes a yard long—take seats and continue to smoke during the recitation. McClure, who could not bear tobacco smoke . . . tried to defend himself against it, but the more he pleaded the more they puffed, until finally the lesson had to be brought to a speedy end."[34]

Biddle, who always aspired toward a taut ship, found his wards no easier to handle than did McClure. These were no teenaged fledglings, but men in their twenties who had been in the navy long enough both afloat and ashore to pick up more sophisticated habits. Their accommodations at the asylum were not such as to induce any kind of a resigned acceptance of restraints. Ammen described their rooms on the first floor of the north wing as "about eight feet square, with partitions eight feet high, separating them from the hall . . . and from each other. . . . The furniture consisted of a small iron bedstead and washstand, a small wooden wardrobe, and whatever we chose to supply in mirrors, carpets, and bedding." The only heat came from two coal-burning stoves in the corridor. Ammen cannot be doubted when he glumly summed up their situation: "We did not live luxuriously." The atmosphere of the rooms, dismal enough at best, was considerably worsened by Biddle's ill-advised act "for the better protection of the young Gentlemen" of placing thick iron bars on all the windows. When he went on to equip the outside doors with heavy bolts, the midshipmen began referring to their quarters as "the Brig," a part of what they jeeringly called "Biddle's Nursery."[35]

At first the Governor had anticipated no trouble in controlling his fractious "inmates." Shortly after the first classes had met he described his rules to the secretary. No midshipman could leave the grounds without permission "after sun-down," cardplaying was forbidden, and lights must be out at 9:00 P.M. Months later he was still deluding himself that all he had to do about discipline was to treat his wards "kindly but firmly. I shall not permit them to frequent the city too much, permitting them however to attend the Evening parties to which they may be invited. The wholesome medium between too much restriction, and too much liberty can I think be attained without great difficulty."[36]

The deportment of his first class, in relation to that of its successors, gave Biddle some hope that he might inch across his disciplinary tightrope. To be sure, there were portents of things to come. Midshipman R. M. Bowland smashed a hole in the wall of his room. Paulding told the Governor to have the damages repaired at Bowland's expense, and "to inform the young Gentlemen at the Asylum that should further complaints of such conduct be made, they will either be dismissed from the Service or forthwith ordered to sea, as it is not the intention of the Department to afford them the means of improvement . . . unless they make a better use of the opportunities afforded them."[37]

A round-robin letter signed by nineteen students gave Biddle notice that his efforts to control them might soon be futile. They emphasized that they had been ordered to attend the school by the secretary on "leave of absence pay." Hence, they "would respectfully inquire if they were still to consider themselves 'under orders,' or at liberty to avail themselves of the privileges hitherto enjoyed by them 'on leave of absence pay.' " While forwarding this to Paulding, Biddle noted: "The purpose of their letter to me is that they should be privileged at their pleasure to disregard your orders and my regulations— in other words that the school might be broken up." The secretary briskly attended to the issue by reminding the students that they were indeed "under orders," and that "the Government was under no obligation to educate them, but has voluntarily not only done this but offered them the strongest inducements to make the most of the means afforded them by honors and rewards to those who were successful." The resentful midshipmen retaliated for this rebuff by growing "mustachios" en masse, a facial adornment forbidden by navy regulations, but shaved them off when assured that their examiners would unquestionably turn such an obvious example of defiance against them in their final grades.[38]

Still, Biddle's entering class was tractable enough for Paulding to comment that according to their commander's first annual report on the progress of his wards, "the conduct of the Midshipmen has been exemplary." They even showered Biddle with encomiums after their graduation:

> The Gentlemen recently attached to this Institution, on leaving, take this opportunity of expressing their high sense of gratitude and respect to Commodore Biddle for his many acts of kindness towards them during the period they were under his command; and entertain the hope that at some future time, they may again have the honor of serving under so distinguished a Commander.[39]

That was about that insofar as "exemplary conduct" was concerned. Evidently discipline at the Asylum School deteriorated considerably during Biddle's final two years there. Commencing late in 1840 his letters to the department are rife with descriptions of his underlings' obnoxious behavior. During that November Paulding was informed that seventeen midshipmen had left the grounds without permission to take up lodgings in town, and that they should be "severely punished." Yet three weeks later all had returned, apparently without penalty. Although Midshipman S. D. Lavallette had been absent without leave for twelve days during March of 1841, he managed to retain his commission, but John V. Hixon resigned from the service shortly after remaining away for only three days. Later the same year Paulding learned that six students were refusing to pay for their room and board at the school, although the records do not say what happened to them. Biddle apparently rid himself so quickly of one Joshua Parker, for being too immature as well as "continually drunk and quarrelsome," that his name does not appear in Hammersly's *List of Officers of the Navy of the United States.*[40]

There is reason to conclude that these individual cases were only the tip of the iceberg. One historian of the Naval Academy summarily concludes: "As for discipline, there was practically none; nor was there anyone specifically charged with its enforcement. The youngsters studied or idled as suited their whims." Efforts to keep the midshipmen on the grounds at night or to control their behavior when they stayed home proved equally fruitless. The students provided themselves with keys to unlock the outside doors, and they soon spotted a place in the wall where the palings were weak enough to be easily pulled aside to allow an exit. Others were more brazen, carrying scaling ladders to clamber over the fence. Once outside they would find a carriage waiting to take them to Jones' Hotel (which they called "Jimmy Haggerty's Ark"), the Philadelphia headquarters for naval personnel. At least one midshipman suffered from his samplings of the city's fleshpots. Biddle told the secretary that Isaac S. K. You had become "venereal."[41]

Those who chose to stay in their rooms flouted Biddle's rules with impunity. The student who was "officer of the day" would yell "Lights out" at nine o'clock, see them extinguished, report to the Governor that all was in order, and return to announce "Lights Up," upon which "the demijohns and cards were taken out of their hiding places for a regular . . . carousal." The same source reports that "the good natured Governor Biddle, finding that the Midshipmen could not be confined by bolts and bars, abandoned the attempt and contented himself with a semblance of authority by forbidding them to trample upon his flower beds." Surely when Biddle wrote the secretary early in his tenure that he realized that "the strictness, indispensable aboard ship, is unsuitable here," he could not have foreseen how thoroughly he would lose control. His later correspondence on the subject of discipline is silent, but he must have looked for an opportunity to rid himself of a situation so compromising to his sense of order and decorum.[42]

Two catastrophes early in 1842 worked to facilitate his exit. In February smallpox broke out at the asylum. No midshipmen died, although Ammen and several others were afflicted. They were promptly vaccinated, but the "vaccine did not take effect but the small-pox did." The chaplain and a few pensioners perished before the disease had run its course, and the asylum was closed for two months. During

April McClure suddenly died of pneumonia. With his school shut down and the better part of his faculty gone, Biddle could notify the department that he was ready to leave the asylum, and he was succeeded by his predecessor, Commodore James Barron. During the latter's term forty-three pensioners lauded both governors for their "good offices," but perhaps it is significant that Biddle's last two classes failed to duplicate the kudos bestowed upon him by his first.[43]

Despite the gloomy finale of his school at the asylum, Biddle's contribution to naval education had been highly significant. To be sure, another forged an even more vital link in the long-delayed and meandering journey toward really effective training for officers in the service. William Chauvenet, an ambitious and able twenty-year-old mathematician and astronomer, replaced McClure, and with Barron's wholehearted cooperation, proceeded to turn the short-lived and somewhat chaotic educational system at the asylum into a permanent and far more intensely professional institution. He expanded the faculty, provided additional space for instruction, inaugurated new courses, and insisted upon a grade for each student in each day's recitation. When naval higher education moved on to new quarters at Annapolis in 1845, Chauvenet had been the prime mover in that accomplishment. Nonetheless, "Biddle's Nursery" had been a crucial step along the way. He could justifiably be designated as one of the important fathers of the U.S. Naval Academy.[44]

The commodore's next residence was at the Philadelphia Club, founded in 1834, of which he had been a charter member. It had been closely modeled on the famous London citadels of masculine separatism, and, as one archivist puts it, "The original membership reads like a who's who of the Philadelphia elite." Biddle lived there for the next three years, serving as its president before leaving on his last cruise in 1845. But what pleasure he may have felt in that capacity was overshadowed by a crisis that threatened his life-style.[45]

For the first time he found himself in financial difficulty. He had participated in some of Nicholas's disastrous investments and when his brother's formerly sizable estate dwindled, much of his more modest fortune went along with it. Although there are many references to the family's fiscal troubles in the papers at Andalusia, the commodore made only one direct mention of it in a note to his brother John during 1842: "Three years ago I was independent of my Navy pay. At present I have scarce [ly] any other income than my pay."[46]

The rise and fall of Nicholas Biddle could have been a subject for Sophocles or Euripides. As one Philadelphia social historian described him: "He makes a fine figure, the darling of the gods . . . at the very height of his glory . . . [when] his hubris is struck down by the lightning of Nemesis." The day after Nicholas died Sydney G. Fisher devoted five pages to him in the printed edition of his Diary: "There have been few instances of a more complete reversal of fortune. . . . How he was followed, praised, worshipped, can scarcely be conceived by those who did not witness the scene in which he was an actor." But this was soon replaced by "remorse, the stings of conscience, the sense of degradation, loss of reputation, of position, of the respect and esteem of society, of the regard of friends, of hope for the future and regret for the past."[47]

The precocity of Nicholas had given expectations of a brilliant career, which in general had not been disappointed. By the time he was fifteen he had completed two advanced courses, the first at the University of Pennsylvania and the second for a degree at the College of New Jersey (Princeton). He then performed diplomatic duties and traveled widely in Europe, where he made a lifelong friend of James Monroe. Editorial work on the *Port Folio* and the journals of Lewis and Clark followed. After the war he ran for both the Senate and House of Representatives as a liberal Democratic-Republican, but was defeated by Federalists. He was briefly considered for secretary of the navy, but his brother's lofty status in that service was probably a deterrent. He found his lasting niche when President Monroe appointed him one of the five directors of the Second Bank of the United States, and became its president in 1823. He continued to direct that establishment under one name or another for the next sixteen years.[48]

The Second Bank, chartered in 1816 for twenty years, was largely privately owned, since the American government could buy only 20 percent of its stock. But as it was the depository for federal funds it was the de facto U.S. treasury, and as such promptly became the nation's financial behemoth. So much political as well as economic power gravitated to the bank as to excite the envy and hatred of politicos in Washington and banking interests in New York. Capitalists on the make throughout the country, particularly in the South and West, who wanted inflation, easy credit, and a lack of centralized financial control resented the bank's more conservative fiscal policies. Biddle, as president, became the natural target of such sentiments.[49]

Nicholas, who had initially supported Jackson as a fellow nationalist, for years brushed aside evidence of the new president's unswerving opposition to his bank, a stand Jackson certainly based more on emotionalism than economics. In June of 1832 Biddle prematurely pushed through Congress a bill rechartering it, four years before it was legally necessary. A month later Jackson's veto killed the measure, for in neither house could the bank's supporters provide the two-thirds necessary to override. Biddle's metamorphosis into a rabid anti-Jacksonian was swift. He described the veto message as having "all the fury of a chained panther biting the bars of his cage. It is really a manifesto of anarchy, such as Marat or Robespierre might have issued to the mob." A few years later he wrote that the "executive power of the government has been wielded by a mere gang of banditti. . . . On the face of the earth there is not a more profligate crew."[50]

An even more devastating blow followed in 1833, when the government stripped Biddle's institution of all federal money, depositing those funds in many "pet banks" around the country. This effectively ended Biddle's control over the national economy and forced him to change from a primarily public banker to a private one. In 1836 his former Bank of the United States went out of existence, being rechartered as "The United States Bank of Pennsylvania" by the legislature of that state. During that same year the victory of the deflationary Locofoco wing of the Jacksonians in the Specie Circular, requiring payment in gold or silver rather than paper money for the purchase of public lands, abruptly shifted the American mood from optimism to pessimism, and headed the country into the great cyclical depression that started in 1837. This, coupled with Biddle's unwise concentration upon agricultural investments in the Southwest, amid allegations of fraud and peculation amounting to $400,000 (charges eventually dropped), portented the Bank's imminent demise; it went bankrupt in 1841.[51]

When Nicholas Biddle, yielding to the entreaties of his wife and children, decided to retire to Andalusia in 1839 he was still an extremely wealthy man, but adverse winds were already buffeting him. Diarist Sydney Fisher commented on that occasion that the "embarrassment of business, the distress of the community, the dangerous position of the banks, all are attributed to him, and he is called a knave & a fool by the very men who a year ago joined the chorus of servile adulation." By 1841, "he was avoided in society, his name was mentioned with contempt & execration, many cut him & refused to speak to him in the street." Biddle's fortune, estimated at its height at "almost a million dollars at the time of his retirement, had evaporated in the general collapse of security and land prices and in the payment of debts."[52]

Nevertheless he was able to keep Andalusia, his magnificent estate located on the bank of the Delaware River some thirteen miles north of Philadelphia, which he had come into through his marriage in 1811 to Jane Margaret Craig. John Craig, her father, had bought that tract and either extensively remodeled an older house or built a new one during 1797 and 1798, with further improvements made as he was dying in 1807. His widow, with whom Biddle was on the most affectionate terms, continued to reside there until her death in 1814, following which her son-in-law and daughter came into full possession of the estate. John Craig had prospered through trade with Spain and the Spanish colonial empire; possibly that explains why it was called Andalusia, although one Philadelphia history attributes the name to James Biddle. He was in southern Spain when he received a letter posing the question of what the estate should be called, and replied, "Why not name the place 'Andalusia,' where I now am?" This story is not mentioned in Nicholas B. Wainwright's authoritative pamphlet on that estate, and may well be apocryphal.[53]

Although he retained a town house in Philadelphia for many years, Nicholas, Jane, and their six children spent more and more time at their summer place, settling there permanently shortly after his retirement in 1839. Andalusia, described in a sales brochure as "the most beautiful and valuable" estate "in the vicinity of Philadelphia," was composed of 113.5 acres. Its most arresting feature was the main house, set well back from the river across extensive lawns with gardens and many trees. Its renovation in 1807 and 1808 had been under the direction of the noted American architect Benjamin H. Latrobe, the chief designer of the Capitol in Washington, while Nicholas's remodeling in 1835 and 1836 had been overseen by Thomas U. Walter, who "extended the wings and the dome of the Capitol from 1851 to 1865." By 1836 the mansion stood much as it does today, "a brick and stone structure, fifty-five feet wide and seventy-three feet deep, with two wings extending forty feet on each side," behind massive white Doric pillars "framing the front and side porches." It was filled with furniture in the French Empire style. Several other edifices dotted the grounds, among them a second sizable mansion and a two-story billiard and card house, the upper story in the form of a Greek temple. Eight servants served the eight members of the Biddle family.[54]

In its heyday Andalusia was practically an agricultural research station. Nicholas was president of the Philadelphia Society for the Promotion of Agriculture. He was also a leading enoculturalist, preserving his grapevines against the local winters in extensive hothouses; a breeder of racehorses; a speculator in mulberry trees, upon which silkworms feed; and the founder of the first American Guernsey herd, in 1842.[55]

A host of luminaries, foreign as well as American, cherished their invitations to visit the famous estate. Nicholas was a host par excellence, "gracious, smiling, easy, gentlemanlylike, a little condescending. . . . His conversation was ready, fluent, elegant & witty." But gradually much of this became the maintenance of a brave public façade while disaster approached. Fisher was sure that his plunge from demigod to devil contributed to his death, for as his income dwindled his health worsened. He suffered psychologically as well as physically: "He felt, it is said . . . more keenly than the abuse and indignation of the multitude, the desertion of those "whom he has most significantly befriended, who owed him their wealth or their escape from ruin & those who had been his most ready tools and flatterers, [who] were loudest in their condemnation when the tide turned."[56]

James, the favorite relative of his brother and sister-in-law, spent more and more days away from the Philadelphia Club at Andalusia, where his quarters were always ready for him, and where he could anticipate a delighted greeting from his two little nieces, who called him "Uncle Commodore." Although it remains unstated in his correspondence, he could only have felt infinite sadness as he watched time run out on what had been his brother's scintillating career. He helped him pass his more healthy hours playing chess and billiards with him. The death of Nicholas was presaged by a severe attack of influenza in June 1843 and his "desperate" illness in October, and by the turn of the new year he was bedridden with "bronchitis accompanied by dropsy." Apparently it was a heart attack that finally killed him on 27 February, for he had been taking digitalis four times a day.[57]

It remained for the commodore, as a trustee of the estate, to restore if he could his brother's shattered reputation and to assuage his sister-in-law's grief. During September of 1844 he wrote to the recently retired secretary of state, Daniel Webster, to whom Nicholas had paid a steady "retainer" so that as senator he would keep up the fight for the Second Bank. James told him that in his final extremity his brother had "repeatedly expressed" to Dr. Nathaniel Chapman, his attending physician, the hope that "his life might be spared until he could finish a vindication of his administration of the Bank." Would Webster write Chapman for information concerning this request and would he publish the answer? On the back of the letter Webster jotted, "What is to be done with this?" He must have concluded "nothing," for the matter seems to have ended there.[58]

The commodore, worried about Jane Biddle's continued desolation over her husband's death and fearing for her health, agreed with her doctor's advice that she should make a long-anticipated and long-delayed European trip. After writing to Secretary of the Navy John Y. Mason asking for permission to accompany her abroad and promising to return quickly, he was given a six-month furlough. But he soon decided that his "duty to see her safe across the Atlantic" was unnecessary, since she would be taking along some of her grownup children, so she sailed without him. This seemingly trivial decision had wide repercussions on Biddle's life. Had he gone to Europe he would not have been available for his culminating experience—his round-the-world cruise from 1845 to 1848.[59]

CHAPTER 10
THE CRUISE OF THE *COLUMBUS:* SUCCESSES IN CHINA, 1845–1846

The grand finale of Biddle's professional life commenced in March of 1845 with a letter from the well-known American historian George Bancroft, serving as secretary of the navy. Biddle was offered command of the ship of the line *Columbus* and the *Vincennes,* a sloop later selected. He was to make a voyage to "the China seas" in order that ratifications could be exchanged of the Treaty of Wanghia, the first Sino-American formal diplomatic agreement, signed the year before. Bancroft made any potential refusal more difficult by his compliments: he wanted this crucial assignment to go to "an officer, distinguished alike for rank and for experience in the public service. I know of no one, to whom I could entrust . . . that command more willingly than to yourself." Biddle read this letter and replied to it on the spot, accepting it as he always did when duty afloat was in prospect, "with pleasure."[1]

From the sidelines Commander Samuel F. Du Pont watched this development with disdain. Ever since the cruise of the *Congress* in 1823, when he had concluded that Biddle's treatment of the ailing Caesar Augustus Rodney had been reprehensible, he had developed an antipathy toward his superior that deepened over the years. He wrote a naval friend that Bancroft's offer of the *Columbus* had been given "in a very flattering letter which tickled the little man abundantly." Warming to his subject, a few weeks later Du Pont told another confidant that the assignment had been the result of a deal between Biddle and Bancroft. Apparently in gratitude for the blandishments contained in the secretary's letter—"which completely turned his head"—Biddle supported the department in its efforts to cashier an unnamed lieutenant, going so far as to bring the subject before

President Polk himself. Du Pont summarized his former commander as "that selfish little viper Commodore Biddle."[2]

Despite whatever reptilian characteristics he possessed, Biddle assumed his new duties quickly and effectively. Within three days of his acceptance he notified the department that he would shortly leave Philadelphia for New York, as he wished to sail as soon as possible in order to get "a favorable monsoon wind." During May, Bancroft sent him some general instructions. He must maintain a taut discipline, while devoting himself to character building and education for the midshipmen, with the usual emphasis upon mathematics. He should collect information from all sites that he might visit in the Far East as to the possibilities of increasing American trade with China, while in the process of "enlarging the bounds of our knowledge" about the mysterious empire.[3]

These mundane chores, however, were secondary to Biddle's chief responsibility: to carry to the environs of Canton Alexander H. Everett, the newly appointed commissioner to China, who would exchange treaty ratifications and set up an American legation and perhaps some new consulates there. Everett, the brother of the famous orator Edward Everett, was a Harvard graduate and had been secretary to John Quincy Adams while the latter was minister to Russia from 1809 to 1811, and shortly thereafter U.S. chargé d'affaires in the Netherlands and then minister to Spain. During the 1830s he had been a capable editor of the influential periodical the *North American Review*. His career then soured: through financial difficulties; his political switch from Whig to Democrat, much resented in his native state of Massachusetts; and the onset of the malady that in July of 1847 would kill him.[4]

Biddle's flagship, the *Columbus* (74 guns but mounting 80), launched in 1819, was one of the first U.S. ships of the line, displacing 2,480 tons, with a complement of 780. The naval architect George Doughty had described her somewhat ambiguously as handling well but "a poor sea boat," but Biddle would find that she could outsail a supposedly faster sloop, the 22-gun, 700-ton *Vincennes,* carrying 190 officers and men. She was the outstanding American globe trotter, having by the time she joined Biddle's little squadron twice circumnavigated the world (first in 1828–29 and then 1835–36), before serving as Lieutenant Charles Wilkes's flagship during his long Pacific explorations from 1838 to 1842. As commodore, Biddle had under him Captain Thomas W. Wyman in command of the *Columbus*'s operations, with Commander Thomas O. Selfridge, personally selected by Biddle, as her executive officer. Captain Hiram Paulding commanded the *Vincennes,* and the fleet surgeon was Dr. Benajah Tichnor, an experienced naval physician who had held a similar position with Biddle in the *Macedonian*'s fever-ridden cruise in the Caribbean during 1822. Tichnor's unpublished Journal provides a wealth of information about the voyage of the *Columbus*.[5]

The commodore's preparations to equip and supply a ship of the line and a sloop must have been exemplary. On 4 June, within ten weeks of his appointment, both vessels were able to clear New York harbor. Shortly before he left, Biddle wrote a sad little note to his brother: "We are all embarked and ready for sea. . . . I expect to be absent about two years and a half. I had supposed that my last cruise (to the Mediterranean) was *the* last."[6]

As they were weighing anchor the commodore asked Tichnor if the health of his people would permit a nonstop cruise to China. The doctor replied that such in all probability would be far too long a stretch at sea, giving ample opportunity for food to spoil, water to run low, and disease to strike. Biddle decided he would put into Rio de Janeiro; later Batavia (Djarkarta) in the Dutch East Indies (Indonesia) would also break the voyage. A rapid passage was mandatory, for according to the terms of the Treaty of Wanghia, Chinese and American ratifications must be exchanged by very early January of 1846. Therefore when Biddle discovered within a month that the slower *Vincennes* was delaying the *Columbus,* he ordered the two ships to part, with each sailing singly for a later rendezvous in the Dutch East Indies.[7]

By that time routine had been established in the flagship and the men were daily "inspected," "instructed," or "exercised at the great guns." On long naval voyages discipline was seldom a problem during the first few weeks, for the spice of novelty could still be tasted. Inevitably, however, as one monotonous day succeeded another tempers began to fray and trouble would start. The officers were by no means immune. Various letters in Biddle's private papers give evidence of his frequent spats with Wyman and Paulding, who also quarreled between themselves. The commodore groused that his midshipmen tended to be "insubordinate" and "disrespectful." As for the crew, the first "All hands to witness punishment" rang out early in July when a sailor endured twelve lashes for "striking a sentry on duty," a remarkably lenient sentence under the circumstances.[8]

The *Columbus* stood off Rio's harbor on the 29th and moored the next day. In general the fifty-six-day, 6,061.5-mile cruise to Brazil had been relatively uneventful. Some idea of seagoing appetites can be gleaned from the flagship's log—en route the men had consumed 193 barrels of beef, 72 barrels of pork, and 29,933 pounds of bread, as well as a variety of other foodstuffs. Their appreciation of Rio's

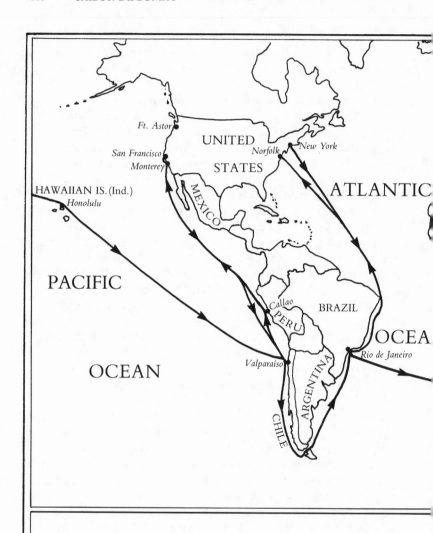

THE CRUISE OF THE *COLUMBUS*,

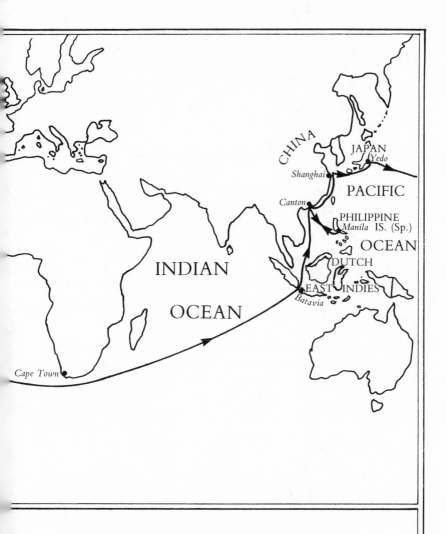

CHINA

JAPAN
Yedo

Shanghai

PACIFIC

Canton

PHILIPPINE
Manila IS. (Sp.)

OCEAN

DUTCH

INDIAN

EAST INDIES
Batavia

OCEAN

Cape Town

4 JUNE 1846–9 MARCH 1848:
68,949.6 MILES

magnificent mountain-rimmed scenery was probably not enhanced when they realized that except for the officers and a handful of others, no one would be granted shore leave. The proprietors of Brazilian fleshpots, saloons, and gambling houses may have wept as they contemplated the profits they would have earned from several hundred sex-starved, thirsty, and comparatively affluent American sailors.[9]

A welcome sight greeted Biddle as he entered the port. Three U.S. warships of the East India Squadron had arrived there from China shortly before, enabling him to absorb the latest information from that part of the world. Commodore Foxhall A. Parker (the same officer whom Biddle had reported for drunkenness some years before) had met in China Caleb Cushing, the American commissioner, who had negotiated the Treaty of Wanghia. As that diplomat had made other plans for his return journey, the squadron left for home without him. Biddle would have liked to have conversed with him, but shrugging off his disappointment, he spent much of the next few weeks conferring with U.S. consul Henry A. Wise about the situation in lower South America. As a gesture of American friendship, the commodore agreed to take six Brazilian naval cadets with him for the remainder of the cruise.[10]

Biddle's major concern while sojourning at Rio was how to handle the matter of Everett's faltering health. The commissioner had suffered continually from seasickness during the southern passage, and while trying to afford him some relief, Tichnor had discovered that his patient had for some time been ailing from a chronic disease; the doctor never revealed precisely the nature of his illness. Once ashore Everett continued to languish. As early as 5 August he told Biddle that he could not continue on his mission, and three days later authorized him to proceed to Canton as acting commissioner with full powers to complete the treaty ratifications, as well as setting up new U.S. diplomatic posts in China. Yet he kept on wavering for another week, his wife arguing that he was well enough to fulfill his obligations personally. He finally gave up on the 16th after Tichnor and two other consulting physicians told him point-blank that it was most unlikely that he could survive so long and arduous a voyage. His equivocation cost him a comfortable passage on the USS *Brandywine,* for Parker had sailed in his flagship on the 10th. A week later the Everetts had to embark for home on a merchantman.[11]

The *Columbus* cleared the harbor on the same day for the Rio-Batavia run. It began auspiciously for the crew but soon turned ugly, according to the reminiscenses of Charles Nordhoff, who had signed on as one of the flagship's "boys" at the age of fifteen. He had great respect for Biddle, writing that "thanks to the kind foresight of the

Commodore" the men enjoyed "fresh beef and vegetables" for several days before returning to their tasteless sea rations. On the other hand, even though no sailors had been permitted ashore at Rio, some had been able to smuggle liquor aboard from boat vendors for immediate consumption. The ship had barely cleared Rio's headlands when punishment started. Twenty-five men received from four to twelve lashes apiece for drunkenness, attempted desertion, "insubordinate language," "sleeping on lookout," and a somewhat nebulous delinquency called "skulking."[12]

As commodore, Biddle had little to do with such matters. Captain Wyman was in charge of discipline and seems to have been a proponent of the theory, "When in doubt, reach for the cat." Before arriving in the Dutch East Indies, either the flagship's log or her Record of Punishment noted floggings on 21 and 26 August; 2, 3, 5, 9, 11, 15, 17, 20, 22, 25, and 27 September; and 6, 10, and 13 October. James E. Valle, in his study entitled *Rocks and Shoals: Order and Discipline in the Old Navy 1800–1860,* uses the "Record of Punishments on board the U.S. Ship *Columbus"* between 26 August and 25 September for his endpapers. The first time young Nordhoff was compelled to watch a man being lashed he was so sickened by the sight that when thereafter called to witness punishment he always kept his eyes closed.[13]

The fifty-nine-day passage from Brazil to Java must have seemed interminable to all concerned. Despite being almost swamped by a gigantic storm off the southwestern tip of Africa, a gale so unrelenting that Nordhoff devoted eight printed pages to it, the *Columbus* was too pressed for time to stop at Cape Town. She finally entered the Straits of Sunda between Sumatra and Java on 14 October, having traversed 16,820 miles from New York. Two weeks later Captain Paulding brought in the *Vincennes* to reunite the squadron. Once again no shore privileges were permitted, although the men on the flagship were sheltered as much as possible from Java's oppressive humidity by shortening their work load and stretching awnings across the deck against the penetrating sun, while providing "free ventilation" for them at night.[14]

Following his usual detail of replenishing depleted stores, over 24 and 25 October Biddle journeyed to Batavia, where he called upon the Dutch governor-general. According to Tichnor he was "very pleased" with his reception, dining sumptuously and escaping the worst of the heat by spending the night at the Dutchman's hillside retreat outside the capital. His host even provided a steam frigate to tow the *Columbus* into open water, enabling her to sail in consort with the *Vincennes* at the end of the month, although by mid-November the flagship was dashing on alone, arriving in China well before the sloop.[15]

A few days out, Biddle called Wyman, Selfridge, Tichnor, and some other high-ranking officers to his cabin, where he brought out a wooden box containing two copies of the Treaty of Wanghia, one in English and the other in Chinese. No effort had been spared to impress the Chinese with the importance which the United States ascribed to the ratification ceremonies. Each copy was encased within a five-inch silver box, enclosed within a velvet covering with a silver chain attached. The reason for the meeting was ostensibly to ascertain how much time remained for the commodore before ratifications must be exchanged, although it is hard to comprehend why this essential information was delayed until the last leg of the voyage. The third of January was the final day possible, so the utmost speed was mandatory.[16]

On Christmas Day the *Columbus* anchored off Lintin Island, the old rendezvous for British vessels carrying opium from India and China, located north of a line between Hong Kong and Macao, and south of the Bogue Forts guarding the mouth of the Pearl River leading north to Canton. Biddle dashed up to the city to busy himself with his diplomatic responsibilities, while over the next weeks the flagship moved back and forth, up toward Canton, back to Lintin, and finally to Portuguese Macao, having been joined by the *Vincennes* on 6 January. There they remained, while the squadron's people were employed in repairing the rigging, scraping iron work, carpentering, caulking, and taking on supplies of food and water. They relished "a large quantity of potatoes and some Chinese beef" that the commodore had sent to them, but once again everyone was kept on board, except for officers and supply parties. For over two months boredom was inescapable; Nordhoff called it "very dull, monotonous."[17]

Biddle, always meticulously well prepared for every overseas assignment, had read everything that he could about the recent history of China. The British quest to open formal diplomatic relations with China had been endlessly frustrated until 1839 when the emperor sent Commissioner Lin Tse-tsü to Canton with orders to smash the primarily British-controlled opium traffic, which was draining his treasury, corrupting his officials, and debauching his people. Lin seized twenty two thousand "chests" (each containing 133⅓ pounds of opium) and burned them. This was the excuse for which London had been waiting, and the spark that lit the Opium War which, despite its name, was fought more to compel the Celestial Empire to negotiate on equal terms than to collect damages for destroyed narcotics. Military and naval operations were waged in a desultory fashion from

1840 to 1842. The Royal Navy had no trouble in converting China's outclassed war junks into kindling, Canton had to be ransomed to save itself from city-leveling bombardment, and the British were able to proceed north along the coast, picking off port after port, until they moved up the Yangtze River toward the central metropolis of Nanking. At this juncture the emperor finally recognized the inevitable and sent envoys to sign the Treaty of Nanking in 1842. This British-dictated agreement, along with further concessions wrested by them at the Bogue Forts the following year, set the pattern for Western domination of China for much of the next century.

In these treaties the British received Hong Kong Island as a colony and a $21 million indemnity, to be paid in installments. More important to the other European nations and the United States, Britons were permitted to reside for purposes of trade in the five cities taken by the Royal Navy during the war: Canton, Amoy, Foochow, Ningpo, and Shanghai. The former system, by which foreigners could do business only in Canton and then through the single agency of the "co-hong" (an amalgamation of a dozen or so Chinese mercantile houses awarded imperial licenses for that purpose) was abolished, and commerce in the five "treaty ports" opened to Englishmen. A low Chinese tariff was imposed so that British exports could not be barred by protective measures. Two additional concessions were especially important to the United States and the others: the principle of most-favored-nation status, and extraterritorial jurisdiction, or "extrality" (Britons accused of committing crimes in China were not subject to that draconian legal code but would be tried in their own consular courts under British law).

London having led the way, some other Western capitals jostled one another in following its footsteps. Washington dispatched Commodore Lawrence Kearney to Canton, where he came just before the Treaty of Nanking had been signed. He met with the imperial commissioner sent by Peking to negotiate with the British, urging successfully that the United States be granted any benefits won by the British under the most-favored-nation policy. Some have thought that Kearney had accomplished a brilliant diplomatic tour de force by gaining this concession, but the Chinese had already decided that such be done, for it was their long-standing procedure to treat all "barbarians" equally.[18]

To ensure that Kearney's informal understanding could be enforced, it had to be put in treaty form. Caleb Cushing, a former congressman from Massachusetts, was selected by President John Tyler to accomplish that end. He sailed in a new steam frigate, the USS *Missouri,* to Gibraltar and was supposed to travel from there to India on his own to meet Commodore Foxhall Parker's East India Squadron at Bombay. But he was so delayed when the *Missouri* was gutted by fire at the Rock that he had to proceed all the way by commercial transportation, coming into Macao during February of 1844. After an irksome and lengthy Chinese-induced delay, during which Cushing implied that he might have to call upon the guns of Parker's men-of-war for backing, he eventually triumphed. On 3 July he was able to sign with Kearney's Chinese negotiator the Treaty of Wanghia, the first Sino-American pact, named after a temple in a village on the border between Macao and China. Americans were awarded the same residential and commercial advantages that the British had won by war, and an even more favorable extrality provision. Copies of the agreement were sent to Washington where, according to Mrs. Tyler, "The Chinese Treaty is accomplished—Hurrah! . . . I thought the President would go off in an ecstasy a minute ago with the pleasant news." Alexander H. Everett's assignment to exchange ratifications of the treaty quickly followed, but his illness compelled Biddle to complete the task.[19]

The day after Christmas, after only a few hours in Canton, Biddle told his Chinese counterpart that he was prepared to effectuate the Treaty of Wanghia as soon as possible, perhaps aboard the *Columbus,* but anywhere ashore should that be preferable. His fellow negotiator was Ch'i-ying (called "Ke-ying," "Ki-ying," and other variations in contemporary English language documents), the same man who had signed understandings with the British, Kearney, and Cushing. He was a veteran bureaucrat, who had served since 1815 in more than a score of increasingly prominent positions and finally became governor-general of Kwangtung and Kwangsi Provinces, "with full power to conduct foreign affairs at the five [treaty] ports."[20]

Ch'i-ying had to walk a tightrope between two extremes: his own recognition that in no way could China withstand the technological superiority of Western arms and his equal awareness that the acute xenophobia of his superiors in Peking would not let them understand that simple fact. His middle course was to recommend to the emperor the continuation of a program to keep the status quo by sowing discord among the Western nations so that British aggression could be neutralized: "If we wish to cause the English barbarians to have some respect and awe, we must first not lose the confidence of the French and American barbarians." Should they be "won over," it might check "the proud and domineering spirit" of the British.[21]

Activated by such sentiments, Ch'i-ying answered Biddle's letter cordially, suggesting that they conclude their business at the Bogue Forts on 7 January 1846, "the lucky 10th day of the 12th month" in

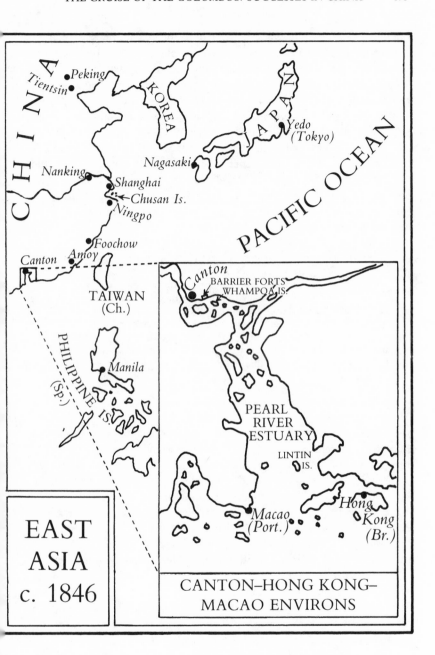

EAST
ASIA
c. 1846

CANTON–HONG KONG–
MACAO ENVIRONS

the Chinese calendar. This was too late to meet Wanghia's stipulation that ratifications must be exchanged by eighteen months after the signing of the treaty. His counterproposal recommended that they wind up their affairs at once, perhaps at the "American consular house" outside Canton. This message was carried by Dr. Peter Parker, medical missionary, legation interpreter, and sometime diplomat, who persuaded the governor-general that haste was essential.[22]

On 31 December Biddle, Parker, Paul S. Forbes, the U.S. consul in Canton, and a few others met Ch'i-ying and his entourage on the outskirts of the city at the palatial home of P'an Shih-ch'eng, a close ally of the governor-general and a former co-hong merchant well known to Americans. The leading missionary publication in China described the ceremonies:

> After the parties had passed the compliments usual when meeting on such occasions, the two copies of the treaty . . . were brought forward, and the Chinese carefully compared one with the other, and, being found to agree, they were exchanged in due form, commodore Biddle, acting commissioner, presenting that from Washington to Kiying, who in his turn delivered that from Peking, the whole party standing. Four copies of a certificate of the exchange, previously prepared in Chinese and English, were then signed and sealed by the commissioners, and two retained by the one, and two by the other. This closed the business of the day. . . . At about 5:00 the party sat down to dinner—one of those rich entertainments that have been so often described by visitors. It was in good style, every way suited to the occasion.[23]

Biddle dispatched his copies to Washington by a homeward-bound American merchant, while Ch'i-ying reported to the emperor that throughout the proceedings the American's "manner and language were very respectful and obedient." He went on to write what he knew the court wished to hear, rather than what had actually occurred. Even though the Treaty of Wanghia carried the clear stipulation that renegotiations could eventually take place, Ch'i-ying said that Biddle was "extremely grateful for Heavenly favor and would maintain the treaty forever without any other proposals whatever."[24]

Dr. Tichnor's Journal makes a quite inexplicable reference to Biddle's behavior during the next week. On 5 January a group of about forty assembled, composed of the commodore, all his officers with him in Canton, Dr. Parker, Forbes, and some other Americans, among them Warren Delano, Jr., and his wife. Delano (Franklin Delano Roosevelt was his descendant) had been U.S. vice-consul in Canton and was a member of the influential American firm of Russell and Company, prominent in the opium trade. They boarded two ferries and went some two miles east from the foreign settlement to "Houqua's" house, situated on the north bank of the Pearl River. Their host, described by the doctor as "hospitable and polite," met them at his dock. Almost at once he asked Biddle how old he was, a most courteous question, for the Chinese venerated longevity. The commodore may have lost a little face, for at not quite sixty-three he was two years the younger.[25]

At five o'clock all sat down to a dinner that featured over twenty courses, including such delicacies as bird's nest soup and bêche de mer (sea slug), the latter famous for rejuvenating fading masculine sexual prowess. Tichnor found some of the offerings "very palatable, while others were far-otherwise, which I have never thought of since without disgust." His last phrase is understandable, for somehow he erroneously concluded that "castor oil [!]" had been used "in the preparation of many of the dishes, to which we attributed the disagreeable effects which most of us experienced the next day." After the first series of courses, the doctor claims, Biddle "made a sudden and unexpected move in behalf of the lady who sat next to him [Mrs. Delano], which caused a great deal of surprise & embarrassment to our host and his friends; and which would have left very unfavorable impressions on their minds respecting American manners if an explanation had not been offered by Dr. Parker. This had the desired effect." Since it is inconceivable that the commodore's lunge could have had any amatory intentions, it is difficult to discern what Tichnor is talking about, and why it should have mortified those Americans present. The most logical explanation would seem to be that Mrs. Delano was choking on a piece of food or had spilled something on her dress, but why should Biddle's hastening to her aid have cast a baleful light on the national etiquette? Sometimes Tichnor's reticence, especially in a private diary, is frustrating.[26]

Biddle was soon occupied with matterrs more essential than dinner-table diversions. On 7 January he met at Dr. Parker's house P'an Shih-ch'eng, his host for the ratification ceremonies, who asked for his advice on how to handle a controversy with the British concerning the dispensation of Chinese money for the recovery of Chinese territory. The Treaty of Nanking had called for the loser's $21 million indemnity to be paid in installments. Until then the British were permitted to occupy Kulangsu Island in Amoy harbor and, of greater importance strategically, the Chusan Islands, close to Ningpo, south of Shanghai, and near the mouth of the Yangtze River. P'an explained that the British had been informed that the final payment would be provided on schedule, but Sir John F. Davis, governor of Hong Kong and superintendent of British trade in China, was changing the rules of the game. He had written Ch'i-ying that those islands would be retained until China promised not to cede them to a third power, the rumor being prevelent that France had an eye out for the Chusans. As P'an put it, "The great inducement to China to pay the large sum . . . was the recovery of Chinese territory occupied by the British." What did the American think should be done?[27]

Biddle's latent anglophobia was immediately alerted. He told P'an that Davis's demand was "offensive both to China and the other foreign powers"; it was "a mere pretext for retaining possession of the islands." He recommended that China pay the final installment and then "require . . . that in fulfillment of the Treaty the British forces should be withdrawn." The evidence shows that Biddle was overly apprehensive about London's supposedly dark designs against China's territorial integrity. After receiving the total indemnity the British evacuated Kulangsu during the next March, and the Chusans in April.[28]

During the same conversation the commodore seized the opportunity to advise Ch'i-ying, through P'an, about three other matters that were worrying him. He thought that it would be much to China's advantage to permit Western envoys to reside in Peking, where they could watch one another. Then, should one diplomat be observed planning some kind of "aggrandizement or conquest against China," the others could so inform their respective governments. They, in turn, could exert concerted pressure against the offender to desist. P'an evidently kept silent. Biddle went on to say that China must lose any war with a European power unless it adopted modern military technology for its armed forces, to which P'an agreed. But the Chinese had no comment on Biddle's third point. This referred to a Sino-British confrontation that was just coming to a head; he recommended that the Chinese defy Davis's demand that the walled city of Canton be thrown open to his people, for that privilege was "not tenable under the Treaty of Nanking."[29]

The "Canton city-entry" problem arose from differing interpretations of the Nanking agreement. The British argued that ever since 1842 they had possessed that right, while the Chinese averred that their copy of the treaty made clear that foreigners would be allowed into the suburbs alone, not into the Chinese walled city itself. Suddenly, however, Ch'i-ying yielded to Davis's pressure, and announced that Britons would be admitted; apparently he was trying to curry favor with Davis to make him more amenable to clearing out of the coastal islands. But instantly he paid for his blatant ignoring of Cantonese public opinion. All classes in the city seem to have exploded simultaneously with denunciations of the governor-general and his underlings. One placard read:

During two centuries our Great Pure Dynasty has enjoyed the happiness of universal peace, and the barbarians, residing quietly at Canton, have never thought of entering the city. . . . Yet our shameless and avaricious officers have [been] persuaded to issue their vile proclamations allowing them to enter! . . . If the rebel barbarians enter the city, we, with united heart and strength, setting at naught official dignity, will grasp and decapitate them; we will rise and act the part of a righteous people.[30]

Violence soon followed. The combined office and residence of the local "prefect," one of Ch'i-ying's party when the ratifications of Wanghia had been exchanged, was sacked, and from 15 through 17 January turmoil raged throughout Canton. The governor-general promptly caved in, announcing on the 16th that no imminent admission of the British was being contemplated. He belatedly told the court that he had done this so as not "to thwart the feelings of the people, and perversely comply with the request of the foreigners."[31]

Biddle observed these events with displeasure, telling the State Department that this unnecessary Sino-British conflict would endanger all Western citizens and their property. He forthwith sent forty of her one hundred Marines from the *Columbus,* moored off the Bogue Forts, to the *Vincennes,* and ordered the sloop to Whampoa Island, twelve miles east of Canton, where the Pearl River's deep water ended. There she joined the frigates *Pluto* and *Vestal,* sent by Davis from Hong Kong. The commodore forecast that this display of Anglo-American power, coupled with Ch'i-ying's conciliatory second pronouncement, would defuse the crisis at Canton. He was right, although the relief was only temporary. To be sure, the governor-general and Davis compromised on the issue during the next April: the British would drop for the time being the Canton city-entry matter in return for a Chinese pledge that the Chusans would not be given to the French or anyone else. But the question kept recurring spasmodically until Canton was occupied in 1858 by the British and French during the Arrow War.[32]

During February Biddle found himself involved in a civil case arising from the Treaty of Wanghia's extrality provision. A Chinese merchant called Shing-ho had come into possession of a tea certificate issued by Wetmore and Company, an American concern. When Shing-ho presented the certificate for payment, senior partner Samuel Wetmore seized the document and kept it. The makeshift nature of commercial law in China was such that Shing-ho could think of no alternative other than to turn his case over to Biddle. Early that month the commodore held a meeting at Parker's house with the doctor, Consul Forbes, Shing-ho, and Wetmore in attendance. The American refused point-blank to surrender the certificate. He then fought back, using language surprisingly discourteous to an East India Squadron commodore and acting U.S. commissioner in China. He told Biddle that not only was he poorly informed about the issues concerned but also that it was no business of his at all:

> We are disposed to deny your right to decide in this matter officially, whether under any general powers, or under any specific authority that may have been delegated to you; for we know of no sufficient powers that can be in your possession in accordance with the Constitution of the United States. . . . However much we value your opinion on general subjects, we will not respect your decision in this case.[33]

Perhaps in part to punish Wetmore for his intransigeance, Biddle, after discussion with Parker and Forbes, lined up solidly on the side of Shing-ho, calling the American's retention of the certificate a clear instance of "injustice and impropriety," and referred the case to Ch'i-ying. He explained his actions to the secretary of state, writing: "Had I refused or neglected to bring it before the public officers of the two nations, the American name and credit in this country would have been affected most injudiciously." Wetmore now had to reconsider his situation. It was one thing to defy a fellow American, no matter how lofty his status, who had no direct control over him; it was quite another to challenge Ch'i-ying and his magistrates. After all, he was in the China trade, and the enmity of local authorities might well ruin him. On the 25th he resolved the controversy by complying with Shing-ho's demands. It should be noted that Biddle's desire to improve Sino-American relations had been strong enough to impel him to support a Chinese against one of his own nationals.[34]

The commodore had passed January and February binding up these loose strings, while living at the American Legation, a building that he had selected in the Foreign Settlement, just southwest of Canton's city walls. On 1 March he moved back to his cabin in the *Columbus,* and left for Macao a week later. There on the 10th he invited a large group of Americans and Britons to his flagship. According to Tichnor, he served "a cold collation of which we partook with keen appetites. Toasts were dealt out in great profusion." In one a Scotsman heaped praise upon his host for his wartime achievements and "equal commendation to his proceedings as a diplomatist." He concluded by hoping that Biddle "might never come into any other collision with the subjects of Great Britain other than a *collision* of *peace.*" The commodore's return toast forecast that war between the two countries would be avoided, but if not, Britain's early advantage would be lost toward the end of the struggle and the United States would be able to annex Canada.[35]

Prospective Anglo-American hostility was very much on Biddle's mind during the spring and early summer of 1846. Even though the Mexican War would break out in May, the earlier correspondence of American naval officers and politicians tended to concentrate upon the quarrel between Washington and London. This conflict had loomed as a definite possibility since December of 1845, when President James K. Polk had given the British the required twelve-month notice abrogating the Anglo-American Convention of 1818, which had opened the huge Oregon Country for settlement by the nationals of both countries. But it had put into abeyance the question of who possessed the area. Originally extended for ten years, it had been continued on an annual basis until 1845. Biddle, in view of his own contribution to American claims by his occupation of the Columbia River's mouth in 1818, would follow the Oregon news with a special rapt attention.

Somewhere in China the commodore received secret instructions from the Navy Department telling him that the crisis with Britain had worsened and there seemed little hope for a bloodless conclusion. He was to proceed as soon as possible to the Oregon coast in order to inspire American settlers there "with a confidence of their nation's protection." The secretary trusted Biddle's "judgment and ability" to handle this crucial matter with "the utmost responsible discretion." Not until he reached Hawaii the next September would he learn that Mexico, not Great Britain, would be his enemy.[36]

His two ships then sailed from Macao to Hong Kong, where Biddle remained for nine days, being most hospitably regaled by British civilians, as well as military and naval personnel. Meanwhile he had sent off the *Columbus* to the Philippines, "as it may be advantageous to the public interest to show the ship." No sooner had she arrived on her six-day visit at Manila than the dreaded "Asiatic cholera" struck, and before it had abated, thirty-three had become infected, of whom twelve died before she returned to China on 11 April.[37]

During this interim, Biddle sailed back to Canton in the *Vincennes* to meet Ch'i-ying for the last time prior to departing for the other Chinese treaty ports. His main purposes were to say good-by and to report that Alexander H. Everett, temporarily in better health, was soon coming from the United States as commissioner. But he took the opportunity to bring forth two of the three recommendations that he had made to P'an Shih-ch'eng. In many instances repeating word for word the same language that he had used the previous January, he urged that Western representatives be welcomed to live in Peking so that each would be on hand to check any anti-Chinese machinations by any other. Ch'i-ying demurred, stressing that although the British had been trying to gain this concession for many years, it could not be granted, for it was "contrary to the laws of the empire." The commodore halfheartedly tried again, but gave up after perceiving that he could make no headway. He once more advised that China must revitalize its armed forces along Western lines for its own protection; perhaps the governor-general tacitly agreed.[38]

By mid-April Biddle had accomplished what he wished in Canton. Appointing Dr. Parker chargé d'affaires until the arrival of Everett as commissioner (who came to China in October and died there the following July), he prepared to embark on his survey of the more northerly ports open to American trade and residence. The *Columbus* and *Vincennes* weighed anchor on the 18th but for five straight weeks the "Easterly monsoon and bad weather" permitted them to proceed no farther than the few score miles to Hong Kong. The same contrary winds continued to hamper them so much that they did not creep into Amoy harbor until 5 June. Little commercial activity could be seen in that sizable port, although it would soon boom as a center of the coolie trade, carrying tens of thousands of Chinese into semi-slavery abroad, especially in Cuba and Peru. Midshipman Daniel Ammen of the *Vincennes* went ashore and described it as "a city of perhaps half a million inhabitants; the streets are narrow . . . and the smells are peculiar and I thought distinctive in every street, and all of them vile."[39]

Ch'i-ying had sent notes to local authorities along the commodore's itinerary saying that "Chief Biddle of the United States was en route to investigate trade conditions in the five ports and everyone should treat him courteously." This suggestion was dutifully obeyed. At each stop Biddle would wine and dine city dignitaries aboard the *Columbus,* and a day or two later his guests would reciprocate ashore. At Amoy he welcomed to his flagship "a party of mandarins," headed by the taotai (superintendent of customs, among many other duties, although Tichnor called him a "Brig. Gen'l of the Army"). The doctor noticed that he drank "sparingly" of Biddle's champagne. Such apparently was not the case when the commodore and some of his officers were given a return banquet the next day. Tichnor sniffed that they came back to the ship at 7:00 P.M., giving "very convincing proof that their entertainer was not a member of a Temperance Society."[40]

Part of Biddle's job in China was to establish permanent U.S. consulates in as many of the four treaty ports north of Canton as he saw fit. Conditions in three of them, however, obviated any effort in that direction. Commerce at Amoy was insignificant, and the only Americans living there were a missionary or two, so he made no consular appointment; not until 1849 was one in residence there. His next destination was supposed to be Foochow, a couple of hundred miles up the coast, but Biddle found that its water depth was insufficient for the *Columbus,* and he decided to bypass the city entirely. Moreover, he knew that an American merchantman had looked into its harbor during 1844 and found that literally no business was being conducted with foreigners; the first U.S. diplomat to be situated there was in 1852. On the 18th he sailed both warships to the nearby Chusan Islands. Remaining there only overnight, he left the flagship for the shallower-drafted *Vincennes* and set out for Shanghai, where he arrived on the 20th.[41]

That city was the northernmost of the five treaty ports and the one closest to China's centers of power. Since its opening to foreigners it had rapidly prospered and was beginning to rival Hong Kong as the leading Western entrepôt in the Far East. During November of 1844 Henry G. Wolcott of Russell and Company had moved to Shanghai, thriving "with the Japanese at Nagasaki in an indirect cotton trade." He had traveled to Canton to meet Biddle, asking for and receiving an appointment as Shanghai's resident U.S. consul.[42]

Wolcott met the commodore as he came in and begged for his help in a local Anglo-American tiff. When he had opened his house and consulate there he had elevated the American flag, an act that evoked a protest from George Balfour, the British consul. The Englishman, pointing out that Wolcott's buildings were located in the "British Concession" just to the north of the Chinese walled city, claimed that by agreement with Shanghai's authorities he was to "govern" all foreigners there. Much to Wolcott's resentment, he had to lower his flag. Biddle sprang to his countryman's defense, writing Balfour: "I am of the opinion that it is the right and duty of Mr. Wolcott to display the flag of his nation within his own premises at all times that he may see fit, and I so informed him." Curtis J. Henson, in his doctoral dissertation entitled "The United States Navy and China, 1839–1861," appears to think that Biddle's intervention was decisive: "The old sailor was obviously delighted in scoring off his former adversaries of the War of 1812." Not so; the commodore tallied nothing in this instance, for the American flag was not raised over the U.S. Consulate in Shanghai until the autumn of 1848.[43]

Although as usual he had little to say about his personal discomfort, Biddle must have welcomed the opportunity to leave for Ningpo on the 24th. According to Ammen, Shanghai had been unbearable: "we had for several days and nights the hottest weather I have any recollection of—over one hundred degrees throughout the nights." Biddle found the consular situation at Ningpo especially confusing.

Wolcott had been offered a vice-consulship there in 1844 by Canton Consul Forbes, his fellow employee in the ubiquitous Russell and Company, and had visited the city briefly before leaving the post vacant in favor of the considerably more important and lucrative position at Shanghai. Biddle discovered that trade at Ningpo was almost totally moribund, so he sensibly made no consular appointment, and that vacancy was not filled on a regular basis until the 1850s.[44]

Liang Pao-ch'ang, governor of Chekiang Province, described Biddle's sojourn at Ningpo to the court in Peking. He reported that the commodore had gone from the *Vincennes* in the harbor to the city proper in a "native fishing craft." His manner was "very respectful. The prefect prepared a dinner for his entertainment and the said chief was very pleased." This may have been the banquet that impelled Biddle to make a tongue-in-cheek observation. While notifying Parker that he was about to depart for Japan and asking him to thank Ch'i-ying for his role in the hospitality that had been so generously extended to him at his every port of call, he added: "The dinner (one at each port) rather made me sick, a proof that they were good, for I defy you or Forbes to show me that a bad dinner ever made a man sick."[45]

Biddle returned to the Chusans and transferred his broad pennant from the *Vincennes* to the *Columbus,* preparing for a quick departure. His reason was an alarming rise in the number of his people who either should be or were in sick bay. Dr. Tichnor reported to him that 150 were down with acute diarrhea, and recommended strongly that they leave the China coast at once. The first portion of his long cruise in the *Columbus* having been completed, Biddle headed for Japan on 7 July.[46]

Biddle's China tour had been accomplished admirably, even though his diplomatic responsibilities had been thrust upon him so unexpectedly while en route to the Far East. He had exchanged ratifications of the Treaty of Wanghia and set up the U.S. Legation at Canton, thereby meeting his two chief requirements. As for consular appointments, he had nothing to do with Canton's, for that had been in existence since 1790. In the four other treaty ports, however, he had judiciously decided that the state of American trade warranted establishing a post at Shanghai only. Had he been given this task a few years later he would doubtless have assigned permanent consuls to Amoy, Foochow, and Ningpo, for by that time increased business activities in those ports would have justified such action.

His Anglophobia was exaggerated, but there was an element of sense in his warning the Chinese to beware of English intentions. Britain may have proven him a little paranoid by withdrawing from

China's coastal islands, but very likely the well-read Biddle recalled the history of India. For more than two centuries the British had expanded their original footholds at Madras, Bombay, and Calcutta by a seemingly insignificant concession gained here, an unimpressive military victory won there, until much of that subcontinent had been brought under their direct rule. Yet when the Canton city riots had menaced Western interests, the commodore had presented China with a unified Anglo-American front by sending the *Vincennes* to join the two Royal Navy frigates at Whampoa.

He had established the most cordial relations with the Chinese. The news must have circulated through China's commercial circles that he had supported Shing-ho against Wetmore, the American. But of far greater essence, by his dignity, decorum, and affability he so impressed Ch'i-ying and Liang Pao-ch'ang that each praised his deportment in separate messages to the emperor. Furthermore, his interviews with P'an Shih-ch'eng and Ch'i-ying cast a revealing light upon the temporarily pro-Chinese policy of the United States and Biddle's well-considered presentation of it. Had his admonitions been followed, it is at least possible that China's humiliations over the next several decades might have been less acute. An earlier presence of Western diplomats in Peking just might have had a mitigating effect upon the virulent antiforeignism of the Hsien-feng court. But with Westerners still denied access to the capital, China's external affairs were conducted most disastrously in Canton during the crucial 1850s by that "die-hard xenophobe," Yeh Ming-ch'en.[47]

Had Biddle's exhortations been heeded as to the need for Western-style reforms, particularly in their army and navy, the Chinese might have been able to start a program of learning from the alien in order to oust him, as the Japanese did. In that case China could possibly have been spared at least some of the rigors emanating from its coming defeat in the Arrow, or Second Opium, War, the consequent imposition of the "unequal treaties" at Tientsin, and further compulsory concessions that kept it weak into the mid-twentieth century.

This is, of course, delving into the "might-have-been" school of history, a futile if fascinating exercise. Considering the dead weight of the Chinese Taoist-Confucianist-Buddhist tradition in the Ch'ing bureaucracy and its massive resistance to change, especially from without, it is almost impossible to see how those reforms could have been effected during Biddle's era or for many years thereafter. Yet it would have been almost as difficult to predict that the Japanese would not have followed a similar policy of all-out resistance to the foreign intruder, even granting that their history had often proven them able to adopt from outside what they wished. Biddle's coming experiences

in Japan would demonstrate that as late as the 1840s their unwillingness to tolerate interference from without was still potent. It would
take the better part of another decade before they began gingerly to
emerge from their 206 years of self-imposed isolation. Moreover,
their xenophobia, at least during the late 1850s and early 1860s, matched
that of the Chinese, as proven by their rabid assaults upon Americans,
Englishmen, Frenchmen, Dutchmen, and Russians alike. Instead, they
dramatically about-faced. During the Meiji Restoration from 1868 to
1912 they sent their people abroad and invited in the foreigners to
learn from the West what they considered essential to recover their
full independence. One illustration of the different results in Japan
and China: the former by the turn of the twentieth century was able
to renegotiate on terms of equality the mid-nineteenth-century treaties
forced upon it, while the latter could not rid itself even of extrality
for another four decades.

It has been a long-standing American myth that the Chinese considered them as somewhat apart from the concession-hungry and con-
quest-minded British, French, and Russians. This view has been well
punctured by modern historians, who conclude that the Chinese looked
upon all Westerners as about the same—avaricious, loud, evil-smell-
ing, long-nosed, hopelessly non-Sinified "barbarians," of whom the
"Starry-flag Barbarians" were as obnoxious as the other varieties.
Despite all American protestations of good will and incessant references to their "Open Door Policy," the Chinese knew that they, with
their "hitchhiking" or "jackal" diplomacy, formed a common front
with the Europeans, trotting after them to claim the same privileges
won by British and French arms under the most-favored-nation program.

Yet there was a difference, however slight, and there is evidence
that the Chinese recognized it. During this period the Far Eastern
policy of the United States had one lodestar: to promote amicable
trade relations. It was adamantly opposed to the possession of overseas colonies or bases, expansionistic though it might have been to
take over relatively empty contiguous territory during the age of
Manifest Destiny from 1845 to 1848. But American democratic re-
publicanism was deemed nonexportable to distant areas already heavily populated by non-Americans. To be sure, an occasional diplomat
(such as Dr. Peter Parker) or a naval officer or two (such as Commodore Matthew C. Perry) worked to get an American colony or
naval base in the Far East, but all such efforts were aborted by their
government.[48]

An episode showing that the Chinese regarded Americans as a
people a little apart from the Europeans occurred early during the

Arrow War in 1856. Chinese batteries in the five huge stone "Barrier Forts" kept firing on neutral American ships passing to and from Canton along the Pearl River. Repeated protests were ignored by Governor-General Yeh Ming-ch'en, so East India Squadron Commodore James Armstrong sent Commander Andrew H. Foote's sailors and marines against these fortifications during that November. He stormed them and dismantled them, stone by stone. Yet throughout, Armstrong kept in touch with the governor-general, refusing to accede to British invitations to join them in the war. After receiving Yeh's tepid promise that American vessels would no longer be fired upon, Armstrong resumed friendly relations with China, acting as if his aggressive action that had annihilated Canton's main defenses had never happened. Early the next year the Hsien-feng emperor wrote to Yeh stating that he could distinguish, despite the Barrier Forts incident, between the British and the Americans, believing that the latter had "no quarrel" with his country. He urged that "intelligent people" be sent to explain to U.S. officials in China that he viewed the British as basically hostile, in contrast to the Americans whom he considered enemies not at all.[49]

Although U.S. policy toward China would oscillate during the rest of the century between trying to support that empire against the Europeans on the one hand and joining them in displays of Western unity on the other, Biddle as well as Cushing and Armstrong had contributed well toward the first. Perhaps they had persuaded Peking that the "Starry-flag Barbarians" were a trifle less barbarous than the others.

CHAPTER 11
THE CRUISE OF THE
COLUMBUS:
JAPAN AND HAWAII,
1846

Biddle's freedom of action in Japan was circumscribed by the nature of his instructions from Secretary Bancroft: "In an especial manner you will take the utmost care to ascertain if the ports of Japan are accessible." He could convey Commissioner Alexander H. Everett with him or go alone, whichever he wished. "Persevere in the design, yet not in such a manner as to excite a hostile feeling or a distrust of the Government of the United States." This meant that his responsibilities there were fact-finding and pacifistic, quite unlike later, more militant orders issued to American commodores heading for that country.[1]

Biddle and his civilian superiors appear less well informed about conditions there than those in China. Actually Japan could be designated a self-withdrawn "hermit kingdom," much like that of the Korea or Tibet of that time. There is no evidence that Biddle or any other American recognized the dual nature of Japanese government; all the commodore's letters were addressed to or concerned someone called "the Emperor." Since the twelfth century, full military and civil power had resided with the "Shogun," a hereditary generalissimo, and the Bakufu, his bureaucracy in Yedo (Tokyo). The emperor had been relegated to conducting religious ceremonies at Kyoto.[2]

It was well known in the West that the Japanese had long isolated themselves from the outside world. Although they had been the first and only Asians to welcome enthusiastically the European and his Christian religion, they had also been the ones to expel both the most violently. Portuguese Jesuits had come there in the mid-1500s and soon converted many thousands in the extreme southwestern part of those islands. But late in the century the tide turned. The Japanese had noticed with increasing suspicion and dislike the inter-Christian quarreling between the Portuguese Jesuits and Spanish Franciscans from the Philippines, complicated by the advent of the Dutch, and further compounded by their conviction that European proselyting was simply a means toward eventual conquest and colonization. By the early 1600s the new Tokugawa shoguns, aware that their opposition was clustered in the most thoroughly Christianized areas, launched a ferocious persecution of that religion, expelled foreigners, and by and large withdrew from contacts with the outside.

From 1638 to 1853 alien merchantmen were fired upon as they approached the Japanese shores and local vessels were restricted to the size of coastal traders or fisherman. The only foreign commerce allowed, and that on a very small scale, was with the Chinese and the nonproselyting Dutch, the latter permitted to maintain a small "factory" on an artificial island in Nagasaki harbor, far to the southwest. One or two Dutch vessels a year could arrive, and this enabled the Japanese to keep in touch with worldwide current events. During the Napoleonic Wars, which shattered the Dutch navy and merchant marine, ships from Salem, Massachusetts, occasionally came to Nagasaki in their stead, and through this means some awareness of that remote people drifted back to the United States. By the 1830s American whalers were operating in North Pacific waters, and Japanese isolation made it impossible for them to procure food or water along that hostile coast; sailors shipwrecked there were sometimes treated with callous severity.

The first U.S. naval interest in Japan was voiced by Commodore David Porter. Just after the end of the War of 1812 he asked the department for permission to open that country. He couched his request in highminded language: "Great changes have since taken place in the world—changes which may have affected Japan. . . . It would be a glory . . . for us, a nation of only forty years standing to beat down their rooted prejudices—to secure to ourselves a valuable trade, and make that people known to the world." Probably his real motive in seeking that assignment, however, was given in his closing words: "The world is at peace. . . . We have ships . . . [and] officers who will require employment." President Madison and Secretary of the Navy Benjamin W. Crowninshield made plans for such an expedition, but the project finally fell through, primarily because of Commodore Oliver H. Perry's refusal to take a subordinate position in Porter's squadron and partly because of a temporary misunderstanding with Spain which called for available U.S. warships to be congregated in the Caribbean. Still, one authority avers that subsequent American naval operations in Japan, including Commodore Matthew

C. Perry's successes in 1853 and 1854, "all developed from the idea which the proposal of 1815 initiated."[3]

U.S. interest in Japan then slumbered until President Jackson sent out Edmund Roberts of Portsmouth, New Hampshire, in the USS *Peacock* between 1832 and 1834 as the first American envoy to Asian capitals. He was to sign what trade treaties he could, and if he wished, Japan might be included. But he never sailed north, concentrating instead on the South Pacific and the Indian Ocean. He was rebuffed at Saigon in modern Vietnam, but was able to conclude America's first Asian pacts, one with Siam (Thailand) and the other with Muscat, the sultan of which ruled Oman in western Arabia and much of the East African coast down to the island of Zanzibar. In 1835 Roberts went out again to exchange ratifications of his treaties. He was also ordered to open negotiations with the Japanese, being outfitted with a letter from Jackson and lavish presents for "the emperor," but he died of cholera off Macao in 1837.[4]

During the same year the American China trading firm of Olyphant and Company dispatched the merchantman *Morrison* to Japan, with the return of seven marooned sailors furnishing a plausible excuse for the voyage. Three eminent Sinologists were aboard: Dr. Peter Parker; S. Wells Williams, who would later write a two-volume history of China that is still worth reading; and the Reverend Charles Gutzlaff, the British legation's Chinese interpreter. But the *Morrison's* errand of mercy proved futile. She sailed directly for Yedo to find hostility rampant; she was fired upon from harbor fortifications. No better reception attended that vessel at Kagoshima at Kyushu Island in the extreme southwest, and she was forced to go back to China with her Japanese sailors still on board.[5]

Captain Mercator Cooper of the American whaler *Manhattan* had a different experience. Shortly before Biddle had arrived in the Far East, Cooper had picked up a few stranded Japanese on a small island off their coast and some others from a floating hulk. He too sailed for Yedo, and after he had explained the purpose of his visit, was allowed to land his refugees and given supplies and presents before being sent on his way. He was, however, warned not to return.[6]

En route to Japan Biddle had to decide whether to go to Nagasaki, the one port open to foreign shipping in the country, or to Yedo, where the real power resided. He opted for the latter, explaining to the department that he felt that the Dutch would do everything possible to hamper his mission in order to keep intact their monopolistic position at Nagasaki. Moreover, that port was so remote that it would take many weeks for any communications with Yedo to pass back and forth.[7]

The *Columbus* and *Vincennes* swept into Yedo's lower harbor on 21 July and, as Biddle reported, almost immediately "an officer with a Dutch interpreter came aboard. He inquired what was my object in coming to Japan. I answered that I came as a friend to ascertain whether Japan had, like China, opened her ports to foreign trade, and, if she had, to fix by treaty the conditions on which American Vessels could trade with Japan." Biddle was asked to put his request in writing, which he had already done. The Japanese next informed the commodore that no American could be permitted ashore, nor could any boats pass between the two American men-of-war. Biddle agreed to the first but refused successfully to countenance the second, although from then on American boats plying back and forth were always accompanied by several watchful Japanese barges.[8]

The next day a higher-ranking official appeared to inform the commodore that it was customary for foreign vessels in Japanese ports to land all their "guns, muskets, swords, etc." for the duration of their stay. Biddle explained that such might be required of merchantmen but could not be expected to apply to warships, and his refusal was accepted. His visitors also told him that his message of the previous day had been forwarded to the "Emperor" and that a reply might be anticipated within a week. Japanese and Americans alike settled down to wait.[9]

Hardly had the *Columbus* and *Vincennes* come to rest than they had been surrounded by hundreds of Japanese armed barges, which hovered close by until the Americans had departed. During the first two days Biddle allowed their occupants to board both of his ships without the slightest hindrance. This was a thoroughly questionable decision, for which he might have paid dearly. Many of those scrambling into the frigate and the sloop wore the two razor-sharp swords carried by the samurai, the armed retainers of the great daimyos (nobles). For Biddle to gamble that their intent was amicable might have cost him his command, possibly his life. But all went well, with the sailors delighting in showing off their ships to the curious onlookers. By the third day, however, no further visitors from the attending barges were welcomed aboard either man-of-war.[10]

While they waited, Americans marveled at the exotic scenes before them—the wooded hills around the bay, the patchwork of impeccably kept farms scattered here and there, and particularly "the cordon of boats, many hundreds of them, lashed stem to stern, forming a compact mass." After dark the spectacle was even more compelling. Many years later one of those in the *Columbus* reminisced:

> The nightly illumination of this encircling and gaily bannered flotilla was a scene to be remembered. Brilliant lanterns of bright colors, thousands

of them . . . each individual light heaving and dancing with the movement of the waves . . . made night on the bay like the witchwork fairy-
land. Our old sailors said one might sail the seas a lifetime and never see
its equal.[11]

It was the Japanese custom to furnish gratis what water and food
was required of foreign vessels in order to speed them on their way
as quickly as possible. Watering commenced very tardily, but finally
it arrived in copious quantities, much to the appreciation of the Americans. Nordhoff described it as "a large supply of the most excellent
drinking water, the best we met with during the whole cruise." He
also commented on the foodstuffs provided:

> Two large junks made their appearance, from the upper harbor, bringing
> us a supply of vegetables of various kinds and several hundred chickens.
> Among the vegetables were sweet potatoes, egg plants, carrots, and
> pumpkins. There was also a quantity of small green apples, the first we
> had since leaving home. A bullock or two would have been most wel-
> come, but the Japanese did not kill or eat their cattle—using them for
> draught and to milk.[12]

Meanwhile Biddle's message had been making its way through
the channels of the bakufu. Evidently it was finally answered by Abe
Masahiro, a leading-member of the shogun's council and later a most
influential advisor in the Japanese decision to negotiate with Perry in
1853, but his reply in 1846 was something else. Biddle notified the
department that on the 27th "an officer, with a suite of eight persons"
came to the *Columbus* with the "Emperor's" response to his letter:

> According to the Japanese laws, the Japanese may not trade except with
> the Dutch or Chinese. It won't be allowed that America make a treaty
> with Japan or trade with her, as the same is not allowed to any other
> nation—Concerning strange lands all things are fixed at Nagasaki, but
> not here in the Bay; therefore you must depart as quick as possible, and
> not come any more to Japan.

Perhaps Biddle's Dutch interpreter was either stupid or lazy in the
above translation. An early twentieth-century Japanese historian cites
a much longer, differently worded, and seemingly more authoritative
version, although its coldly inhospitable tone persists:

> The object of this communication is to explain the reasons why we
> refuse to trade with foreigners who come to this country across the ocean
> for this purpose.
> This has been the habit of our nation since time immemorial. In all
> cases of a similar kind that have occurred, we have positively refused to
> trade. Foreigners have come to us from various quarters, but have always

been received in the same way. In taking this course in regard to you, we only pursue our accustomed policy. We can make no distinction between different foreign nations—we treat them all alike—and you, as Americans, must receive the same answer with the rest. It will be of no use to renew the attempt, as all applications of the kind, however numerous they may be, will be steadily rejected.

We are aware that our customs are in this respect different from those of some other countries, but every nation has a right to manage its affairs in its own way.

The trade carried on with the Dutch at Nagasaki is not to be regarded as furnishing a precedent for trade with other foreign nations. The place is of few inhabitants and very little business, and the whole affair is of no importance.

In conclusion, we have to say that the Emperor positively refuses the permission you desire. He earnestly advises you to depart immediately, and to consult your own safety by not appearing again on our coast.[13]

The *Vincennes* carried presumably the first version of the Japanese reply to China. Commissioner Everett commented on it in a letter to Washington shortly after his arrival in the Far East. He stressed that Biddle's proposal had been rejected "not only with decision but with rudeness and incivility." He went on:

This document . . . has been prepared with an evidently studied and intentional disregard of the rules of courtesy. . . . The paper is addressed to no one by name either within or without. The phrase *Explanatory Edict* is written on the cover, which as you will perceive, was not sealed. There is no signature, and no date of time or place, or any other indication of the quarter from which the document proceeds, excepting that it purports to speak the sentiments of the Nation, which can regularly be done only by the Government, and is called an *Edict* which can properly be applied only to an act of the Emperor.[14]

Despite its scarcely veiled antagonism, Biddle accepted the rebuff with equanimity, telling the bakufu's messenger that the United States wanted a trade treaty with Japan only if that nation also desired one. He had come to Yedo solely for information, which he now possessed. As the Japanese had refused point-blank to enter any formal negotiations of any kind, he would sail away when convenient for both parties.[15]

During this exchange Biddle found himself involved in what he termed "an occurrence of an unpleasant character." Indeed it was, and proved to be by far the most controversial episode of his entire cruise. As he explained it, he had been asked to come to a nearby junk to meet the Japanese message bearer. He refused, and sent his interpreter with that information to the Japanese, demanding that the letter be brought to his flagship. Unfortunately within an hour he changed his mind and "went along in the Ship's Boat in my uniform. At the moment I was stepping on board a Japanese on the deck of the junk gave me a blow or a push which threw me back into the boat." The shaken and furious commodore demanded that the offender be arrested, and at once returned to the *Columbus*. The Japanese officers hurriedly followed him and protested that they had not known that he was coming to visit them. They assured him that the one responsible for the outrage was a mere "common soldier" who had acted on his own initiative. He would be "severely punished." Biddle replied that in this circumstance he would abide by "the laws of Japan," but emphasized that he held the officials themselves partly responsible by not being present to greet him when his boat came in. He was "careful to impress upon them all the enormity of the outrage that had been committed, and how much they owed to my forbearance."[16]

Biddle soon decided to drop the matter. He told the secretary that the Japanese had "manifested great anxiety and apprehension, and endeavored in every way to appease me," including the "Governor of Yedo," who hoped that "I would not think too seriously of the affair." The commodore concluded that "the conduct of the man was inexplicable," and that he was "convinced that the outrage had been committed, without the procurement or knowledge of the Japanese officers, as every atonement that I could expect or desire was promptly tendered."[17]

A few expedition members both amplified and in some cases disagreed with his version of the occurrence. Tichnor truthfully states that Biddle left for the junk "without having given any previous notice of his intention" to the Japanese. As an unannounced intruder the commodore should have been prepared for an unfriendly reception. Midshipman Ammen of the *Vincennes* asserted that the entire affair had been deliberately planned, since "a Japanese official at the gangway laid his hand upon his sword, with a plain intention of its use should further effort be made to come on board."[18]

At least eyewitnesses were as one about the commodore's state of mind when he came back to the *Columbus*. Tichnor wrote that he was "greatly exasperated." Edward S. Burton, one of the *Columbus*'s sailors, recalled many years later: "When he came over the side he was the hottest little old man I ever saw. He stamped into his cabin in great rage, and I thought at one time he was going to open up the batteries on them." Ammen agreed, reporting that the commodore had indirectly threatened to use force, pointing this out to Japanese officers who joined him immediately after the incident. He told them that his cannon could "blow them out of the water." They acknowledged that he could "destroy them," but that such an act could have no justification.[19]

Biddle's unwillingness to make his embarrassment a major issue with the Japanese—especially by not demanding and witnessing his offender's execution—has received mixed reactions from contemporary and later commentators. Some justified his tolerance. Stephen B. Luce, a midshipman on the flagship and later one of the Navy's most influential admirals, ignored the incident, apparently considering it of little importance. In 1905 he wrote about his admiration for his commander: "There can be no doubt but that the interchange between Commodore Biddle and his officers, and the Japanese officials, and the total absence on the part of the American officers of any hostile intention, must have impressed the Japanese officials with our friendly disposition and disposed them to receive with favor the overtures of American officers who visited Japan a few years later." Ammen also thoroughly approved of Biddle's conduct in Japan:

> When, eight years later, Commodore Perry appeared and made no demands of apology or statement of intended injury, it was quite apparent to the Japanese that we had no desire to foment a misunderstanding, and perhaps on that account the government was more disposed to listen to what Commodore Perry had to say. . . . [Biddle's] expedition, indeed, had the effect of entirely changing the relation of the Asiatic nations to Europeans and others which might otherwise have remained isolated.[20]

While somewhat critical of Biddle, Charles O. Paullin, the early-twentieth-century historian of naval diplomacy, in general compliments him:

> The presence of an armed fleet in the bay of Yedo and Biddle's amiable and judicious relations with the Japanese officials gave them a favorable impression of the strength, candor, and justice of the great Western republic. Biddle must be awarded the distinction that attaches to the pioneer, for he was the first American naval officer to anchor a fleet in the waters of Japan, to hold intercourse with the officials of that country, and to acquire a first-hand knowledge of its people and customs. Those who came after him had the advantage of his experience.[21]

The negative chorus has been even louder. Early in 1850 a Philadelphia newspaper described a meeting of the Royal Asiatic Society held in London the previous December. The Reverend Charles Gutzlaff, the Chinese interpreter for the British and a passenger in the *Morrison* some years before, informed its members that Biddle had been *"struck with much violence by a sailor,* whose insolence, in all probability, was induced, as it was certainly protected, by the Government." He went on to narrate an incident a little later that lowered the commodore's reputation even more. Fifteen of the American whaler *Ladoga*'s crew had deserted in a boat and were apprehended by the Japanese off their northwestern coast. According to their story, they were considered spies and after having been taken to Nagasaki they were treated so inhumanely that one hanged himself. They might all have died had not the chief Dutch official there exerted himself in their behalf. When the American prisoners had tried to coerce the Japanese into better treatment by forecasting that their country would soon avenge them, they were told: "We treated Commodore Biddle as we liked, and your Government took no notice of it, and how then should they care for common sailors?" The Philadelphia editors knew that Biddle "was never wanting in spirit," but in this instance he had been used by the Japanese "to the disparagement of the American name."[22]

Some of Biddle's diplomatic, commercial, and naval contemporaries were also uncomplimentary. Alexander Everett, when he finally arrived in China, learned about the commodore's acceptance of the insult and wrote the secretary of state that he thought that Biddle had been both indiscreet and inept, thereby making a commercial treaty with Japan that much more difficult to conclude. Aaron H. Palmer, an American businessman promoting the U.S. presence in the Far East, told the State Department that Biddle had accepted "the gross indignity . . . at the hands of a common Japanese boat guard." By so doing, he "left an unfavorable impression on the public authorities and people of Japan respecting the American character, which can only be erased by an imposing mission." Without mentioning Biddle by name, Matthew C. Perry planned to make sure that he would avoid any similar embarrassment:

> I had, before reaching the coast, fully considered and determined upon the course I should pertinaciously pursue in concluding the delicate and responsible duties which had been entrusted to my charge. It was to adopt an entirely contrary plan of proceedings from that of all others who had hitherto visited Japan on the same errand: to demand as a right and not to solicit as a favor those acts of courtesy which are due from one civilized nation to another; to allow none of those petty annoyances which have been unsparingly visited upon those who preceded me, and to disregard the acts as well as the threats of the authorities if they in the least conflicted with my own sense of what was due to the dignity of the American flag.[23]

A nineteenth-century history of Japan says that during 1849 exaggerated rumors circulated through the Ryukyu Islands between Japan and Taiwan about the insult offered with impunity to the "American chief" in Yedo. A Japanese observer, reflecting on the incident during the early twentieth century, is scathing:

> Commodore Biddle's mission was worse than a mere failure. It had the effect of lowering the dignity of his country in the mind of the oriental. The defiant and haughty tone running through the foregoing note [the answer to Biddle's letter delivered to him on 27 July] was, I dare say, the result of insult which he had accepted without strong demonstration. It may be that he only meant to be cautious, and that his caution was misconstrued. . . . A stronger attitude on his part might have ended in his reaping the glory of opening Japan.

This historian is wrong. Since the episode of the "blow or a push" occurred while the bakufu's letter was being received by Biddle, in no way could the incident have contributed to its "defiant and haughty tone." Nor is there the slightest reason to believe that Japan could have been "opened" in 1846, no matter what the commodore's behavior.[24]

An American diplomatic historian of the early 1930s was also critical, if less so:

> The magnanimous conduct of Commodore Biddle appears to have been misinterpreted by the Japanese as weakness and a lack of dignity. Accounts of the insult, magnified and misunderstood, spread not only through Japan but even to the Lew Chews [Ryukyus] and the Americans were made to appear as having accepted an insult with complacency. It was believed that Biddle's visit left matters in a "less favorable position" than before.

Samuel Eliot Morison, Perry's modern biographer, is very hard on Biddle, constantly contrasting Perry's austere dignity to the " 'soft stuff' that Biddle handed out." He calls Biddle "no diplomat," who had "messed up negotiations with Turkey," which he most assuredly had not. Why had he failed in Japan? Primarily because of his "palsy-walsy approach," which will do as an example of regrettable phraseology.[25]

The anti-Biddle clique has focused upon the difference between his conduct in Japan during 1846 and that of another American naval officer in 1849. Commander James Glynn was ordered to go from Hong Kong to Nagasaki in the sloop *Preble* to recover the castaways from the *Ladoga* and another ship or two still imprisoned there. That April he sailed into Nagasaki harbor, anchored in front of the forts, and after negotiating for a few days, during which he adopted an air of cold disdain, obtained their release. Glynn used his own triumph to cast aspersions upon his predecessor, writing to President Millard Fillmore: "I have every reason to believe that the effect of the [Biddle] visit upon the people of that country [Japan] has been very unfavorable to the interests of the United States." Morison seems to have erred again when he claims that Glynn went so far as to threaten to open fire on Nagasaki. This is completely at variance with Charles O. Paullin's long verbatim rendition of the conversations between Glynn and several Japanese officials. In this the American did no more than to warn that if rebuffed he would leave "and report to my government that you decline complying with my demand for the release of the men," which could hardly be more different than issuing a threat to level a city in a country with which the United States was at peace.[26]

The critics of Biddle and the advocates of Glynn appear to have overlooked the contrasting nature of the orders under which each was operating. Glynn had been instructed by East India Squadron Commodore David Geisinger to demand the liberation of his fellow countrymen held in Nagasaki. If he could accomplish nothing there, he was to carry his case to the highest authorities in Yedo in a "conciliatory but firm" manner. In short, Glynn had a specific duty. Biddle, to the contrary, had been sent to Japan only to see if it wished to emulate China and sign trade treaties with the United States and the other Western powers. He was particularly admonished to do nothing "to excite a hostile feeling" against his nation. Had he forcibly overreacted in response to a "blow or a push," Washington's negative reaction might be imagined: very likely a court of inquiry followed by a court-martial conviction and Biddle's suspension.

The acid test in evaluation of Biddle's performance in Japan may be seen in the response of his own government. Secretary Bancroft jotted a comment in the margin of one of the commodore's letters to him: "Although he did not succeed in inducing the Japanese to open their ports and establish commercial relations with us, his prudent and judicious conduct at Yedo merits the strong approbation of the Department."[27]

Egged on by his reluctant hosts and with no reason to tarry further in Japan, Biddle took advantage of their offer to speed his departure. On 29 July the *Columbus,* facing contrary winds, was towed to open water by hundreds of the attending barges. The *Vincennes* was similarly aided the next day, and the two men-of-war parted for good on the 31st, as Captain Hiram Paulding's sloop had been ordered to remain in the Far East for a while longer. She visited Guam in the Spanish Mariana Islands for three weeks in September, went on to China, where she remained for October and part of November, sailed for home on the 15th, and ended her cruise at New York on 9 April 1847.[28]

Long before the squadron had divided, evidence was plentiful that Biddle was at sword's points with his three major subordinates: Paulding of the *Vincennes,* Thomas Wyman, and Commander Thomas Selfridge, captain and chief executive officer respectively of the *Columbus*. Tichnor observed the commodore's last meeting with Paulding: "The parting scene . . . was the coldest I have ever witnessed, the cause was known only to themselves." Actually they had been on terms of veiled hostility for some time. Biddle's private letters during 1845 and 1846 carry oblique references to this. More to the point, his reports to the secretary mention three specific clashes. Shortly after the squadron had been reunited in China, Paulding told his superior that the *Vincennes* had been sent to sea in no condition for a long cruise. Furthermore, he had been forced to sail without either "a force pump or fire engine." The commodore responded with a single frosty question: Had he reported these serious omissions to anyone in the department prior to his departure? When the captain admitted that he had not, he knew that Biddle had scored against him. A second instance of their mutual dislike happened when Paulding sent Biddle a petulant note objecting to his having been criticized for "extravagance" while resupplying his ship at Rio, adding sourly that he had hoped without success for "the professional sympathy of my commanding officer." The third occurred in April when Paulding bypassed his superior by sending a letter directly to the Navy Department. Biddle called the delinquency to the secretary's attention, for all squadron communications from officers were supposed to go to the commodore before being forwarded to Washington. Little wonder that Tichnor had looked upon a "parting scene" so icy.[29]

Biddle was no friendlier with Wyman. Probably the enforced intimacy of so long a cruise was primarily responsible for their estrangement. This too had been compounded by their conflicts of authority. The commodore was supposed to restrict himself to directing overall squadron operations, but according to Nordhoff, Biddle regularly interfered with Wyman's day-by-day running of the ship. One incident inspiring mutual resentment happened early in the voyage. Wyman asked for the right to flog Biddle's steward for "disrespectful language to me in the presence of others, neglect of duty, positive disobedience of my orders, and lesser offenses committed by him on several occasions." Biddle refused to comply with his request, and his reason was simple: his steward ranked as a petty officer and anyone in that category could not be whipped, for such was prohibited by "the printed rules of the service." There is nothing in the records to suggest that Biddle even admonished the offender, and that must have added to the captain's resentment. Moreover, the commodore's files at Andalusia contain occasional negative references to Wyman. But he, unlike the liberated Paulding, had no choice but to suffer along with his commanding officer for the remainder of the cruise.[30]

Executive Officer Selfridge also had no escape from his commodore's displeasure, at least until the flagship reached California. Only a single reference to their relationship is extant, but one is enough. During the run from Honolulu to Valparaiso Biddle criticized Selfridge for not being on deck to oversee the hoisting of the topsails, for neglecting to collect rainwater to the amount ordered, and for not correcting a "deck officer" when the latter was clearly in error. It is easy to guess their later attitude toward one another when the captain answered the commodore's castigations immediately: since he had not "disobeyed any order, nor infringed any regulations, I must consider the imputations, you have been pleased to make, as unwarranted and unjust."[31]

The *Columbus* had to undergo a long passage from Yedo to Honolulu, for Biddle complained that he had had "no westerly wind" after leaving Japan. Forced to sail well to the north before being able to head southeast, the flagship took forty days to reach Hawaii, not coming into that port until 9 September. Despite his differences with Biddle, Wyman appears to have allowed more relaxed shipboard conditions during this leg; only on 22 and 29 August were punishments inflicted. Once at Honolulu, however, the crew again remained penned inside their wooden walls, although for the first time Nordhoff and the other "Ship's Boys" were permitted to stretch their legs on solid ground. Biddle lost no time in going ashore, where he remained for most of his sojourn.[32]

The independent kingdom of Hawaii (the former Sandwich Islands) was ruled by an indigenous Polynesian dynasty from its establishment in the late eighteenth century down to the American-sponsored revolution of 1893, followed for the next five years by the Hawaiian Republic, until its annexation by the United States in 1898. It had been founded by King Kamehameha I, the so-called "Napoleon of the Pacific," who had conquered all the other islands from his base at "the Big Island" of Hawaii, save for Kauai (which was absorbed shortly after his death). While Biddle was there, Kamehameha III occupied the throne.

The U.S. influence in Hawaii had remained strong since the first American missionaries had arrived in 1819, just after Kamehameha I had died. This impact was reinforced by the scores of whalers from Nantucket Island and New Bedford in Massachusetts, which made

Honolulu on Oahu and Lahaina on Maui their supply and recreational headquarters. But the kingdom's military and naval weakness, augmented by its isolated position, attracted European interest. During the early nineteenth century, twice the British, twice the French, and once the Russian flags had been elevated over one or another of the islands, only to be lowered by altered circumstances or foreign protests. As the United States was still refusing to colonize remote, heavily populated areas, no serious consideration could be given to annexing Hawaii. To be sure, European encroachments must be resisted so that the islands would remain independent, but only under American guidance. Biddle would do his bit to bring that fact to the king's attention.

Kamehameha III visited the *Columbus* a few days after her arrival, and was received with appropriate honors. He reciprocated with a banquet at his palace. The toasts offered gave the affair some importance. The first was offered by Anthony Ten Eyck, an attorney, a loyal Democrat, and congressman from New Jersey, 1823 to 1825, who was serving as U.S. commissioner in Hawaii. He eulogized the commodore for his services during and after the War of 1812, telling the Hawaiians how lucky they were to have had President Polk send so noteworthy an American to visit them. In his answering remarks, Biddle warned the king that U.S. influence in his islands was and would remain predominant. He was pleased that relations between the two countries were so amicable and stressed that Ten Eyck, a personal friend of the president, spoke for his nation. He informed Kamehameha that should any disagreement arise between him and Ten Eyck, "the Government of the United States would be slow to believe that he, and not His Majesty's Government, were to blame." The king diplomatically replied that his entire association with the American envoy had given him "great satisfaction," and that he was determined "by doing what was right" to avoid any controversy with him or his country.[33]

Having promoted a little his nation's mid-Pacific policy, Biddle was eager to go on his way. While in Honolulu he received a secret letter from the secretary of the navy notifying him that the Oregon crisis with Britain would probably be settled peacefully, but that the United States had just declared war against Mexico. Instead of the Northwest coast, he was now to proceed to either "California or Sonora" unless other instructions should reach him. Tichnor confirms this when he says that it was in Hawaii that the men first learned about the Mexican War.[34]

But Biddle had second thoughts as he mulled over the department's message, written just as the conflict was starting. It would take him a month more or less to reach either California or northern Mexico, and conditions there would have changed over the five months since the secretary had dispatched his letter. By then his responsibilities might range from fighting off California to a speedy return around Cape Horn for service in the Gulf of Mexico. He decided that it would be more prudent for him to sail for Valparaiso, where he could anticipate that more recent orders would await him. Many months later Tichnor found out that new instructions directing the commodore to head straight for California had come into Honolulu just two days after the *Columbus* had left. Had they been received in time, he grumbled, "we should have saved about sixteen thousand miles sailing and reached California in October instead of March." Biddle, however, had made his decision, and with Chile as his destination, pulled out of Honolulu on 29 September. Homesick, and anticipating service in a war he considered a national disgrace, he looked toward a future that appeared bleak.[35]

CHAPTER 12
THE CRUISE OF THE
COLUMBUS:
CALIFORNIA AND HOME,
1846–1848

In Hawaii Biddle must have been able to read the latest American newspapers about the outbreak of the Mexican War. Always up-to-date concerning political and diplomatic matters, he doubtless recalled the background to that conflict. Ever since the 1820s the United States had kept an acquisitive eye on the comparatively empty Mexican province of Texas, where by the mid-1830s Americans heavily outnumbered Mexicans. The Texan declaration of independence in 1836, the annihilation of Americans at the Alamo and Goliad, Samuel Houston's well-fought victory over General Antonio Lopez de Santa Anna at San Jacinto, and the successful establishment of the "Lone Star Republic" would have been an old story to him. As a Northern Whig he quite likely opposed that nation's nine-year quest for annexation by the United States and objected to its admittance as a slave state in 1845. He would also have been familiar with the clashes between Washington and Mexico City over unpaid claims owed by Mexico to Americans; the disputed territory between the Nueces River and the Rio Grande; the refusal of the Mexicans late in 1845 to receive John Slidell, Polk's envoy; and the president's ill-concealed desire to annex Mexican California. The most current dispatches would have told about Polk's sending General Zachary Taylor across the Nueces to the Rio Grande, where he built a fort and blockaded the river. Fighting started when the Mexicans attacked Taylor, followed by the U.S. declaration of war. But there is no evidence that Biddle recognized that both nations had been aggressive; the records show that in strife-torn Mexico at that time no faction could have seized and retained power on a platform of peace with the United States.[1]

Biddle certainly knew where he stood on the Mexican War—in

225

strong opposition to it. He would probably have judged it an expansionistic plot of the southern Democrat Polk to expand slavery (although his correspondence contains no strictures against that "peculiar institution"). En route from Hawaii to Chile he expressed his sentiments about the war to the wife of his nephew, Lieutenant James S. Biddle:

> I am on my way to Valparaiso. Where I shall go next will depend upon the information I may receive at Valparaiso of the unjust war we have provoked with Mexico. I hope to hear that it is at end. It would be disreputable in us not to make it short, tho' I think our countrymen will find the capture of the city of Mexico not so easy as they imagine. It will cost us a good many lives. One of the bad results of this war will be that the man who plants our flag upon the walls of the city of Mexico will be our next President, tho' he be as unfit as was Jackson.

In a letter written when the *Columbus* was almost home, he reminisced about his experiences from 1812 to 1815, and briefly alluded to the present conflict: "During the war (not this wretched Mexican war). . . ."[2]

On 2 December 1846 the flagship entered Valparaiso harbor, and during his stay of almost three weeks, if Biddle had any keen memories of his troubles there with Admiral Cochrane almost twenty years before, he never mentioned them. In Chile the crew had good reason for both disappointment and jubilation. Dispatches from Washington awaiting the commodore ordered him to proceed to California, thereby extending the *Columbus*'s cruise for many months. Tichnor must have spoken for the vast majority of his shipmates when he described how ardently he had hoped to sail directly home. Half the crew, however, could rejoice over the news that, having sailed 39,795 miles from New York, and having been kept on board for 559 straight days (except for officers, supply details, and the "Boys" at Honolulu), they were granted shore leave. The rest of the men would have to wait for Callao, their next stop.[3]

A bacchanalia was the result. The doctor observed with distaste that those ashore passed their time "as man-of-war sailors do, by getting drunk." Young Nordhoff wondered if his liberty had been worthwhile:

> Here was a ship which had gone quite around the world . . . had visited various ports in the Brazils, the East Indies, China, and the Sandwich Islands, and now, when nearly two years from home, the crew was for the first time allowed to set foot on shore . . . and saw—what? Speaking from my own experience: First, I saw a lot of drunken sailors. Next, a number of very fierce looking fellows, with long swords and villainous

countenances, whose principal duty (so far as I could ever discover) was to keep said sailors within proper bounds. Thirdly, I had seen a few trees, a little grass, a number of grog-shops and ten-pin alleys, the cathedral, the calaboose, and the plaza.[4]

The flagship had come into Valparaiso about the same time as the "razee" *Independence,* a former sister of the *Columbus,* reduced from a ship of the line to a frigate by the razing of one deck to make her ride higher in the water and to require the services of fewer men. She was carrying Commodore William B. Shubrick to assume command of the Pacific Squadron operating off the western shores of the hemisphere. He had been appointed by Secretary Bancroft to replace Commodore John D. Sloat in that position, unless Biddle arrived from the Far East, in which case the latter, as senior officer, would have precedence. Biddle of course was the last person Shubrick wished to meet in the Pacific, but temporarily submerging his disappointment, he agreed to sail on to Californiᴬ and await Biddle's appearance.[5]

While in port Biddle became aware that since the United States was at war, the Brazilian midshipmen whom he had welcomed on board a year and a half before must not continue their cruise with him, for their country was at peace with Mexico. He took advantage of a homeward-bound U.S. Navy sloop to transport them. The following April Henry A. Wise, the resident American consul at Rio, reported their safe arrival and that all had been "immediately promoted." He said that their "Minister of Marine" had asked him to pass along to Biddle "the most grateful acknowledgement for the 'proper and judicious treatment of the Brazilian Midshipmen' . . . and for the 'delicate manner' in which you have returned them to their Gov't. . . . Thus . . . you and your officers have made everlasting friends among the *future* naval heroes of Brazil!"[6]

In Chile the commodore was informed that additional orders had been addressed to him at Callao. On the 21st the *Columbus* departed and came into Lima's seaport on 1 January 1847. Biddle went ashore, where he read no more than that the secretary had confirmed his priority of command in California. Meanwhile the sailors who had missed shore leave at Valparaiso were given liberty in Callao. So enticing were the bars and bagnios there, Tichnor reported that many "had to be brought on by force." On the 9th the *Columbus* set out on a long but unremarkable haul to Monterey. A Protestant pastor in that city watched her come in on 3 March 1847: she "entered our bay in stately majesty this morning. She came in before a light breeze, under a vast cloud of canvas, and rounded in splendid style near the *Independence.*"[7]

"Monumentally confused" might be an apt phrase to describe American naval and military conditions along Mexico's west coast, which consisted of Alta and Baja California (north and south respectively of the present international boundary. Robert E. Johnson well entitles his Mexican War chapter "Too Many Commodores" in *Thence Around Cape Horn: The Story of U.S. Naval Forces on Pacific Station, 1818–1923.* Indeed, within two years there were *five* commodores assigned to that quarter: Sloat, Stockton, Shubrick, Biddle, and Jones, often with conflicting jurisdictions. The absentmindedness and inefficiency of the Navy Department under secretaries Bancroft and his successor, John Y. Mason, were responsible for this superfluity of commanders in the Pacific. On the other hand, naval operations in the Gulf of Mexico under commodores David Conner and Matthew C. Perry (both Biddle protegés) were much better organized.

At the start of the war on the Pacific Commodore John D. Sloat, Biddle's lieutenant who had saved the *Congress* during the hurricane at La Guaira in 1822, hesitated for many weeks before taking offensive actions against the Mexicans. Although he had ample reason to think that hostilities had begun, he had no official word of it. For his inertia, Secretary Bancroft later castigated and replaced him. Perhaps this was unfair, for Sloat had before him the memory of a premature American action in California that could have started a war. During October of 1842 Captain Thomas ap Catsby Jones harkened to rumors that such a conflict had already started. He sailed from Callao to Monterey in the USS *United States,* occupied the town, ran up the American flag, and proclaimed its annexation. Within a day or so he learned to his embarrassment that peace still prevailed. He lowered the American flag and sailed away, leaving in his wake some thoroughly bewildered Mexicans. He was lucky not to have been cashiered from the navy for such unauthorized and impulsive behavior.[8]

To be sure, Sloat was by no means totally inactive, for during July of 1846 men under his command occupied without resistance Monterey and San Francisco ("Yerba Buena" at the time). But then the commodore's already shaky equanimity was disturbed by the appearance of two Royal Navy men-of-war, the sloop *Juno* and the ship of the line *Collingwood,* the latter carrying the admiral's flag of Sir George F. Seymour. For a short, panicky interval Sloat assumed that they had come to interfere with his operations in California, with implications of an Anglo-American war. But Seymour had looked in only to satisfy his curiosity and within a week put out to sea.[9]

The dilemmas of the aged and ailing Sloat were most assuredly not simplified by the arrival in Monterey of Colonel John C. Frémont, the flamboyant and insubordinate "Pathfinder of the West." For some

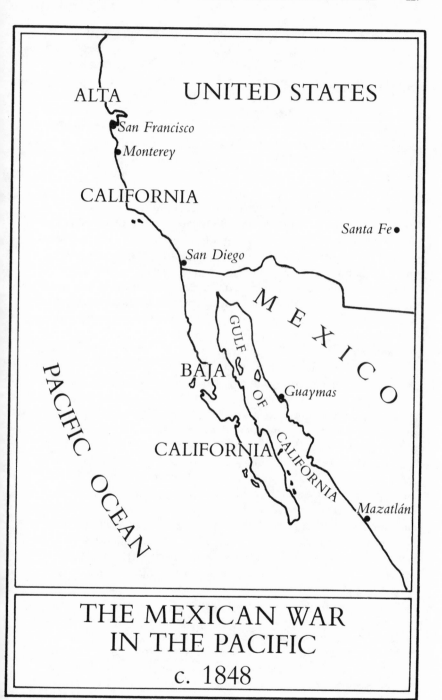

ALTA

UNITED STATES

San Francisco

Monterey

CALIFORNIA

Santa Fe •

San Diego

M E X I C O

GULF

BAJA

OF

Guaymas

CALIFORNIA

CALIFORNIA

PACIFIC OCEAN

Mazatlán

THE MEXICAN WAR
IN THE PACIFIC
c. 1848

months he had been marching around California with his small detachment of army engineers, ostensibly to improve East–West Coast communications. Instead, he had concentrated upon stirring up anti-Mexican sentiments among Americans under that rule that culminated in the proclamation of the independent "Bear Flag Republic" in northern California just as the Mexican War was breaking out. In Monterey Frémont urged Sloat to start widespread offenses, but the commodore refused until he had received official word to start shooting.[10]

In late July the frigate *Congress* sailed into Monterey, bearing Robert F. Stockton, the second commodore of the wartime Pacific Squadron. He was an experienced officer whose career had already demonstrated that he was able, active, and impulsive; later he would serve as an influential senator from New Jersey. Sloat thankfully took his leave after turning over command to him. Stockton proceeded to carry out brilliantly his military and naval campaigns, but his political impositions boomeranged. Working hand in hand with Frémont, he picked off all the other major ports in Alta California, proclaiming the area American territory, instituting civil as well as military rule, and appointing himself governor, with Frémont as his commander-in-chief of armed forces ashore. But his haughty and supercilious attitude toward Mexican Californians provoked many uprisings, one of which temporarily recaptured Los Angeles.[11]

At this juncture confusion was heightened by the appearance of General Stephen W. Kearney, who had led his little "Army of the West" all the way from Kansas and seized Santa Fé along his route. But having sent most of his men on other assignments, he came into southern California with a mere "100 Dragoons." Only with the timely aid of Stockton's sailors was he able to beat off a strong Mexican assault near San Diego early in December. Of greater import, however, Kearney brought with him a letter from President Polk naming him to army command in the Far West. Inevitably Stockton and Frémont, well satisfied with their own authority, lined up against Kearney. By the time that first Shubrick and then Biddle arrived, the jurisdictional situation among the American armed forces in California was little short of absurd. Three naval commandants and two high-ranking army officers were all on hand at the same time, each with some sort of claim to predominance.[12]

Stockton tried to ingratiate himself with Biddle to avoid being replaced at the top position. Learning that his superior had appeared at Monterey early in March of 1847 he wrote him at once, starting with a none-too-subtle avowal: "My claim to your regard" was that he had been a "firm and unflinching friend" of the commodore's brother Nicholas. Stockton went on to blast Sloat who, he said, had left him "in the midst of an outraged and exasperated people without provisions or resources of any kind," neatly ignoring his own role in instigating rebellion among the Mexican Californians. As for Kearney, that officer claimed "Supreme Authority," even though sailors had saved him at San Diego and Stockton himself had received him "in the most generous and kindest manner." Could he retain his command until definite orders to the contrary were received from Washington? Evidently Biddle did not bother to reply to this sycophantic appeal, and within a few days Stockton recognized the inevitable, offering the feeble excuse that when he had written his first letter he had not realized that Biddle planned to remain in California. He promised to vacate his command soon, and did.[13]

Meanwhile Biddle had conversed at length with Shubrick, reviewed what Stockton had to say, learned about Frémont's activities, and met Kearney. He came down foursquare for Shubrick and Kearney. Dr. Tichnor lauded his decision to oppose Stockton and Frémont. The former had put into effect "a system of coercion, which was altogether unnecessary, and which had excited . . . a feeling of hostility in the natives. . . . Colonel Frémont, it was reported, had acted in concert with Stockton, and had caused much ill-will" among the local Mexicans. Biddle, however, had "put things on the right track by sustaining Gen. Kearney in the exercise of his authority." The doctor's evaluation of the dramatis personae has been pretty well confirmed by modern commentators on the Mexican War in the Pacific.[14]

But Biddle still had to deal with yet another unhappy commodore. Not only had Shubrick clashed with Stockton, but during the weeks since first meeting the commodore at Valparaiso he had brooded over his unfair treatment by Secretary Bancroft. He asked Biddle to order him back to Washington, since the department seemed to have no faith in his talents. His superior handled this awkward situation impeccably. He warned Shubrick that being sent away from a post during wartime would ruin his future prospects in the navy. To make his agreement more palatable, Biddle promised his junior what amounted to an independent command to direct West Coast operations, including the conquest of Baja California. Biddle would stay well to the north, immersing himself in the more prosaic requirements of the service. Furthermore, he would soon depart for home, leaving Shubrick in full control. As one authority puts it: "Commodore Biddle took no direct part in the operations of the squadron, but his tact in dealing with the angry Shubrick probably saved a valuable officer for the United States Navy."[15]

One of Biddle's most commendable accomplishments during his

tenure in the Pacific was to review what his predecessor had done in regard to captured ports and prizes. Stockton had slapped duties on foreign vessels and cargoes coming into them, which evoked protests from abroad; Biddle let the impositions stand. But he struck down Stockton's blockade that had been proclaimed the previous August affecting "all ports, harbors, bays, inlets, outlets . . . on the west coast of Mexico south of San Diego." When Biddle realized that this interdicted some 2,500 miles of shoreline and was patrolled by only two sloops, the USS *Cyane* and *Warren,* he very likely remembered his own frustrations with the paper blockades off Chile and Peru in 1818 and 1819, and those off Brazil and Argentina from 1826 to 1828. So he rescinded Stockton's unenforceable proclamation, telling Shubrick to blockade only the two ports of Mazatlán and Guaymas in the Gulf of California by the warships actually stationed off those harbors. The Pacific Squadron had also nabbed a few Mexican prizes, and Biddle simplified matters for their takers by setting up a prize court in Monterey where they could be "judged and sold or released," thereby saving their captors from having to escort them around Cape Horn for adjudication in the United States.[16]

Another of Biddle's praiseworthy efforts in the West Coast was to avoid in areas under his command the atrocities committed against Mexican civilians by Americans elsewhere that later became sources of national shame. He mentioned to Shubrick that he wanted his men to behave differently than had the British during the War of 1812:

> Our enemy at the city of Washington made war upon public edifices devoted exclusively to civil purposes, and upon the public library, and within the waters of the Chesapeake carried on a plundering and burning system of warfare against non-combatants and their families. I mention this as an example to be carefully shunned by us in all our hostilities against Mexico. By imitating such an example, we should certainly bring disgrace upon our country and probably prolong the war.[17]

During and after Biddle's service in California Shubrick justified his superior's trust in his abilities. With the *Independence,* the *Congress,* and three sloops he occupied the towns of Baja California one by one. During the spring of 1848, however, he was replaced by Thomas C. ap Jones as commodore, the fifth wartime commander in the Pacific. But much to Shubrick's disgust, his able work had been in vain. By the Mexican-American Treaty of Guadalupe Hidalgo, ending the war in February 1848, Mexico lost Alta California, Nevada, Utah, most of Arizona, and parts of New Mexico, Wyoming, and Colorado. It retained all of Baja California, however, and American conquests there had to be returned.[18]

Biddle had taken time to meet his responsibilities in California. Tichnor, who once again unquestionably spoke for most of his fellows, thought that the commodore had dallied at Monterey far longer than necessary before leaving for San Francisco on 13 June. Then he took ten days for a passage that the doctor estimated should take only two. Biddle informed him that he wanted the men to dry out from their alcoholic excesses at Monterey, an explanation that Tichnor considered "preposterous," since no liquor could be purchased at San Francisco.[19]

The *Columbus* remained inside the Golden Gate for another month and a half, waiting for Shubrick, according to the commodore. Although Tichnor accused Biddle of tarrying "for the purpose of exploring the countryside and purchasing estates," no other documentation supports his allegation. When they finally sailed for home on 25 July the doctor glumly summed up his experiences in a place that he hated ("California is much over-rated"):

> Thus terminates our long & tedious stay on the coast of California, which has been protracted three months after the Commodore had received orders from Washington to return home. For this long delay, no satisfactory reason could be assigned; the presence of the ship, according to the Commodore's own declaration, being altogether unnecessary; everything having been done before our arrival on the coast which could have required his agency.

Walter Colton, the clergyman at Monterey who had briefly clashed with Biddle over the behavior of some of his sailors ashore, agreed with Tichnor: "The *Columbus,* Commodore Biddle, left for the United States having done nothing on the coast of California save consume stores, and carry them off when she left."[20]

These negative evaluations of Biddle's work in the Pacific during 1847 seem unfair. Both of his accusers had their own very good reasons for judging him harshly. Colton thought the commodore remiss in maintaining discipline and had quarreled with him. Tichnor's Journal shows that he almost ached to go home and would probably have been critical of anyone who delayed his departure. But Biddle himself was no less eager to end his interminable cruise, writing to a relative from between Honolulu and Valparaiso:

> I have become heartily tired of the sea, and all its anxieties and all its discomforts. I am aware that life at sea is just what it was *forty-six* years ago, when I first knew and liked it, and that the change is not in it but in me. . . . When I get home you need not ask me to go to Andalusia *by water.* I shall go by land and not look towards the river while there. Dear Andalusia![21]

He had submerged his personal preferences, in order to perform what he thought to be his duty. It was reasonable for him to delay his departure until he was able to evaluate Shubrick's performance while the latter was cruising as commodore for the first time. Once satisfied, then he could weigh anchor for "dear Andalusia!"

Old and tired though he was, Biddle had served well his government in California. He had helped Shubrick to overcome his potentially self-destructive self-pity by giving him practically a free hand to conduct naval operations most capably off Baja California. He had replaced Stockton's sweeping paper blockade with one restricted enough to be enforceable. By setting up a prize court at Monterey he had saved his fellow officers thousands of needless miles in taking captives to the East Coast. His active support for Kearney had assisted in ridding California of the impulsive Frémont. He had paved the way for Shubrick's accomplishments in the Pacific by refusing to permit the erratic Stockton to remain in command of naval forces there. By his role in dismissing that hotheaded duo he had made easier the imposition of a more moderate civil government on the West Coast. Through his admonitions to treat the local Mexican population well he had aided in soothing postwar racial tensions. All in all, Biddle's last active service for the navy composed a fitting climax to a career stretching across almost half a century.

The return voyage of the *Columbus* may be described as briefly here as it was undoubtedly endless for her people. She stopped for almost a month at Valparaiso, where three Americans were given passage back to the States. Enjoying good weather around Cape Horn in November, she came into Rio just before Christmas. The men slaked their thirst for the last time until reaching Virginia two months later, while Biddle may have had a reunion with his "*future* naval heroes of Brazil," but if so, the records do not mention it. Early in February 1848 the *Columbus* "crossed the Equator for the Sixth time this Cruise."[22]

During the trek from Valparaiso to Rio Biddle once more proved that he was anything but the most self-sacrificing and tolerant of roommates, as Caesar Augustus Rodney had discovered a quarter-century before. One of the American trio, identified by Tichnor only as "Dr. Crump," shared the commodore's cabin, and was continually seasick. When the ship left Brazil Crump moved in with Captain Wyman, because of Biddle's "almost incessant smoking segars," intolerable to one "laboring under seasickness." At least the men should have relished their final leg of the voyage more than the queasy Dr. Crump did. Wyman seems to have forgotten about his whip, well used throughout the earlier part of the cruise. Nordhoff described conditions as more relaxed than ever before. Disciplinary measures were eased to such an extent that no one was flogged.[23]

On 3 March the entrance to Chesapeake Bay was sighted, ending the *Columbus*'s thirty-three-month cruise around the world, during which she had sailed precisely "68,949.6 miles." She anchored outside Hamptom Roads on the 8th and the next day two steam tugs towed her into Norfolk. On the 9th: "At 11:45 Com. Biddle left the ship. hauled down the Broad Pennant & saluted him with 13 Guns." On the 15th the midshipman keeping the ship's journal allowed the sheer joy shared by all on board to appear in his final entry: "At 10:00 paid the Crew off and struck the Pendant and Colors & started for Home!!!"[24]

Biddle's last active duty in the U.S. Navy ended, as had so many others, in an intraservice feud. Just before vacating the *Columbus* he had addressed a contingent of marine officers and men. He told them that the acquittal of one marine private in California by a court-martial upon which Lieutenant William A. T. Maddox had sat had been "a ridiculous finding and sentence," and that "any intelligent court" would have decided otherwise. Maddox wrote to Secretary of the Navy John Y. Mason that he considered Biddle's remarks "ill judged and improper," calling upon the department "to guard and protect a subordinate from so wanton and unjustifiable an attack upon his personal as well as official feelings from so gross an insult of an unanswerable superior." Mason passed this letter along to the commodore, asking for his version of the incident. The marine in question had asserted that his enlistment had expired, Biddle explained, and so "he refused to do duty." Since all had signed on for the duration of the cruise, the commodore wished no precedent to be set that might cause "further trouble" in the squadron over that issue. Hence, the court-martial acquittal had been a judicial error. A final flash of his old disdain illuminated Biddle's conclusion about Maddox: "I have formed a most unfavorable opinion of his character, altho' I deem L̺ Maddox' letter to you indecorous and improper yet I willingly take his word for all he alleges that I said on the occasion to which his letter refers."[25]

Biddle knew that his round-the-world cruise terminated his active career, and welcomed the prospect of his retirement. While crossing the Pacific toward Chile he had written home about it:

> I am beginning to wonder where and how I shall locate myself in Philadelphia. I think of mooring ship in the Washington Hotel in Ches[t]nut Street above 7th. I shall require two cabins upon one deck, and then I shall not turn out, let what will come to pass. It may blow and be d———d, the anchor may drag and be d———d, the cable may part and be d———d. Let those look out who have watch on deck. I shall keep the watch below, and sleep on. I shall be just like the old Negro in Jamaica, "the more massa call me, the more I won't come."

Instead of rooms at the Washington Hotel, however, he resided in a

house at "Portico Row, in Spruce Street above 9th," although undoubtedly he frequently visited the widowed Jane Craig Biddle and
her children at Andalusia and at their Philadelphia town house which
they had also managed to retain.[26]

Toward the end of the commodore's life a second woman of some
meaning to him appears—Mrs. Eliza A. Hirst, whether a widow or
still married is uncertain from the scanty documentation about her
that has survived. Perhaps she is the one referred to in a letter sent to
Biddle from one of his Philadelphia friends shortly after his departure
for Brazil in mid-1845: "I occasionally meet *our* fair friend in the
street—poor girl she . . . grieves your absence. I told her to look
ahead—she tells me she will write to you."[27]

Only three of Mrs. Hirst's letters to or about Biddle are in the
Andalusia archives. The first, written late in 1847, chided him for
writing to her only once in two years, expressed the hope that he had
not forgotten "your neglected friend," promised to meet him at whatever port he came into, and was signed, "adieu my dear, dear friend
and believe me that I am still your affectionate Eliza." The second, a
forlorn note, is addressed to his nephew Charles Biddle shortly after
the commodore's death on 1 October 1848: "Knowing the tender
friendship that has existed between your deceased uncle and me and
I crave from you permission to see him if it [is] possible before he is
removed from me forever." The last, dated the following spring, tells
Charles that she and the commodore had met, and "he then told me
that in case he never got well and did not live he would make provision for me and I never knew him to tel[l] me any things that was
not true." Had he made any bequest for her? There is nothing to
indicate that Charles ever answered her appeal, and Biddle's will contained no reference to her.[28]

The letters of Mrs. Hirst, quite unlike those of Mary Chapman,
are replete with misspellings and grammatical errors. Furthermore,
she was clearly of a lower social and economic standing than the
Biddles or Chapmans. By 1849 she was reduced to "trying to get a
living by keeping house but find it impossible as my health is very
bad." The nature of her association with the patrician commodore
can be only guessed, as in the case of Mary Chapman, the mere fact
that her letters were retained in the family papers lends credence to
the assumption that her role in Biddle's life was of some significance.[29]

On 1 October 1848 the commodore died of unannounced causes
at Andalusia, with Dr. Nathaniel Chapman as his attending physician.
According to Mrs. Hirst, when they met—probably in the late summer of 1848, as he had just returned from Cape May, New Jersey—
he feared that he might not recover from whatever ailments were

afflicting him. One would assume that the rigors and deprivations of his almost three-year voyage could well have broken him physically. He had been occasionally indisposed ever since his siege of illnesses following his overland trips in Turkey in 1830. Dr. Tichnor, however, expressed his "great surprise" upon hearing that "he died of a disease contracted during his last cruise." To the contrary, he wrote Chapman, when the commodore had left the *Columbus* on 9 March, he had examined him and found that "he was in as good health & spirits that I have ever known him to be, and seemed to have a fair prospect of enjoying the high degree of happiness which he had promised himself." What was the reason for his death? Evidently Chapman never replied. Nicholas B. Wainwright suspects that a heart condition was what felled him: "He suffered from shortness of breath as did Nicholas Biddle who took digitalis for that condition," and such would seem as good a guess as any.[30]

James's last will, dated 24 March 1848, was short, containing only four provisions. He released Nicholas's estate from any claims from "some money" which he had given before and after his brother's death. His entire library, books and cases alike, went to his nephew Craig Biddle. James S. Biddle, his nephew in the navy, received his sword awarded by the State of Pennsylvania, the silver "vase" from personal friends in 1812, and the "medal presented to me by the United States" (presumably his gold one for the *Hornet-Penguin;* he does not mention his silver medal for the *Wasp-Frolic*). The remainder of his estate was divided in half, one share going to his sister, Ann Hopkinson, and the other to his sister-in-law, Jane Craig Biddle. It appears odd that Mary Biddle, his widowed sister, received nothing, but possibly she was financially independent by that time. In September of 1849 his nephew Charles Biddle, his executor, reported the estate as worth $51,926.67. This is $18,255 less than the commodore's figures of 1848, which amounted to $70,181, $46,881 in assets, and "about $23,400" in outstanding loans to relatives. Supporting documentation appended to the will describes the disposition of the estate over the next decade. Brother John eventually repaid his obligation of $5,600, but there is no mention of collecting anything from Cadwalader's $13,000, or executor Charles's $2,500, or Hopkinson's $2,200. Probably James had written them off before he died.[31]

His funeral, on 4 October, was everything that the nineteenth century, with its profound emphasis upon the proper rites of passage, would desire. A procession, watched by a sizable crowd, wound from Jane Biddle's home on Pine Street, to which his remains had been brought, to Christ Church cemetery, where he was interred in his father's crypt. Army, navy, and marine units, accompanied by a band playing dirges, had marched behind clergymen and "a sailor who carried the Commodore's broad pennant in front of a coffin upon the shoulders of other sailors." Secretary Mason ordered that all flags in warships and at naval installations ashore be lowered to half-mast, a thirteen-gun salute be fired, and all officers wear "crape" on their left arms for one month. A leading Washington daily quoted the Philadelphia *Public Ledger*'s eulogy:

> It has been the distinguished character of this gentleman to exert in the public service an unwearied activity and an ardent enterprise which surmounted every obstacle and crowned his enterprises with success. Com. Biddle was a man of slight frame and delicate constitution, but of an indomitable spirit, which sustained him through trials and hardships under which greater physical strength might have failed. As an officer, he was unsurpassed in courage, acquirements, and skill; and as a man, his spotless honor and noble qualities of mind and heart gave him a distinction not inferior to his professional reputation. Philadelphia may well mourn the loss of one of its most distinguished of her sons.[32]

CHAPTER 13
BIDDLE: THE MAN,
THE OFFICER,
AND THE DIPLOMAT

Biddle possessed the mottled pattern of pluses and minuses of us all in appearance, personality, and character. He may be described as short, slender, well educated, intellectually if not aesthetically inclined, immersed in his family circle, unmarried but appreciative of feminine beauty, emotionally taciturn, self-contained, financially well off, conscious of his own social standing, occasionally droll, paternalistic toward his sailors and junior officers, but thin-skinned in his relations with his naval equals or superiors. He was in short more to be respected and even admired than liked or loved. His careers as a naval officer and a diplomat were less flawed; in both he generally met his responsibilities masterfully.[1]

According to the form releasing him from British imprisonment in Bermuda during 1812, Biddle was five feet, four-and-a-half inches tall; though not unusually short for that day, he certainly gave that impression. Only *Analectic Magazine*'s November 1815 issue differed by calling him "of middle size," but immediately added, "or perhaps a little below it." Edward Shippen's 1883 article said that he was "small in stature"; all the rest used the word "little," ranging from marine Private William Ray's devastating "little, captious, amphibious animal" in 1803 through Jesse D. Elliott's "high minded gallant little fellow" in 1826 and Samuel F. Du Pont's "little man" and "selfish little viper" in 1845, to sailor Edward S. Burton's "hottest little old man I ever saw" a year later. His slimness probably enhanced this impression, for he was variously limned as "slender in his make" (*Analectic,* 1815), "a man of slight build" (Philadelphia *Public Ledger,* 1848), and "slight in person" (Henry Simpson, *Lives of Eminent Philadelphians Now Deceased,* 1859). All three publications qualified that characterization with some such phrase as "indomitable in spirit" that allowed him to compensate for his unimpressive physical appearance.[2]

Biddle's educational training appears sound, even though he did not graduate from the University of Pennsylvania. Well grounded in the Latin classics and with an apparently innate flair for self-expression, throughout his life he was able to write clearly and correctly, seldom erring in either spelling or grammar. His French was fluent enough to allow him to protest against the slipshod use of that language in the Turkish-American Treaty of 1830, although he seems to have read French works in translation.

Despite his complaints about the unreliability of newspapers, he was a journalistic patron, not only of the Philadelphia press but of Washington's *National Intelligencer,* which he probably scanned from its inception, for it supported his own political predilections. Above all, he became an omniverous and eclectic devourer of books, as proven by his personal library of 2,329 volumes amassed by 1845. As there is no evidence that he used libraries regularly, he probably had standing orders with booksellers in Philadelphia and other cities in which he resided for new works across a gamut of topics, representing his catholicity of interests.[3]

At first Biddle's itemized catalogue of his holdings, totaling fifty-seven handwritten pages, maintained clear topical divisions in his collection. He commenced by listing 67 histories (none American); 135 biographies, of which 17 were American (including his brother Richard's *Life of Sebastian Cabot* and—perhaps surprising for the very proper James—9 lives of Byron); 133 travel and descriptive narratives, of which 42 were American (for some reason he placed works on American history and politics here, including Tocqueville's *Democracy in America*); 111 on foreign locales, heavily concentrated on the British Isles, France, and Italy, and to a lesser extent on the Middle East, India, and the Far East (11 on China but only 1 on Japan); 8 geographies and atlases; 34 on Pacific, African, and polar explorations (among them Porter's *Journal of a Cruise to the Pacific Ocean,* which he must have read with snorts of indignation and disbelief); and 50 professional works about naval judicial procedures, international law, seamanship, gunnery, navigation, and military regulations.[4]

The commodore's ownership of more than 400 novels demonstrates how addicted he was to this form of literary expression. All the major English classics are there, from Defoe and Richardson to Dickens—although most assuredly John Cleland's *Fanny Hill* does not appear. He had his obvious favorites: 12 by Captain Frederick Marryat (better known in the United States for his long *Diary in America,* 1839); 14 by Sir Walter Scott; 21 by James Fenimore Cooper; and the astonishing total of 27 George P. R. James, who for many years churned out an annual potboiler based "on accurate historical settings." After maintaining his divisions for most of the catalogue, toward the end Biddle must have become bored with his task of careful differentiations, for he began lumping all categories together: essays, sketches of naval life, more histories and travel accounts, treatises on political science and economics, scientific works, medical texts, collections of poetry and drama, Latin classics, and scores of bound volumes of the leading British and American periodicals.[5]

One might imagine that a man so intellectually active would have regularly attended the plays, operas, and musicales flourishing in Philadelphia and other American cities during his era, but if he did, he says nothing about them. He seems to have had little interest in music per se, and although he willingly sat for his portraits by Joseph Wood, Charles Willson Peale, and Thomas Sully, except for commissioning Horatio Greenough in Italy to do the busts of Washington he is generally silent about any form of aesthetical enjoyment. Apparently he was satisfied with his reading and some other diversions: playing chess (not well, he admitted) and billiards (no comment on his proficiency), incessant smoking of cigars, and wine drinking—but hard liquor never since Tripoli in 1805.

Beyond his reading and his other unexceptional amusements, Biddle's greatest interest was immersing himself in the affairs of his sizable, affectionate, and well-knit clan. During 1818 he summed up this lifelong lodestar in a letter to his father, "God bless my dear family." Whether its members were related to him by consanguinity or affinity made little difference to him. Thomas Cadwalader, his relative by marriage, was his favorite confidant except for his brother Nicholas, and his letters in the Cadwalader Collection are among the most revealing.

Biddle was never happier than when living in the room always ready for him at Andalusia, for he particularly loved Nicholas and obviously adored his wife, Jane. He wrote her his gracious and affecting, "When people are discontented, it is not unusual I believe to be the most discontented with those they love most . . . and hence it is perhaps why I am now quarreling with you." Because of his worry about her following Nicholas's death, he planned to accompany her to Europe, and had he done so, he would have thrown away the greatest opportunity of his career—commanding the East India Squadron during 1845 and 1846. He was especially close to his sisters Mary and Ann, consoling Mary on the death of her husband, and distraught that he could do no more to assuage her grief. He watched carefully over the naval prospects of his nephew, James S. Biddle, telling him in mid-1846: "I am on my last cruise—my very last—and when I return home and get surveyed and condemned as unseaworthy the family will depend on you for all its naval honors." Through this fortunate solicitude we have the commodore's summary of his life, written to James S. only seven months before he died.[6]

He put his affection for his kin into tangible form by purchasing expensive presents for them overseas at every opportunity. For instance, during the first four months of his Mediterranean command in 1829, he spent close to $1,500 on gifts. When coming home almost terminally ill a few years later he packed much of his forty-two cases of personal possessions with similar mementos. Even more to the point, his family knew that his bank account was open to them when they were in financial trouble. Shortly before he died he estimated those "loans" at "about $23,300" to four close relatives. He made no mention here about Nicholas's estate, but in his will he excused any repayment of "some money" advanced to his brother during the early 1840s.[7]

This strong attachment to his family is probably a major reason that Biddle never married. Whether this committed him to celibacy is, of course, impossible to say, but he was never unaware of the female presence, the more attractive the better. Nor was he averse to a little self-promotion along such lines. Diarist Jeremy Robinson noted that off Chile in 1818 he "played the great man among the ladies." Even in his sixties he was an appreciative observer of the opposite sex. In the same letter cited above he wrote his nephew James, "I find here a married lady who claims me as a relative. . . . I have admitted her claim as she is young and handsome." The enigmatic nature of his associations with Mary Randolph Chapman and Eliza A. Hirst has already been explored.[8]

One clear-cut reason why his biographer finds his relationships with women so hard to discern is the commodore's almost morbid reticence about expressing his own emotions. Illustrations to support this generalization abound. His single reference to the family tragedy in 1801 was his telling his father that he was "too much distressed" to write about his brother Edward's death. Seven years later he summed up his impressions of exotic China with, "I dislike Canton." In 1811 he says nothing at all about his diplomatic assignment to Europe, even though he is said to have been introduced to Napoleon I. He shrugged off his neck wound suffered while fighting HMS *Penguin* in 1815, and at the end of his life summarized his brilliant War of 1812 service with "I was in two actions, both of them successful." He did not mention how close he came to losing his frigate *Congress* in the hurricane at La Guaira in 1822. His single extant remark about the excruciatingly stupid death of his brother Thomas in the duel with Pettis in 1831 was that as soon as he heard about it, "I declined the civilities offered me at Malta, and on the same account sailed from Malta sooner than otherwise I should." His brush with financial insolvency in 1842 merited no more than, "Three years ago I was independent of my Navy pay. At present I have scarce[ly] any other income than my pay."

Furthermore, his irritating reluctance to put his thoughts on paper hampers our understanding him more fully. Although he was an Episcopalian, religion almost never comes up in his correspondence, the single exception being his musings in 1816 after the murderer Lieutenant Richard Smith had been hanged while his even guiltier paramour Ann Carson had escaped unscathed: "She cannot be made to suffer in this life all that is due her offenses. Will not Vengeance therefore be pursued after death?" Although we know that he was a rabid anti-Jacksonian in politics and that he saw no justification for the Mexican War, his sentiments about other vital issues remain unexpressed. We may surmise that he was against slavery and its expansion into new territory, but there is no documentary proof that he was. Nothing that Biddle may have said about the Barron–Decatur duel has survived, nor have his reactions to the sensational news in 1842 that Commander Alexander S. Mackenzie had hanged on the high seas three of his crew accused of attempted mutiny in the USS *Somers,* among them the son of J. C. Spencer, Tyler's secretary of war at the time. We know where the commodore stood on temperance, but that is about all in reference to the spirited controversies that were convulsing the navy during his latter years: the eradication of flogging, the abolition of the Board of Navy Commissioners in favor of five naval bureaus, the increasing use of steam to augment or replace sails in warships, or the need for the introduction of armor plating, rifled cannon, and exploding shells.

There were naturally many exceptions to his restraint in letting his feelings be known. He was always candid in his letters to his brother Nicholas. He was verbose enough in telling Cadwalader how close he had come to "Davy Jones" in the *John Adams* at Pensacola in 1825. He spared no ink in describing the many faults of David Porter, John Rodgers, Isaac Hull, Caesar Augustus Rodney, and Lord Cochrane. But in general he was so closemouthed that important aspects of his public, as well as his private, life remain in shadows, much to his biographer's regret.

Biddle's patrician sense of belonging to a breed apart was probably a leading cause of his reticence, for very likely he considered that those whom he viewed as his inferiors had no reason or right to be admitted to his innermost thoughts. As a Biddle he was automatically a member of the top layer of the class-conscious Philadelphia of his era. Nor would his lifelong familial and social interactions with the Craigs, Cadwaladers, Ettings, Ingersolls, Willings, and Whartons have done anything to lower his self-esteem. As a bona fide War of 1812 hero he was able to move onto the national stage where he knew and was known to most of the political, legal, military, mercantile, planting, and increasingly business-dominated clique that ran the country. Since 1815 he had been at the top in naval ranking, and as a captain and commodore his shipboard quarters would have revealed the chasm that stretched between him and the other officers, to say nothing of the men. His accommodations ashore were equally comfortable, and even today one cannot lunch at the Philadelphia Club, or stand on Andalusia's porch beside its massive Doric pillars to view across its expansive lawns and gardens the Delaware River rolling by, without recognizing that Biddle enjoyed a special way of life that contributed to his serene awareness of his own self-importance.

Save for a brief period of financial embarrassment early in the 1840s, he was always well off. Shortly before he died he scrawled a list of his assets, amounting to $46,881 in stocks, bonds, and annuities, as well as the $23,300 loaned to relatives, for a total of $70,181. Nor was he a wastrel. A second page of that list itemizes his expenses from 1839 to 1847 as $20,591. But his navy income for the same years came to $30,921, leaving him a net of $10,300 for investment or bequeathal. So he could and did live the life of a country gentleman. His bills for cigars, wine (he always brought home cases from Europe), and his collection of more than 2,300 books must have been high. Some idea of how sumptuously he could entertain even on board ship is given by the inventory of his silver service carried to the *Columbus* shortly before his departure in 1845. It numbered 233 separate pieces.[9]

One negative consequence of Biddle's lofty social, economic, and professional status was that it turned him into a snob. There are only a few instances of this in his letters, but they are enough to justify the epithet. Du Pont called attention to his aloofness with some of his younger colleagues in 1822. According to the commodore, the Rodney family was "crass, vulgar, and indecent." He was at his worst when he expressed concern that Porter's wife and sister-in-law might come aboard the *Congress* in 1824, admitting, "I abhor the idea of having in my ship two daughters of a tavern-keeper," even though their father had been a four-term congressman. Some of his colleagues recognized and resented his snobbishness. After he had first promised to back John Shaw in 1822 and then refused to do so, Jesse D. Elliott sarcastically referred to him as "high-minded" and "gallant." Sinclair, after extracting an apology from him to avoid a duel, jeered at *"His High Mightiness."* The same unattractive trait probably influenced him politically. Even without the troubles Nicholas had with the Jacksonians, the commodore would have been likely to oppose their leveling influences. Perhaps he felt threatened not so much economically as socially. The Democratic party's success in every presidential election save one from 1828 to Biddle's death twenty years later would naturally evoke a siege mentality among America's quasi-aristocracy, within which he would certainly have included himself.

If his condescending air of superiority marks a flaw in Biddle's character, his humor was a saving grace. It appeared as neither raucous joke telling, nor a self-deprecatory stream of personal reminiscences, nor the mock-classical or biblical exaggerations in which Bainbridge reveled. Biddle specialized in wry analogies and understated allusions. Probably the wife of the U.S. consul in Hong Kong was too kind when she wrote to him in 1846 thanking him for "your bright and happy flow of wit and humor," but it was there. Although he would soon see nothing comical in the superfluity of Rodney's unattached girls, he told Cadwalader that "it is not genteel nor respectable in any man to have nine unmarried daughters." He assured Dr. Peter Parker that the lavish overabundance of food at his Chinese banquets made him ill, "a proof that they were good, for I defy you and Forbes to show me that a bad dinner ever made a man sick." Before the onset of the awful epidemic of yellow fever in the *Macedonian* off Cuba, he compared his opinion of Havana to a failed marriage: "I dislike Havana most cordially & shall leave it with no other regret than that I ever knew it, as a certain man said of his wife, after they had been divorced." Perhaps the best example of his humor is in a letter he sent to the mother of one of his midshipmen in 1828:

> Last Wednesday I gave the *Macedonian* and all on board of her to Captain [Commander] Hoffman. It cost me much emotion, but emotions do not last forever; they do not last a week, for already I am tolerably composed altho this is only the fourth day. Your landswomen do not comprehend the affection which a commander feels for his frigate, and yet that affection is so *pure*. I cannot read of Napoleon's embracing with transport his *wooden* eagles at Fontainbleau without using my pocket handkerchief.[10]

Sometimes he overreached himself in this direction. After losing one-third of his personnel off Cuba in 1822 he was little short of morbid in writing Josiah Quincy a few months later: "The weather here begins to feel wintry and I sigh for the climate of Havana." His father thought it a splendid "joke" when his son, after helping Decatur prepare a speech for a public dinner at Philadelphia in 1813, proceeded to recite it verbatim from memory just before Decatur himself was to deliver it. Anyone who has studied Decatur becomes aware of his overweening pride as he strutted the national stage, and it strains credulity to think that he accepted his embarrassment "in great good humor." Somewhat later, the commodore told a service colleague: "When a prudent man thinks of getting married he looks out for a suitable father in law as being necessary above all other things, to domestic ease and comfort." One momentarily wonders if so strange a standard of marital values might help account for his failure to wed. But he wrote it in the context of an explanation for his cousin John B. Chapman's having broken up with a previous love, so one may describe it as an example of his subtlety of wit.[11]

Little of his drollery, however, is manifested in his personal relations in the navy. As for his sailors, although he regarded them as among the lower forms of homo sapiens, he maintained a paternalistic determination to treat them well. Save for his early brutality toward his men in 1803, abating as he gained confidence and experience, he falls into the category of a relatively mild disciplinarian, like Decatur. When in port he recognized that sexual frustration could raise havoc with morale, so he allowed prostitutes to come on board at Valparaiso and in the Mediterranean. But when time was essential, as in the *Columbus*'s dash to the Far East, he permitted no shore leaves for the sailors for over a year and a half. He tried to help his bluejackets overcome their chronic addiction to drunkenness with his temperance campaign of the early 1830s, which succeeded, temporarily at least, in exchanging grog rations for cash payments; he crowed that every man on the *John Adams* had taken that alternative.

There is evidence that his solicitude was recognized by his men. The crew of the *Java* thanked him for his "kind treatment," and claimed that the service would never lack willing recruits while it had "commanders like Biddle." Toward the end of his career he became almost benign, his greatest praise coming from young Nordhoff, who noted that throughout the cruise of the *Columbus* he was always sending back fresh meat, vegetables, and fruit for the men. Warming to the subject, Nordhoff wrote: "Our commodore . . . often interfered in the general management of our ship, and always in favor of the crew. For this he was much beloved by all hands and it was a common saying among the old salts, when the commodore was about to leave the vessel for a time, as he frequently did, 'now the old fellow has gone away, we'll see some hard times,' a prophecy which was generally fulfilled."[12]

The same respondent narrates a revealing story of how Biddle could handle with flair a threat to the ship's order. While the *Columbus* was anchored off Batavia in 1845 under the punishing equatorial sun, depleted supplies necessitated a cutback in drinking water to only three pints a day for each man. Some of the bluejackets "conceived a brilliant idea of making an appeal to the humanity of the commodore" by informing him that thirst had reduced them to imbibing salt water. A little later Biddle asked for the names of those who had been driven to such an extremity. Convinced that this meant that their water ration would be increased, a number of them hastened to sign the list. Instead, the call "All hands to witness punishment" forecast their lot. According to Nordhoff:

> Directly the commodore came out of the cabin, and walked to the gangway, looking as fierce as a trooper. Surveying the crowd ranged before him a moment, he said:
>
> "H———m, so you fellows drank salt water, did you?" looking at a paper. "Here John Jones."
>
> "Here, sir," answered that worthy.
>
> "Did you drink salt water, my man?"
>
> "Yes, sir, a little," answered John Jones, willing to crawl out of the scrape, but unable to see the slightest crevice.
>
> "How much?"
>
> "Only about a pint, sir."
>
> "Master-at-arms, strip John Jones."
>
> And John Jones was seized up and received six with the cats. And so the whole list of *seaman . . .* was gone through, each one receiving half dozen. . . .
>
> After the flogging was through, the commodore said:
>
> "Now, I suppose, you fellows want to know why you have been punished. I'll tell you. It's for drinking salt water. I want you to know, that aboard my ship no one is allowed to drink anything but fresh water. . . . I use only the regular allowance . . . myself; and if any man is really suffering, I'll divide my water with him—but you *shan't drink salt water.* . . . Boatswain, pipe down."
>
> It is scarcely necessary to add, that no more reports of that kind were sent up to head-quarters. It *didn't pay.*[13]

On the other hand, Biddle's concern for his "tars" was always coupled with his insistence that, in comparison to his own standing, their social inferiority and lowly position in the naval hierarchy must be upheld. He showed what he really thought of them when he called the girls he provided while in port for their sexual release, "women of their own class in society." He was appalled when Secretary of the Navy Branch in 1830 invited the men in the *Java* to evaluate him as a commander: "God help the Service if Sailors are permitted" to make such comments. When the same bluejackets had subscribed $100 to buy him a sword, he refused the offering with a frosty, "I disapprove of officers receiving presents from the crew."

His associations with commissioned officers must be described on two levels: those with his juniors, and those with his equals or superiors. In a report to the department in 1830 he summed up what he deemed his responsibilities to his juniors: "To cherish honorable and gentlemanly feelings among the young Midshipmen, to stimulate their ambition, to aid their professional acquirements that they become qualified to fulfill the future hopes and just expectations of their country, I regard as the most important duties entrusted to me."

To a large degree he met his own high aspirations for them, especially in his long-standing interest in their education and his work as a leading forerunner at the Naval Asylum of the U.S. Naval Academy. His letters at Andalusia and to the secretary confirm that he both recommended and interceded for deserving underlings. As a commander he sometimes tried to influence decisions of the department as to promotions or disciplinary actions leading to courts-martial and possible dismissal from the service. For example, he urged that Midshipman Moores receive no further punishment than being sent home for his fracas with Admiral Pacheco in Brazil, even though his troubles had been brought on in part by his being "a little excited by liquor." While commodore of the Mediterranean Squadron he overrode Captain Wadsworth's refusal to approve David Dixon Porter's midshipman's warrant. Some of those who served under him became permanent admirers, modeling themselves after him as an ideal officer.

But Biddle suffered two major breakdowns in his efforts to cultivate the "honorable and gentlemanly feelings among the young Midshipmen." While commodore in the Mediterranean, despite his threats, his lower rankers continued to be noisy, drunken, pugnacious, duel prone, and debt ridden, although the captains under him must share responsibility for this disciplinary failure. In the second instance, however, the fault was his own. At "Biddle's Nursery" at the Naval Asylum he clearly failed to recognize that his wards were officers seasoned by several years of navy experience, and he should have realized that his bars and bolts, ban on cardplaying, and lights out at nine o'clock had no chance of acceptance. By 1840 his classes were ignoring his regulations, reducing him to "forbidding them to trample on his flower beds." By his last cruise the combination of the commodore's mildness and the captain's harshness, despite their personal animosity, evidently worked well enough to control their juniors. Little similar to the open flouting of authority in the Mediterranean and at the asylum is recorded in Biddle's letters to the secretary or entries in the "Smooth Log" of the *Columbus*.

Biddle's high sense of his own social importance that came through as snobbishness made his relations with his equals and superiors often touchy, although a partial reason for this may have been that his absorption in the activities of his family made outside associations less important to him than to most other persons. He had warm friends, of course. He and Bainbridge remained close from the time of their shared incarceration in Tripoli until the elder's death in 1833. George Read was a confidant. David Conner, who served as Biddle's first lieutenant in the *Hornet* and the *Ontario,* admired him. John D. Sloat, who thanked his captain for his "many kindnesses" in the *Congress* during 1823, referred to him almost a quarter of a century later as "my oldest and most intimate friend" in the navy. Of his diplomatic associates, Hugh Nelson was apparently the one who liked him the best and supported him throughout the controversy with Rodney. U.S. minister to Argentina John M. Forbes, Jeremy Robinson in Chile, and General Stephen A. Kearney were others who expressed their appreciation for favors that Biddle had put himself out to do for them.[14]

The list of his enemies is longer. This work is dotted with his uncomplimentary remarks about Porter and Rodgers, his pet detestations. Secretary Smith Thompson, Hull, Decatur, and Sinclair incurred his strong dislike. Du Pont, who first rather admired him, soon came to regard him with utter contempt. Two of his diplomatic colleagues, Prevost and Rhind, clashed with him for what they considered, perhaps correctly, his intrusions into their own bailiwicks. His short association with Lord Cochrane was characterized by a mutal antipathy. Biddle comes across as selfish insofar as his own comfort or convenience was concerned. Even granting the noisome conditions in the captain's cabin that Rodney caused, his treatment of that desperately ill old man was merciless. It made no difference to him that the perpetually seasick Dr. Crump needed fresh air in 1847, and he kept his cabin filled with cigar smoke until the other was literally driven out of it. Indeed, Biddle does not seem to have sweetened with age, save in his regard for his sailors. Although Dr. Tichnor's Journal in the *Columbus* is somewhat ambivalent about him, with both compliments and derogations, the three officers most closely associated with him on that cruise—Paulding, Wyman, and Selfridge—all ended on terms of hostility with him. In many, if not most of his personal relationships, those with his family excepted, he often comes across as cold, self-centered, and cantankerous.

These unattractive aspects of his character and personality, however, cannot detract from his sterling achievements as a naval officer and a diplomat. As a professional seafarer Biddle can be summed up as superb in navigation, gunnery, courage, and administrative ability.

Throughout his cruises in the *Hornet, Ontario, Macedonian, Congress, Macedonian* again, *Java, Brandywine,* and *Columbus,* one looks in vain for such mishaps as running aground, and only rarely are there indications of faulty planning for supplies of food, water, and other necessities. Biddle's serene confidence in his own nautical mastery may be implied from his official correspondence with the Navy Department. He almost never referred to adverse weather conditions, quite unlike the carpings of Porter and Bainbridge on that subject. Three times he rounded ferocious Cape Horn without complaint, nor did he even mention the massive storm off South Africa in 1845 that so terrified the adolescent Nordhoff that he devoted several hundred words to it in his later book. Biddle's escape from HMS *Cornwallis* in the *Hornet* composes the most conspicuous example of his seafaring mastery. His court of inquiry on the matter described this achievement as deserving "the greatest applause" for his "persevering gallantry and nautical skill, evinced in escaping, under the most disadvantageous circumstances, of a long and arduous chase by a British line-of-battle ship."

As only once did he command a warship in hostile action, his tactical skill with his guns can quickly be summarized. Racing in with the *Hornet* on the *Penguin,* he withheld his broadsides until the distance of "a musket shot" separated them, but once his men commenced their "quick and well directed" fire into their hapless adversary, she was hulled again and again while her most essential masts were either shot away or so damaged as to be useless. Theodore Roosevelt summed up Biddle's competency well in this regard, saying that his "excellent gunnery" enabled him "to destroy an antagonist of equal force in such an exceedingly short time."

Biddle had three wartime and one peacetime opportunities to demonstrate different kinds of courage. When he became the first officer to climb from the *Wasp* to the *Frolic* and personally hauled down her flag he proved his physical bravery. The second occasion demonstrates courage of another sort. After understanding that the *Penguin* had surrendered, he was poised on a rail when a British musket ball sliced along his chin and through his neck. Yet he remained on deck, tied a sailor's shirt around his throat to staunch the blood, and saw to it that his own wound was the last to be dressed by the surgeons. The third was his refusal to panic when for many hours a contrary breeze appeared to make it inevitable that the mighty *Cornwallis* would either sink or force the surrender of his ship. Repeatedly he pulled ahead, gaining precious inches by the well-timed jettisoning of his movables and the use of his crew as shifting ballast until a change in the wind permitted him to escape from his dogged pursuer.

Nor was it his fault that he had no other opportunities to prove his valor against the British. At the start of the war he even hired a boat to chase Commodore Rodgers so that he might sail in the USS *President*. When that failed, he commenced his long enmity with Porter after the latter refused to let him sign on as a lieutenant in the *Essex*. During his enforced fifteen months of idleness at New London he grew increasingly critical of Decatur's torpor in not daring to hazard a dash through the British blockaders. For weeks he strove for a prearranged single-ship encounter between his *Hornet* and the *Loup Cervier*. Meanwhile he was beating on the door of the Navy Department until he was given permission to take out his sloop, thereby enabling him to embark on his last "successful action" of the war.

The situation during his final opportunity to garner honors in battle was quite unlike that of thirty-odd years before. Instead of being outnumbered in warships some forty to one, as in 1812, the United States possessed overwhelming naval superiority over the Mexicans. So the aged commodore recognized that there was neither reason nor need to emulate his derring-do against the British. Instead, he allowed his younger colleagues to carry on what little fighting was necessary in the Pacific, remaining in port throughout his entire tenure. He served well in this nonbelligerent capacity, persuading Shubrick to stay at his post, aiding in removing the erratic Stockton and Frémont in favor of the levelheaded Kearney, lifting a paper blockade, and refusing to countenance a scorched-earth policy against Mexican civilians.

Biddle's peacetime bravery occurred at Valparaiso in the summer of 1819, and it was accompanied by nerve-wracking tension. His *Ontario* carried over $200,000 in specie, while out in the bay rode two Chilean frigates, outgunning his sloop by at least three to one. He had just received a warning that the talented but avaricious and unscrupulous Lord Cochrane, ever ready to violate neutral rights for his own advantage, was planning to board him. This threat was made plausible by the ominous movements of Cochrane's frigates as they came into positions to intercept or attack. Biddle, however, "did not choose to be deterred from sailing." Suspense must have been mouth-drying for the Americans, for the *Ontario* had to pass "within half gun shot" of the larger frigate before making her way to open water unscathed.

Biddle was the most active of his period's higher-ranking naval officers. Not once in his career spanning almost a half-century did he turn down a seagoing assignment, although over thirty years separated his first command from his last. To be sure, his relative affluence made available to him greater options than those open to the majority of his colleagues, but it was primarily his record that eventually allowed him to pick and choose among the department's offerings. When no duty afloat was available, he was content to remain on inactive status in Philadelphia among his relatives and friends until foreign opportunities again beckoned.

Unlike many of his confreres he had little interest in administration per se, especially ashore. He never strove, as far as the record indicates, to become a highly paid navy commissioner, nor did he hanker for navy yard commands, in contrast to Rodgers, Hull, Porter, Barron, Bainbridge, and Chauncey, among others. The only times the secretary could wheedle him into accepting such posts were when they were located in Philadelphia. For about a year between 1825 and 1826 he commanded ably the navy yard in that city. He was "Governor" of the Navy Asylum there for four years, and in the process considerably improved its physical plant.

His managerial ability was equally effective at sea. He usually obeyed the department's orders to the letter, but when he realized that circumstances had changed, he was self-confident enough to disregard them. His reports to the secretary were typically short and to the point, only lapsing into verbosity when he felt that lengthy explanations were mandatory. The general lack of complaints about his direction of his several squadrons suggests that he met their needs well, purchasing supplies, accounting for expenditures, planning the movements of his ships and their repairs, and, with a couple of exceptions, maintaining morale and discipline.

There are some flaws in his service record. It was most uncharacteristically rash of him to permit Japanese from hundreds of armed barges aboard the *Columbus* and *Vincennes* at Yedo. Much worse was his obtuseness in keeping the *Macedonian* close to Cuba's febrile shore for so long in 1822, making him chiefly responsible for turning his ship into a deathtrap. This was followed by his odd inertia in failing to pursue pirates after he returned to the West Indies a few months later. But these errors in judgment do no more than lower him a notch from top-drawer ranking.

Biddle's potential contributions to the service were recognized early. Prior to attaining his own commands, he was evaluated by several of those under whom he had worked. All recognized him as a sterling prospect for the navy. In 1805 Bainbridge had predicted that because of his junior's "talents," he must "one day be conspicuous in the service of his country." A few months later the fact that he was "very attentive" to his gunboat duties made Commodore Alexander Murray's cruise "much more to our satisfaction." The

Wasp's Captain Jacob Jones reported that major reasons for his triumph over the *Frolic* had been Biddle's "active conduct," "exact attention to every department," and particularly his "animating example to the crew by his intrepidity."

The department evaluated him with the most concrete examples of approval possible—promotions and commands. His progress up the ranks was swift, from midshipman in 1800 to lieutenant in 1807, master commandant in 1813, and post captain in 1815, thereby reaching the highest official grade in the service. He first trod the quarterdeck of his own command in 1813 when he was thirty and walked down the gangway of his last in 1848 at the age of sixty-five. From 1815 to 1845 he was either captain or commodore in eight American warships. He was the only officer to command four men-of-war between 1815 and 1823. His government honored him not only with prize money but with a silver medal for the *Wasp-Frolic* and a gold one for the *Hornet-Penguin*. As a naval officer his achievements were little short of singular.

Biddle was fortunate in having many opportunities to prove himself an adroit and accomplished diplomat. His less important assignments, such as those questioning the Russians in the *Kutuzov* off Monterey in 1818, the Spaniards near Gibraltar in 1823, and the Hawaiians at Honolulu in 1846, may be sidelined in order to evaluate him for his activities in which he was able to make major contributions to American foreign policy—his negotiations with royalist and rebel authorities at Valparaiso, Santiago, and Lima during the Chilean and Peruvian wars of independence against Spain in 1817 and 1818; with primarily Spanish representatives in the Caribbean during 1822 and 1823; with Latin Americans off Montevideo and Buenos Aires from 1826 to 1828; with the Turks at Smyrna and Constantinople in 1829 and 1830; with Chinese and Britons at Canton and other ports in China from 1845 to 1846; and with the Japanese at Yedo harbor in 1846. Of these six opportunities, Biddle failed to serve his nation well in only one, attaining inconclusive results in another.

The Chilean and Peruvian uprisings against their Spanish masters plunged Biddle into a maelstrom of complications, and it is to his credit that he eased his way through it without being capsized. He later summarized his difficulties at the time and place: "I believe it impossible for any American commanding officer to be in the Pacific without giving offense to one side or the other. The royal party, knowing the general feeling of our countrymen, are jealous of them; the Patriots, on the other hand, expecting too much, are dissatisfied." To be sure, he had been hoodwinked by Viceroy Pezuela when he transported royalist spies to Chile, and had irritated some of the patriots by his tiffs with Calderón and Cochrane. But through the formulation of his close friendship with Pezuela he had saved American property amounting to "nearly a million" and had freed some of his fellow countrymen from Peruvian jails. Historian Edward Billington is correct when he describes the beneficial consequences of this relationship: Biddle "had carefully refrained from making unreasonable or exaggerated claims that would denigrate the authority of the viceroy. . . . On his part, Pezuela, recognizing in the naval officer a man of reason and integrity, was willing to concede any requests that could be justified under international usage and were not contrary to Spanish laws." King Ferdinand VII himself had thanked him "in his royal name." Yet he had done this without a break in rebel-American relations. None other than Bernardo O'Higgins, "Supreme Dictator" of Chile, called him "as good a republican as any one."

It should be pointed out that although four other Americans were in lower South America at the time engaging in some sort of diplomatic activity—Prevost, Worthington, Robinson, and Bland—these attainments had been Biddle's alone. Prevost asserted that the kudos should be his own, but Secretary of State Adams disagreed: "Biddle's conduct . . . was to the account of his countrymen, for whom he saved and rescued property to a very large amount. He obtained the release of many citizens of the United States who were prisoners. Prevost has never saved a dollar nor obtained the release of a man."

In the midst of these tribulations he had sped to the mouth of the Columbia River in Oregon during the summer of 1818 to accomplish all that his government had asked of him by entering a strong American claim to at least the southern portion of that vast area.

What Biddle did off the Atlantic coast of South America while Brazil and Argentina were at one another's throats was also praiseworthy, granting that the situation there was less complex than that on Pacific shores a decade before. He had handled skilfully the Moores-Pacheco imbroglio, which might have wildfired into an international incident. He had managed to retain the amity of both antagonists while mitigating the impact of Brazilian blockades on American shipping. Secretary of the Navy Southard had characterized his tenure there as demonstrating his "intelligence[,] fidelity, and discretion."

Biddle had been able to conduct essentially a one-man show in both of his Latin American tours. In Turkey during 1829 and 1830, however, he was a member of a latter-day succession of American naval and civil officials who had worked off and on for a Turkish treaty since the days of Bainbridge in 1801. Of the trio who had hammered out the final details of the pact in 1830, Rhind was clearly more important than Biddle and Offley. Yet the other two contributed effectively toward its later ratification by the Senate when they made vocal their opposition to Rhind's secret naval clause. This was obviously against America's long "no alliance" tradition, or, as Adams said, "incompatible with the neutrality of the United States." Biddle's objections helped to enable the Senate to accept the vital public provisions without having to include Rhind's article.

In China he was once again on his own. Even though his diplomatic responsibilities had been dumped upon him unexpectedly by Everett's illness in Brazil, he was able to execute them with judicious competency. He made himself persona grata with all the Ch'ing authorities with whom he came in contact. He had advised them well as to what tactics they might use vis-à-vis the British occupation of the Chusan Islands and the Canton city entry question. He had recommended to them courses of action for their country that, if adopted, might have made late-nineteenth-century Chinese history less doleful. He had demonstrated that his nation could deal fairly in commercial matters by opposing Wetmore in his controversy with Shing-ho. He had set up the U.S. Legation at Canton and the American consulate at Shanghai, the only treaty port with enough American trade to warrant such a station. He permitted a bit of iron to show through the velvet by sending the *Vincennes* to join two British frigates at Whampoa Island when the Canton riots threatened to go out of control.

His single abject failure in diplomacy was in the Caribbean during 1822 and 1823. One might offer convincing arguments to explain why his behavior there was so atypical. His orders were both confusing and hampering, the makeup of his squadron was quite inadequate to destroy the shallow-draft hit-and-run corsair vessels, he was shattered by the awful losses from yellow fever in the *Macedonian* and embittered by the Navy Department's treatment of him in his quarrels with Hull and Sinclair. All this, however, cannot gainsay the simple fact that his efforts proved sterile. He was unable to persuade Captain General Mahe to grant him the essential right of landing on Spanish soil when in active pursuit of pirates. He could not achieve the same degree of naval cooperation with the British that Warrington was able to enjoy a few years later in ridding Caribbean waters of that menace. Biddle's squadron may have made a few captures during his first tour there, but from late 1822 into the spring of 1823 he cruised for 112 days without apprehending a single outlaw vessel.

To complete the final diplomatic assignment of his life, Biddle had sailed directly from his triumphs in China to somewhat mixed results in Japan, but with a greater degree of success than failure. His attempts to bring the Japanese a bit out of their isolation by writing a trade treaty with them were futile, but it is difficult to see how any other American officer could have done better in 1846. He had accepted a physical assault from a Japanese soldier without violent response, not even ensuring that his assailant would be promptly executed. For this he has been criticized both then and now for causing America to "lose face." But his mission was fact-finding only, and had he reacted truculently to the "blow or a push" he would have disobeyed his instructions, which specifically enjoined him against any conduct that might "excite a hostile feeling or distrust of the Government of the United States." Indeed, had he done so, Perry might have been received quite differently when he sailed into Yedo harbor seven years later.

Biddle's hauteur, aloofness, and confidence in his impeccable social standing, irksome to many of his American associates, served him well in meeting foreign dignitaries. Almost all of those with whom he negotiated were noblemen of one kind or another, for the world was still monarch-ridden during the early nineteenth century. Clearly considering himself an innate part of an American aristocracy, he felt at no disadvantage in discussions with his titled counterparts. He always moved with ease and confidence among them (Lord Cochrane, of course, excepted) from the time Sir Alexander Ball interceded in his behalf in Tripoli, then in his efforts with Admiral Sir Thomas Hardy to arrange a ship-to-ship duel off New London, in his warm friendship with Viceroy Pezuela, and, finally, in his attracting the approval of mandarins Ch'i-ying and Liang Pao-ch'ang.

In all his diplomatic negotiations Biddle never hesitated to show that he had, as Billingsley puts it, "clothed himself in the authority and power of the country he so proudly represented." Whenever he thought that his nation's honor had been impugned he hastened to retaliate, as in his refusals to salute Calderón or Cochrane after the former had not responded to the *Ontario*'s guns when first entering a Chilean port. His pro-Americanism made him somewhat xenophobic. His difficulties with Latin-Americans in the Caribbean and lower South America impelled him to admit, "I despise the Spaniards," and a few years later, "Next to the Portuguese-Americans, the most suspicious people in the world are Spanish-Americans." He approved of the French takeover of Algeria in 1830, forecasting that its results would be beneficial for the local populace. On the other hand, he enthusiastically prepared to war against them during the spat of the early 1830s over unpaid French claims.

Biddle's opinion of the British is ambivalent. He manifested Anglophobia while in China during the mid-1840s, erroneously concluding that they were plotting to retain the Chusan Islands. Yet when

Western interests were apparently menaced by the rioting in Canton he lined up with them until calm was restored to the city. He had objected vehemently, if in vain, against the British ban on hoisting the American flag over the U.S. consulate in Shanghai. As late as the summer of 1846 he had predicted war with Britain over Oregon, a conflict he thought his nation could eventually win. On the other hand, he had recognized them as worthy antagonists from 1812 to 1815, deploring though he did their campaigns against noncombatants in Chesapeake Bay and elsewhere. He summarized his estimation of them in 1830: "With all her faults, including those toward us, I still admire England. Her fall or decline would be a calamity to the people of every country in Europe. But for its strenuous and enlightened friends among the English the cause of representative government in Europe would soon go to the bottom."[15]

Though somewhat muted, Biddle's patriotism was always there. He may have refused to indulge in some of the more blatant and chauvinistic flag-waving of so many of his contemporaries, nor could he go all the way with Decatur's famous, "Our country . . . may she always be in the right, but our country, right or wrong," as he considered the Mexican War a national disgrace. Still, he meant it when he wrote toward the end of his last cruise, "There is but one country in the world which I wish to see again, and that country is my own."

Biddle's diplomatic career can be summed up as four triumphs, one partial success, and one failure. The secretary of the navy wrote at the end of his Japanese assignment that his "prudent and judicious conduct . . . merits the strong approbation of the Department." This evaluation may be applied to all his other responsibilities, save that in the West Indies, as an accurate judgment as to his contributions to U.S. foreign policy.

Considering Biddle's eventful life and meaningful contributions to the advantage of the Navy and State departments, why has he been so largely forgotten? Prior to this work, no full-length biography of him had ever been published. This is surprising, as lives have been written of so many of his naval contemporaries, some by several authors, both in their own day and since. Nor has his own navy honored him. There have been four U.S. warships named *Biddle,* but all of them commemorate his uncle Nicholas for the *Randolph-Yarmouth* battle on 7 March 1778. Bainbridge, for example, has had four named after him, including the world's first nuclear-powered surface fighting ship, a guided missile cruiser still on active service at this writing. Six American towns and cities are called Bainbridge, and the one in Maryland contains the Bainbridge Naval Training Center. To carry his family name Biddle has only two hamlets, one in western Pennsyl-

vania and the other in southern Montana, and both probably commemorate not him, but his brother Nicholas.[16]

The reasons for his relative oblivion are many. He was physically
unimpressive, lacking the attractive magnetism of Decatur and Porter
or the glowering eminence of Truxtun and Rodgers. He was no orator, no coiner of memorable phrases, never emulating Oliver H.
Perry's "We have met the enemy and they are ours," or Decatur's
"Our country . . . right or wrong." That Biddle was always publicity
shy is perhaps the chief explanation for his lack of impact upon his
country's memory. Save when forced to defend himself in controversies, he refused to beat his own drum. This was in the sharpest
contrast to so many of his gaudier and more theatrical colleagues:
Decatur, who would so ruthlessly manipulate or ride over others who
threatened his public reputation; Porter, who captured international
attention by his startling irruption into the Pacific, his desperately
fought but ill-starred defeat at Valparaiso, and his book about his
exploits, which instigated controversy on both sides of the Atlantic;
Bainbridge, who aroused national sympathy for the mishaps that dogged
his early career and thereafter never left the national eye; Hull, who
became the public's darling as the first to demonstrate that the Royal
Navy was not indefatigable; and Rodgers, who ensured his national
reputation by his stranglehold for so many years as head of the prestigious Board of Navy Commissioners.

The timing and nature of Biddle's exploits did not promote his
later remembrance. His wartime achievements were won in sloops,
not in the superfrigates that inspired so much national adulation. His
only victory won on his own was fought in the distant South Atlantic,
occurring many months after the end of the war. He never commanded America's favorite combat vessel, the USS *Constitution*. Most
of his triumphs were gained in peacetime naval and diplomatic assignments, effective in the long run but arousing little contemporary
interest. For the better part of a quarter-century to most Americans
the name Biddle denoted the banker, not the officer, for Nicholas
was bathed in the nation's spotlight, particularly during his struggle
with the Jacksonians over rechartering the Second Bank of the United
States. The manner of James's death was prosaic, both as to time and
circumstance. He lived on for decades after his wartime achievements,
unlike Oliver H. Perry or Macdonough who died prematurely, while
the memories of Lakes Erie and Champlain were still vivid. He was
killed by natural causes, unlike Decatur, tragically slain by Barron's
pistol; his uncle Nicholas blown to pieces battling a British ship of
the line; or Lawrence, crying in the agony of his mortal wound,
"Don't give up the ship!" Never marrying, he had no direct descen-

dants, as did Porter and Macdonough, to write books exaggerating the abilities and glossing over or even omitting the failings of their close relatives. When his accomplishments rather than his public relations are studied, however, it is clear that he deserves to have made a more lasting impression upon the national memory.

From his correspondence and other documentation, generalities about Biddle may be stated and adjectives applied with some degree of confidence. But to state a truism that should be recognized by any biographer, penetrating the innermost thoughts or satisfactorily explaining the actions of his or her subject is a chancy enterprise. His deliberate reticence ensures even more that Biddle the private individual must remain somewhat shadowy. One is upon more solid ground in evaluating him on his generally excellent naval and diplomatic record. The America in which he lived provided him with a lofty social status, a comfortable way of life, and ample opportunities to contribute to the aspirations of the Navy and State departments. As Bainbridge had forecast during the summer of 1805, Biddle would be "conspicuous in the service of his country," and the interaction between the man and his nation would profit both.

APPENDIX

1. Since the first time I put to sea, I have been in England, France, Spain, Portugal, Italy, and Turkey in Europe—Tunis, Algiers, Tripoli, and Turkey in Asia—Sicily, Malta, Gibraltar, Majorca and Minorca—Colombia, Brasil, Banda Oriental [Uruguay], Chile, Peru, California, Oregon, and the Sandwich islands—China and Japan—English, Dutch, and Portuguese possessions in the East Indies—English, French, Dutch, Spanish, Swedish, and Danish islands in the West Indies, besides the black island of St. Domingo. To many of these places I have been oftener than once.

I have been once round the world, five times round the Cape of Good Hope, three times round Cape Horn, and crossed the Equator twenty times. I have commanded on all the naval stations, the Mediterranean, the Brasils, the Pacific, the East Indies, and the West Indies. I signed the treaty with Turkey, exchanged the treaty with China, had authority to conclude a treaty with Japan. During the war with Great Britain, I was in two actions, both of them successful. During the war with Tripoli, I was upwards of 19 months a prisoner. At this moment I am the only officer afloat who was a commanding officer in the War of 1812. I was made a Commander when 13 years in the Navy and *Post* when 15 years.

I have been 48 years in the Navy, twice a prisoner of war, once severely wounded in action, never fought a duel, never was tried by a court martial, never drank a glass of grog. At the time I entered the Navy, grog drinking was almost universal.

During the war (not this wretched Mexican war), I was promoted out of my turn. I have received two medals from the government of the United States, a sword from the Commonwealth of Pennsylvania, a piece of plate from some of my personal friends in Philadelphia, a public dinner from some of the citizens of New York, was slandered by the Legislature of Delaware, and burnt in effigy by the people of Wilmington.

In 1807 I went to China on a merchant ship as 1st officer. In July 1811 I went to Lisbon as a supercargo. In December 1811, I went to Paris as a bearer of dispatches. In 1824 I went passenger to Italy with my brother-in-law who was sent abroad for his health. There is but one country in the world that I wish to see again, and that country is my own. I am now on my way to it. Shall I ever leave it again? I think not, certainly not willingly.

—James Biddle to James S. Biddle, 12 February 1848, from Nicholas Biddle's Personal Letters, vol. 5, p. 40 (Historical Society of Pennsylvania)

2. Statement of Rodney Family Luggage to be put aboard the USS *Congress*, 1823.

1 new Carriage with Harness
1 old Phaeton with Harness
1 old Cart with Harness
1 Plough
2 Churns for making butter (old)
1 Patent washing machine (old)
1 Wooden Horse for drying Cloths (old)
2 Hampers contents unknown
4 Casks contents unknown
3 Quarter Casks wine
1 Quarter Cask Vinegar
1 large Crate supposed to be Crockery ware
1 large Tierce [42-gallon cask] of Kitchen utensils
2 large quilting frames (old)
1 large Chest
26 Trunks
1 Side Board
4 Mattress' (old)
1 Ship with ordnance
4 dogs. 5 Goats
1 mans Saddle (old)
1 mans Saddle (new)
1 Female Saddle (old)
86 Boxes Contents of most of them unknown
54 barrels Contents of most of them unknown
16 Kegs contents unknown
2 Jars contents unknown
1 Role Blankets (old)
1 Bundle Bedquilts (old)
2 Mahogany Candle Stands (old)
8 washing tubs (old)
4 wash stands (old)
4 Pails (old)
3 Horse Buckets (old)

11 Bureaus
1 Secretary and Book case (old)
8 Pine Board Book cases (old)
1 Set Pine board shelves (old)
1 large Walnut Desk (old)
1 Piano Forte (old)
1 large Mirror
1 large easy chair (old)
107 Chairs 47 of them old
1 Sofa
2 Settees
1 Fancy stool
2 foot Stools
11 Bedsteads (old)
3 Pine Cotts
6 Sacking bottoms (old)
2 Bed cords (old)
1 Cradle (old)
2 Setts of Testers [bed canopies] (old)
10 Beds (old)
2 Kitchen tin Roasters
3 Tubs jars containing pickles
7 Baskets of different sizes
5 Waiters [trays] (old)
1 Tea Canister
1 Tea Chest empty
1 Demijohn
2 Oil Cloths (old)
1 old Carpet
1 Hearth rug (old)
3 pair of Tongs (old)
3 pair of Andirons (old)
3 Shovels (old)
3 Shafing dishes (old)
1 Iron pot (old)
1 Chopping knife
1 Frying pan (old)
1 Wine cooler (old)
1 Coffee mill broken

5 Crickets [wooden footstools] &
Arms Chairs for Children (old)
1 Seal Press
17 Tables

1 Fish Kettle (old)
1 Knife tray (old)
2 drip Stones [sills]
2 small Bags of Stores

—"Statement of Capt. Biddle respecting Mr. Rodney" (written by a clerk), n.d., Cadwalader Collection (Historical Society of Pennsylvania) in Nicholas Biddle Wainwright's "Voyage of the Frigate *Congress*, 1823," *Pennsylvania Magazine of History and Biography* (Philadelphia), vol. 75 (April 1951), 172–73.

NOTES

ABBREVIATIONS USED IN THE NOTES

ASP   *American State Papers: Documents Legislative and Executive, 1789–1838*, 38 vols. (Washington: 1832–61).

BDP   DFL, *Nothing Too Daring: A Biography of Commodore David Porter, 1780–1843* (Annapolis, Md.: 1970).

BW   USND, *Naval Documents Related to the United States Wars with the Barbary Powers: Naval Operations, Including Diplomatic Backround from 1785–1807,* 6 vols. (Washington: 1939–44).

BWB   DFL, *Ready to Hazard: A Biography of Commodore William Bainbridge, 1774–1833* (Hanover, N.H. and London: 1981).

CB   Charles Biddle, Commodore James Biddle's father.

CBA   CB, *Autobiography of Charles Biddle, Vice-President of the Executive Council of Pennsylvania, 1745–1821,* 2 vols., ed. by James S. Biddle, (Philadelphia: 1883).

CC   Cadwalader Collection, HSP.

CD   USDS, Diplomatic Despatches, China, M 69, NA.

CL   USND, Letters Received by the SN from Captains, RG 45, M 125, NA, and USNA.

DAB   Allen Johnson and Dumas Malone, eds., *Dictionary of American Biography,* 22 vols. (New York: 1928–44).

DFL   David F. Long, author of this work.

DNB   Leslie Stephen and Sidney Lee, eds., *Dictionary of National Biography,* 22 vols. (London: rev. ed., 1959–65).

DP   David Porter.

EISL   USND, East India Squadron Letters, RG 45, M 89, NA.

HLNO   L. R. Hamersly Co., *List of Officers of the U.S. Navy and of the Marine Corps* (New York: 1900).

HSP   Historical Society of Pennsylvania, Philadelphia, Pa.

JB   James Biddle, the subject of this biography.

JBJO   Journal Kept by James Biddle in the *Ontario,* 4 October 1817–22 March 1819, USND, RG 45, roll M 902, NA.

JBPA   JB Papers at Andalusia, the Biddle family estate near Philadelphia.

"JBSB"   "Commodore James Biddle and His Sketch Book," *PMHB*, vol. 90 (January 1966), 3–50.

JQA   John Quincy Adams.

JQAM   Charles Francis Adams, ed., *Memoirs of John Quincy Adams*, 12 vols. (Philadelphia: 1877).

LC   Library of Congress, Washington, D.C.

LBV   "Log Book of the U.S. Ship *Vincennes*, Captain Hiram Paulding," USND, RG 45, app. D, no. 78, vol. 13 (1 May 1845–9 April 1847), NA.

NA   National Archives, Washington, D.C.

NB   Nicholas Biddle, the banker, James's brother.

NBW   Nicholas Biddle Wainwright.

NWR   *Niles' Weekly Register,* Baltimore, Md.

NYHS   New-York Historical Society, New York, N.Y.

PMHB   *Pennsylvania Magazine of History and Biography*, Philadelphia, Pa.

RG   USND, Record Group, NA.

SLC   "Smooth Log of the United States Ship *Columbus,* Thos W. Wyman, bearing the broad pennant of Commodore James Biddle," vols. 6–8 (26 April 1845–15 March 1848), JBPA, vols. 9–11.

SN   Secretary of the Navy.

SNL   Letters Sent by the SN to Officers, 1798–1868, USND, RG 45, M 149, NA.

SS   Secretary of State.

TJ   Benajah Tichnor, "Journal, 1845–48, on Board the *Columbus* on a Voyage from New York to the East Indies," ms. vol., Benajah Tichnor Collection, Yale University.

USDS   U.S. Department of State.

USNA   U.S. Naval Academy, Annapolis, Md.

USND   U.S. Navy Department.

USNIP   *U.S. Naval Institute Proceedings,* Annapolis, Md.

WB   William Bainbridge.

WC   Winterthur Collection, Eleutherian Mills Historical Library, Greenville, Del.

PROLOGUE

1 Smooth Log of the *Columbus* (SLC), 12 February 1848, James Biddle Papers at Andalusia (JBPA), 16 vols, vol. 8 (11 November 1847–15 March 1848).

2. James Biddle (JB) to James S. Biddle, 12 February 1848, Nicholas Biddle (NB), Personal Letters, vol. 5, Historical Society of Pennsylvania (HSP).

CHAPTER 1

1. *Autobiography of Charles Biddle, Vice-President of the Executive Council of Pennsylvania, 1745–1821 (CBA)*, ed. by James S. Biddle (Philadelphia: 1883), 377, 366–367; Thomas P. Govan. *Nicholas Biddle: Nationalist and Public Banker, 1786–1844* (Chicago: 1959), 3.

2. Nathaniel Burt, *The Perennial Philadelphians: The Anatomy of an American Aristocracy* (Boston: 1963), 46; "Clement Biddle," *Dictionary of American Biography (DAB)*, 22 vols. (New York, 1928–44), vol. 2, 239–40; David Porter (DP) to Samuel Hambleton, 12 October 1811 (DP Papers), David Dixon Porter Papers, Library of Congress (LC); "James Wilkinson," *DAB*, vol. 20, 225.

3. Nicholas B. Wainwright (NBW), "Commodore James Biddle and His Sketch Book" ("JBSB") *Pennsylvania Magazine of History and Biography (PMHB)*, vol. 90 (January 1966), 33.

4. William B. Clark, *Captain Dauntless: The Story of Nicholas Biddle of the Continental Navy, 1740–1778* (Baton Rouge: 1949), 5.

5. *CBA*, 57; Govan, 3.

6. Govan, 3; *CBA*, 116–17; Govan, 4; *CBA*, 371–73.

7. Govan, 4.

8. Clark, 36–70.

9. Ibid., 71–239.

10. Ibid., 240

11. Ibid., 240–46.

12. James Fenimore Cooper, *History of the Navy of the United States*, 3 vols. (New York: 1864), vol. 1, 120.

13. NB to his brother James, 16 June 1776, in Clark, 134.

14. Francis J. Dallett, University of Pennsylvania archivist, letter to David F. Long (DFL), 4 December 1980; *Port Folio Magazine*, vol. 6 (November 1815), 429; *Analectic Magazine and Naval Chronicle*, vol. 6 (November 1815) 383; Henry Simpson, *The Lives of Eminent Philadelphians Now Deceased* (Philadelphia: 1859), 70; "JBSB," 33.

15. Eugene S. Ferguson, ed., *A Description of the* [Thomas] *Truxtun–*[Charles] *Biddle Letters in the Collection of the Library Company of Philadelphia* (Philadelphia: 1947), passim. These letters have since been moved to the HSP.

16. Truxtun to CB, 3 December 1799, Truxton-Biddle Letters, HSP, *CBA*, 286; Truxtun to CB, 24 June 1800, Truxtun-Biddle Letters, HSP, *CBA*, 286–87; Aaron Burr Papers, 1756–1836, series I, Correspondence and Public Papers, July 1800, microfilmed, University of New Hampshire Library; *CBA*, 286–87.

17. DP, *Constantinople and Its Environs: in a Series of Letters Exhibiting the Actual State of the Manners, Customs, and Habits of the Turks, Armenians, Jews, and Greeks—by an American Long Resident at Constantinople*, 2 vols. (New York: 1835), vol. 2, 10–11.

18. David Dixon Porter, *Memoir of Commodore David Porter of the United States Navy* (Albany, N.Y.: 1875), 19–20; Eugene S. Ferguson, *Truxtun of the Constellation: The Life of Commodore Thomas Truxtun, 1755–1822* (Baltimore: 1956), 207, 210.

19. *CBA,* 290–91.

20. "Extract of a letter from a gentleman on board the frigate *President,* 20 November 1800," in *Port Folio,* 430; Ferguson, *Truxtun,* 211–12; *CBA,* 292.

21. Truxtun to CB, 4 January 1800, Truxton-Biddle Letters, HSP; Charles O. Paullin, *Paullin's History of Naval Administration, 1775–1911* (Annapolis: 1968), 132.

22. "JBSB," 7; JB to NB, 7 June 1801, JBPA, vol. 1, #2490; JB to NB, 7 July 1801, in Thomas P. Govan, "Nicholas Biddle at Princeton," *Princeton University Library Chronicle,* vol. 9 (February 1948), 54.

23. JB to NB, 7 June 1801.

24. "A Journal Kept on Board the United States Frigate *Constellation,* Alexander Murray, Esquire, Commanding, by James Biddle, Midshipman," USND, *Naval Documents Related to the United States Wars with the Barbary Powers: Naval Operations, Including Diplomatic Background, from 1785 to 1807 (BW),* 6 vols. (Washington: 1939–44), vol. 2, passim.

25. In Leonard F. Guttridge and Jay D. Smith, *The Commodores* (New York, Evanston, and London: 1959), 67.

26. *Port Folio,* 451.

27. Ray's reference is undoubtedly to Daniel Mendoza (1764–1836), a British prizefighter well known during his day for introducing a new style of pugilism, in which clever boxing partially superseded the slugging contests so typical of the bare-knuckle era. "Daniel Mendoza," *Dictionary of National Biography (DNB),* 22 vols. (London, 1959–65), vol. 13, 250; William Ray, *Horrors of Slavery, or, American Tars in Tripoli* (Troy, N.Y.: 1808), 60, 64.

28. Ray, 70, 69.

29. "Act of Congress, 19 March 1804," *BW,* vol. 3, 503.

30. I have narrated the details of the *Philadelphia*'s grounding and capture, as well as her personnel's nineteen months' imprisonment, in my biographies of David Porter *(BDP),* 22–32, and William Bainbridge *(BWB),* 70–102. Here I shall confine myself in general to matters concerning Biddle personally.

31. *BWB,* 70–77.

32. Ray, 82; *Port Folio,* 432.

33. James Fenimore Cooper, "Bainbridge," *Graham's Magazine,* vol. 21 (November 1842), 250.

34. William Bainbridge (WB) to Edward Preble, 16 February 1804, *BW,* vol. 3, 409; WB to ?, 18 February 1804, ibid., 433.

35. James Renshaw to John Rodgers, 6 November 1804, ibid., vol. 5, 124–25; in Thomas Appleton to Robert E. Livingston, U.S. minister to France, 12 April 1804, ibid., vol. 4, 22; JB to NB, 10 April 1805, JBPA, vol. 1, #2528.

36. Jones to NB, 16 April 1805, JBPA, vol. 1, #2531; JB to NB, 10 April 1805, *Port Folio,* vol. 2 (December 1813), 570.

37. Thomas Harris, *The Life and Services of Commodore William Bainbridge, United States Navy* (Philadelphia: 1837), 104–7.

38. *BWB*, 78–80; WB to Preble, 12 November 1803, *BW,* vol. 3, 174.

39. BWB, 24–31, 40–54.

40. WB to JB, n.d., JBPA, vol. 16, #6063.

41. *CBA,* 300; Truxtun to CB, 10 March 1804, Truxtun-Biddle Letters, HSP, *CBA,* 300; Phineas Bond to the secretary of the Navy (SN), 14 March 1804, JBPA, vol. 1, #2522.

42. "Alexander Ball," *DNB,* vol. 1, 990–91; Ball to CB, 22 August 1804, JBPA, vol. 1, #2523; JB to NB, 10 April 1805, ibid., #2528; Jones, Hunt, and JB to NB, 16 April 1805, ibid., #2531.

43. WB to Tobias Lear, 11 April 1805, *BW,* vol. 5, 503; Cowdery Journal, 13–15 April 1805, ibid., 509; ibid., 14 May 1805, ibid., vol. 6, 14; Smith to Jefferson, 19 September 1805, Thomas Jefferson Papers, in Christopher McKee, *Edward Preble: A Naval Biography* (Annapolis: 1972), 334.

44. "Treaty of Peace and Amity Between the United States and Tripoli," 4 June 1805, *BW,* vol. 6, 81–82.

45. "Court of Inquiry, Testimony and Report," 29 June 1805, ibid., vol. 3, 191–94.

46. WB to Dr. John Ridgely, 27 January 1806, WB Papers, National Historical Foundation Collection, LC.

47. WB to SN, 23 September 1805, *BW,* vol. 6, 286.

CHAPTER 2

1. *CBA,* 312; SN to Murray, 31 July 1805, *BW,* vol. 6, 199.

2. Charles O. Paullin, *Paullin's History of Naval Administration 1775–1911* (Annapolis: 1968), 143, 148.

3. Ibid., 134; E. K. Eckert, "William Jones and the Role of the Secretary of the Navy in the War of 1812" (unpublished Ph.D. dissertation, University of Florida, 1969), 23–27; JB to NB, 17 August 1813, JBPA, vol. 1, #2667; Charles W. Goldsborough, *United States Naval Chronicle* (Washington: 1824), 322–29; JB to NB, 17 August 1813; Stephen Decatur to WB, n.d., in Leonard F. Guttridge and Jay D. Smith, *The Commodores,* (New York, Evanston, and London: 1959), 109–10.

4. SN to Murray, 31 July 1805; *Spectator* (Boston), 27 October 1804, in John B. McMaster, *History of the People of the United States from the Revolution to the Civil War,* 8 vols. (New York: 1883–1913), vol. 3, 195–97.

5. Murray to SN, 16, 1 December 1805, *BW,* vol. 6, 319, 314.

6. JB to SN, 17 April 1806, Jonathan Williams Collection, Indiana University.

7. *Port Folio,* vol. 6 (November 1815), 434; "JBSB," 8.

8. JB to SN, 21 January 1807, Letters Received by the SN from Officers Below the Rank of Commander, USND, RG 45, M 148, roll 3, #40, N.A; L. R. Hamersly Co., *List of Officers of the U.S. Navy and of the Marine Corps (HLNO)* (New York: 1900), 56.

9. *United States Gazette* (Philadelphia), 1 May 1807, p. 3, col. 2; "JBSB," 8; "George Washington Biddle, Feb. 21, 1779–Aug. 16, 1811," ms. biographical sketch by Jacques Downs, enc. in a letter, Downs to DFL, 5 October 1979; Phyllis R. Abrams, assistant to the curator, Girard College, Philadelphia, letter to DFL, 25 April 1980.

10. George Biddle to JB, 5 September 1807, JBPA, vol. 1, #2558.

11. JB to WB, 19 April 1808, Connaroe Collection, HSP.

12. Jonathan Goldstein, *Philadelphia and the China Trade, 1682–1840: Commercial, Cultural and Attitudinal Effects* (University Park, Pa.: 1978), letter to DFL, 14 February 1979.

13. JB to WB, 19 April 1808; Downs, "George Washington Biddle"; JB to NB, 6 February 1811, JBPA, vol. 1, #2573.

14. JB to WB, 19 April 1808; JB to SN, 24 April 1808, Letters Received by the SN from Officers Below the Rank of Commander, roll 3, #190.

15. DP to SN, 15, 18 February 1809, Letters Received by the SN from Commanders, USND, RG 45, M 147, roll 3, unnumbered.

16. Collector to WB, 1 November 1808, enc. in WB to SN, 2 November 1808, Letters Received by the SN from Captains (CL), ibid., M 125, roll 13, #190.

17. JB to George Read, 13 September 1808, Naval Mss., Historical Society of Delaware.

18. In an ironic twist of fate Bainbridge sat as one of Barron's judges, voting for the conviction of the man who had presided over his own court of inquiry three years before which had found him guiltless for grounding and surrendering the *Philadelphia*. Stephen Decatur was also a member of Barron's court-martial and so publicly assailed the accused, then and later, that he started an intermittent quarrel that finally culminated in the famous duel of March 1820 when Barron killed him.

19. WB to JB, 4 February 1809, War of 1812 Collection, University of Michigan; WB to John Rodgers, 27 November 1809, Rodgers Correspondence, roll 1, New-York Historical Society (NYHS).

20. WB to DP, 29 January 1810, WB Papers, Naval Historical Society Collection, NYHS; WB to SN, 11, 13 March 1810, CL, roll 18, #79, 85.

21. *Analectic Magazine*, vol. 6 (1815), 387; *Port Folio*, 434–35; "JBSB," 8; JB to Rodgers, 12 April 1811, Rodgers Family Papers, Rodgers-Meigs-Macomb Family Mss., Series 1, LC; *United States Gazette*, 15 April–30 May, 1 July–11 September 1811, passim.

22. SN to JB, 27 November 1811, SNL to Officers Below the Rank of Commander, pp. 511–12; *United States Gazette*, 20 November 1811, p. 3, col. 3; ibid., 5–6 December 1811, p. 3. col. 3.

23. Joel Barlow to Secretary of State (SS), 4 January 1812, *American State Papers: Documents Legal and Executive, 1798–1838, (ASP)* 38 vols. (Washington: 1832–61), Class 1, *Foreign Relations*, vol. 3, 517; *Port Folio*, 435; Charles Morris, *Autobiography of Charles Morris* (Boston: 1880), 45–49.

24. "Joel Barlow," *DAB*, vol. 1, 609–13; Bradford Perkins, *Prologue to War: England and the United States, 1805–1812* (Berkeley, Los Angeles, and London: 1970), 367–68.

25. *Independent Chronicle* (Boston), 23 May 1812, p. 2, col. 4; *Niles' Weekly Register* (*NWR*) (Baltimore), 23 May 1812, vol. 2, 200; Perkins, 400.

CHAPTER 3

1. *Port Folio*, 435; *CBA*, 336; *BDP*, 63; *Port Folio*, 435; *Analectic*, 338; DP to SN, 29 June 1812, USND, Letters Received by the SN from Master Commandants, M 147, roll 14, unnumbered.

2. SN to JB, 23 July 1812, SNL, roll 10, p. 114; *NWR*, 18 July 1812, vol. 2, 335; "Jacob Jones," *DAB*, vol. 10, 176–77; *Analectic*, vol. 2 (1813), 76–78; K. Jack Bauer, *Ships of the Navy, 1775–1969*, 2 vols. (Troy, N.Y.: 1969), vol. 1, 34.

3. Theodore Roosevelt, *The Naval War of 1812*, 3rd ed. (New York: 1910), 100.

4. "Thomas Whinyates," *DNB*, vol. 26, 6–7; Whinyates to J.B. Warren, 23 October 1812, in *Navy Chronicle* (London: 1813), vol. 29, 76–77; William James, *The Naval History of Great Britain from the Declaration of War against France in 1793 to the Accession of George IV*, 6 vols. (London: 1878 ed.), vol. 5, 338.

5. James, 338; Roosevelt, 101; Jones to SN, 24 November 1812, JBPA, vol. 2, #2712; Whinyates to Warren, 23 October 1812.

6. *Port Folio*, 436; Jones to SN, 24 November 1812; Whinyates to Warren, 23 October 1812; Jones to SN, 24 November 1812.

7. James, 391; *Analectic*, vol. 6 (1815), 399; James Fenimore Cooper, *History of the Navy of the United States*, 3 vols. (New York: 1864) vol. 2, 64; Jones to SN, 24 November 1812.

8. Whinyates to Warren, 23 October 1812; Jones to SN, 24 November 1812; Cooper, 65; Roosevelt, 103; Alfred T. Mahan, *Sea Power in Relation to the War of 1812*, 2 vols. (Boston: 1919), vol. 1, 414; James, 391–92; Jones to SN, 24 November 1812.

9. Jones to SN, 24 November 1812; Roosevelt, 104.

10. Beresford to Warren, 18 October 1812, in *Annual Register for 1812* (London: 1813), 252; C.S. Forester, *The Age of Fighting Sail: The Story of the Naval War of 1812* (New York: 1956), 102–3.

11. *NWR*, 7, 28 November 1812, vol. 3, 156, 203; Benson J. Lossing, *The Pictorial Field-Book of the War of 1812* (New York: 1869), 451; *NWR*, 5 December 1812, vol. 3, 221.

12. Lossing, 453; James Williams, president of the Society of the Cincinnati, to JB, 12 November 1813, and D. Lennox, president of the Pennsylvania chapter, to JB, 5 July 1813, JBPA, vol. 1, #2687, 2644; SN to JB, 1 February 1837, SNL, vol. 25, 445; Lossing, 452; *ASP, Naval Affairs*, vol. 1, 564.

13. *HLNO*, 56; SN to JB, 31 March 1813, JBPA, vol. 1, #2620; SN to JB, 25 April 1813, SNL, vol. 10, 374; Howard I. Chappelle, *The History of the American Sailing Navy* (New York: 1949), 212–14. Long guns and carronades were the largest cannon used by the navies of that era. The former could hurl heavy shot with considerable accuracy for up to a mile. The latter, named after the Carron River in Scotland where they were first developed, were short-barreled and short-ranged, throwing a broadside with shattering impact at close quarters. They were lighter than the long guns, permitting more of them to be mounted on the decks. This is the chief reason that the U.S. superfrigates, designated as 44s, invariably carried sufficient extra carronades to bring their totals as high as 55.

14. *The Times,* 20 March 1813.

15. S.W. Jackson, review of Michael Lewis, *A Social History of the [British] Navy,* 1793–1815, in *American Neptune,* vol. 22 (April 1962), 148; Forester, 134.

16. "Thomas W. Hardy," *DNB,* vol. 8, 1242–46.

17. Douglas S. Jordan, "Stephen Decatur at New London: A Study in Strategic Frustration," *United States Naval Institute Proceedings (USNIP),* vol. 93 (October 1967), 61–63.

18. Francis M. Caulkins, *History of New London, Connecticut, from the First Survey of the Coast in 1612 to 1852* (New London: 1852), 634–35; *Port Folio,* 429.

19. JB to John and Richard Biddle, 6 January 1814, JBPA, box J, folder, "Com. James Biddle," Miscellaneous Papers; *CBA,* 349, *n.*

20. Mends to JB, 24 January 1814; JB to Mends, 25 January 1814, JBPA, vol. 2, #2515–17; *Port Folio,* 440–41; James, *History,* vol. 6, 194–96.

21. Jordan, 195; JB to William Jackson, 20 July 1814, William Jackson Papers, box 1, folder, "James Biddle, 1783–1848," Yale University.

22. JB to John and Richard Biddle, 6 January 1814.

23. Dudley W. Knox, *A History of the United States Navy,* rev. ed. (New York: 1948), 129–30.

24. *Newburyport* (Mass.) *Herald,* 27 January 1815, p. 2, col. 3; *Daily National Intelligencer* (Washington, D.C.), 7 July 1815, p. 2, col. 5; JB to CB, 31 March 1815, JBPA, loose in vol. 1.

25. William James, *A Full and Correct Account of the Naval Occurrences of the Late War Between Great Britain and the United States of America* (London: 1817), 493–94; Roosevelt, 173 *n*; "Private Letter of an Officer in the Peacock," 10 April 1815, in Abel Bowen, *The Naval Monument, Containing Official and Other Accounts of the Battles Fought Between the Navies of the United States and Great Britain During the Last War; and an Account of the War with Algiers* (Boston: 1830), 187; Lieutenant James McDonald to ? (probably Vice Admiral Charles Tyler, commanding British forces in South African waters), 6 April 1815, in James, *Naval Occurrences,* app., p. cc, no. 111.

26. JB to Decatur, 25 March 1815, in Bowen, 185; McDonald to ?, 6 April 1815; James, *History,* 263–64.

27. James, *Naval Occurrences,* 489, 499; *NWR,* 12 August 1815, vol. 8, 417.

28. "Private Letter," 10 April 1815; JB to CB, 9 April 1815.

29. *Port Folio,* 445; JB to Decatur, 25 March 1815; McDonald to ?, 6 April 1815.

30. JB to Decatur, 25 March 1815; *Port Folio,* 445; *Analectic,* vol. 6 (1815), 395–96; JB to CB, 31 March, 8 April, JBPA, loose in vol. 1.

31. JB to SN, 15 August 1815, CL, roll 45, #115.

32. JB to Decatur, 25 March 1815; "Journal of the *Hornet*," 21 March 1815, David Conner Papers, Franklin D. Roosevelt Library; JB to CB, 8 April 1815; SN to JB, 14 December 1815, SNL, roll 12, p. 238; "David Conner," *DAB,* vol. 4, 349.

33. Roosevelt, "The War with the United States, 1812–1815," in William L.

Clowes, *The Royal Navy: A History from the Earliest Times to the Present,* 7 vols. (London: 1901, repr. 1966), vol. 6, 175.

34. "William James," *DNB,* vol. 10, 665; Review of William James, *Naval History of Great Britain,* in the *Edinburgh Review,* vol. 73 (1840), 125; Henry Simpson, *The Lives of Eminent Philadelphians Now Deceased* (Philadelphia: 1859), 71.

35. James, *History,* 264–65.

36. *Daily National Intelligencer,* 30 January 1815, p. 3, col. 5; JB to CB, 8 April 1815; JB to Decatur, 10 June 1815, enc. in JB to SN, 10 June 1815, CL, roll 45, unnumbered (between 19 and 19½).

37. "From the Private Journal of one of the *Hornet*'s Officers," 9 May 1815, in Bowen, 195; JB to Decatur, 10 June 1815, enc.; "Private Journal," 9 May 1815; Forester, 276.

38. Warrington was able to reach the Indian Ocean, where he took four richly laden ships of the British East India Company. He went on to the Dutch East Indies, where on 20 June in the Straits of Sunda he encountered the tiny armed brig *Nautilus* of the British Company. Evidence exists that Warrington was told that the war was over but he claimed to have disbelieved it, firing into the *Nautilus,* killing seven. Theodore Roosevelt holds that there was "no excuse whatever" for Warrington's violence and it is hard to fault that statement. Roosevelt, "1812–1815," in Clowes, 176; Forester, 278; JB to Decatur, 10 June 1815, enc.; Forester, 277.

39. JB to Decatur, 10 June 1815, enc.; "Private Journal," 9 May 1815; Forester, 277.

40. JB to Decatur, 10 June 1815, enc.; "Private Journal," 9 May 1815.

41. "Private Journal," 9 May 1815; JB to Decatur, 10 June 1815, enc.; Roosevelt, *Naval War of 1812,* 435.

42. James, *History,* 266; "Private Journal," 9 May 1815; *Naval Chronicle,* vol. 34 (1815), 377.

43. JB to SN, 29 July 1815, CL, roll 45, #82; *HLNO,* 56.

44. SN to JB, 19 August 1815, SNL, roll 12, p. 190; Court of inquiry decision, 23 August 1815, in Bowen, 197.

45. *Port Folio,* 499.

46. SN to JB, 10 February 1820, JBPA, vol. 2, #2920; JB to NB, 27 February 1820, ibid., vol. 15, #6063.

47. JB to James S. Biddle, 12 February 1848, NB, Personal Letters, vol. 5, HSP.

CHAPTER 4

1. CB to Dallas, 12 August 1815, Benjamin W. Crowninshield Papers, box 8, #6, Peabody Museum, Salem, Mass.; Dallas to CB, 13 August 1815, ibid., #64; Commander Tyrone G. Martin, 57th in command of USS *Constitution,* letter to DFL, 10 March 1980; SN to JB, 20 November 1815, SNL, roll 12, p. 121.

2. SN to JB, 8 May 1816, SNL, roll 12, pp. 316–17.

3. For Wood's portrait of JB, see "JBSB," 18; for Peale's, Charles W. Sell-

ers, "Portraits and Miniatures of Charles Willson Peale," *Transactions of the American Philosophical Society*, vol. 22, pt. 1 (1952), 340, and "Charles Willson Peale," *Concise DAB* (New York: 1964), 775; for Sully's, Pennsylvania Academy of the Fine Arts, *Catalogue of the Memorial Exhibition of Portraits by Thomas Sully*, 2nd ed. (Philadelphia: 1922), #97, 68.

4. *Columbian Centinel* (Boston, Mass.), n. d., in *Poulson's American Daily Advertiser* (Philadelphia), 4 September 1816, p. 3, col. 4; JB to Thomas Cadwalader, 10 August 1816, Cadwalader Collection (CC), box 2T, folder, "Letters of Commodore James Biddle," HSP; *Poulson's*, *Relf's Philadelphia Gazette*, *Daily National Intelligencer*, *NWR*, February, May–September, November 1816, passim.

5. JB to Cadwalader, 10 August 1816, CC.

6. JB to SN, 10 April, 19 May 1817, CL, roll 53, #6, 87; K. Jack Bauer, *Ships of the Navy, 1775–1969* (Troy, N.Y.: 1969), vol. 1, 24.

7. SN to JB, 21 July 1817, SNL, roll 13, pp. 51–52; Edward W. Billingsley, *In Defense of Neutral Rights: The United States Navy and the Wars of Independence in Chile and Peru* (Chapel Hill, N.C.: 1967), 19–20. This is a superb monograph, well researched and intelligently written.

8. John C. Pine, "The Role of United States Special Agents in the Development of a Spanish American Policy" (unpublished Ph.D. dissertation, University of Colorado, 1955), 238.

9. SN to JB, 30 September 1817, Confidential Letters Sent by the SN to Officers, 1813–22, 1840, 1843–79, NA; John Quincy Adams (JQA), *Memoirs of John Quincy Adams (JQAM)*, ed. by Charles Francis Adams, 12 vols. (Philadelphia: 1877), 28 September 1817, vol. 4, 11; JB to JQA, 2 October 1817, USDS, South American Missions, vol. 1, in Arthur P. Whitaker, *The United States and Latin America, 1800–1830* (Baltimore: 1941), 242, *n* 30.

10. JB, Journal kept by James Biddle on the *Ontario*, 4 October 1817–22 March 1819 (JBJO), 1, USND, RG 45, roll M 902, NA; Billingsley, 17.

11. "John Stuart Skinner," *DAB*, vol. 17, 200; for an extended discussion of this topic, see *BDP*, 189–202.

12. *BDP*, 189–202.

13. Ibid., 194; Laura Bornholdt, *Baltimore and Early Pan-Americanism: A Study in the Background to the Monroe Doctrine* (Northampton, Mass.: 1949), 102; *BDP*, 199–200; *JQAM*, 2 November 1818, vol. 4, 160.

14. JQA to Worthington, 7 February 1819, USDS, Despatches to Consuls, vol. 2, in Pine, 94–95; Billingsley, 10; Pine, 95–96; Henry M. Wriston, *Executive Agents in American Foreign Policy* (Baltimore: 1929; repr. 1962), 419–20.

15. JB to Thomas Cadwalader, 23 November 1817, CC; JB to NB, 23 November 1817, JB Papers, HSP; JBJO, 14; Log Book of the *Ontario*, 1 December 1817, JBPA, vol. 16, #2715–17; JB to SN, 26 January 1818, CL, roll 57, #35; "JBSB," 58; David Conner, "Journal of the *Ontario*, James Biddle, Esq., Master Commandant, by Her First Lieutenant, David Connor, U.S.N.," 4 October 1817–20 February 1819, Franklin D. Roosevelt Library.

16. JBJO, 1; Billingsley, 20–21.

17. JBJO, 1–2; *NWR*, 12 May 1818, vol. 14, 168; JBJO, 2.

18. Billingsley, 19, 23; Pine, 346.

19. JBJO, 3; Billingsley, 24–26.

20. Billingsley, 30–31; Jeremy Robinson, Diary, 19 June 1818, Peter Forbes Collection, LC.

21. Henry Hill, *Recollections of an Octogenarian* (Boston: 1884), 87; JBJO, 3–5.

22. JBJO, 5–6; Billingsley, 31–33, 34–35; Robinson, Diary, 24 May 1818.

23. Pine, 394; JB to NB, 11 April 1818, James Monroe Papers, vol. 26, LC.

24. Pine, 399; Robinson, Diary, 19 June 1818.

25. JBJO, 7–8; Billingsley, 41–42.

26. JB to SN, 26 June 1819, CL, roll 63, #51; Joaquin de la Pezuela, *Memoria de Gobierno,* 259, in Billingsley, 219, *n* 9.

27. Pezuela, *Memoria,* 260, in Billingsley, 219, *n.* 18; JB to SN, 12 June 1818, CL, roll 58, #32.

28. JBJO, 10–11.

29. Billingsley, 46–47; Pezuela, *Memoria,* 281–83, in Billingsley, 220, *n* 42; JBJO, 11; William L. Neumann, "United States Aid to the Chilean Wars of Independence" (unpublished Ph.D. dissertation, University of Michigan, 1947), 76.

30. David Conner, Journal of the *Ontario,* 14 June 1818, 150.

31. JBJO, 11; Robinson, Diary, 7, 9, 15 June 1818; JBJO, 11.

32. JB to Monroe, 16 August 1819, *ASP, Naval Affairs,* vol. 1, 669; JB to SN, 2 August 1820, CL, roll 67, #106; Calhoun to JB, 4 November 1818, SN, Confidential Letters.

33. SN to JB, 30 September 1817, SN, Confidential Letters.

34. Thomas P. Govan, *Nicholas Biddle: Nationalist and Public Banker, 1786–1844* (Chicago: 1959), 22–23.

35. Frederick W. Longstaff and W. Kaye Lamb, "The Royal Navy on the Northwest Coast, 1813–1850," *British Columbia Historical Quarterly,* vol. 9 (1945), 3; David Lavender, *Land of the Giants: The Drive to the Pacific Northwest* (Garden City, N.Y.: 1956), 104–5.

36. *BDP,* 123, 152–57, 143.

37. Longstaff and Lamb, 3–4.

38. Barry M. Gough, *The Royal Navy and the Northwest Coast of North America* (Vancouver: 1971), 25; *JQAM,* 29 September 1817, vol. 4, 11.

39. JBJO, 12–13.

40. Ibid., 13.

41. "Commodore John Aulick," *American Historical Record,* vol. 3 (1874), 292–93; Robinson, Diary, 24 October 1818.

42. JBJO, 13–14.

43. Nicolai N. Bolkovitinov, *The Beginnings of Russian-American Relations, 1775–1815* (Cambridge, Mass.: 1975), 352–53; Hector Chevigny, *Russian America: The Great Alaskan Venture, 1741–1867* (New York: 1965), 156–59.

44. McGillivrary to "Ambassador," 15 November 1817, in Katherine B. Judson, "The British Side of the Restoration of Fort Astoria," *Oregon Historical Quarterly,* vol. 20 (1919), 309; Joseph Schafer, "The British Attitude toward the Oregon Question," *American Historical Review,* vol. 16 (January 1911), 282.

45. Gough, 125–26.

46. Frederick Merk, "The Genesis of the Oregon Question," *Mississippi Valley Historical Review,* vol. 36 (March 1950), 606.

47. Ibid., 611.

48. Richard J. Cleveland, *Voyages and Commercial Enterprises of the Sons of New England* (New York: 1855), 284–85; "Invoice of the Cargo of the Ship *Beaver,*" 30 June 1817, in Kenneth W. Porter, *John Jacob Astor: Businessman,* 2 vols. (Cambridge, Mass.: 1931), vol. 2, 1150–51; Cleveland, 285; Porter, 649; Whitaker, 283–84.

49. Porter, 649; Billingsley, 29; JBJO, 12; Cleveland, 323.

50. JBJO, 16–17; Billingsley, 54; Porter, 651; Cleveland, 337–38.

51. JBJO, 16–18.

52. Ibid., 18–19.

53. Billingsley, 57.

54. JBJO, 19; William R. O'Byrne, *A Naval Biographical Dictionary: Comprising the Life and Services of Every Living Officer in Her Majesty's Navy from the Rank of Admiral of the Fleet to that of Lieutenant Inclusive* (London: 1849), 314; F.C. Lynch, "Admiral Lord Cochrane: A Hero for Today's Professionals," *USNIP,* vol. 101 (February 1975), 65–66; William S. Clowes, *The Royal Navy: A History from the Earliest Times to the Present,* 7 vols. (London: 1901), vol. 5, 379.

55. Hill, 117; *JQAM,* 8 July 1820, vol. 5, 164.

56. David Porter was the most famous American equivalent of Cochrane, resigning his commission in the U.S. Navy during 1825 after a court-martial conviction for exceeding his orders and insubordination. He took command of the Mexican navy fighting Spain from 1826 to 1829, a purgatorial assignment that wrecked him financially and almost cost him his life. *BDP,* 256–83.

57. JB to NB, 19 May 1819, JBPA, vol. 2, #2908; Cochrane to JB, 27 December 1818, *NWR,* 18 May 1819, vol. 16, 204; JBJO, JB to Cochrane, 28 December 1818, ibid., 21.

58. Cochrane to JB, 28 December 1818, JBJO, 20–21; JB to Cochrane, 28 December 1818, ibid., 21; Cochrane to JB, 28 December 1818, ibid.; *NWR,* 5 June 1818, vol. 16, 247.

59. JBJO, 26.

60. Ibid., 28–29.

61. JB to Monroe, 16 August 1819, CL, roll 64, #6; William R. Manning, ed., *Diplomatic Correspondence of the United States Concerning the Independence of the Latin American Nations,* 3 vols. (New York: 1925), vol. 1, 134, n 1.

62. *Daily National Intelligencer,* 4 May 1819, p. 2, col. 4; JBJO, 27; Billingsley, 65.

63. JBJO, 27.

64. JB to SN, 13, 15 June 1819, 2 April 1820, CL, roll 63, #32, 36, 106; JBJO, 27–28; *NWR,* 1 May 1819, vol. 16, 223.

65. JB to James and Thomas Perkins, 20 May 1819, *Charleston Courier,* 7 June 1819, in Billingsley, 233, n 36; JBJO, 25.

66. WB to JB, 5 May 1819, JBPA, vol. 2, #2904; WB to JB, n.d. in *NWR,* 5 June 1819, vol. 16, 247, n.

67. *BW,* vol. 2, 68, 96, 129, 123; *NWR,* 12 June 1819, vol. 16, 272. As JB's career would not again interrelate with Cochrane's, a word about that fiery Briton's later life is in order. Brilliant as before in strategy and tactics, he swept Spanish sea power from the Pacific, aiding greatly in ensuring the independence of Chile and Peru. But as always, he quarreled with a superior—San Martín in this case—and resigned his commission late in 1822. He then directed with equal distinction the Brazilian fleet against the Portuguese from 1823 to 1826, but left after another personal clash. He next commanded the Greek navy battling the Turks from 1826 to 1829, but found to his distress that for the first time he could accomplish little. He became the tenth earl of Dundonald in 1831 and was reinstated in the Royal Navy the following year. He lived on and on, dying in 1860 at the age of eighty-five, spending his final years in collecting only partially the large sums that he claimed were owed to him by Chile and Brazil, described at tiresome length in his whining and self-serving autobiography. Christopher Lloyd, *Lord Cochrane: Seaman—Radical—Liberator: A Life of Thomas, Lord Cochrane, 10th Earl of Dundonald* (London: 1947), passim; "Thomas Cochrane," *DNB,* vol. 4, 621–31; Earl of Dundonald, *Narration of Services in the Liberation of Chili, Peru, and Brazil from Spanish and Portuguese Domination,* 2 vols. (London: 1859), vol. 2, passim.

68. JBJO, 30–31; Astor to JB, 5 May 1819, in *NWR,* 5 June 1819, vol. 16, 250.

69. Prevost to JQA, 20 March 1819, in Pine, 423, *n* 83; Echevarria to Prevost, 16 March 1818, ibid.; Billingsley, 222, *n* 31–32.

70. JB's five defenses were JB to SN, 13, 15, 26 June 1819, CL, roll 63, #32, 36, 51; 2 April 1820, ibid., roll 64, #166; JB to Monroe, 16 August 1819, ibid., #6. Of these the letter of 2 April 1820 is the most authoritative.

71. JB to SN, 2 April 1820, CL, roll 64, #166.

72. Henry Clay, "Resolutions of South American Independence," 4 April 1820, *The Papers of Henry Clay,* ed. by James F. Hopkins and Mary Hargreaves, 5 vols. (Lexington, Ky.: 1963–73), vol. 2, *The Rising Statesman,* 817–18.

73. Ibid., 854–55.

74. De la Cerna to JB, 8 October 1819, enc. in JB to SN, 27 November 1819, CL, roll 63, #82; Worthington to JB, 26 February 1820, *ASP, Naval Affairs,* vol. 1, 673.

75. Homans to Monroe, 16 August 1819, enc. in JB to Monroe, 16 August 1819, CL, roll 64, #6; SN to Clay, 8 April 1820, *ASP, Naval Affairs,* vol. 1, 672; *JQAM,* 8 July 1821, vol. 5, 164–65.

76. NB to Monroe, 14 June 1821, Monroe Papers, vol. 30, LC; SN to JB, 26 March 1822, USND, SN, Confidential Letters.

CHAPTER 5

1. JB to Oscar Bullus, 25 June 1821, Maine Historical Society; NB to Monroe, 14 June 1821, NB Papers, General Correspondence, HSP; Monroe to NB, 5 December 1821, ibid.; SN to JB, 26 March 1822, USND, SN, Confidential Letters.

2. K. Jack Bauer, *Ships of the Navy, 1775–1969* (Troy, N.Y.: 1969), vol. 1, 316; Robert E. Johnson, *Thence Around Cape Horn: The Story of the United States Naval Forces on Pacific Station, 1818–1923* (Annapolis: 1963), 25.

3. *NWR*, 19 April 1823, vol. 24, 98; "An Account of piracys [*sic*] committed on American Vessels near the Island of Cuba," February 1822, encl. in JB to SN, 24 July 1822, CL, roll 76, #68.

4. *NWR*, 20 October 1821, vol. 21, 419.

5. *BDP*, 205; SN to JB, 26 March 1822, USND, SN, Confidential Letters; *Annual Report of the SN*, 1 December 1822, *ASP Naval Affairs*, vol. 1, 804.

6. SN to JB, 26 March 1822, USND, SN, Confidential Letters.

7. *NWR*, 30 April 1822, vol. 22, 128; JB to Mahe, 30 April 1822, *ASP Naval Affairs*, vol. 1, 805; Mahe to JB, 2 May 1822, ibid., 806.

8. JB to SN, 6 May 1822, *ASP, Naval Affairs*, vol. 1, 805; JB to SN, 18 May 1822, CL, roll 78, #91.

9. *JQAM*, 20 July 1818, vol. 4, 113; JB to SN, 16 May 1822, CL, roll 78, #88.

10. JB to SN, 30 June 1822, CL, roll 78, #125; JB to SN, 31 May 1822, ibid., #106; JB to Thomas Cadwalader, 21 May 1822, CC.

11. John Warner to C. A. Rodney, 20 February 1822, Monroe Papers, in Philip J. Foner, *A History of Cuba and Its Relations with the United States*, 2 vols. (New York: 1967), vol. 1, 140; JB to Monroe, 3 August 1822, in ibid., 141.

12. *JQAM*, 27 September 1822, vol. 6, 70–74.

13. Charles L. Lewis, *David Glasgow Farragut: Admiral in the Making* (Annapolis: 1941), 163.

14. DP to SN, 10 May 1823, in *BDP*, 215; David McCulloch, *The Path Between the Seas: The Creation of the Panama Canal* (New York: 1977), 140.

15. JB to SN, 4 June 1822, CL, roll 78, #108; Charles Gauntt, "*Macedonian* Journal," 21 March–20 June 1822, LC; *HLNO*, 683.

16. JB to SN, 24 July 1822, CL, roll 79, #8.

17. Ibid., *NWR*, 30 November 1822, vol. 23, 205–6.

18. JB to SN, 24 July 1822, CL, roll 79, #8.

19. *Columbian Centinel* (Boston), 17 August 1822, p. 2, col. 4.

20. SN to JB, 8 August 1822, SNL, vol. 14, 359; DP to JB, 8 August 1822, JBPA, vol. 3, #2994.

21. Cornelius Comegys to JB, 12 August 1822, in *New-York Evening Post*, 25 August 1822, p. 2, col. 3; JB to Comegys, 18 August 1822, ibid.

22. JB to NB, 8 August 1822, JBPA, vol. 3, #2996; Decatur to Barron, 19 October 1819, *Correspondence Between the Late Commodore S. Decatur and Commodore J. Barron Which Led to the Unfortunate Meeting of 22 March 1820* (Washington: 1820), 12.

23. Benjamin Homans, Chief Clerk of the USND, to JB, 10 September 1822, SNL, vol. 14, p. 376; JB to Sinclair, 13, 15 August 1822, enc. in Sinclair to SN, 22 August 1822, CL, roll 79, #29.

24. Sinclair to JB, 15 August 1822, enc. in Sinclair to SN, 22 August 1822; JB to SN, 15 August, ibid.; Sinclair to SN, 22 August 1822, ibid., #29.

25. Sinclair to JB, 17 September 1822, CL, roll 79, #48; Sinclair to John Shaw, 3 February 1823, John Shaw Papers, LC.

26. On 22 March 1820 Barron, although badly hurt himself, had mortally wounded Decatur, the nation's favorite naval hero. Strangely, Biddle never refers to this sensational event in the many of his surviving letters dating from this period. Monroe to NB, 4 September 1822; NB to Monroe, 8, 12 September 1822, courtesy of Nicholas Biddle, Jr., Narberth, Pa.; Monroe to NB, 29 September 1822, ibid.; WB and C. A. Rodney to SN, 12 October 1822, enc. in Sinclair to SN, 17 October 1822, CL, roll 79, #55.

27. JB to Sinclair, 12 October 1822, enc. in Sinclair to SN, 17 October 1822; Sinclair to Shaw, 9 February 1823, John Shaw Papers; NB to Monroe, 12 October 1822, Gratz Autograph Collection, HSP.

28. For background material on the Bainbridge-Hull rivalry, see *BWB,* chaps. 10 and 11.

29. *Trial of John Shaw, by the General Court-martial, Holden on Board the U.S. Ship* Independence, *at the Navy-Yard, Charlestown, Massachusetts, upon Charges Preferred Against Him by Captain Isaac Hull* (Washington: 1822), 4–5.

30. JB to Shaw, 26 February 1822, John Shaw Papers.

31. *Trial of John Shaw,* passim.

32. *Trial of Lieutenant Joel Abbot, by the General Court-martial, Holden on Board the U.S. Ship* Independence, *at the Navy-Yard, Charlestown, Massachusetts, on Allegations Made Against Him by Captain David Porter, Navy Commissioner* (Boston: 1822), passim; DP to SN, 3 June 1822, Samuel L. Southard Letter Book, New York Public Library.

33. JB to Shaw, 3 October 1822, John Shaw Papers; Jesse D. Elliott to Shaw, 23 July 1823, ibid.

34. *Minutes of the Proceedings of the Court of Inquiry into the Official Conduct of Capt. Isaac Hull, etc.* (Washington: 1822), passim.

35. JB to NB, 5 February 1823, JBPA, vol. 3, #3028.

36. JB to Thomas Cadwalader, 5 February 1823, CC. It is a bit ironic in view of his above sentiments to see that Biddle served as one of Rodgers's pallbearers at his funeral in 1838, telling the widow: "It was gratifying to my feelings to manifest in the recent meaningful occasion, my respect for the character and services of Commodore Rodgers." JB to Mrs. Rodgers, 16 August, Rodgers Family Papers, Rodgers-Meigs-Macomb Family, LC.

37. *NWR,* 1 November 1822, vol. 23, p. 129.

38. JB to Quincy, 26 October 1822, Josiah Quincy Papers, Massachusetts Historical Society.

39. Maury D. Baker, Jr., "The United States and Piracy During the Spanish-American Wars of Independence" (unpublished Ph.D. dissertation, Duke University, 1947), 182–85; Gregory to JB, 24 August 1822, *ASP, Naval Affairs,* vol. 1, 806; William A. Morgan, "Sea Power in the Gulf of Mexico During the Mexican and Colombian Wars of Independence"

(unpublished Ph.D. dissertation, University of Southern California, 1969), 110.

40. *JQAM,* 26 October 1822, vol. 6, 85–86; SN to JB, 1 November 1822, SNL, roll 14, p. 391.

41. Baker, "The United States and Piracy," 201–2.

42. Bauer, 14; SN to JB, 1 November 1822, SNL, roll 14, p. 391; JB to SN, 27 November 1822, CL, roll 79, #77; JB to SN, 9 December 1822, ibid., #93; Samuel Lockwood, "Journal of the U.S. Frigate *Congress,* James Biddle, Esq., Commander," 19 December 1822, Samuel Lockwood Papers, Yale University.

43. Samuel F. Du Pont to Charles Du Pont, 3 January 1823, Winterthur Collection (WC), Eleutherian Mills Historical Society, Greenville, Del.

44. Lockwood, Journal, 20 December 1822.

45. Edwin A. Sherman, *Life of Rear Admiral John Drake Sloat of the U.S. Navy* . . . (Oakland, Calif: 1902), 25.

46. S. F. Du Pont to Victorine Du Pont Bauduy, 4 January 1823, WC; JB to SN, 5 February 1823, CL, roll 80, #60; S. F. Du Pont to Charles Du Pont, 13 April 1823, WC; SN to JB, 7 January 1823, SNL, roll 14, p. 416.

47. S. F. Du Pont to Charles Du Pont, 13 April 1823, WC; Caspar F. Goodrich, "Our Navy and the West Indian Pirates: A Documentary History," *USNIP,* vol. 43 (1916), 490–91, 493.

48. JB to Thomas Cadwalader, 5 February 1823, CC; Baker, "The United States and Piracy," 195–96.

49. JB to William Biddle, 22 January 1823, JBPA, vol. 3, #6168 [*sic*]; JB to Thomas Cadwalader, 5 February 1823, CC.

CHAPTER 6

1. JB to Thomas Cadwalader, 16 January 1824, JBPA, vol. 3, #3078.

2. SN to JB, 4, 24 April 1823, SNL, roll 14, pp. 457, 467.

3. Cadwalader, a major-general of the Pennsylvania militia during the war and later a director of the Second Bank of the United States, had become embroiled in a controversy between two doctors. Granville S. Pattison, a Scottish adventurer who was a professor at the University of Maryland Medical School, had originally been sponsored by Nathaniel Chapman, a well-known and well-liked physician, long connected with the University of Pennsylvania Medical School. Later they quarreled so bitterly that Pattison challenged Chapman. Somehow the latter managed to wriggle out of any combat, but within a few years Pattison concentrated his enmity on Cadwalader, a Chapman advocate. In their encounter, probably on 5 April 1823, the "Scotch Villain," as Biddle called him, shot his adversary with a bullet "that lodged in the elbow-joint, and which from its position could not be removed. The irritation from its presence gradually undermined his constitution," and undoubtedly caused in part his premature death. For amplification of this duel, see *NBW,* "Affair with Professor Pattison," *PMHB,* vol. 64 (July 1940), 330–34. JB to

Cadwalader, 20 April 1823, CC; *Encyclopaedia of Contemporary Biography of Pennsylvania,* 3 vols. (New York: 1888–93), vol. 3, 299; JB to Cadwalader, 20 April 1823; SN to JB, 2, 14 May 1823, SNL, roll 14, pp. 475, 481.

4. "Hugh Nelson," *DAB,* vol. 12, 416–17.

5. "Caesar Augustus Rodney," ibid., vol. 16, 82–83; JB to Cadwalader, 16 May 1823, CC.

6. "Statement of Capt. Biddle respecting Mr. Rodney" (written by a clerk), n.d., in NBW, "Voyage of the Frigate *Congress,* 1823," *PMHB,* vol. 75 (April 1951), 172–73; JN to SN, 13 February 1824, JBPA, vol. 3, #3054.

7. JB to SN, 13 February 1824, JBPA, vol. 3, #3054; *Salem Gazette,* 16 December 1823, p. 3, col. 1; *National Gazette,* 16 December 1823, in NBW, "Voyage of the Frigate Congress," 179, *n* 17.

8. JB to SN, 13 February 1824.

9. Samuel F. Du Pont to Victorine Du Pont Bauduy, 21 July 1823, WC.

10. JB to John G. Biddle, 23 July 1823, JBPA, box J, uncatalogued, "JB, John, and Richard Biddle Letters;" JB to Jane Biddle, 13 October 1823, ibid., vol. 3, #3008.

11. JB to John G. Biddle, 23 July 1823; JB to SN, 13 February 1824.

12. JB to SN, 13 February 1824; S. F. Du Pont to Victorine Du Pont Bauduy, 21 July 1823, WC; JB to Jane Biddle, 13 October 1823; JB to SN, 13 February 1824.

13. "Log of the Congress," HSP. Biddle says the 14th (JB to SN, 13 February 1824) but his memory erred; S. F. Du Pont to Charles Du Pont, 31 July 1823, WC; JB to SN, 13 February 1824.

14. JB to SN, 13 February 1824.

15. The news that Cadiz had fallen and the possibility that the French might sail from there to restore its American colonies to Spain was a major reason for the Cabinet meetings in Washington that resulted in the pronouncement of the Monroe Doctrine the next December.

16. SN to JB, 24 April 1823, SNL, roll 14, p. 467; JB to SN, 28 July 1823, CL, roll 83, #34.

17. JB to SN, 13 February 1824.

18. Nelson to Charles J. Ingersoll, 10 November 1823, JBPA, vol. 3, #3061; S. F. Du Pont to Charles Du Pont, 31 July 1823; *NWR,* 24 January 1824, vol. 25, 321.

19. "Log of the *Congress*"; JB to SN, 13 February 1824.

20. S. F. Du Pont to Victorine Du Pont Bauduy, 27 September 1823, WC.

21. JB to SN, 13 February 1824.

22. *Journal of the House of Representatives of the State of Delaware,* 9 January 1824, Delaware Historical Society; JB to SN, 13 February 1824; SN to JB, 6 May 1823, SNL, roll 14, p. 477.

23. S. F. Du Pont to Charles Du Pont, 6 October 1823, WC; JB to SN, 13 February 1824; "Log of the *Congress.*"

24. S. F. Du Pont to Charles Du Pont, 17 December 1823, WC; S. F. Du Pont to JB, 7 July 1824, ibid.; S. F. Du Pont to Alexander S. Mackenzie, 1 June 1845, ibid.

25. *NWR,* 17 May 1823, vol. 24, 161; ibid., 24 January 1824, vol. 25, 321.

26. JB to SN, 13 February 1824.

27. *Journal of the House of Representatives of the State of Delaware,* 9 January 1824; *National Gazette,* n.d., in *NWR,* 24 January 1824, 321; ibid., 322.

28. *NWR,* 24 January 1824, 321, 322.

29. JB to Thomas Cadwalader, 25 December 1823, CC.

30. "Wilmingtonian," in *American Watchman,* 30 January 1824, p. 3, col. 1, Historical Society of Delaware; JB to James S. Biddle, 12 February 1848, NB, Personal Letters, vol. 5, HSP.

31. Ingersoll to Nelson, 10 November 1823, JBPA, vol. 3, #3060–61; Nelson to Ingersoll, n.d. [24 January 1824], ibid.

32. Gordon to JB, 20 January 1824, ibid.; *NWR,* 14 August 1824, vol. 26, 394.

33. JB to Thomas Cadwalader, 16 January 1824, JBPA, vol. 3, #3060–61.

34. "Langdon Cheeves," *DAB,* vol. 4, 63; Cheeves to Cadwalader, 29 May 1824, JBPA, vol. 3, #3102.

CHAPTER 7

1. JB, Testimony, 27 August 1824, *ASP, Naval Affairs,* vol. 2, 513; Edward B. Billingsley, *In Defense of Neutral Rights: The United States Navy and the Wars of Independence in Chile and Peru,* (Chapel Hill, N.C.: 1967) 184–92.

2. JB, Testimony, 27 August 1824; Billingsley, 193.

3. JB to SN, 1 October 1824; CL, roll 88, #145; JB to Thomas Cadwalader, 23 January 1827, CC; JB to SN, 1 October 1824; JB to SN, 4 March 1825, ibid., roll 91, #23; "JBSB," 24; JB to Cadwalader, 23 January 1827.

4. JB to SN, 14 March 1825, "Private Letter," Samuel L. Southard Collection, Princeton University; JB to SN, 6 May 1825, CL, roll 92, #64.

5. SN to DP, 23 June 1825, SNL, roll 16, p. 96. For extended discussions of Porter's troubles in the West Indies and Washington, see *BDP,* chaps. 8 and 9, passim.

6. James Monroe, "Rough Notes," 18 July 1825, Monroe Papers, vol. 34, LC; *JQAM,* 24 December 1824, vol. 6, 453–54.

7. David Dixon Porter, *Memoir of Commodore David Porter, of the United States Navy* (Albany, N.Y.: 1875), 417.

8. DP, *Journal of a Cruise Made to the Pacific Ocean by Captain David Porter in the United States Frigate Essex in the Years 1812, 1813, and 1814, Containing Descriptions of the Cape de Verd[e] Islands, Coasts of Brazil, Patagonia, Chile and Peru, and of the Galapagos Islands,* 2 vols. (Philadelphia: 1815), vol. 2, passim; *National Intelligencer,* 3 August 1816, p. 2, cols. 3–4; JB to Thomas Cadwalader, 10 August 1816, CC; JB to Cadwalader, 23 November 1817, ibid.

9. Beverly Kennan, Testimony, 24 February 1824, in *BDP,* 226–27; JB to Thomas Cadwalader, 4 January 1824, ibid.; "William Anderson," *Biographical Directory of the American Congress, 1774–1971* (Washington: 1971), 516.

10. WB to JB, 5 June 1825, WB Papers, Naval Historical Society Collection, NYHS.

11. *Minutes of the Proceedings of the Courts of Inquiry and Court Martial in Relation to Captain David Porter Convened at Washington, D.C., on Thursday, the Seventh Day of July, A.D. 1825* (Washington: 1825), passim; Archibald D. Turnbull, *Commodore David Porter, 1780–1843* (New York and London: 1929), 16; *BDP*, 241–47.

12. *BDP*, 247.

13. Richard S. West, *The Second Admiral: A Life of David Dixon Porter, 1813–1891* (New York: 1939), 16; "Court Martial of Commodore David Porter, 7 July–10 August 1825," USND, (Records of General Courts Martial and Courts of Inquiry of the Navy Department, 1799–1867, M 273, roll 19, vol. 17 (21 June–5 September 1825), NA, passim.

14. D. D. Porter, *Memoir*, 343; see *BDP*, chap. 10, for Porter in Mexico; chap. 11 for his Turkish experiences.

15. Warrington had just finished his tenure as West India Squadron commodore. He had succeeded where JB and DP had failed. Enjoying much better cooperation from Spanish authorities than had his predecessors, as well as the closest collaboration with the Royal Navy, he played a major role in the practical eradication of piracy in the Caribbean by the late 1820s. William A. Morgan, "Sea Power in the Gulf of Mexico during the Mexican and Colombian Wars of Independence," 200–206; SN to WB, Warrington, and JB, 15 September 1825, SNL, roll 16, pp. 204–5; JB to Thomas Cadwalader, 27 November 1825, CC.

16. JB to SN, 1 April 1826, CL, roll 99, #115; JB to WB, 19 April 1826, Charles Roberts Autograph Collection, Haverford College; JB to SN, 21 April 1826, CL, roll 100, #64 (Researchers using CL for 1826 will find them misnumbered chronologically); JB to SN, 16 May 1826, ibid., #54; W. S. Robertson, *Hispanic American Relations with the United States*, n. p., in Donald W. Griffin, "The American Navy at Work on the Brazil Station, 1827–1860," *American Neptune*, vol. 19 (October 1959), 239.

17. "Thomas Cochrane," *DNB*, vol. 4, 361; Clarence T. Harris, *Empire in Brazil: A New World Experiment with Monarchy* (Cambridge, Mass.: 1958), 20–21.

18. John Street, [José Gervasio] *Artigas and the Emancipation of Uruguay* (Cambridge, U.K.: 1959), 344–46.

19. SN to JB, 1 June 1826, SNL, roll 16, pp. 420–24.

20. JB to Elliott, 15 August 1826, enc. in ibid. For some reason much of JB's official correspondence for 1826 had been placed in the NA's CL, roll 100, labeled "Letters from Capt. Isaac Hull, Jan. 19–Dec. 10, 1826, and Capt. James Biddle, Aug. 16–Dec. 17, 1826," some letters numbered, some not. A word of warning for scholars using CL, roll 100 and after. Rolls may not be ordered on interlibrary loan from the NA, but may be from the USNA Nimitz Library. But starting with roll 100 those at Nimitz differ slightly in roll numbers from those at the NA. Orders placed there should refer to the dates needed rather than the roll numbers listed in the invaluable *National Archives List of Microfilmed Publications*, 1961 ed., the last to give both the roll numbers and the dates.

21. Street, *Artigas*, 349; John Armitage, *The History of Brazil from the Period*

of the Arrival of the Braganza Family in 1808 to the Abdication of Don Pedro the First in 1831, 2 vols. (London: 1836), vol. 1, 309–14.

22. JB to SN, 1 September 1826, "Private Letter," Samuel Southard Collection.

23. Lawrence F. Hill, *Diplomatic Relations Between the United States and Brazil* (Durham, N.C.: 1933), 44–45, 52; JB to SN, 13 April 1827, "Private Letter," Samuel Southard Collection; *JQAM,* 10 January 1828, vol. 7, 401.

24. JB to SN, 10 November 1826, "Letters from . . . Hull . . . and Biddle . . . ," NA; *HLNO,* 434.

25. Levy (1792–1862) was one of the more notable members of the navy, for during most of his professional life he was the only Jewish officer in the service. Anti-Semitism, coupled with his own hot temper involved him in several courts-martial, as well as two resignations from and reappointments to the navy. Shortly before his death he finally won his commodore's pennant with the Mediterranean Squadron. But Levy's claim to national remembrance is that he, a lifelong admirer of Jefferson for his role in the Bill of Rights principle of religious toleration, in 1836 bought the former president's lovely estate at Monticello, Virginia, for $2,500 and restored it. Monticello remained in the Levy family until purchased in 1923 by the Thomas Jefferson Memorial Foundation, which operates it today. Mary Cable and Annabelle Prager, "The Levys of Monticello," *American Heritage,* vol. 29 (February–March 1978), 32–39; "Uriah Phillips Levy," *DAB,* vol. 11, 203–4; Levy to JB, 16 November 1826, enc. in JB to SN, 20 November 1826, "Letters from . . . Hull . . . and Biddle . . . ," NA.

26. Levy to JB, 16 November 1826.

27. JB to SN, 20 November 1826; *HLNO,* 389.

28. JB to Ann Biddle Hopkinson, 18 February 1827, JBPA, vol. 4, #3177.

29. JB to SN, 20 October 1827, "Private Letter," Samuel Southard Collection.

30. *JQAM,* 19 December 1827, vol. 7, 385; "Memorandum of American Vessels Seized . . . ," enc. in JB to SN, 19 November 1827, CL, roll 117, #87.

31. "William Brown," *DNB,* vol. 3, 36; Alvaro de Alzogaray, *Diario de Operaciones de la Escuadra Republicana Compare Del Brasil, 1826–1828* (Montevideo: 1934), passim; JB to Hoffman, 12 November 1827, enc. in JB to SN, 9 December 1827, CL, roll 119, #24; Hoffman to JB, 8 December 1827, enc. in ibid.

32. Forbes to SS, 10 December 1827, USDS, Despatches from U.S. Ministers to Argentina, M 69, roll 4, #54, NA; Forbes to SS, 27 December 1827, ibid., #55; SN to JB, 11 April 1828, Samuel L. Southard, Letter Book to Officers, 19 May 1826–1 November 1828, 240–41, NYHS; *JQAM,* 8 April 1828, vol. 7, 500; for instance, JB to Rodrigo Pinto Guedes, "Baron of la Plata," 11–18 January 1828 (10 large pages), enc. in JB to SN, 22 January 1828, CL, roll 120, #72.

33. Street, *Artigas,* 246–47; John H. Hann, "Brazil and the Rio de la Plata, 1808–1829" (unpublished Ph.D. dissertation, University of Texas, 1967), 425–28; Armitage, vol. 1, 326–27; Harris, 35.

34. Benajah Tichnor, "Sickness Report," 25 October 1828, enc. in JB to SN, 25 October 1828, "Private Letter," Samuel Southard Collection; JB to SN, 25 October 1828.

35. SN to JB, 1 November 1828, Samuel L. Southard Letter Book.

CHAPTER 8

1. JB to SN, 18 June 1829, CL, roll 136, #67.

2. JB to SN, 10 July 1829, ibid., roll 137, #42; *NWR*, 2 January 1830, vol. 37, 296; "Louis McLane," *DAB*, vol. 12, 113–15; "William Cabell Rives," ibid., vol. 15, 635–37.

3. Enoch C. Wines, *Two and a Half Years in the Navy, or, a Journal of a Cruise to the Mediterranean and Levant on Board the U.S. Frigate* Constellation, *in the Years 1829, 1830, and 1831,* 2 vols. (Philadelphia: 1832), vol. 1, 132–34.

4. JB to SN, 29 October 1829, CL, roll 149, #76; *NWR*, 16 January 1830, vol. 37, 342.

5. SN to JB, 24 July 1829, SNL, roll 18, pp. 319–21; JB to Officers, 22 October 1828, CL, roll 140, #76.

6. JB to SN, 14 November 1829, CL, roll 141, #42; JB to NB, 12 February, n. d. [1830], JBPA, vol. 15, #6056. In this reticence Biddle was mirroring William Bainbridge, who visited Tripoli both in 1815 and 1820 without any written recollections of his captivity. Indeed, in neither instance did he even bother to go ashore. As for Yusuf, his days as bashaw were numbered. In 1832 he was toppled from his throne by his son Ali, who was in turn ousted by the Turks three years later. Under the name of Libya, Tripoli was ruled by the Ottoman sultan until it was annexed as an Italian colony in 1911.

7. JB to SN, 14 November 1829; JB to NB, 7 August 1830, JBPA, vol. 5, #3594–95.

8. SN to JB, 9 April 1830, SNL, roll 18, pp. 489–90.

9. JB to SN, 17 August 1830, CL, roll 149, #50; SN to JB, 27 November 1830, SNL, roll 19, p. 177.

10. JB to NB, 14 February 1830, JBPA, vol. 6, #3624.

11. JB to NB, 30 September 1831, ibid., #3762; JB to Mrs. James S. Biddle, 10 November 1846, NB Papers, Personal Correspondence, vol. 5, HSP.

12. Robertson to JB, 14 November 1834, JBPA, vol. 7, #3997; Sloat to JB, 13 August 1840, ibid., vol. 8, #4220.

13. JB to SN, 1 February 1832, CL, roll 165, #1; *Sailor's Magazine*, vol. 5 (1832–33), 293.

14. JB to SN, 10 March 1830, CL, roll 144, #42. Unless otherwise identified, all references to officers in this chapter are taken from *HLNO*, listed alphabetically. The Foxhall A. Parker mentioned here is not to be confused with his son, Foxhall Alexander Parker, the author of works on naval technology and strategy, who died in 1879 while superintendent of the U.S. Naval Academy at Annapolis. "Foxhall Alexander Parker," *DAB*, vol. 14, 200.

15. "Extracts of the Proceedings of the Court Martial, 16 September 1831," JBPA, vol. 6, #3647–48; JB to SN, 31 March 1830, CL, roll 144, #87.

16. JB to SN, 1 May 1830, CL, roll 146, #3; JB to SN, 8 September 1830, ibid., roll 150, #26; JB to SN, 5 January 1831, ibid., roll 153, #21.

17. "JBSB," 28; JB to SN, 19 September 1830, CL, roll 150, #51.

18. JB to SN, 31 March 1830, CL, roll 144, #87.

19. Ibid.

20. JB to SN, 3 September 1830, ibid., roll 150, #9; JB to SN, 31 March 1830, ibid., roll 144, #87.

21. JB to NB, 17 September 1830, JBPA, vol. 5, #3609; Walsh to JB, 13 July 1830, ibid., #3584; JB to SN, 14 January 1832, CL, roll 164, #65.

22. JB to SN, 24 August 1830, CL, roll 149, #78; JB to SN, 8 September 1830, ibid., roll 150, #26; JB to SN, 19 September 1830, ibid., #51.

23. JB to SN, 31 March 1830, ibid., roll 144, #87; Richard W. Meade to JB, 10 May 1831, enc. in JB to SN, 1 October 1831, ibid., roll 162, #4.

24. Euclid Borland, Robert J. Ross, John Weems, and William C. Spencer to JB, 4 January 1832, "Winter Regulations at Mahon," NYHS; JB to Borland, Ross, Weems, and Spencer, 7 January 1832, ibid.

25. American Daily Advertiser, n. d., in Daily National Intelligencer, 17 September 1832, p. 3, col. 3.

26. "Spencer D. Pettis," Biographical Directory of the American Congress, 1774–1971, 1536; Daily National Intelligencer, 13 September 1831, p. 3, col. 2; Globe (Washington), 16 September 1831, p. 2, col. 6.

27. Daily National Intelligencer, 12 September 1831, p. 3, col. 3; ibid., 13 September 1831, p. 3, col. 2; ibid., 12 September 1831; Globe, 16 September 1831.

28. "Niagara," in Globe, 16 September 1831, p. 3, col. 1.

29. JB to SN, 14 January 1832, CL, roll 164, #65.

30. "David Offley," DAB, vol. 13, 634–35.

31. Charles O. Paullin, Diplomatic Negotiations of American Naval Officers, 1778–1883 (Baltimore: 1912), 122–26; BWB, 40–52, 254–55.

32. BDP, 296 n; David H. Finnie, Pioneers East: The Early American Experience in the Middle East (Cambridge, Mass.: 1967); James A. Field, Jr., America and the Mediterranean World (Princeton: 1969), 141–53.

33. Paullin, 138.

34. René Ristelbueber, A History of the Balkan Peoples (New York: 1971), 85–87; Charles and Barbara Jelavich, The Establishment of the Balkan National States, 1804–1920 (Seattle and London: 1977), 48–49; National Aegis (Worcester, Mass.), 26 December 1827, p. 3, col. 1.

35. Andrew Jackson, Proclamation, 12 September 1829, U.S. Congress, 22nd, 1st Session, 1829–30, House of Representatives, Executive Document No. 250, Treaty with the Sublime Porte, 74; SS to JB, 12 September 1829, ibid., 76; Jackson to SN, 12 September 1829, ibid., 74–75.

36. "Charles Rhind," DAB, vol. 15, 529–30; James A. Hamilton, Reminiscenses of James A. Hamilton, or, Men and Events, at Home and Abroad, during Three Quarters of a Century (New York: 1869), 136, 207.

37. Hamilton to JB, 15 October 1829, JBPA, vol. 5, #3456; Hamilton to JB, 17 October 1829, ibid., #3462; Paullin, 145; Field, 149–50.

38. JB to SS, 8 September 1830, JBPA, vol. 6, #3702; Rhind to Jackson, 10 May 1830, *Executive Document 250*, 77–78; ibid., passim.

39. Rhind to Jackson, 10 May 1830, *Executive Document 250*, 78–94.

40. D. Hunter Miller, ed., *Treaties and Other International Acts of the United States of America, 1776–1863*, 8 vols. (Washington: 1932–39), vol. 3, 558–59.

41. JB to SS, 8 September 1830; "Charles Rhind's Separate and Secret Article," Miller, vol. 3, 580–81; Finnie, 60–61.

42. Paullin, 149; Finnie, 62.

43. JB and Offley to Jackson, 8 June 1830, *Executive Document 250*, 95; JB to SS, 8 September 1830, JBPA, vol. 6, #3702; JB to NB, 3 June 1830, ibid., #3714.

44. *JQAM*, 26 December 1830, vol. 8, 255; Finnie, 61; Paullin, 150.

45. Finnie, 62–63.

46. *BDP*, 273–76; DP to SS, 20 August 1830, DP Papers, David Dixon Porter Papers, LC.

47. Richard S. West, *The Second Admiral: A Life of David Dixon Porter, 1813–1891*, 16–17, 28–29; R.C. Wilcocks to JB, 15 April 1845, JBPA, vol. 9, #4407.

48. *BDP*, 284–316; Phyllis D. Wheelock, "Henry Eckford (1775–1832), an American Shipbuilder," *American Neptune*, vol. 7 (July 1947), 186–95; Finnie, 75–81.

49. JB to NB, 30 September 1831, JBPA, vol. 6, #3762.

50. SN to JB, 28 July 1831, ibid., #3736; JB to SN, 28 September 1831, ibid., #3760; SN to JB, 22 October 1831, CL, roll 162, #70.

51. JB, "Itemization of Presents," ? December 1829, JBPA, vol. 5, #3477; Greenough to Morse, 23 April 1832, Nathalia Wright, *Letters of Horatio Greenough: American Sculptor* (Madison, Wisc.: 1972), 118; ibid., 59, *n* 6; "JBSB," 28, *n* 62.

52. JB to SN, 12 July 1832, CL, roll 170, #53; "JBSB," 31; *Sailor's Magazine*, vol. 5 (1832–33), 113; JB to SN, 23 November 1832, JBPA, vol. 7, #3882.

53. JB to Kendall; Kendall to JB, 5 December 1832–21 January 1833, JBPA, vol. 7, #3884–905; Perry to SN, 28 July 1833, ibid., #3927; John Boyle to Williamson, 29 August 1833, ibid., 3942.

54. *Sailor's Magazine*, vol. 3, 151, in Harold D. Langley, *Social Reform in the United States Navy, 1798–1862* (Urbana, Ill.: 1967), 87; Voorhees to JB, JB to Voorhess, 1 March 1832, JBPA, vol. 6, #3832.

CHAPTER 9

1. NB to Patterson, 20 August 1833, JBPA, loose in vol. 1; JB to Jackson, 12 July 1833, James S. Biddle Papers, HSP.

2. Edward Shippen, "Some Account of the Origin of the Naval Asylum in Philadelphia," *PMHB*, vol. 7 (1883), 129; Dillard to Chapman, 9 August

1833, JBPA, vol. 7, #3939; Jane Biddle to NB, ? [late summer of 1833], ibid., loose in vol. 1.

3. JB to George C. Read, 21 May 1833, Richard Dale Papers, American Philosophical Society; BWB, 310–11; NB to Patterson, 20 August 1833, JBPA, loose in vol. 1.

4. JB to John Aulick, 31 March 1834, Charles Roberts Autograph Collection, Haverford College; Dillard to JB, 5 August 1834, JBPA, vol. 7, #3993.

5. Nicholas Biddle, Jr., Narberth, Pa., letter to DFL, 29 October 1980; "Nathaniel Chapman," DAB, vol. 4, 20; JB to George C. Read, 21 May 1833.

6. Mary Chapman to JB, 30 August 1833, JBPA, vol. 7, #3942.

7. M. Chapman to JB, 12 January 1834, ibid., #3964; M. Chapman to JB, 26 January 1834, ibid., box J, uncatalogued, "JB, John, and Richard Biddle Letters," folder, "Commodore James Biddle–John Chapman Letters."

8. John B. Chapman to JB, 22 May 1835, ibid., vol. 7, #4019; J.B. Chapman to JB, 4 June 1835, ibid., #4021; M. Chapman to JB, 4 June 1835, ibid.

9. M. Chapman to JB, 6 December 1835, ibid., #4052.

10. J.B. Chapman to JB, 9 September 1836, ibid., vol. 8, #4120.

11. Brockenbrough to JB, 9 September 1836, ibid., #4124.

12. JB and Dandridge, Duel Terms, 15 September 1836, ibid., #4126; DFL, "William Bainbridge and the Barron-Decatur Duel: Mere Participant or Active Plotter?" PMHB, vol. 103 (January 1979), 47, 49.

13. New York Commercial Advertiser, 19 September 1836, p. 2, col. 3; Columbian Centinel, 21 September 1836, p. 2, col. 2.

14. M. Chapman to JB, 21 September 1836, JBPA, vol. 8, #4029. Mary's death in 1837 is from the Pennsylvania Academy of Fine Arts, Catalogue of the Memorial Exhibition of Portraits by Thomas Sully (Philadelphia: 1922), 27. Although her difficulties after the birth of her daughter may have contributed to her demise, no specific causes have been discovered. According to Peter Parker, HSP, letter to DFL, 10 December 1982, nothing about Mary appears in either the Randolph or Chapman genealogies at HSP.

15. JB to SN, 20 December 1834, Mahlon Dickerson Papers, New Jersey Historical Society.

16. William C. Murrell, Cruise of the Frigate Columbia Around the World, Under the Command of George C. Read, in 1838, 1839, and 1840 (Boston: 1840), 55, 209; "George Campbell Read," DAB, vol. 15, 424.

17. JB to SN, 2 June 1835, Mahlon Dickerson Papers; "Read," DAB, 424.

18. JB to SN, 8 April 1837, JBPA, vol. 8, #4153; SN to JB, 11 April 1837, ibid.

19. In William Stanton, The Great United States Exploring Expedition of 1838–1842 (Berkeley, Los Angeles, and London: 1975), 53.

20. SN to JB, Hull, and Aulick, 12 December 1837, JBPA, vol. 8, #4163; Stanton, passim.

21. SN to JB, 10 September 1835, JBPA, vol. 8, #4031; JB to SN, 18 September 1835, CL, roll 210, #46.

22. SN to JB, 18 July 1838, JBPA, vol. 8, #4179; JB to SN, 10 August 1838, CL, roll 244, #204.

23. Albert Gleaves, "The United States Naval Asylum, Philadelphia," *US-NIP*, vol. 57 (1931), 474; Edward Shippen, "Naval Asylum," *PMHB*, vol. 7, 130.

24. Charles H. Stockton, *Origin, History, Laws, and Regulations of the United States Naval Asylum, Philadelphia* (Washington: 1886), 11; Daniel Ammen, *The Old Navy and the New* (Philadelphia: 1891), 95.

25. Shippen, 131; American Guide Series, *Philadelphia: Guide to the Nation's Birthplace* (repr., St Clair Shores, Michigan: 1939), 502–5.

26. Shippen, 135; JB to Navy Commissioners, 22 November 1838, USND, RG 45, Entry 211, Letters of JB to the Navy Commissioners, 1838–42, NA; Sydney G. Fisher, *A Philadelphia Perspective: The Diary of Sydney George Fisher Covering the Years 1834–1871,* ed. by NBW (Philadelphia: 1967), 81.

27. JB to Navy Commissioners, 22 November 1838, 7 August 1839, 3 August 1841, 2 November 1840, USND, RG 45, Entry 231; Elliott to JB, 14 August 1838, ibid.; American Guide Series, *Philadelphia,* 503; JB to Navy Commissioners, 2, 14 November 1840, 5 November 1841, Entry 231.

28. *BWB,* 216.

29. Samuel F. Du Pont to "Friend," 8 May 1823, WC; JB to SN, 19 March 1837, CL, roll 225 (USNA), #47. It should be reemphasized that the Captains' Letters of the Naval Academy's Nimitz Library differ slightly in roll numbers from those at the National Archives. Those from the Nimitz are designated (USNA).

30. SN to JB, 5 July 1838, SNL, roll 29, p. 106; JB to SN, 11 July 1839, roll 253 (USNA), #47; Judge J. K. Kane to Harry D. Gilpin, n. d., in Thomas J. Ford, "History of the United States Naval Academy," ms. volume in Nimitz Library's Special Collections, p. 31. Pages given are from the ms.'s typed copy.

31. JB to SN, 10 September 1840, CL, roll 269 (USNA), #85; Ford, 43.

32. Park Benjamin, *The United States Naval Academy* (New York and London: 1900), 120; Ford, 35.

33. Ammen, 95; Benjamin, 122; SN to JB, 10 June 1841, SNL, roll 32, pp. 471–72.

34. "Seventeen Midshipmen to McClure," 15 June 1840, in Ford, 35; Ford, 42–43.

35. Ammen, 94–95; Ford, 41, 42.

36. Henry L. Burr, *Education in the Early Navy* (Philadelphia: 1939), 156–57; JB to SN, 5 February 1840, CL, roll 260 (USNA), #14.

37. JB to SN, 9 March 1840, CL, roll 261 (USNA), #37; SN to JB, 14 March 1840, SNL, roll 30, p. 394.

38. Midshipmen to JB, 21 February 1840, enc. in JB to SN, 24 February 1840, CL, roll 260 (USNA), #81; SN to JB, 29 February 1840, SNL, roll 30, pp. 369–70; Ford, 43–44.

39. SN to JB, 4 June 1840, SNL, roll 31, p. 154; Midshipmen to JB, 9 July 1840, in Gleaves, "United States Naval Asylum," 475.

40. JB to SN, 3 November 1840, CL, roll 269 (USNA), #17; JB to SN, 22 November 1840, ibid., #125; JB to SN, 25 March 1841, ibid., roll 275 (NA), #115; HLNO, 324; JB to SN, 30 January 1814, CL, roll 275 (USNA), #117; HLNO, 268; JB to SN, 22 October 1841, CL, roll 280 (USNA), #106; JB to SN, 19 January 1841, ibid., roll 283 (USNA), #83.

41. Benjamin, 120–21; Ford, 44; JB to SN, 22 November 1840, CL, roll 269 (USNA), #125.

42. Ford, 44–45; JB to SN, 1 June 1840, CL, roll 264 (USNA), #10.

43. Ammen, 96; JB to SN, 21 March 1842, CL, roll 285 (USNA), #112; Charles O. Paullin, Diplomatic Negotiations of American Naval Officers, 1778–1883 (Baltimore: 1912), 193; Burr, 123; JB to SN, 1 April 1842, CL, roll 288 (USNA), #4; Paullin, 193; Pensioners to Barron, 4 February 1843, James Barron Papers, box 9, #39, College of William and Mary.

44. Benjamin, 124–27; Burr, 159–61.

45. Rules and Regulations for the Government of the Philadelphia Club (Philadelphia: 1834), passim; Bruce C. Compton, HSP, letter to DFL, 19 June 1980.

46. "JBSB," 33, 35; JB to John Biddle, 27 March 1842, JBPA, vol. 8, #4246.

47. Nathaniel Burt, The Perennial Philadelphians: The Anatomy of an American Aristocracy (Boston: 1963), 52; Fisher, Diary, 28 February 1844, 154, 156.

48. "Nicholas Biddle," DAB, vol. 2, 243–44; Bray Hammond, Banks and Politics in America from the Revolution to the Civil War (Princeton: 1957), 290–91.

49. Hammond, 534–40.

50. Thomas P. Govan, Nicholas Biddle: Nationalist and Public Banker, 1786–1844 (Chicago: 1959), 107; Hammond, 399–400; Govan, 202–3, 281.

51. Hammond, 438–39, 538–39, 526, 501.

52. Fisher, Diary, 31 October 1838, 28 February 1844, 88, 155; Govan, 406.

53. NBW, Andalusia: Countryseat of the Craig Family and of Nicholas Biddle and His Descendants (Philadelphia: 1976), 3–19; Harold B. Eberlein and Cortlandt Van Dyke, Portrait of a Colonial City: Philadelphia, 1670–1838 (Philadelphia, London, Toronto, and New York: 1939), 548; NBW, Andalusia, passim.

54. NBW, Andalusia, 4, 24 n, 1, 24–25; James Biddle, ex-president of the National Trust for Historic Preservation, who owns Andalusia, very kindly permitted JB's and other family files to be taken to the HSP in Philadelphia, where I was able to peruse them. During the summer of 1979, through the aid of Mary Graham of Cliveden in Germantown, I spent a day at Andalusia, examining the main house and grounds, while rechecking some of the JB correspondence, which by that time had been moved back to Andalusia from Philadelphia.

55. NBW, Andalusia, 26–44.

56. Fisher, Diary, 28 February 1844, 154, 157.

57. NBW, letter to DFL, 7 March 1980; "JBSB," 34; Govan, 411; NBW, Andalusia, 46.

58. JB to Webster, 30 September 1844, Daniel Webster Papers, New Hamp-

shire Historical Society, microfilmed ed., roll 19, "Correspondence, 1843–1844, #25967.

59. JB to SN, 20 February 1845; SN to JB, 22 February 1845, in JB's "Library Catalogue, 13 April 1845," courtesy of NBW.

CHAPTER 10

1. SN to JB, 17 March 1845; JB to SN, 18 March 1845, JBPA, vol. 9, #4391.

2. Samuel F. Du Pont to G. I. Pendergast, 6 April 1845; S. F. Du Pont to Alexander S. Mackenzie, 1 June 1845, WC.

3. JB to SN, 20 March 1845, CL, roll 321, #100; SN to JB, 22 May 1845, JBPA, vol. 9, #4489.

4. "Alexander Hill Everett," *DAB*, vol. 6, 220–21.

5. K. Jack Bauer, *Ships of the Navy 1775–1969* (Troy, N.Y.: 1969), vol. 1, 6–7, 25; Dudley D. Knox, *A History of the United States Navy* rev. ed., (N.Y.: 1948), 151–56; JB to SN, 19 April 1845, George Bancroft Papers, box 1845, Massachusetts Historical Society; Benajah Tichnor, "Journal, 1845–1848, on Board the *Columbus* on a Voyage from New York to the East Indies" (TJ), ms. volume, Benajah Tichnor Collection, journal 5, Yale University.

6. SLC, vol. 9; JB to John Biddle, 30 May 1845, NB Papers, "Personal Letters," vol. 5, HSP.

7. TJ, 4, 30 June 1845, pp. 12–13, 16; "Log Book of the U.S. Ship *Vincennes, Captain Hiram Paulding*" (LBV), 5–8 July 1835, USND, RG 45, app. D, #78, vol. 13 (1 May 1845–31 October 1846), NA.

8. SLC, 4–30 June 1845, passim; JB to SN, 2 August 1845–11 February 1846, JBPA, vol. 10, passim; SLC, 5, 30 July 1845; TJ, 29 July 1845, p. 20.

9. SNL, 30 July 1845.

10. Charles O. Paullin, *Diplomatic Negotiations of American Naval Officers, 1778–1883* (Baltimore: 1912), 205–10; Knox, 163; JB to SN, 14 August 1845, USND, RG 45, M 89, East India Squadron Letters (EISL), roll 3, pp. 34–35.

11. TJ, 30 July 1845, p. 16; Everett to JB, 5 August 1845, JBPA, vol. 10, #4591; Everett to JB, 8 August 1845, enc. in Everett to SS, 25 September 1845, USDS, China Despatches (CD), M 69, NA, vol. 3, in Jules Davids, ed., *American Diplomatic and Public Papers, The United States and China*, 21 vols. (Wilmington, Del.: 1973), series 1, vol. 2, *The Treaty of Wanghia*, #46, p. 336; Everett to SS, 16 August 1845, EISL, p. 37; TJ, 4–17 August 1845, pp. 20–24; Tekong Tong, *United States Diplomacy in China, 1844–1860* (Seattle: 1964), 10.

12. SLC, 17 August 1845; Charles Nordhoff, *Nine Years a Sailor, With Sketches of Personal Reminiscences in the United States Naval Service, the American and British Merchant Marine, and the Whaling Service* (Cincinnati: 1857), 143. After almost a decade afloat, Nordhoff left the sea for a productive later career as a popular author and editor of the *New York Evening Post* before,

during, and after the Civil War. He spent the rest of his life as the trusted and effective Washington correspondent of the *New York Herald,* dying in 1890 at the age of 60. "Charles Nordhoff," *DAB,* vol. 13, 548; SLC, 18 August 1845.

13. Nordhoff, 139–40.

14. Ibid., 154–55; SLC, 14 October 1845; LBV, 25–27 October 1845; Nordhoff, 161–66; TJ, 26 October 1845, pp. 57–58.

15. SLC, 30 October 1845; LBV, 29 October, 19 November 1845.

16. TJ, 9, 25 December 1845, pp. 69–70.

17. SLC, 26 December 1845–8 March 1846; LBV, 6 January 1846; SLC, 30 December 1845; Nordhoff, 181–82.

18. John K. Fairbank, *Trade and Diplomacy on the China Coast: The Opening of the Treaty Ports, 1842–1854* (Cambridge, Mass., 1953), 195–96.

19. Britain's extrality rights applied only to criminal cases; America's gained civil as well as criminal jurisdiction. Claude M. Fuess, *The Life of Caleb Cushing,* 2 vols. (New York: 1923), vol. 1, 422–25, 442, 448.

20. JB to Chi-y'ing, 26 December 1845, in Davids, *Wanghia,* #49, p. 346; Arthur Hummel, ed., *Eminent Chinese of the Ch'ing Period, 1644–1912,* 2 vols. (Washington: 1943–44), vol. 1, 132–34.

21. Chi-y'ing to emperor, 17 January 1846, in Earl Swisher, ed., *China's Management of the American Barbarians: A Study in Sino-American Relations, 1841–1861* (New Haven: 1953), 183.

22. Chi-y'ing to JB, 29 December 1845, in Davids, *Wanghia,* #50, pp. 347–48; JB to Chi-y'ing, 31 December 1845, ibid., #51, pp. 349–50.

23. Tong, 11, *n* 36; *Chinese Repository* (Canton), vol. 14 (December 1845), 500–501.

24. JB to SS, 8 January 1846, in Davids, *Wanghia,* #54, p. 354; Chi-y'ing to emperor, 18 February 1846, in Swisher, 184–85. One of the more blatant instances in which Ch'ing officials, terrified to be bearers of bad news (which had been known to result in a death sentence), embroidered reports to Peking occurred late in 1856. Yeh Ming-ch'en, governor-general of Kwangtung and Kwangsi provinces, told the emperor about a battle between his forces and the British early in the Arrow War: "Our troops blew up a warship, killed their admiral, Michael Seymour, and killed or wounded 400 barbarians and rebels." Imperial Edict, 12 December 1856, in Swisher, 328. This was a complete fabrication. No British man-of-war was lost; Seymour lived until 1887, and he reported his losses in the above engagement as 1 killed and 4 wounded. Seymour to secretary of the Admiralty, 14 November 1856, Great Britain, *Parliamentary Papers, 1857,* vol. 12, *Naval Forces,* #2163, (Harvard University). p. 99; "Michael Seymour," *DNB,* vol. 17, 1264.

25. Curtis J. Henson, *The United States Navy and China, 1841–1861* (Ann Arbor: 1972), 82. There were two Chinese co-hong merchants, father and son, known as "Houqua" or "Howqua," both of whom maintained cordial relations with Americans compared to other foreigners. Wu Ping-chen (1769–1843) established the family fortune, which was expanded by Wu Ch'ung-yueh (1810–63). The son, in addition to carrying on his far-flung business enterprises, was renowned for the quality of his hospitality, entertaining not only foreigners but aspiring Chinese poets and artists

as well, for he was an enthusiastic patron of the arts. Hummel, vol. 2, 876–77, 867–68; "JBSB," 37.

26. TJ, 5 January 1846, pp. 75–77.

27. JB to SS, 8 January 1846, in Davids, *Wanghia*, #54, pp. 354–56; Emmanuel C. Y. Hsü, *The Rise of Modern China* (New York, London, and Toronto: 1970), 249.

28. JB to SS, 8 January 1846; Fairbank, 203.

29. JB to SS, 8 January 1846, pp. 357–58.

30. Tyler Dennett, *Americans in Eastern Asia: A Critical Study of the United States, with Reference to China, Japan, and Korea in the Nineteenth Century* (New York: 1931), 294–95; *Overland Friend of China* (Hong Kong), 31 January 1846, p. 27, cols. 1–2; *Chinese Repository*, vol. 15 (January 1846), 50–51.

31. Hsü, 249; Chi-y'ing, Proclamation, 16 January 1846, enc. in JB to SS, 28 January 1846, in Davids, *Wanghia*, #69, pp. 370–71. This was the beginning of the end for Chi-y'ing. By 1848 the combined impact of his intimate association with Chinese concessions in the treaties with the West and his apparent continuous favoring of the "barbarians" over his own people resulted in his ouster as governor-general. With the advent of the xenophobic Hsien-Feng, emperor two years later, he was forced into retirement. But he was brought back to serve as a sacrificial lamb during the negotiations at Tientsin in 1858 that resulted in treaties between China and Great Britain, the United States, France, and Russia, the terms of which were abhorrent to the court. Almost at once the emperor invited Chi-y'ing to commit suicide, which he did, evidently by poison. Hummel, "Chi-y'ing," vol. 1, 134.

32. TJ, 11 February; 846, pp. 90–91; *Overland Friend of China*, 31 January 1846, p. 27, col. 2; JB to SS, 28 January 1846, pp. 371–73; *Chinese Repository*, vol. 15 (April 1846), 224; Hsü, 249.

33. Parker to JB, 20 February 1846, in Jules Davids, ed., series 1, *The Treaty System and the Taiping Rebellion*, vol. 10, *Extraterritoriality*, #57, pp. 120–122; Wetmore to JB, 17 February 1846, in ibid., #54, pp. 115–16.

34. JB to SS, 28 February 1846, in Tong 14, *n* 39; 40; JB to Wetmore, 24 February 1846; Forbes to JB, 25 February 1846, in Davids, *Extraterritoriality*, #59, 60, pp. 125–26.

35. Eldon Griffin, *Clippers and Consuls; American Consular and Commercial Relations with Eastern Asia, 1845–1860* (Ann Arbor: 1938), 241; SLC, 8 March 1846; TJ, 12 March 1846, p. 95.

36. SN to JB, 12 February 1846, USND, Record of Confidential Letters from the SN to Officers, vol. 1 (12 September 1843–26 February 1849), NA, pp. 169–70.

37. "JBSB," 38; JB to Wyman, 12 March 1846, enc. in JB to SN, 21 March 1846, EISL, #13, p. 47; TJ, 26–31 March 1846, pp. 101–2; Nordhoff, 186; SLC, 11 April 1846.

38. Everett did come to China in October 1846 and died there the next July. "Alexander Hill Everett," *DAB*, vol. 6, 221; JB to SS, 14 April 1846, in Davids, *Wanghia*, #62, pp. 375–78.

39. JB to SS, 18 April 1846, in Davids, *Wanghia*, #62, pp. 379–80; JB to SN, 3 July 1846, EISL, p. 69; SLC, LBV, 18 April–24 May 1846; TJ, 24

May 1846, p. 129; SLC, LBV, 5 June 1846; Fairbank, 215–19; Ammen, *The Old Navy and the New* (Philadelphia: 1891), 135.

40. In Liang Pao-ch'ang, Governor of Chekiang Province, to emperor, 25 August 1846, in Swisher, 185; TJ, 6 June 1846, pp. 138–40.

41. Tong, 60–61; JB to SN, 3 July 1846, EISL, #18, p. 69; Tong, 62–63; SLC, 17–18 June 1846; LBV, 20 June 1846.

42. Tong, 59–60; Griffin, 258.

43. Tong, 60; JB to Balfour, 1 July 1846, in Henson, 99; Dennett, 195–97; Tong, 60.

44. LBV, 24 June 1846; Ammen, 137; Griffin, 298; Tong, 62.

45. Liang to emperor, 26 August 1846, in Swisher, 185–86; JB to Parker, 5 July 1846, in Henson, 99–100.

46. TJ, 27 June 1846, p. 154; SLC; LBV, 7 July 1846.

47. Fairbank, 277.

48. Washington's aversion to expansionism made it easy for the U.S. government to relegate to oblivion a petition to the House of Representatives signed by "Granville R. Rosebery and one hundred and nine other citizens of McKean County, in the State of Pennsylvania . . . praying for the annexation of China to the United States." U.S. Congress, 29th, 1st session, 1846, *Journal of the House of Representatives* 494, in Henson, 98, *n* 18.

49. DFL, "A Case for Intervention: Armstrong, Foote, and the Destruction of the Barrier Forts, Canton, China, 1856," Craig L. Symonds, et al., eds. *New Aspects of Naval History: Selected Papers Presented at the Fourth Naval History Symposium, United States Naval Academy, 25–26 October 1979* (Annapolis: 1981), 220–37; Imperial Edict, 23 April 1857, in Swisher, 330–31.

CHAPTER 11

1. SN to JB, 22 May 1845, in "Cruise of the *Colimbia* [*sic*] and *Vincennes* to the Coast[s], of China, Inida [*sic*], and [the] East Indian Islands," USND, RG 45, subject file 00, box 3, 1845, NA.

2. In the catalogue of his large private libary Biddle listed eleven histories and travel works on China, but only one on Japan. JB, "Catalogue, 13 April 1845,"

3. DP to SN, 31 October 1815, in *BDP*, 173–74; Albert B. Cole, ed., "Captain David Porter's Proposed Expedition to the Pacific and Japan, 1815," *Pacific Historical Review*, vol. 9 (1940), 65.

4. Charles O. Paullin, *Diplomatic Negotiations of American Naval Officers, 1778–1883* (Baltimore: 1912), 220–22.

5. Tyler Dennett, *Americans in Eastern Asia* (N.Y.: 1931), 247–48.

6. Paullin, 219.

7. JB to SN, 31 July 1846, EISL, roll 3, #17, pp. 60–62.

8. Ibid.

9. Ibid.

10. Ibid.

11. H. Valette Warren, "Commodore James Biddle's Visit to Japan—Another Recollection," *Independent Magazine,* vol. 59 (2 November 1905), 1044.

12. Charles Nordhoff, *Nine Years a Sailor* (Cincinnati: 1857), 205–6. In the late nineteenth century the butchers of Tokyo erected a small memorial to Townsend Harris, the first U.S. consul-general in Japan during the 1850s, as practically their patron saint for having introduced meat-eating into Japan. I have seen it where it still stands at Harris's house in the small town of Shimoda, south of Tokyo.

13. Samuel E. Morison, *Old Bruin: Commodore Matthew Calbraith Perry* (Boston and Toronto: 1967), 319; JB to SN, 31 July 1846, p. 61; Nitobe Azano, "American-Japanese Intercourse Prior to the Advent of Perry," *Annual Report of the American Historical Association for the Year 1911,* 2 vols. (Washington: 1913), vol. 1, 138.

14. Everett to SS, 26 October 1846, in Nitobe Azano, 138.

15. JB to SN, 31 July 1846.

16. Ibid.

17. Ibid.

18. TJ, 28 July 1846, p. 161; Daniel Ammen, *The Old Navy and the New* (Philadelphia: 1891), 140.

19. TJ, 28 July 1846; Edward S. Burton, "Commodore James Biddle's Failure to Enter Japan in 1846," *Independent Magazine,* vol. 59 (31 August 1905), 502; Ammen, 141.

20. Stephen B. Luce, "Commodore James Biddle's Visit to Japan in 1846," *USNIP,* vol. 31 (1905), 599; Ammen, 140.

21. Paullin, 232.

22. *American and Gazette,* 2 February 1850, p. 3, cols. 1–2, in JBPA, box "Letters Received for James Biddle," folder, "Commodore James Biddle Correspondence." A Japanese authority, however, after examining the pertinent documentation about the matter, has concluded that most foreign castaways were accorded sympathy and leniency while in Japan. He finds that the *Ladoga's* men had earned their harsh treatment by incessant quarreling among themselves and with their guards, as well as by constant attempts to escape. Shunzo Sakamaki, "Japan and the United States, 1790–1853," *Transactions of the Asiatic Society of Japan,* vol. 18 (1939), 50–55.

23. Everett to SS, 5 January 1847, in Merrill J. Bartlett, "Commodore James Biddle and the First Naval Mission to Japan, 1845 [sic]–1846," *American Neptune,* vol. 61 (January 1981), 32; Palmer to SS, 17 September 1849, ibid.; [Matthew C. Perry], *The Japan Expedition, 1852–1854: Personal Journal,* ed. by Roger Pineau (Washington: 1958), 92.

24. James Murdoch, *History of Japan,* 3 vols. (repr., London: 1926), vol. 3, 571; Nitobe Azano, 138–39.

25. Dennett, 250; Morison, 303, 265, 322.

26. Paullin, 233–34; Glynn used his own triumph to cast aspersions upon his predecessor, writing to Fillmore, "I have every reason to believe that the effect of the [Biddle] visit upon the people of that country [Japan] has

been very unfavorable to the interests of the United States." Glynn to
Fillmore, 10 June 1851, in Bartlett, 32; Morison, 266; Paullin, 238–42.

27. JB to SN, 16 September 1846, EISL, #20.

28. SLC, 29–31 July 1846; LBV, vol. 1 (through 31 October 1846); vol. 2 (1
    November 1846–9 April 1847), passim.

29. TJ, 31 July 1846, p. 166; JBPA, vol. 10 (2 August 1845–11 February
    1846); vol. 11 (12 February–26 July 1846), passim; Paulding to JB, 13
    January; JB to Paulding, 14 January; Paulding to JB, 20 January 1846,
    EISL, pp. 47–53, enc. in JB to SN, 1 February 1846, ibid., #11, pp.
    44–45; Paulding to JB, 14 January 1846, in ibid., pp. 55–56. For some
    reason this letter was enclosed in JB's April rather than January corre-
    spondence. JB to SN, 6 April 1846, ibid., #16, p. 54.

30. Wyman to JB, 24 November; JB to Wyman, 25 November 1846, JBPA,
    vol. 10, #4685; JBPA, vols. 10–11, passim.

31. JB to Selfridge; Selfridge to JB, 2 November 1846, ibid., vol. 12, #5153.
    Selfridge soon made his escape from the *Columbus* to serve as commander
    of the sloop *Dale* operating off Baja California late in 1847. K. Jack Bauer,
    The Mexican War, 1846–1848 (New York and London: 1971), 346.

32. JB to James S. Biddle, 20 September 1846, NB, Personal Correspon-
    dence, vol. 5, HSP; SLC, 1 July–9 September 1946, passim; Nordhoff,
    216; TJ, 10 September 1846, p. 167.

33. Nordhoff, 220; "Anthony Ten Eyck," *National Cyclopaedia of American
    Biography,* 59 vols. to date (New York: 1893–   ), vol. 12, 259; TJ, 27–28
    September 1846, pp. 180–81.

34. SN to JB, 16 May 1846, USND, Record of Confidential Letters from
    the SN to Officers, vol. 1 (12 September 1843–28 February 1849), p.
    179. TJ, 14 September 1846, p. 171.

35. TJ, 23 April 1847, pp. 202–3; SLC, 29 September 1846.

CHAPTER 12

1. JB's hunger for information was so acute that just before leaving the
   United States in 1845 he ordered a two-year subscription to Washington's
   Daily National Intelligencer to be sent to Philadelphia so that he could
   catch up on all the news when he returned. JB to Edward L. Clark, 18
   April 1845, War of 1812 Collection, University of Michigan.

2. JB to Mrs. James S. Biddle, 10 November 1846, NB, Personal Correspondence, vol. 5, HSP; JB to James S. Biddle, 12 February 1848, ibid.

3. SLC, 2 December 1846; TJ, 2 December 1846, p. 186.

4. TJ, 30 December 1846, p. 187; Charles Nordhoff, *Nine Years a Sailor*
   (Cincinnati: 1891), 231.

5. *BDP,* 216; John L. Betts, "The United States Navy in the Mexican War"
   (unpublished Ph.D. dissertation, University of Chicago, 1955), 272.

6. Wise to JB, 16 April 1847, JBPA, vol. 14, #5764.

7. SLC, 1 January 1847; TJ, 2 January 1847, p. 191; Walter Colton, *Deck
   and Port: or Incidents of a Cruise in the United States Frigate* Congress (New
   York: 1850), 186; SLC, 9 January–3 March 1847.

8. Russell B. Nye, *George Bancroft: Brahmin Rebel* (New York: 1944), 159; C.G. Hatheway, "Commodore Jones' War," *History Today*, vol. 16 (March 1966), 194–201.

9. Robert E. Johnson, *Thence Around Cape Horn: The Story of the United States Naval Forces on Pacific Station, 1818–1923* (Annapolis: 1963), 77–79.

10. K. Jack Bauer, *The Mexican War, 1846–1848* (New York and London: 1971), 164–72.

11. Ibid., 183–86; Allen Nevins, *Frémont: Pathfinder of the West* (New York and London: 1939), 305–11.

12. Nevins, 186–89.

13. Stockton to JB, 17, 25 March 1847, JBPA, vol. 13, #5553, 5616.

14. TJ, 4 January 1847, pp. 195–97.

15. Johnson, 91.

16. Ibid., 81–82; Daniel J. O'Neil, "The United States Navy in the Californias, 1840–1850" (unpublished Ph.D. dissertation, University of Southern California, 1969), 263–66; TJ, 16 March 1847, p. 197; Johnson, 89.

17. JB to Shubrick, 17 April 1847, in "JBSB," 46.

18. Betts, 275.

19. SLC, 13 June 1847; TJ, 13 June 1847, p. 208.

20. TJ, 13, 25 June 1847, pp. 215, 217; Colton to JB; JB to Colton, 22 March 1847, JBPA, vol. 13, #5594; Walter Colton, *Three Years in California* (New York: 1856), 163.

21. JB to James S. Biddle, 10 November 1846, NB, Personal Correspondence, vol. 5, HSP.

22. SLC, 11 November 1847–15 March 1848, passim; Nicholas H. Van Zandt, "Journal Kept by Midshipman Nicholas H. Van Zandt Aboard USS *Columbus,* Flagship of Commodore Biddle, on Voyage from Valparaiso to Hampton Roads, 14 October 1847–15 March 1848," USND, subject file, app. D, NA, #78, passim.

23. TJ, 1 November 1847, 2 February 1848, pp. 227, 232; Nordhoff, 272.

24. Van Zandt, "Journal," 2, 9, 15 March 1848.

25. Maddox to SN, 9 March 1848, JBPA, vol. 15, #6010; JB to SN, 17 March 1848, ibid., #6023. This is JB's last letter in the Andalusia collection.

26. JB to James S. Biddle, 20 September 1846, NB, Personal Correspondence, vol. 5, HSP; "JBSB," 50.

27. B. Henry to JB, 22 August 1845, JBPA, vol. 16, #6288.

28. Eliza Hirst to JB, 12 December 1847; to Charles Biddle, n. d.; to C. Biddle, 28 June 1849, ibid., uncatalogued, box "James, John, and Richard Biddle Letters," folder, "Mrs. Eliza Hirst"; JB "Last Will and Testament," 24 March 1848, Registry of Wills, City Hall, Philadelphia.

29. Eliza Hirst to Charles Biddle, 28 June 1849.

30. Ibid; Tichnor to Chapman, ? October 1848, Letterbook, 1844–54, #14, p. 62, Benajah Tichnor Papers, series 2, roll 3, Yale University; NBW to DFL, 17 February 1981.

31. JB, "Last Will and Testament"; JB note, n. d. (sometime after 15 March 1848), p. 2, JBPA, loose in vol. 1.

32. "JBSB," 50; *Daily National Intelligencer,* 11 October 1848, p. 3, col. 4; ibid., 5 October 1848, p. 3, col. 3.

CHAPTER 13

1. The only footnote references in this chapter are to sources not previously cited or to those used for a different purpose.

2. "JBSB," 32, *n* 73.

3. Ibid., 33.

4. JB, "Catalogue, 13 April 1845."

5. "George Payne Rainsford James," *DNB,* vol. 10, 646–47; JB "Catalogue."

6. JB to James S. Biddle, 20 September 1846, NB, Personal Correspondence, vol. 5, HSP.

7. JB, note, n. d. (sometime after 15 March 1848), p. 1, JBPA, loose in vol. 1; JB, "Last Will and Testament," 24 March 1848, Registry of Wills, City Hall, Philadelphia.

8. Jeremy Robinson, Diary, 20 November 1818, Peter Forbes Collection, LC; JB to James S. Biddle, 20 September 1846.

9. JB, note, n. d., pp. 1–2; "List of Commodore Biddle's Silver," ibid., vol. 9, #4945.

10. Ann Rawles to JB, 31 March 1846, ibid., vol. 11, #4945; JB to Mrs. Elwyn, 6 April 1828, in "JBSB," 25.

11. JB to George C. Read, 21 May 1833, Richard Dale Papers, American Philosophical Society.

12. Charles Nordhoff, *Nine Years a Sailor* (Cincinnati: 1857), 52–53.

13. Ibid., 170–73.

14. Sloat to JB, 3 April 1823, JBPA, vol. 3, #3038; Sloat to Richard Biddle, 15 January 1847, ibid., loose in vol. 1.

15. JB to NB, 7 August 1830, ibid., vol. 5, #3594–95.

16. Commander Tyrone G. Martin, 57th in command of USS *Constitution,* gave me the information about ships named *Biddle,* letter to DFL, 28 August 1981.

INDEX